THE PUBLICATIONS
OF THE AMERICAN TRACT SOCIETY

VOLUME IV

SOLID GROUND CHRISTIAN BOOKS
BIRMINGHAM, ALABAMA USA

THE

PUBLICATIONS

OF THE

AMERICAN TRACT SOCIETY.

VOL. IV.

"The benefits to be derived from Education may be greatly assisted by the dispersion of small cheap Tracts on religious and moral
duties."   BISHOP OF DURHAM.

PUBLISHED BY THE

AMERICAN TRACT SOCIETY,

AND SOLD AT THEIR DEPOSITORY, NO. 87 NASSAU-STREET, NEAR
THE CITY-HALL, NEW-YORK; AND BY AGENTS OF THE
SOCIETY, ITS BRANCHES, AND AUXILIARIES, IN
THE PRINCIPAL CITIES AND TOWNS
IN THE UNITED STATES

Solid Ground Christian Books
PO Box 660132
Vestavia Hills AL 35266
205-443-0311
sgcb@charter.net
www.solid-ground-books.com

The Publications of the American Tract Society
Volume IV – Tracts 94 – 127

Published by the American Tract Society, New York

First Solid Ground Christian Books Edition Dec. 2007

Cover design by Borgo Design, Tuscaloosa, AL
Reach them at borgogirl@bellsouth.net

ISBN: 1-59925-1078

CONTENTS.

VOL. IV

CONTENTS.

FIRST LINES OF HYMNS IN THIS VOLUME.

INTERESTING HISTORY

OF

MRS. TOOLY,

AN EMINENT CHRISTIAN LADY IN LONDON.

"God bless you, my dear child."—*Page 4.*

PUBLISHED BY THE

AMERICAN TRACT SOCIETY,

AND SOLD AT THEIR DEPOSITORY, NO. 150 NASSAU-STREET, NEAR
THE CITY-HALL, NEW-YORK; AND BY AGENTS OF THE
SOCIETY, ITS BRANCHES, AND AUXILIARIES, IN
THE PRINCIPAL CITIES AND TOWNS
IN THE UNITED STATES.   A

HISTORY OF MRS. TOOLY.

THE late Mr. Thomas Bradbury happened to dine one day at the house of Mrs. Tooly, an eminent Christian lady in London, who was famous, in her day, for religion, and for the love she bore to Christ and to all his servants and people. Her house and table were open to them all, being another Lydia in that respect. Mr. Timothy Rogers, who wrote the book on religious melancholy, and was himself many years under that distemper, happened to dine there the same day with Mr. Bradbury; and after dinner, he entertained Mrs. Tooly and Mr. Bradbury with some stories concerning his father, who was one of the ejected ministers in the year 1662, and the sufferings he underwent on account of his nonconformity. Mr. Rogers particularly related one anecdote that he had often heard his father, with much pleasure, tell to himself and others, concerning a deliverance which he had from being sent to prison, after his *mittimus*, as they call it, was written out for that purpose.

He happened to live near the house of one Sir Richard Cradock, a justice of the peace, who was a most violent hater and persecutor of the Dissenters; one who laid out himself to distress them by all the means which the severe laws then in being put in his power, particularly by enforcing the law against conventicles. He bore a particular hatred to Mr. Rogers, and wanted above all things to have him in his power; and a fair opportunity, as he thought, offered itself to him. He heard that Mr. Rogers was to preach at a place some miles distant; and he hired two men to go as spies, who were to take the names of all the hearers they knew, and to witness against Mr. Rogers and them.

The thing succeeded to his wish; they brought the names of several persons who were hearers on that occasion; and Sir Richard sent and warned such of them as he owed particular spite, and Mr. Rogers, to appear before him.—Accordingly they all came with trembling hearts, expecting the worst; for they knew the violence of the man.

While they were in his great hall, expecting to be called upon, there happened to come into the hall a little girl, a grandchild of Sir Richard's, about six or seven years of age. She looked at Mr. Rogers, and was much taken with his venerable appearance; and he being naturally fond of children, took her on his knee, and made a great deal of her; and she was fond of him. At last Sir Richard sent one of his servants to inform the company, that one of the witnesses had fallen sick, and could not be present that day, and therefore warned them anew to come on another day, which he named to them.

Accordingly they came; and the crime, as the justice called it, was proved. He ordered their *mittimus* to be written, to send them all to jail. Mr. Rogers, before he came, expecting to see the little girl again, had brought some sweetmeats to give her; and he was not disappointed; for she came running to him, and was fonder of him, than she was the day before. She was, it seems, a particular favourite of her grandfather's, and had got such an ascendency over him that he could deny her nothing. She was withal a child of a violent spirit, and could bear no contradiction, as she was indulged in every thing. Once, when she was contradicted in something, she ran a penknife into her arm, that had near cost her either her life, or the loss of her arm. After which Sir Richard would not suffer her to be contradicted in any thing.

While she was sitting on Mr. Rogers' knee, and eating the sweetmeats which he gave her, she looked wishfully on him, and said, " What are you here for, Sir ?" He answered, " I believe your grandfather is going to send me, and my friends whom you see here, to jail." " To jail !" said she ; " why, what have you done ?" " Why, I did nothing but preach at such a place; and they did nothing but hear me." " But," said she, " my grandpapa shan't send you to jail." " Ay, but, my dear," said he, " I believe he is now making out our *mittimus* to send us all there."

She ran immediately to the chamber where her grandfather was, and knocked with her head and heels till she got in, and said, " What are you going to do with my good old gentleman here in the hall ?" " That's nothing to you," said her grandfather ; " get you about your business." " But I won't," said she ; " he tells me that you are going to send him and his friends to jail; and if you send them

I'll drown myself in the pond as soon as they are gone; I will, indeed." When he saw the girl was resolute and peremptory, it shook him, and overcame even the wicked design he had formed to persecute the servants of the Lord. He stepped into the hall, with the *mittimus* in his hand, and said, "I had here made out your *mittimus* to send you all to jail, as you deserve; but at my grandchild's request, I fall from the prosecution, and set you all at liberty."

They all bowed, and thanked his worship. But Mr. Rogers stepped up to the child, and laid his hand upon her head; and lifting up his eyes to heaven, said, "God bless you, my dear child; may the blessing of that God whose cause you did plead, though as yet you know him not, be upon you in life, at death, and throughout eternity." And then he and his friends went away.

Mrs. Tooly listened with uncommon attention to the story; and looking on Mr. Rogers, said, "And are you that Mr. Rogers' son?" "Yes, madam," answered he, "I am." "Well," said she, "for as long as I have been acquainted with you, I never knew that before. And now I will tell you something you never knew before. I am the very girl your dear father blessed in the manner you have now related. It made an impression on me, I could never forget." Upon this double discovery, Mr. Rogers and Mrs. Tooly found they had a superadded tie of love and affection to each other, beyond what they had before. And then he and Mr. Bradbury were desirous to know how she, who had been bred up with an aversion to the dissenters and to serious religion, made now such a figure among them, and was so eminent for religion.

She complied with their request, and very freely told them her story. She said, that after her grandfather's death, she was left sole heiress of his great estate; and being in the bloom of youth, and having none to control her, she ran after all the fashionable diversions of the time in which she lived, without any manner of restraint. But at the same time she confessed, that at the end of them all, she found a dissatisfaction, both with herself and them, that always struck a damp to her heart, which she did not know how to get rid of, but by running the same fruitless round over and over again: but all in vain.

She contracted some slight illness, upon which she thought she would go to Bath, hearing that that was a place for pleasure, as well as health. When she came there, she was led in providence to consult an apothecary, who happened to be a very worthy, religious man. He inquired what she ailed? "Why," said she, "Doctor, I don't ail much as to my body; but I have an uneasy mind, that I can't get rid of." "Truly," said he, "Miss, I was so too till I met with a book that cured me of it." "Books!" said she; "I get all the books I can lay my hand on, all plays, novels, and romances I can hear of; but, after I have read them, my uneasiness is the same." "That may be," said he, "Miss, I don't wonder at it. But this book I speak of, I can say of it what I can say of no other I ever read. I am never tired of reading it; but can begin to read it again, as if I never had read it before. And I always see something new in it." "Pray," said she, "Doctor, what book is that?" "Nay, Miss," answered he, 'that is a secret I don't tell to every one." "But could not I get a sight of that book?" said she. "Yes," said he, 'Miss, if you speak me fair, I can help you to it." "Pray get it me then, Doctor, and I'll give you any thing you please." "Yes," said he, "if you will promise one thing, I'll bring it you; and that is, that you will read it over carefully; and if you should not see much in it at first, that you will give it a second reading."

She promised faithfully she would. And after raising her curiosity by coming twice or thrice without bringing it, he at last brought it, took it from his pocket and gave it her. It was a New Testament. When she looked on it, she said, "Poh, (with a flirt,) I could get that any time." "Why, Miss, so you might" replied the Doctor; "but remember, I have your solemn promise that you will read it carefully." "Well," said she, "though I never read it before, I'll give it a reading."

Accordingly, she began to read it; and it soon attracted her attention. She saw something in it which she had a deep concern in; and if she was uneasy in her mind before, she was ten times more so now; she did not know what to do with herself. So she got back to London, to see what the diversion there would do again. But all was in vain.

She was lodged at the court end of the town, and had a gentlewoman with her by way of a companion. One Sabbath they set out with a design to attend public worship, but without fixing on any particular church, and after passing by several, were providentially led into the Old Jewry. Mrs. Tooly's attention was much excited by the solemn manner of Mr. Shower, who was then minister of the place; and when he rose to pray, she was deeply affected. Having finished prayer, he took for his text, Psalm cxvi. 7. "*Return unto thy rest, O my soul; for the Lord hath dealt bountifully with thee.*" In the hearing of this sermon, God met with her soul in a saving way and manner ; and she at last obtained what she in vain sought for elsewhere—rest to her soul, in him who is the life and happiness of souls

———

THE life of this illustrious character is a literal comment on that declaration of eternal truth—"*Wisdom's ways are ways of pleasantness, and all her paths are peace: wisdom is better than rubies ; and all the things that may be desired are not to be compared to it.*" That living godliness communicates to the heart a happiness infinitely more refined, and solid, and satisfactory, than the world can bestow on her most favourite children. This lady was born to fortune, was eminently the child of parental fondness and indulgence, and nursed from infancy in the lap of ease and affluence. By her the experiment was fairly made, whether any thing, beneath the uncreated Jehovah, is a portion equal to the desires of an immortal spirit. She early commenced her career in the pursuit of happiness, and eagerly sought it, *now* in reading the enchanting novel ; *again* by mingling with the social circle, and frequenting the fashionable amusements of the age. But the experiment was not more presumptuous than vain. Each source of earthly enjoyment proved literally *a broken cistern*, soon exhausted, from which her thirsty soul returned unsatisfied; or like the bubble that plays upon the waters, it instantly eluded her grasp, and mocked her expectation.

Important instruction may be derived from this example ; instruction peculiarly interesting to those who move in the higher circles of life, and have been charmed with the false glare of earthly grandeur, or earthly joy ; who, like the lady above mentioned, have too long expected happiness in the sportive dance, the polite assembly, or other refined gratifications. Be persuaded, ye that are such ; be persuaded, from the testimony of thousands, from the testimony of Mrs. Tooly, " *that all on earth is a shadow;*" that while your expectations are fastened on any terrestrial portion, disappointment will be your unavoidable doom. The immortal principle within your bosom is too dignified in its nature, too enlarged in its desires, too lasting in its duration, to be satisfied with any created good. Ye votaries of pleasure, whose expectations have hitherto been deceived, make her last experiment; try, for a time, those expedients to which her soul, after her numerous and painful disappointments, was driven by a blessed necessity. Exchange your novels for the Scriptures of the holy Jesus: here are cordials to refresh, under the most exquisite sorrows of life: here is rest for the weary, and balm for the bleeding heart: here peace is proclaimed, through the blood of Calvary, to the awakened, anxious conscience; a peace which passeth all understanding; which tongue cannot utter, nor pen describe, nor heart comprehend; a peace, which all who enjoy it, esteem as a most precious, precious treasure; and which none would barter for ten thousand worlds. Here joys are proclaimed to the dejected, disquieted heart; joys unspeakable and full of glory; joys which are beyond description; which are refreshing below, and the earnest, the certain earnest, of all that our capacities can receive in the regions of immortality. " *Search the Scriptures,* therefore, *for in them ye think ye have eternal life. And they are they which testify of Jesus; more to be desired are they than gold, yea, than much fine gold; sweeter also than honey, and the honey-comb.*" The royal David could appeal to the Searcher of hearts; and thousands and thousands, under the sealing influences of the same Spirit, can bear the same testimony—" *Thy statutes have been my song in the house of my pilgrimage: I have chosen thy testimonies as mine heritage for ever; they are the rejoicing of my heart.*"

Again, make an experiment of our Lord Jesus Christ; try if that happiness is not to be enjoyed in him, which you have unprofitably sought in the circle of worldly amusements.—Brother, sister, what does thy soul desire ? *Believe in the Lord Jesus,* and this desire will be gratified. Embrace him in his offices, and promises, and salvation; and thy capacities, however enlarged, shall be filled *to the very uttermost.* Are pleasures the object of your pursuit ? In Jesus are pleasures the most refined, the most ennobled and unfading; in him are *everlasting consolations, fulness of joy, and pleasures for evermore.* Are honours the desire of your heart? Here are honours more distinguished and durable than creation can afford: each living member of the ever glorious Redeemer, *is a son, a daughter of God*, an heir of never ending glory. They are introduced, in the very moment of their *marriage to the Lamb, to the general assembly and church of the first-born ; to an innumerable company of angels ; to God, the Judge of all.* They receive from the hands of Christ the Mediator, a title to the *house eternal in the heavens ; to an inheritance incorruptible ; and a crown of glory that fadeth not away ;* a title written in his own blood, which *neither life, nor death, nor things present, nor things to come, shall be able* to destroy.

Ye sons, ye daughters of pleasure, we appeal to your own ingenuousness. Are joys thus refined, are honours thus lasting to be found in your splendid round? In all your research after happiness, have you experienced any thing in which you can rejoice, as a *ll-sufficient* portion? Any covert from every outward storm, of which you can deliberately say—*Soul, shelter thyself here for time and for eternity !* With your hands laid upon your hearts, are you not obliged ingenuously to reply—*We have not ; all is vanity*, doubly *vantiy and vexation of spirit.* Then I urge the expostulation—Make an experiment of Jesus, the friend of sinners. Behold! a *fountain of living waters* is presented to your view! Why will you *labour in vain, and spend your* time, your precious time, and *strength, for nought and in vain?* Millions have drunk in this fountain, and been refreshed; and yet it is unexhausted, undiminished; eternally flowing, eternally full. " *Ho every one that thirsteth, come ye to the waters ; the Spirit and the bride say come ; let him that heareth come ;* let him that readeth come ; *let him that is athirst come ; and whosoever will, let him take of the waters of life freely.*" May that same Spirit, Jehovah, who sweetly constrained Mrs. Tooly, constrain each of you *in his own method, and in his own time*, to resolve with the once militant but now triumphant Psalmist—" *Return unto thy rest, O my soul, for the Lord hath dealt bountifully with thee.*"

END.

NOW OR NEVER.

BY REV. RICHARD BAXTER.

" Whatsoever thy hand findeth to do, do it with thy might."—Eccl. 9 : 10.

WHO knoweth not that time cannot be recalled? That which once was, will be no more. Yesterday will never come again. To-day is passing, and will not return. You may work while it is day; but when you have lost that day, it will not return for you to work in. While your candle burneth, you may make use of its light; but when it is done, it is too late to use it. No force of medicine, no orator's elegant persuasions, no worldling's wealth, no prince's power, can call back one day or hour of time. If they would, what endeavors would there be used, when extremity hath taught men to value what they now despise! What bargaining would there be at last, if time could be purchased for any thing that man can give! Then misers would bring out their wealth, and say, " All this will I give for one day's time of repentance more." And lords and knights would lay down their honors, and say, " Take all, and let us be beggars, if we may have but one year of the time that we mispent." Then kings would lay down their crowns and say, " Let us be equal with the lowest subjects, so we may but have the time again that we wasted in the cares and pleasures of the world." Kingdoms would then seem a contemptible price for the recovery of time.

The time that is now idled and talked away; the time that is now feasted and complimented away; that is unnecessarily sported and slept away; that is wickedly and presumptuously sinned away; how precious will it one day seem to all!

The profanest mariner falls a praying when he fears his time is at an end. If importunity would then prevail, how earnestly would they pray for the recovery of time, that formerly derided praying! What a liturgy would death teach the trifling. time-despising gallant; the idle, busy, dreaming, active, ambitious, covetous lovers of this world, if time could be entreated to return! How passionately then would they pour out their requests: "O that we might once see the days of hope, and means and mercy, which once we saw, and would not see! O that we had those days to spend in penitential tears and prayers, and holy preparations for an endless life, which we spent at cards, in needless recreations, in idle talk, in humoring others, in the pleasing of our flesh, or in the inordinate cares and business of the world! O that our youthful vigor might return! that our years might be renewed! that the days we spent in vanity might be recalled! that ministers might again be sent to us publicly and privately, with the message of grace which we once made light of! that the sun would once more shine upon us! and that patience and mercy would once more reassume their work!"

If cries or tears, or price or pain would bring back lost, abused time, how happy were the now distracted, dreaming, dead-hearted, and impenitent world! If it would then serve their turn to say to the vigilant believers, "Give us of your oil, for our lamps are gone out;" or to cry, "Lord, Lord, open to us," when the door is shut, the foolish would be saved as well as the wise. But this is "the day of salvation!" this is "the accepted time" While it is called to-day, hearken, and harden not your heart. Awake, thou that sleepest, and use the light that is afforded thee by Christ; or else the everlasting utter darkness will shortly end thy time and hope.

One life is appointed us on earth, to despatch the work on which our everlasting life depends, and we shall have but one. Lose that, and all is lost for ever: now you may hear, and read, and learn, and pray; but when this life is ended, it shall be so no more. You shall rise from the dead, indeed, to judgment, and to the life that you are now preparing for; but never to such a life as this on earth: your life is as the fighting of a battle that must be won or lost at once. There is no coming hither again to mend what is done amiss. Oversights must be presently corrected by repentance, or else they are everlastingly past remedy. Now, if you be not truly converted, you may be; if you find that you are carnal and miserable, you may be healed; if you are an enemy, you may be reconciled to God : but when once the thread of life is cut, your opportunities are at an end. Now you may inquire of your friends and teachers what you must do to be saved; and you may receive particular instructions and exhortations, and God may bless them to the illuminating, renewing, and saving of your soul. But when life is past, it will be so no more. O then, if departed souls might but return, and once more be tried with the means of life, what joyful tidings would it be! How welcome would be the messenger that brought it! Had hell but such an offer as this, and would any cries procure it from their righteous Judge, O what a change would be among them! How importunately would they cry to God, "O send us once again to the earth! Once more let us see the face of mercy, and hear the offers of Christ and of salvation! Once more let ministers offer us their help, and teach, in season and out of season, in public and in private, and we will refuse their help and exhortations no more; we will hate them, and drive them away from us no more. Once more let us have thy word and ordinances, and try whether we will not believe them, and use them better than we did. Once more let us have the help and company of thy saints, and we will scorn them, and abuse them, and persecute them no more. O for the great invaluable mercy of such a life as once we had! O try us once more with such a life, and see whether we will not contemn the world and close with Christ, and live as strictly, and pray as earnestly, as those that we hated and abused for so doing! O that we might once more be admitted into the holy assemblies, and have the Lord's day to spend in the business of our salvation! We would plead no more against the power and purity of the ordinances; we would no more call that day a burden, nor hate them that spend it in works of holiness, nor plead for the liberty of the flesh therein."

He that would have Lazarus sent from the dead to warn his unbelieving brethren on earth, no doubt would have strongly purposed himself on a reformation, if he might once more have been tried; and how earnestly would he have begged for such a trial, that begged so hard for a drop of water? But alas! such mouths must be stopped for ever with—"Remember that thou, in thy life-time, receivedst thy good things."

"It is appointed unto men once to die, but after this the judgment." There is no return to earth again: the places of your abode, employment, and delight, shall know you no more. You must see the faces of your friends, and converse in flesh with men no more. This world, those houses, that wealth and honor, as to any fruition, must be to you as if you had never known them.

You must assemble here but a little while. Yet a little longer, and we must preach, and you hear the Gospel invitation no more for ever. That therefore which you will do, must presently be done, or it will be too late. If ever you will repent and believe, it must be now. If ever you will be converted and sanctified, it must be now. If ever you will be pardoned and reconciled to God, it must be now. If ever you will reign, it is now that you must fight and conquer. "O that you were wise, that you understood this, that you would consider your latter end!" And that you would let those words sink down into your heart, which came from the heart of the Redeemer, as was witnessed by his tears: "If thou hadst known, even thou, at least in this thy day, the things which belong unto thy peace! but now they are hid from thine eyes."

There is no doing this work hereafter. Heaven and hell are for other work. The harvest doth presuppose the seed-time, and the labor of the husbandman. It is now that you must sow, and hereafter that you must reap. It is now that you must work, and then that you must receive your wages.

Is this believed and considered by the thoughtless world? Alas! do you live here as men that must live here no more? Do you work as men that must work no more, and pray as men that must pray no more, when once the time of work is ended? What thinkest thou? Will God command the sun to stand still while thou rebellest or forgettest thy work and him? Dost thou expect he should pervert the course of nature, and continue the spring and seed-time, till thou hast a mind to sow? Will he renew thy age, and make thee young again, and c_il back the hours that thou hast prodigally wasted on thy lusts and idleness? Canst thou look for this at the hand of God, when nature and Scripture assure thee of the contrary? If not, why hast thou not yet done with thy beloved sins? Why hast thou not yet begun to live? Why sittest thou still, while thy soul is unrenewed, and all thy preparation for death and judgment is yet to be made? Wilt thou hear and be converted in the grave and hell? or wilt thou be saved without holiness? that is, in despite of God, that hath resolved it shall not be. O ye sons of sleep, of death, of darkness, awake, and live, and hear the Lord, before the grave and hell have shut their mouths upon you! Hear now, lest hearing be too late! Hear now, if you will ever hear. Hear now, if you have ears to hear.

Look about you, and see what you have to do, and do it with your might.

1. Trifle not, but do it presently, without unnecessary delay.

2. Do it resolutely: remain not doubtful, unresolved, in suspense, as if it were yet a question with thee whether thou shouldst do it or not.

3. Do it with thy most awakened affections, and the serious intention of the powers of thy soul. Sleepiness and insensibility are most unsuitable to such works.

4. Do it with all necessary forecast and contrivance; not with a distracting, hindering care; but with such a care as may show that you despise not your Master, and are not regardless of his work; and with such a care as is suited to the difficulties and nature of the thing, and is necessary to the due accomplishment of it.

5. Do it not slothfully, but vigorously, and with diligence. "Hide not thy hand in thy bosom" with the slothful, and say not, "There is a lion in the way." The negligent, and the vicious, the waster and the slothful, differ but as one brother from another. As the self-murder of the wilful ungodly, so also "the desire of the slothful killeth him, because his hands refuse to labor." "The soul of the sluggard desireth and hath nothing; but the soul of the diligent shall be made fat." Be not slothful in business, but be "fervent in spirit, serving the Lord."

6. Do it with constancy, and not with destructive pauses and intermissions, or with weariness and turning back. "The righteous shall hold on his way, and he that is of clean hands shall be stronger and stronger." "Be steadfast, unmoveable, always abounding in the work of the Lord, for as much as you know that your labor is not in vain in the Lord." "Be not weary in well-doing: for in due season we shall reap if we faint not."

Apply these quickening precepts to all the duties of the Christian course. Be religious in good earnest, if you would be found such when you look for the reward. "Work out your salvation with fear and trembling." "Strive to enter in at the strait gate; for many shall seek to enter, and shall not be able." Many run, but few receive the prize: so run that you may obtain. "If the righteous scarcely be saved, where shall the ungodly and sinner appear?" Let the doting world deride your diligence, and set themselves to hinder and afflict you: it will be but a little while before experience change their minds, and make them talk differently. Follow Christ fully: be diligent and lose no time. The Judge is coming. Let not words, nor any thing that man can do, prevail with you to sit down, or stop you in a journey of such importance. Please God, though flesh, and friends, and all the world should be displeased. Obey God, though all the world forbid you. No power can save you from his justice; and none can deprive you of his reward. One thing is necessary: do that with speed, and care, and diligence, or you are lost for ever. They that are now against your much and earnest praying, will shortly cry as loud themselves in vain. When it is too late, how fervently will they beg for mercy, that now deride you for valuing and seeking it in time! But "then they shall call upon God, but he will not answer; they shall seek him early, but shall not find him: for that they hated knowledge, and did not choose the fear of the Lord: they would none of his counsel, but despised all his reproof." Up, therefore, and work with all thy might. Let unbelievers trifle, that know not that the righteous God stands over them, and know not that they are *now* to work for eternity, and know not that heaven or hell is at the end. Let them delay, and laugh, and play, and dream away their time, that are drunk with prosperity, and mad with fleshly lusts and pleasures, and have lost their reason in the cares, and delusions, and vain-glory of the world. But shall it be so with thee, whose eyes are opened, who seest the God, the heaven, the hell, which they do but hear of as unlikely things? Wilt thou live awake, as they that are asleep? Wilt thou do in the day-light as they do in the dark? Shall freemen live as Satan's slaves? Shall the living lie as still and useless as the dead? Work then while it is day, " for the night cometh, when none can work."

If your mind is sluggish, and you are forgetting your God and your latter end, and religion seems a lifeless thing, and you do your duty as if it were in vain, or against your will—*stir up your soul with the urgency of such questions as these:*—

Question 1. Can I do no more than this for *God*, who gave me all? who deserveth all? who seeth me in my duties and my sins? When he puts me purposely on the trial what I can do for his sake and service, can I do no more? Can I love him no more, and obey, and watch, and work no more?

Question 2. Can I do no more than this for *Christ?* for him that did so much for me? that obeyed so perfectly; walked so meekly; despising all the baits, and honors, and riches of the world? that loved me to the death ; and offereth me freely all his benefits, and would bring me to eternal glory? Are these careless, cold, and dull endeavors, my best return for all his mercy?

Question 3. Can I do no more, when *my salvation* is the prize? when heaven or hell depends upon it? when I know this beforehand, and may see, in the glass of the Holy Scriptures, what is prepared for the diligent and the negligent, and what work there is, and will be for ever, in heaven and hell, on these accounts? Could I not do more, if my house were on fire, or my estate, or life, or friend, were in danger, than I do for my salvation?

Question 4. Can I do no more for the *souls of men,* when they are undone for ever, if they be not speedily delivered? Is this my love and compassion to my neighbor, my servant, friend, or child?

Question 5. Can I do no more for the *church of God?*
for the public good? for the peace and welfare of the
nation, and our posterity? in suppressing sin? in praying
for deliverance? or in promoting works of public benefit?

Question 6. Can I do no more, that have loitered so
long; and go no faster, that have slept till the evening
of my days, when diligence is the one certain evidence
of my repentance?

Question 7. Can I do no more, that know not now but
I am doing my last? that see how fast my time makes
haste, and how I must be quickly gone? that know it
must be *now* or *never?*

Question 8. Can I do no better, when I know beforehand what a vexatious and heart-disquieting thing it will
then be, to look back on time as irrecoverably lost, and
on a life of trial as spent in vanity, while the work that
we lived for, lay undone? Shall I now, by trifling, prepare such tormenting thoughts for my awakened conscience?

Question 9. Can I do no more, when I am sure I cannot do too much, and am sure there is nothing else to be
preferred?

Question 10. Can I do no more, that have so much
help? that have mercies of all sorts encouraging me,
and creatures attending me? that have health to enable
me, or affliction to remind and excite me? that have such
a Master, such a work, such a reward? Who is less ex-
cuseable for neglect than I?

Question 11. Could I do no more, if I were sure that
my salvation lay on this one duty? that according to this
prayer, it should go with me for ever? or if the soul of
my child, my servant, or my neighbor, must speed for
ever, as my endeavors speed with them now for their
conversion? For aught I know, it may be thus.

Alas! it is nothing but intoxicating prosperity, and
sensual delights, and worldly diversions, that make you
think well of ungodly slothfulness, and make you think
contemptuously of a heavenly life.

Methinks I even see how you will passionately rage
against yourself, and tear your heart with self-revenge, (if
grace prevent it not by a safe repentance,) when you think,
too late, how you lived on earth, and what golden times of

grace you lost, and vilified all that would not lose them as foolishly as you. O how will you wonder at yourself, that ever you could be so blind and senseless, as to be no more affected with the warnings of the Lord, and with the forethoughts of everlasting joy and misery! To have but one small part of time to do all that ever must be done by you for eternity, and say all that ever you must say, for your own or others' souls, and to have spent this in worse than nothing! To have but one uncertain life, in which you must run the race that wins or loses heaven for ever; and that you should be tempted with a thing of nought to lose that one irrecoverable opportunity, and to sit still or run another way, when you should have been making haste with all your might! O the thoughts of this will give you unutterable anguish in the day of judgment. That you had a time in which you might have prayed, with promise of acceptance, and had no heart to take that time! That Christ was offered to you as well as to them that entertained him; that you were called on, and warned, as well as they, but obstinately despised and neglected all! That life and death were set before you, and everlasting joys were offered to your choice, and you might have freely had them if you would, and were told that holiness was the only way, and that it must be *now* or *never;* and yet that you chose your own destruction! These thoughts will be part of hell to the ungodly.

Come away, then, from the snares of sinners, and the company of deceived, hardened men. Heaven is before you! Death is at hand! The eternal God hath sent to call you! Mercy doth yet stretch forth its arms! You have stayed too long, and abused patience too much already: stay no longer! O now please God, and save yourself by resolving that "this shall be the day," and faithfully performing this your resolution. " Up and be doing:" believe, repent, obey, and do all this with all your might. Love him that you must love for ever, and love him with all your soul and might. Seek that which is truly worth seeking, and will pay for all your cost and pains, and seek it first with all your might, remembering still it must be *now* or *never.*

And now that I should conclude, I am loath to end,

for fear I have not yet prevailed with you. What are you now resolved to do, from this day forward? It is work of endless consequence that we have been speaking of, which must be done, and quickly done, and thoroughly done. Are you not convinced that it is so? that ploughing and sowing are not more necessary to your harvest, than is the work of holiness in this day of grace to your salvation? You are blind, if you see not this; you are dead, if you feel it not: what then will you do? O hear the God of heaven, if you will not hear us, who calleth to you, Return and live! O hear him that shed his blood for souls, and tendereth you now salvation by his blood! O hear without any more delay, before all is gone, and you are gone, and he, that now deceiveth you, torment you! Hold on a little longer in a carnal, earthly, unsanctified state, and it is too late to hope, or pray, or strive for your salvation. Yet a little longer, and mercy will have done with you for ever; and Christ will never invite you more, nor ever offer to cleanse you by his blood, nor sanctify you by his Spirit. O what shall I do to show you how near you stand to eternity, and what is now doing in the world that you are going to, and how these things are thought on there! What shall I do to make you know how time is valued, how sin and holiness are esteemed, in the world where you must live for ever! What shall I do to make you know these things *to-day?* If every word I write were accompanied with bitter tears, I should not think it too dear, if I could but help you to such a sight of the things we speak of, that you might truly understand them as they are: that you had but a true awakened apprehension of the shortness of your day, of the nearness of eternity, and of the endless consequence of your present work, and how holy labor and sinful loitering will be regarded in the world to come for ever. But when we see you sin, and trifle, and no more regard your endless life, and see also what haste your time is making, and yet cannot make you understand these things; when we know that you will shortly be astonished at the review of your present sloth and folly, and when we know that these matters are not thought of in another world, as they are among sleepy sinners here, and yet know not how to make you know it, whom it doth so exceedingly concern, this amazeth us, and almost breaks our heart.

Sinner, whatever the devil and raging passion may say against a holy life, God and your own conscience shall be our witnesses, that we desired nothing unreasonable, or unnecessary, at your hands.

The question that I am putting to you, is not whether you will be for this form of church-government, or for that: but it is, whether you will hearken in time to God and conscience, and be as busy to provide for heaven, as ever you have been to provide for earth? It is godliness, serious and practical godliness, that thou art called to. It is nothing but what all Christians in the world are agreed in. That I may not leave thee in any darkness which I can deliver thee from, I will tell thee distinctly, though succinctly, what it is that thou art thus importuned to; and tell me, then, whether it be that which any Christian can make doubt of.

1. That which I entreat of thee, is but to live as one that verily *believeth there is a God;* and that this God is the Creator, the Lord and Ruler of the world; and that it is incomparably more our business to understand and obey his laws, and as faithful subjects to be conformed to them, than to observe or be conformed to the laws of man: and to live as men that do believe that this God is almighty, and that the greatest of men are less than crawling worms to him; and that he is infinitely wise, and the wisdom of man is foolishness to him; and that he is infinitely good and amiable; that his love is the only felicity of man, and that none are happy but those that do enjoy it, and none that do enjoy it can be miserable; and that riches, and honor, and fleshly delights, are brutish vanities, in comparison of the eternal love of God. Is any of this a matter of controversy or doubt? Not among Christians, I am sure: not among wise men. It is no doubt to those in heaven, nor to those in hell, nor to those that have not lost their understandings upon earth. Live then according to these truths.

2. Live as men that verily believe *mankind is fallen into sin and misery;* and that all men are corrupted, and under the condemnation of the law of God, till they are delivered, pardoned, reconciled to God, and made new

creatures, by a renewing, restoring, sanctifying change.
Live but as men that believe that this cure must be
wrought, and this great restoring change must be made
upon ourselves, if it be not done already. Live as men
who have so great a work to look after; and is this a
matter of any doubt or controversy? Sure it is not
to a Christian: and methinks it should not be to any man
else that knoweth himself, any more than to a man in a
dropsy, whether he be diseased, when he feels the thirst
and sees the swelling. Did you but know what cures and
changes are necessarily to be made upon your diseased,
miserable soul, if you care what becomes of it, you would
soon see cause to look about you.

3. Live but as men that verily believe the *Son of God
hath suffered* for sin, and brought the tidings of pardon
and salvation, which you may have, if you will give up
yourself to him who is the Physician of souls, to be healed
by him. Live as men that believe that the infinite love
of God, revealed to lost mankind in the Redeemer, doth
bind us to love him with all our hearts, and serve him
with all our restored faculties, and to work as those that
have the greatest thankfulness to show, as well as the
greatest mercies to receive, and misery to escape. Live as
those that believe that if sinners, who, without Christ,
could have had no hope, shall now love their sins and
refuse to leave them, and to repent and be converted,
and unthankfully reject the mercies of salvation, so dearly
bought and freely offered them, their damnation will be
doubled, as their sin is doubled.

Live but as men that have such redemption to admire,
such mercy to entertain, and such a salvation to secure,
and that are sure they can never escape, if they continue
to "neglect so great salvation." And is there any
controversy among Christians in any of this? There is
not, certainly.

4. Live but as men that believe *the Holy Ghost is
given* by Jesus Christ to convert, to quicken, and to sanctify all that he will save; that "except ye be born again"
"of the Spirit, you shall not enter into the kingdom of
heaven;" and that "if any man have not the Spirit of
Christ, he is none of his;" and that without this, no
mending of your life, by any common principles, will

serve for your salvation, or make you acceptable to God. Live as men that believe that this Spirit is given by the hearing of the word of God, and must be prayed for, and obeyed, and not resisted, quenched, and grieved And is there any controversy among Christians in any of this?

5. Live but as men that believe that *sin is the greatest evil*, the thing which the holy God abhoreth; and then you will never make a mock of it, as Solomon saith the foolish do; nor say, What harm is in it?

6. Live but as men that believe *no sin is pardoned without repentance;* and that repentance is the loathing and forsaking of sin; and that if it be true, it will not suffer you to live in any sin, nor to desire to keep the least infirmity, nor to be loath to know your unknown sins.

7. Live as those that believe that there is *a life everlasting*, where the sanctified shall live in endless joy, and the unsanctified in endless punishment and wo: live but as men that verily believe a heaven and a hell, and a day of judgment, in which all the actions of this life must be revised, and all men judged to their endless state. Believe these things heartily, and then think a holy diligence needless, if you can. Then be of the mind of the deriders and enemies of godliness, if you can. If one sight of heaven or hell would serve without any more ado, instead of other arguments, to confute all the cavils of the distracted world, and to justify the most diligent saints in the judgment of those that now abhor them, why should not a sound belief of the same thing in its measure do the same?

8. Live but as those that believe this life is given us *as the only time to make preparation* for eternal life: and that all that ever shall be done for your salvation, must be now, just now, before your time is ended: live as those that know and need not faith to tell them, that this time is short, and almost at an end already, and stayeth for no man, but, as a post, doth haste away. It will not stay while you are taken up at stage-plays, in compliments, in idle visits, or any impertinent, needless things: it will not tarry while you spend yet the other year, or month, or day, in your worldliness or ambition, or in your

lusts and sensual delights, and put off your repentance to another time. O, for the Lord's sake, do but live as men that must be shortly buried in the grave, and their souls appear before the Lord; and as men that have but this little time to do all for their everlasting life, that ever must be done. O live as men that are sure to die, and are not sure to live till to-morrow: and let not the noise of pleasure or worldly business, or the chat or scorns of miserable fools, bear down your reason, and make you live as if you knew not what you know; or as if there was any doubt about these things. Who is the man, and what is his name, that dares contradict them, and can make it good? O do not sin against your knowledge: do not stand still and see your glass running, and time making such haste, and yet make no more haste yourselves, than if you were not concerned in it. Do not O do not slumber, when time and judgment never slumber; nor sit still, when you have so much to do, and know all that is now left undone must be undone for ever! Alas, how many questions of exceeding weight have you yet to be resolved in! whether you are truly sanctified? whether your sins be pardoned? whether you shall be saved when you die? whether you are ready to leave this world and enter upon another? I tell you, the answering of these, and many more such questions, is a matter of no small difficulty or concern. And all these must be done in this little and uncertain time. It must be *now* or *never*.

9. Lastly, Will you but live as men that believe that *the world and the flesh are the deadly enemies of your salvation?* and that "if any man love the world," (so far) "the love of the Father is not in him?" and as men that believe that, "if ye live after the flesh, ye shall die; but if by the Spirit ye do mortify the deeds of the body, ye shall live;" and that those who are in Christ Jesus, and are freed from condemnation, are such as "walk not after the flesh, but after the Spirit?" Will you live as knowing that we must "make no provision for the flesh to fulfil the lusts thereof;" and must not "walk in gluttony and drunkenness, in chambering and wantonness, in strife and envying;" but must "have our hearts where our treasure is," and our conversation in heaven; and being

risen with Christ, must seek the things that are above,
and set our affections on them, and not on the things
that are on earth?

Will you say that any of this is our singular opinion,
or matter of controversy and doubt? Are not all Christians agreed in it? Do you not, yourself, profess that
you believe it? Live then but as those that do believe
it, and condemn not yourself in the things that you
confess.

O that you would hear us! Though we speak not to
you as men would do that had seen heaven and hell,
and were themselves in a perfectly awakened frame, yet
hear us while we speak to you the words of truth, with
some seriousness and compassionate desire for your salvation. O look up to your God! Look out unto eternity:
look inwardly upon your souls: look wisely upon your
short and hasty time; and then bethink you how the
little remnant of your time should be employed; and
what it is that most concerneth you to despatch and
secure before you die. Now you have sermons, and
books, and warnings: it will not be so long. Now you
have the Lord's day to spend in holy exercises, for the
edification and solace of your souls. O what invaluable mercies are all these! O know your time, and use
these with industry, and improve this harvest for your
souls! For it will not be thus always: it must be *now* or
never. You have yet time and leave to pray and cry to
God in hope: yet if you have hearts and tongues, he
hath a hearing ear; the Spirit of grace is ready to assist
you. It will not be thus always: the time is coming,
when the loudest cries will do no good. O pray, pray,
pray, poor needy miserable sinner; for it must be *now*
or *never*.

Would you not be loath to be left to the despairing
case of many poor distressed souls, that cry out, "O it is
now too late! I fear my day of grace is past; God
will not hear me now, if I should call upon him: he hath
forsaken me, and given me over to myself. It is too late
to repent, too late to pray, too late to think of a new
life; all is too late." This case is sad; but yet many of
these are in a safer and better case than they imagine;
and it is not too late, while they cry out, "It is too late;"

out if you are left to cry out in hell, "It is too late;" alas, how long and how doleful a cry and lamentation will it be!

O consider, poor sinner, that God knoweth the time and season of thy mercies. He giveth the spring and harvest in their season; and all his mercies in their season; and wilt thou not know thy time and season for love, and duty, and thanks to him?

Consider that God, who hath commanded thee thy work, hath also appointed thee thy time. And this is his appointed time. To-day, therefore, hearken to his voice, and see that thou harden not thy heart. He that bids thee repent and believe in Christ, doth also bid thee do it now. Obey him in the time, if thou wilt be indeed obedient; he best understandeth the fittest time. One would think, that to men that have lost so much already, and loitered so long, and are so lamentably behindhand, and stand so near the bar of God and their everlasting state, there should be no need to say any more to persuade them to be up and doing. I shall add but this: "You are never like to have a better time." Take this, or the work will grow more difficult, more doubtful, if, through the just judgment of God, it become not desperate. If all this will not serve, but still you will loiter till time be gone, what can your poor friends do but lament your misery! The Lord knows, if we knew what words, what pains, what cost would tend to your awakening, and conversion, and salvation, we should be glad to submit to it; and hope we should not think our labors, or liberties, or our lives too dear, to promote so blessed and so necessary a work. But if, when all is done that we can do, you will leave us nothing but our tears and moans for self-destroyers, the sin is yours, and the suffering shall be yours. If I can do no more, I shall leave this upon record, that we took our time to tell you, that *serious diligence* is necessary to your salvation; and that God is the "Rewarder of them that diligently seek him;" and that this was your day, your only day. It must be NOW or NEVER.

THE

SAILOR'S FRIEND.

—✺—

SAILOR, will you permit a friend to converse with you seriously a few moments? Your life is a life of danger. To-day you may be sailing under a cloudless sky; to-morrow the storm may rage around you, and put your life in jeopardy. But there is a danger to which you are exposed, that is still more awful—*the danger of losing the soul.* A Saviour has, however, been provided, who not only delivers from this danger, but raises superior to the fear of every other. The following pages are intended to draw your attention to the danger alluded to, and to the only way of escaping it.

While the children of men are universally depraved, this depravity is not manifested by every individual in the same manner. One follows one vicious inclination, another, another. There are characteristic crimes attached to many professions, and yours has not failed to be thus distinguished. The crime of swearing, for example, has become common among sea-faring people, to a proverb. Many of you are guilty of habitual swearing; and you attempt to apologize for your conduct by saying, "We mean no harm:" but the Lord hath said that he "will not hold him guiltless who taketh his name in vain." Others of you indulge in violent anger upon the least opposition, and often gratify your rage in the most degrading manner; and you will even glory in this as a display of courage: or should the thought come across your mind that such conduct is condemned by the Divine law, you endeavour to quiet your consciences with such reflections as the following: "No man is perfect;"—"You do not keep anger;"—"You are no hypocrite;"—and, upon the whole, "You have a good heart." There are others of you who take exquisite pleasure in riotous mirth and brutal dissipation. "Who hath woe? who hath sorrow? who hath contentions? who hath babbling? who hath wounds without cause?" Is it not frequently the dissipated Sailor? Is not this a just description of some of your revellings, banquetings, and riotous meetings? And mark the baneful effects which result from them even in this world. "Thou shalt be as he who lieth down in the midst of the sea, or as he that lieth on the top of a mast. They have stricken me, thou shalt say, and I was not sick; they have beaten me, and I felt it not: when shall I awake? I will seek it yet again." Prov. xxiii. 29. 34, 35. Many, however, who would be shocked so far to transgress the bounds of external decency, are, nevertheless, "foolish and disobedient, serving divers lusts and pleasures, living in malice and envy, hateful and hating one another." Your conduct may be upright and honourable among men, but how does your heart stand affected towards God? Is He the object of your supreme delight? Or is your heart wholly set on earthly things? Are you grateful to your fellow-men for the favours they bestow upon you; but feel no gratitude to Him who bestows upon you life, and breath, and all things? If you say you are grateful to God, let me ask if your gratitude be proved to be genuine by searching his word to know his will, and by obeying all his commandments? He who searcheth and knoweth the heart, requires that you should love him with all your heart, and your neighbour as yourself. Whatever you may think of yourself, when tried by this righteous law you must be found guilty. For in place of loving God, "the carnal mind" (and this is the mind which all the children of men are possessed of by nature) "is enmity against God, for it is not subject to the law of God, neither indeed can be." It is further declared, that "there is none righteous, no, not one; all have sinned, and come short of the glory of God:" and this is written, "that every mouth may be stopped, and all the world become guilty before God."

Allow me now to warn you of your extreme danger, if you have hitherto neglected the great salvation. We presume you will acknowledge, from the view which has been given of the divine law, that you are a sinner. Hear then the solemn denunciation of Jehovah: "Cursed is every one who continueth not in all things written in the book of the law to do them." There is only this life between you

and that world where this curse shall be put in execution.
And " what is our life? it is a vapour which continueth for
a little time, and then vanisheth away." A thousand un-
foreseen accidents may land us in an eternal world, before
we are aware. And you not only stand exposed to the diseases and calamities common to man, but from the perilous
nature of your employment, you may be said to be " in
deaths oft." The swelling sea may in a moment wash you
into the bosom of the great deep. Perhaps you have been
more than once in scenes of the greatest danger: when
the stormy winds appeared to carry death on their wings,
and every billow seemed fraught with destruction; and
possibly, in spite of every effort, you were nearing a coast
under the fearful apprehension of being dashed in pieces.
You may have seen vessels, with which you were in company, hoist signals of distress, and been unable to afford
any relief to those who were ready to perish—yea, out of
a wreck you may have escaped, while you saw some of
your shipmates sink like lead in the mighty waters. In
such calamitous scenes, have you not felt the pangs of a
guilty conscience, and the fearful forebodings of a future
judgment? Have you not been sensible, that although religion may be despised in life, it is indispensably necessary
at the approach of death? In the hour of danger, have you
not formed the resolution, that, if spared, you would never
be the same again? But the storm has no sooner subsided,
than you, like Pharaoh, have hardened your heart, returned
to your old courses of iniquity, and become fully as unconcerned about an eternal world as before. "And do ye thus
requite the Lord, O foolish people and unwise? They
who go down to the sea in ships, and do business in great
waters; these see the works of the Lord, and his wonders in
the great deep. He commandeth, and raiseth the stormy
wind, which lifteth up the waves thereof. They mount up
to the heavens, and go down again to the depths, their
souls are melted because of trouble. They reel to and
fro, and stagger like a drunken man, and are at their wits'
end. Then they cry unto the Lord in their trouble, and
he bringeth them out of their distresses. He maketh the
storm a calm, so that the waves are still; then are they
glad, because they are quiet, and he bringeth them to their
desired haven. O that men would praise the Lord for his

goodness, and for his wonderful works to the children of men!" See Psalm cvii. 23—32.

You are thus every moment in danger of being hurried into an eternal world, and into misery with which all the sufferings endured in this world are not for a moment to be compared. Those who perish in their sins, perish for ever. The Scriptures represent all mankind as in a lost condition! and what renders their situation still more awful is, they are neither aware of their danger, nor at all concerned about it. Thus it was with the antediluvians, "they planted and builded, they bought and sold, they married and were given in marriage, until the day that Noah entered the ark, and the flood came and swept them all away." And although "the heavens and the earth which are now, are reserved unto fire against the day of judgment and perdition of ungodly men," yet the same carelessness about an eternal world still continues. But however much men may put off the evil day, it is certain that "upon the wicked God shall rain fire and brimstone, and a horrible tempest; this shall be the portion of their cup." "The Lord Jesus shall be revealed from heaven, in flaming fire, taking vengeance on them who know not God, and who obey not the Gospel; who shall be punished with everlasting destruction from the presence of the Lord and from the glory of his power." 2 Thes. i. 7—9. What are all the desolations which the most dreadful storms ever produced, when compared with this? The dismal shrieks of the crew, when their vessel is going to pieces, can convey but a very faint idea, indeed, of the wreck of dissolving worlds; when men shall be calling to the rocks and mountains to fall on them, and cover them from the wrath of God and of the Lamb.

Do you ask, how shall I be safe at that day? There is no way of safety for any sinner, except the atonement of Jesus. "He is a hiding-place from the wind, and a covert from the tempest. He is a strength to the poor, and a strength to the needy in their distress, a refuge from the storm, and a shadow from the heat, when the blast of the terrible ones is as a storm against the wall." Isa. xxv. 4. "God so loved the world, that he gave his only begotten Son, that whosoever believeth in him might not perish, but have everlasting life." Jehovah's equal Son assumed our nature, and endured that wrath which sin deserves. " He did no sin, neither was guile found in his mouth; yet it pleased the Lord to bruise him, and to put him to grief." The Lord laid on him the iniquity of all his people. The Saviour died for sinners that they might live; and in proof of the Father's approbation of his atonement, He was raised from the dead, and " exalted to the Father's right hand, a Prince and a Saviour, to give repentance and the remission of sins."

Sailor! this is the only haven of safety for your immortal soul. His name is a strong tower, to which the righteous run and are safe, and there is no other refuge: for " there is no other name given under heaven among men, by which you can be saved, but the name of Jesus; and by him, all who believe are justified from all things. Their sins and their iniquities God remembers no more." Permit me then to ask, *What think you of Christ?* Ponder the question; both your present and eternal happiness hinge upon right views of the Saviour. If he be your refuge and righteousness, he will be " altogether lovely" in your esteem; but if you still consider him " as a root out of dry ground," an object unworthy of either your faith or affection, you stand unsheltered from the wrath of God. We are warranted to affirm, that without faith in the Redeemer, and supreme love to him, you can neither live in safety, nor die in security: for it is written, " If any man love not the Lord Jesus Christ, he shall be anathema maranatha"— accursed at the coming of Christ. But praised be his name the way of access to him yet is open. Jesus is still saying, " Come unto me, all ye that labour and are heavy laden, and I will give you rest. Therefore, take with you words, and turn to the Lord, and say, Take away all iniquity, and receive us graciously, and we will render unto thee the offerings of our lips."

You have frequently felt the advantage of a well sheltered roadstead, or safe harbour, during a disastrous storm. And when danger was apprehended, the desire of self-preservation has induced you to steer with all possible speed for a place of safety. May we not then entreat you to act as wise a part for the salvation of your soul, as in many instances you have done for the preservation of your life? Take an example of prudence from Noah, who " by faith, when he was warned of God of things not seen as yet, prepared an ark to the saving of his house, by which he condemned the world, and became heir of the righteousness which is by faith." If you take shelter under Immanuel's wings, you will experience " that there is now no condemnation to them who are in Christ Jesus, who walk not after the flesh, but after the Spirit. Flee, therefore, for refuge, to lay hold on the hope set before you in the Gospel." A drowning man would gladly lay hold of a rope cast to him as the means of deliverance—he would neither hesitate about the strength of the cord, nor question the compassion or ability of him who threw it. He might be disappointed; but if you lay hold on the glorious Gospel of the blessed God, you will most certainly be delivered from the gulf of eternal misery, and enjoy everlasting life.

Do not then delay attending to the things which belong to your everlasting peace; for although the Lord bears long with the negligence and wickedness of men, yet his longsuffering is daily drawing to a close. " The Lord is not slack concerning his promise, as some men count slackness, but is long-suffering to us-ward, not willing that any should perish, but that all should come to repentance. Who art thou, O man, who despisest the riches of the forbearance of God, not knowing that the goodness of God leadeth thee to repentance?" Perhaps, Reader, you have grown old in the service of Satan; if so, it is surely time to listen to the voice of earnest entreaty: " O ye sons of men, how long will ye turn my glory into shame? How long will ye love vanity, and seek after lies? This has been thy manner from thy youth." And as time is short, death certain, and eternity at hand, the question ought to be urged upon your attention, " How long, ye simple ones, will ye love simplicity? and ye scorners delight in your scorning! and ye fools hate knowledge! Turn ye at my reproof, saith the Lord; behold, I will pour out my Spirit upon you, I will make known my words unto you. Seek ye the Lord while he may be found: call ye upon him while he is near. Let the wicked forsake his way, and the unrighteous man his thoughts; and let him return unto the Lord, and he will have mercy upon him; and to our God, for he will abundantly pardon. Behold, now is the accepted time; behold, now is the day of salvation; to-day, if ye will hear his voice, harden not your hearts." If the reader is young, let him attend to the following gracious words of the Lord: "I love them who love me, and they who seek me early shall find me." If riches and honours are the objects of your pursuit, seek them where they are to be found. "Riches and honour are with me; (saith Wisdom;) yea, durable riches and righteousness. My fruit is better than gold, yea, than much fine gold; and my revenue than choice silver. I lead in the way of righteousness, in the midst of the paths of judgment: that I may cause them that love me to inherit substance; and I will fill all their treasures." There is a thousand fold more to be enjoyed in the unsearchable riches of Christ, than the most sanguine expectations can anticipate. To have the soul "filled with all the fulness of God," puts more gladness into the heart of the righteous, than the wicked enjoy when their corn and wine and oil are increased. "O taste and see that God is good; they are blessed who trust in him."

In order to animate the hopes, draw forth the prayers, and stimulate the exertions of the church of God for the conversion of Seamen, God hath declared to Zion: "Then thou shalt see and flow together, and thy heart shall fear and be enlarged, because the abundance of the sea shall be converted unto thee, and the forces of the Gentiles shall be brought unto thee." Isa. lx. 5. The achievement of such a noble conquest upon the watery world, where Satan has long swayed an almost universal sceptre, is calculated to make heaven and earth resound with joy. And the Sailor's profane swearing shall give place to the praises of the Lord, from a pure heart. "Sing unto the Lord a new song, and his praise from the ends of the earth; ye that go down to the sea, and all that is therein; the isles and the inhabitants thereof." Isa. xlii. 10.

It is worthy of remark, that in these eventful days in which we live, the Lord is blessing the word of his grace in no ordinary degree, for the conversion of Seamen. They are now putting their trust in him, "who is the confidence of all the ends of the earth, and of those who are afar off upon the sea." Psalm lxv. 5. God is granting to Sailors "repentance unto life." This is calculated to afford you the most heart-melting encouragement to return to the Lord, and confide in his mercy.

And consider, Reader, that the Gospel will prove either the means of salvation to you, or the means of increasing your punishment at last. The time is not far distant, when the hand of the writer shall moulder into dust, and the eye of the reader shall be closed in death : they may never meet but at the judgment-seat of Christ. Then, the reception which has been given to the truths contained in these pages will be disclosed before an assembled world. If they be the means of leading to the oracles of God, and to Him, " to whom all the prophets gave witness," their design will be fully answered. But, if the reader live and die in the neglect of the great salvation, they will be an additional witness against him, in the great and notable day of the Lord; and will add to his eternal anguish. We would, therefore, " beseech you to be reconciled unto God. For he hath made Christ, who knew no sin, to be sin for the guilty, that they might be made the righteousness of God in him." If you believe the declarations of the Scriptures concerning the death of Christ as an atonement for sin, and receive him as your Redeemer, you will enjoy the favour of God and the good hope of everlasting life ; and death will, in consequence, be stripped of all its terrors. In the midst of the stormy ocean your mind will be at peace, trusting in Him who can say to the proud waves of the sea, " Peace, be still." You will be convinced that " not a hair of your head can perish without your Father;" and that although he should see fit to allow you to perish in the sea, your spirit will immediately join those of " the just made perfect :" and at the great day, when " the sea shall give up the dead which are in it," your body, " fashioned like the glorious body of the Son of God, will be caught up to meet the Lord in the air ; and so be for ever with the Lord."

A

Parting Address

TO A

SABBATH-SCHOOL CHILD.

PUBLISHED BY THE

AMERICAN TRACT SOCIETY,

AND SOLD AT THEIR DEPOSITORY, NO. 150 NASSAU-STREET, NEAR
THE CITY-HALL, NEW-YORK; AND BY AGENTS OF THE
SOCIETY, ITS BRANCHES, AND AUXILIARIES, IN
THE PRINCIPAL CITIES AND TOWNS
IN THE UNITED STATES.

PARTING ADDRESS.

As you are now about to leave the school in which you have been taught a considerable time, we cannot part with you till we have given you a few hints of counsel and caution, which we trust you will receive as a token of our affectionate good-will towards you, and our desire to promote your prosperity.

Here let us remind you of *four* things:

1. You are a *rational* creature. You can think, and reason, as well as feel. God hath made you " wiser than the fowls of the air and the beasts of the field." Job, xxxv. 11.

2. You are a *sinful* creature. You have done that which you ought not to have done, and have left undone what you ought to have done. Does not your conscience bear witness that what we now say is true?

3. You are an *accountable* creature. Your soul is not your own. God hath said, " All souls are mine." Ezek. xviii. 4. Every tie of duty, of gratitude, and of love, binds you to him who is your Creator and your Father in heaven. Forget not that he who is now your Preserver and Benefactor, will soon be your Judge. "For we must all appear before the judgment seat of Christ." 2 Cor. v. 10.

4. You are an *immortal* creature. Though your body will soon die and turn to dust, your soul will live for ever, and for ever feel either the happiness enjoyed in heaven, or the misery endured in hell. How solemn is the prospect of *eternity*, which the Bible opens!

All these things you have been taught in this school. Do you understand them now?

I. *Consider what you have been taught.*

You have been taught to read " the Holy Scriptures, which are able, through faith in Christ Jesus, to make you wise unto salvation." You have been taught that God sees you by day and by night; that he is always present

with you; that with almighty power he can reward or punish; that he is " able to save and to destroy." The ten
commandments, containing the will of God concerning
you, have been explained. The sins into which you are
most liable to fall, (such as falsehood, dishonesty, profaneness, and filthy speaking,) have been clearly pointed out.
It has been shown that all your sins spring from the corruption of your nature, and that your nature is corrupt in
consequence of the fall of Adam, the fall of us all, who
broke the covenant of our God. You have heard of the
great love of God in sending his Son Jesus Christ to save
sinners. You have been told that he was born at Bethlehem, of the Virgin Mary, in circumstances of poverty;
that his life was perfectly holy, just and good, exemplify-
ing all the precepts of the law; that as he grew in stature,
he grew in wisdom, and in favour with God and man; that,
when twelve years of age, he was found in the temple listening to the elders, and asking questions; that he went
back to Nazareth with his parents, and was subject to
them; that he was a preacher of righteousness, explaining
by parables, and in other forms, the wonders of the reign
of God on earth; and that he was despised and rejected of
men, though the miracles he wrought were grand, instruc-
tive, and eminently beneficial. You have heard of his
agony and bloody sweat in the garden of Gethsemane, the
treachery of Judas, the shameful flight of the other apostles, the cruel mockings he endured in the hall of Caia-
phas and in the palace of Herod, the hypocrisy of the
priests and elders, the injustice of Pontius Pilate, the insults of a barbarous rabble, and the tortures of crucifixion
on Mount Calvary. There, after carrying his own cross
to the place of execution, he was fastened to it. They
pierced his hands and his feet with the cruel nails. The
cross was lifted up, and being placed between the crosses
of two malefactors, Jesus " was numbered with transgressors." " He suffered, the just for the unjust, that he might
bring us to God."

You have heard many urgent and pressing exhortations,
to mourn over the corruption of your nature; to flee for
refuge to Jesus, the all-sufficient Saviour of sinners, that
you may be washed in the fountain of his blood; and to
pray for the purifying influences of the Holy Spirit. Par-

don and purification are equally necessary. For if not pardoned, you must be sent to the prison of hell on account
of your sins. And there is no forgiveness of sins but
through the precious blood of Christ. Again, if not purified, you cannot go to heaven. Nothing unclean shall enter the New Jerusalem above.

You have been instructed not only in the school, but
also by the minister in the place of worship which you
have constantly attended. Remember that you have been
often exhorted to keep holy the Sabbath day as long as you
live. You have heard a great many public sermons, as well
as more private exhortations; and have you heard all in
vain ?

You have seen good children rewarded, and the disobedient reproved and punished. Some may have been so
intolerably wicked, that, because their temper and behaviour were infectious, in kindness to you they were expelled.
Some may have been restored, when they have appeared
to repent, and have earnestly begged to be admitted again.
Some may have died since your own admission. What
effect have these things produced upon you? Some may
have died happily in the Lord. You heard perhaps their
last words repeated; their sorrow for their sinfulness, their
trust in Christ, and their love to him, their prayers for you,
and their thankfulness to their teachers and benefactors.
Did you not feel, on such occasions, a desire that your last
end, if called to die soon, might be like theirs? Did you
not resolve to live in obedience to the will of God? Forget
not those tender moments when you retired to pray alone;
and pray without ceasing, that the impressions then made
may be revived and confirmed; that the good seed then
sown, may not be lost, but be ripened into useful fruit.

II. *Consider what is now justly expected from you.*

Your *parents* expect that you will be more dutiful and
affectionate to them, and more kind to your brothers and
sisters, than if you had not been instructed. " Honour
thy father and thy mother; which is the first commandment with promise." Eph. vi. 2. Your *teachers* will expect that you inform them of your situation, and that if
Providence bring you from a distance into the neighbourhood, you will call at the school. They who have labour-

ed so much for your good, and are therefore so much interested in your welfare, will be always glad to see you again.
The *neighbours* in general who know you, expect that your
conduct will be more regular and becoming than if you
had not received these advantages. Your *heavenly Father*
will require that you make a suitable return of gratitude to
him for this favour. It is he who has put it into the hearts
of your teachers to spend a part of their time in giving you
instruction. He brought them into this neighbourhood.
He gave you health, and opportunity, and ability, to learn
what you have learned. With these cords of love he draws
you to himself; and will not this encourage you to study
the more to please him?

III. *Consider your present prospects.*

You expect to be men and women. Remember that
humility, honesty, modesty, diligence, cheerfulness and
piety, are the principal qualities of every good man and
woman. Make much of public worship. Constantly attend upon it. Fail not to pray, in secret, to your Father
in heaven. For he will hear if you pray in the name of
Christ, and ask for those things which he has promised;
and " this will prove a source of consolation to you, when
no other ear listens to your complaint, when no other friend
is nigh to sympathize with you." Be very careful of forming acquaintances. Beware of wicked young men and
wicked young women. Be a companion to no one that
despises God; for it is written, " a companion of fools shall
be destroyed." Prov. xiii. 20. Good men will say, " Come
thou with us, and we will surely do thee good, for the
Lord hath spoken good concerning Israel." Num. x. 29.
Perhaps you have some pious relatives, who are watching,
hoping, praying for you; deeply interested in your temporal welfare, and longing for your final salvation.

The time is coming when your principles and temper
will be severely tried. It will be seen when you are
tempted, and it cannot be known till then, except to him
that knoweth all things, whether you are prepared to stand
fast in the hour of temptation. It will be seen very soon
whether you love truth and integrity, or not; whether you
love and honour good men, or not; whether you have a
sincere attachment to the house of God, or whether you

prefer roving about on the Sabbath with those who fear
not God.

If your parents are pious, you will see what additional
obligations lie upon you to every good word and work.
Has your immortal soul been precious in their eyes? Have
they laboured to instil sentiments of piety and virtue into
your heart in a suitable manner, as you were able to receive them? Have they been accustomed to call you to
join in family worship? Has their example been such, that
they might say, in humble imitation of the great apostle,
" Be ye followers of me, even as I am of Christ?" Have
they governed and corrected you with wisdom, sometimes
mingling their tears with their admonitions, avoiding with
equal care the extremes of foolish fondness and cruel severity? Have they, in a word, trained you up in the " nur-
ture and admonition of the Lord?" How anxiously, then,
will they follow you in their thoughts, while you enter into
new and hitherto untrodden paths, which are beset with
so many snares! Wherever Providence places you, let it
be your aim to make all happy around you. Study propriety in your behaviour towards your superiors, your
equals, and your inferiors; and you will be respected by
all. Never indulge a censorious or slanderous tongue.
Never speak evil of any one, except you see clearly that
you are called to do so for some valuable purpose. It is
written, " Whoso keepeth his mouth and his tongue, keepeth his soul from troubles." Prov. xxi. 23.

Remember, death will soon overtake you. " The judge
standeth at the door." Heaven is near; and hell is also
near. What God will do with you, we know not. Indeed,
where he may appoint your lot even in this life, we cannot
tell. Some of our children may be in the *East* Indies, and
some in the *West*. Many will be scattered through the
different parts of this country, and we may not again see
them till we all stand before the judgment seat of Christ.
Our prayers shall follow you, that you may do worthily in
your generation. Go, and the Lord be with you. " If
thou be wise, thou shall be wise for thyself; but if thou
scornest, thou alone shalt bear it." Prov. ix. 12.

And now, my dear child, stop and think. Many children
read much, but do not think of what they read. Think
how great a mercy you possess in being able to read the

Bible. Think what a great blessing a Sabbath-school is, by which a child may become learned in the knowledge of God, of Jesus Christ, and of heaven. Think, how a poor sinful child like you, may become happy by trusting in Christ, and keeping his commandments. Think how needful it is for you to be prepared to die ; since many children die when they are young.

To be prepared to die, you must think of God, and love him : be sorry for your sins, trust in Christ, and serve him.

There are many reasons why you should begin to do this *now*.

The first is, that if your heart is not thinking of good things, it will be thinking of evil things.

The second is, if you begin now to fear God, and you should live long, you will be more happy, and do more good to others, and honour God the longer; and God will very kindly reward you for ever.

The third reason why you should now remember God is, it is a very great sin to forget God; and this one sin will make you commit other sins; and it may provoke God to punish you, to take away your life, and send you to the place of torment.

The fourth reason why you should now begin to seek the Lord, is, that it will make you very happy to think of God, as the glorious Being who is in every place; whose eye always sees you, night and day; who hears your prayers, protects your life, gives you food and clothes, Grace and Heaven.

The child who believes that God is in every place, who trusts his word, hopes in his mercy through Jesus Christ, and loves to do his will, may be patient, thankful, and happy, when he is sick, and thinks he shall die. The wicked child, who forgets God when he is in health, will be afraid of God as his enemy, and think that God will not take him to heaven, but send him to hell for his sins.

You should remember, God is present with you night and day, in every place, to make you thankful to him for his mercies, and contented with what he gives you, and also to make you afraid of evil words, evil actions, and evil thoughts; because God is holy, and hates all kind of sin. And if some men and women, who do not love God, should see that *you*, though so young, are afraid to offend him, it may do them good, and convince them of their wickedness.

You should remember and seek God now you are young, because your life is uncertain. You must die. You may die soon. Perhaps you may die this year, or this month. You may die this week—this day, or this very hour. And if you should die without fearing or loving God, without trusting in Christ to save your soul from sin and hell, you will be miserable for ever.

Dear young Reader, what do you think of religion? What do you *feel*? What do you *desire*? Do you wish to die safe and happy? Trust in the grace of Christ to save you from the love of sin, the practice of sin, and the punishment of sin. Do not suppose that you are too young to think of religion. The evil days may come while you are young. You are not too young to repent of sin, to be converted to God, to believe in Christ as your Saviour, your Lord, and your example. You are not too young to suffer, and to die. You are not too young to be punished for your sins; not too young to be saved from them.

You may ask, What shall I do to be saved? Repent of all your sins, trust in Jesus Christ for pardon, and keep his commandments. Read his holy word, and pray for the Holy Spirit to enable you to understand it. Lord, teach me to pray, and make me truly sorry for every sin. Show me the evils of my heart, and change it. Help me to love thee as my Creator and my Father. O may I trust in Jesus Christ to save me from sin and from hell. Send thy good Spirit into my heart, to make me wise to salvation; to make me holy, happy, and useful, in life and death; and if I live, may I live to the honour of Christ my Saviour; and when I die, may I die joyful in the Lord, and be with him for ever. Lord, grant me these mercies for the sake of Jesus Christ! AMEN.

END.

THE NEW BIRTH.

WHOEVER reads the Scriptures with serious attention, will perceive that some kind of *change* must take place in every person, in order to his becoming a real Christian. This change is described by a variety of names, the most remarkable of which is *Regeneration*, or *the New Birth*. The necessity of this change is often insisted on in the Bible, and no where more strongly than in our Saviour's discourse with Nicodemus, recorded in the third chapter of St. John's Gospel, where he says to that ruler, *Verily, verily, I say unto you, except a man be born again, he cannot see the kingdom of God.*

As this change is absolutely necessary to salvation, it is of great importance to know what it is ; especially as there is much reason to fear that many mistake its true nature, and take the shadow for the substance. Be it observed, then, that,

1. *The new birth is a* GREAT *change ;* the term must signify so much; it signifies that we must be very different from what we were before; we begin *a new kind of life.* Elsewhere, the same change is described by "passing from darkness to light," and "from death to life." All these expressions strongly denote a very great change. And this ought to be seriously considered; for what a light matter passes for religion in general ! a few lifeless forms, a little outward decency, or some faint desires, make the whole of it. But the Scripture expressions of "a new creation," and "a second birth," surely imply something more. They certainly denote *a very great change.*

2. *The new birth is a* UNIVERSAL *change.*

Many are the devices of Satan. If he cannot keep sinners in total blindness and security, he tries to pervert their views of religion by causing them to mistake appearances for realities ; or, by putting a part for the whole. Many are ruined forever, by mistakes of this kind. Most men have, at one time or another, some serious thoughts about their souls, and religion, and eternity ; and therefore do some things, and abstain from others, to still their fears and quiet their consciences. But this *partial* change

C 2

in point of morals, is often owing to some natural change
in age, temper, and situation.   Some men only exchange
one sin for another which they love better.   And others
are very diligent in religious duties, to atone for the indulgence of their lusts, and to cover them from their own
observation ; and the more unwilling they are to part with
a darling sin, the more ready are they to overdo in such
duties as do not oppose the present current of unsanctified
affections.

3. *The new birth is an* INWARD *change.*   It is far more
than a strict and regular course of outward actions or outward duties.   It does not consist in partial *Reformation*
only, so that a man is less wicked than he was before ;
but there is a complete and essential change of his whole
character. God looks at the *heart*. " My son," says Solomon, " give me thine *heart*."   The great sum of the law
is, " Thou shalt love the Lord thy God with all thy *heart*."
The prayer of the penitent is, " Create in me a clean *heart*,
O God ;" and the grand promise of the covenant is, " *A
new heart* will I give you."   Now the new birth consists
in having this new heart.   If you ask what a new heart
is : It is a heart set on new objects.   The affections of the
mind are turned from the world to God, and from the supreme love of self to the love of our fellow men, and from
living to ourselves to living to the glory of God.

This is very different from an *outward* change, which
may arise from mere selfishness.   A man may avoid excess
in some sins, and practise some duties, for the sake of his
health or his reputation among men, or from the slavish
fear of hell.   Without any real hatred to a sin, as sin, he
may forsake it for fear of burning in hell for it ; and without any love to God, he may perform religious duties ; for
though they are a heavy burden to him, he thinks it more
tolerable than hell will be.

4. *The new birth is a change, wrought by the operation of
the Holy Spirit.*   We are by nature in a state of enmity
against God, and this is what we cannot of ourselves remove, or overcome, because we love our sins.   It is the
sinfulness of man that interposes the obstacle to his regeneration ; and for this he is criminal and inexcusable.
And this is an obstacle which nothing but the grace of
God can surmount.   Hence the apostle John, speaking of

true believers, says, " They were born, not of blood, nor of the will of the flesh, nor of the will of man, but of God." John i. 13. This doctrine is indeed greatly disliked by many, because it gives so humbling a view of our own character and state, and so much opposes our own pride and self sufficiency. It is, however, the truth of God; and if we give any credit to the Scriptures, we must yield to it. Real Christians are said to " be born of God;" " born from above ;" born of the Spirit. They are also said to be " quickened, who were dead in sin." All which expressions plainly show that Regeneration is the work of God, and not the work of man.

These remarks are intended to caution the reader against wrong notions of the nature of religion. Let us now go a step further, and point out with as much plainness as possible, *what is the change* which is wrought in all the people of God, without exception : what it is which makes the difference between one who *is*, and one who is *not* born again.

The design of this change is to make man holy. Man was made at first in the image of God, in knowledge, righteousness, and holiness ; and he then enjoyed the most happy fellowship and communion with him. His duty and delight were the same. But by the fall he became obnoxious to the divine wrath, and disobedient to the divine will in his prevailing inclinations. He became disinclined to communion with God, and preferred the creature before the Creator. The design of regeneration is to restore man to the image of God, and to the exercise of love to him, so that his prevailing disposition may be the same as it was before the fall. The change therefore consists in these two things : that our supreme and chief end be to serve and glorify God ; and that the soul rest in God, as its chief good.

1. Our *supreme and chief end must be to serve and glorify God ;* and every other aim must be subordinate to this.

All things were made for the glory of God, that is, for the display of divine perfection ; and every reasonable creature ought to seek this. But no natural man seeks it. The sin of man consists in withdrawing his allegiance from God, and refusing subjection to his will. The language of his heart and practice is, " Our lips are our own. who is lord over us ?" But the renewed person sees and owns his dependance upon God, his Maker's right to rule, and the obligation of all creatures to submit to his will.

In regeneration, God gives this disposition of mind; and gives it such force that it will prevail. The natural man seeks his own happiness supremely. This determines his choice of employments, enjoyments, companions. His religious actions are not chosen, but submitted to, for fear of worse. In short, he hath forgotten his subjection : God is dethroned ; and self is honoured, loved, and served, in his room. Hence our Lord so much insisted on self-denial. " If any man, said he, will come after me, let him deny himself, and take up his cross, and follow me." To honour God in the heart then, and to serve him in the life, is the first and highest desire of him that is born again. And hence we may learn the reason why profane and worldly men are generally self-righteous, while the truly pious abhor themselves, on account of sin. Natural men have no just sense of their obligation to glorify God in their thoughts, words and actions ; and therefore, whatever they do in religion, they look upon as meritorious, and think that something is due to them on that account. On the other hand, those who are born of God, know it is their duty to love God with all their heart, and serve him with all their might. They see that could this be perfectly done, it is no more than their duty, and there could be no plea of merit. But when they consider their sins, and how far short of duty they come in every instance, they ask for mercy, and not for reward.

2. In regeneration, the soul is brought to *rest in God as its chief happiness*, and habitually to prefer his favour to every other enjoyment. The believer sees that those, and those alone, are happy, whose God is the Lord, and that those who are afar off from him must perish. All natural men place their supreme happiness in something that is not God. In this they all agree, though the ways in which they seek for worldly happiness are innumerable. There is but one way to peace, and if that is neglected, the insufficiency of all worldly enjoyments makes them fly from one earthly comfort to another, till they feel by sad experience the vanity of them all.

The change that takes place in regeneration, in no small degree consists in a strong inward conviction of the vanity of worldly enjoyments of every kind; and a persuasion that the favour and enjoyment of God is infinitely superior to them all. Whatever other differences there may be, this will be found in every child of God, from the highest to the lowest, from the richest to the poorest; and from the oldest to the youngest. Every such one will be able to say, with the Psalmist, "There be many that say, who will show us any good? Lord, lift thou up the light of thy countenance upon me. Thou hast put gladness in my heart, **more than** in the time that their corn and wine increased."

Thus it appears that in Regeneration there is a renewal of the moral image of God upon the heart. The renewed man loves him supremely, serves him as his highest end, and delights in him as his chief good. This recovery, however, is but begun on earth. It is gradually improved in the progress of sanctification, and shall be fully completed at the resurrection of the just. The sum of the moral law is, to love the Lord our God with all our heart, and soul, and strength, and mind. This is the duty of every creature, and regeneration consists in communicating this love to the soul, which gradually gains the ascendency, and habitually prevails over its opposite.

We may now consider by what steps and by what means this change is brought about. It is true it may be wrought at any time, in any manner, and by any means that to Infinite Wisdom shall seem proper. "The wind bloweth where it listeth, and thou hearest the sound thereof, but canst not tell whence it cometh, and whither it goeth : so is every one that is born of the Spirit." John iii. 8. We shall only speak of such steps in the change, as are, in substance, common to all true converts.

I.

There must be a discovery of the real nature of God.

Those who are in a natural state, are often described as lying in ignorance and darkness. They know not God. They have "the understanding darkened, being alienated from the life of God through the ignorance that is in them, because of the blindness of their hearts." Eph. iv. 18. In the change which the Holy Spirit accomplishes, this darkness, ignorance, and blindness, are dispelled. The understanding is enlightened ; the true character and nature of God are discovered; and his glorious perfections seen in all their lustre. It will be easily perceived how indispensable is this part of the momentous work ; for it is impossible that should be a man's chief motive of action, or supreme object of desire, of which he has no degree of knowledge. God must be known in his real character, such as he is; and no false image placed in his stead. He must be seen in his spiritual nature as almighty in his power, unsearchable in his wisdom, inviolable in his truth ; but, above all, he must be seen as infinite in his holiness and hatred of sin, as impartial in his justice, and determined to punish it.

II.

There must be a discovery of the infinite glory of God.

He must not only be seen to be such a being as he really is, but there must be a sense of the infinite worth, beauty, and perfection of his character. It is one thing to know, and another to approve. Men may know things which they hate ; and it must be so, when natures are opposite, the one sinful and the other holy. There are many who cannot endure the scriptural representation of God, as holy and jealous. They oppose it by carnal reasonings, and give it the most odious names. The reason is plain. Such a view of God sets the opposition of their own hearts to him in the strongest light. The consequence is, God or themselves must be held in abhorrence. There must, therefore, be a discovery of the glory and beauty of the divine nature; an entire approbation of every thing in God, as perfectly right and faultless. No man can love that which doth not appear to him lovely. And this is the very foundation on which this change is built. While men continue in the love of sin, it is impossible they should see the beauty of infinite holiness; they will hate holiness, and fly from a holy God, as our first parents did in the garden.

III.

There must be a conviction of sin and danger.

If an entire change be necessary, there must be a dissatisfaction with our past character : whoever is pleased with it, will neither desire nor accept of a change. Those who are not humbled for sin, will treat with contempt a purchased pardon and a crucified Saviour. This our Lord tells us in the plainest terms. " They that are whole need not a physician, but they that are sick." "I came not to call the righteous but sinners to repentance." To these his invitation is particularly addressed : " Come unto me, all ye that labour and are heavy laden, and I will give you rest."

From these passages and many others, it is evident, beyond contradiction, that there must be a deep humiliation of mind and sense of guilt and wretchedness, before a sinner can be brought unto God. The source of this humiliation is *a sense of the evil and desert of sin.* This is found in true penitents, and it is this that distinguishes repentance unto life from every counterfeit. Many have trembled through fear of punishment from God, who lived and died strangers to this change: they had no just sense of the evil of sin in itself; no cordial approbation of the holiness of God's nature and law, or of the justice of that condemnation which stands written against every transgressor. Here, O Christian, is the cardinal point on which true repentance turns. Without this there may be a slavish terror, but no true humiliation. There is often as great, or a greater degree of terror, in convictions that prove fruitless, as in others which end in a saving change. The passion of fear in Cain or Ahab, was perhaps equal in degree to the fear of any true penitent recorded in Scripture. It is the principle that distinguishes their nature, and produces opposite effects. The one is alarmed through fear of the wrath of an angry God ; the other is truly sensible of sin in all its malignity, and feels the sanction of a righteous, but violated law. The one feels himself *a miserable creature ;* the other confesses himself *a guilty sinner.* The one is terrified, and the other humbled.

IV.

There must be an acceptance of salvation through the cross of Christ.

This is the last and finishing step of the glorious work. When this is attained, the evidence of the change is completed, the new nature exhibits all its parts. The spiritual seed is implanted, and hath taken root; and it will arrive, by degrees, in every vessel of mercy, to that measure of maturity which it pleaseth God each shall possess before he be carried hence.

Before conviction of sin, the Gospel of Christ almost always appears to be foolishness. Or, if education and example prompt the sinner to speak with reverence of a Saviour, there is no distinct perception of the meaning, nor any inward relish of the sweetness of Gospel truth. But those who have been wounded in spirit, begin to perceive its unspeakable value. The helpless state of the sinner makes him anxiously inquire, " What must I do to be saved ? I have no excuse to offer, nor any shelter to fly to: the works, the word, and the providence of God, seem all to be against me. O, how fearful a thing it is to fall into the hands of the living God ! I have awaked as out of a dream, and find myself fast hastening to the pit of destruction. What would I not do, what would I not give, for good ground to believe that my guilt were taken away, and my peace made with God !"

With what eagerness before unknown, does the sinner now inquire after the way of life? With what solicitude does he go forth by the footsteps of the flock ? The Sabbaths, and ordinances, and word of God, are now quite different things from what they were before. No more waste of that sacred time, in business or in play. No more serenity of heart because he had been regularly and constantly at church; but an astonishing view of the sins of his holy things; his careless, formal, heartless worship. No more indifferent, slothful, or critical hearing the word, that he may commend the ability, or deride the weakness of the preacher. Now he hears that " God was in Christ, reconciling the world to himself." The very news of salvation, the bare mention of pardon, is now a joyful sound. It rouses his attention, and he sets himself to weigh the important intimation. He hears that " God so loved the world that he gave his only begotten Son, that whosoever believeth in him should not perish, but have everlasting life." " Is there then," says he, " hope of mercy with God, whom 1 have so long forgotten, and so greatly offended ? Hath he indeed loved a guilty world ? Hath he loved them in so amazing a manner as to send his only begotten Son to save them from destruction? How great is the giver, how wonderful the gift, and how undeserving the objects of his love!"

This is a brief sketch of the steps by which this great change is effected in the heart. It may be proper, before we close, to mention some of the principal

EVIDENCES AND FRUITS OF REGENERATION.

The heart being renewed, the life will, of course, be reformed; and holiness, in all manner of conversation, will be its natural and genuine effect. He who is born again, discovers his new nature and life, by new apprehensions of God—of himself—of the world—of Jesus Christ,—and of the ordinances of his appointment.

The regenerate person has new views of *God.* He really and inwardly believes the being, presence, power, and providence of God. Formerly, God was seldom in his thoughts; now, he can scarcely look upon any thing, without considering its relation to him. What a lustre and glory does his opened eye behold in all the divine perfections? Above all, what an astonishing view he has of the divine goodness and love, which he sees in all his mercies, of the least of which he is not worthy?

He has quite new apprehensions of *himself.* Before, he thought himself his own master; but now he sees that he belongs to God. He remembers his Creator, confesses his obligations, and mourns for his transgressions. A converted sinner stands astonished at his former conduct. He wonders at the boldness of a poor guilty rebel, perhaps cursing and blaspheming, perhaps rioting in sensuality and lust. He wonders that the power of God did not arrest him in his course; and by some signal stroke make him a dreadful monument of his righteous indignation. He trembles to think of his former state; and it excites a lively acknowledgment of the riches of divine grace.

This is connected with, and increased by his views of the *world,* and of *worldly men.* The charm is now broken; the false colours are taken off from the world and all its enjoyments. How ardently did he once love them! How eagerly did he pursue them, and how did he envy the possessors of them! But now, he can never separate the idea of riches from temptation; and often considers the dread-

ful change of those who are clothed in purple and fine
linen, and fare sumptuously every day; but will be, in a
little time, tormented in hell-fire.   Formerly, he valued
persons by their station, genius and wealth; but now, a
Christian in a cottage appears more amiable than a blasphemer in a palace.

Further; the regenerate person has new apprehensions
of *Eternity*.   Formerly, the vanities of time engaged his
thoughts, and eternity was seldom in view: but now, it is
frequently and strongly upon his mind, so as to correct the
false representations of sense, and oppose the unjust claims
of earthly gratifications.   Formerly, unseen things were
treated as fabulous; now there is such a discovery of
them, as weighs down all created things, and makes them
feel light as a feather in a balance.

The regenerate person has also new views of *Jesus
Christ*, the great and only Saviour of sinners.   Before, he
was "without form or comeliness," all the truths relating
to his person and offices were treated with indifference;
but now the name of a Saviour is precious.   The strongest language is too weak to express his gratitude and
breathe out his love.   "He is the chief among ten thousand; yea, he is altogether lovely."

Again, the regenerate person has new views of the *ordinances* of Christ's appointment.   They were formerly
his burden; now they are his delight.   Before, the Sabbath wore a sable garb, and an offensive gloom; now, he
calls it a delight, the "holy of the Lord, and honourable."
Now he thirsts after the water of life, esteems, loves, and
desires the word of God.   He now readily joins the holy
Psalmist in the fervent expressions of his affection to the
truths and ordinances of God.   "O how love I thy law;
it is my meditation all the day.   My soul thirsteth for
thee.   To see thy power and thy glory, so as I have seen
thee in the sanctuary."

In short, a change takes place in his whole character
and conduct.   "The love of God is shed abroad in his
heart, by the Holy Ghost;" and is the commanding principle of all his future actions.   The love of God is the
source, the sum, and the perfection of holiness.   All other
duties naturally flow from it; nay, all other duties are nothing but the expressions of it.   The believer is under the

constant influence of gratitude to God. It is not merely thankfulness to a bountiful benefactor for mercies which have not been deserved; but a deep sense of obligation to a Saviour, who "loved him, and washed him in his own blood:" so that his language is, "Lord, what wilt thou have me to do? O that I knew how I might repay some small part of my infinite obligations! O.that I knew by what means I might magnify and do thee honour. Write thy laws in my heart, and enable me in every possible way to show that I love thee, because thou hast first loved me."

This plainly includes in it, and will certainly produce, the most sincere and fervent love to his fellow creatures. If they are *bad* men, the same love to God, the same concern for his glory, which fills the Christian with grief and indignation at their daring offences, inspires the most ardent desire for their recovery and salvation. And as to *good* men, they are united by the tenderest and strongest ties, and love one another with a pure heart fervently.

Thus we have taken a brief view of this important subject: a subject in which every reader is deeply interested. Let me now earnestly entreat every one who peruses these pages, to bring the matter to a trial with regard to himself. As all men are either regenerate or unregenerate, let him ask, to which of these classes do I belong? We are dropping into the grave from day to day, and our state is then fixed beyond the possibility of a change. What astonishing folly to continue in uncertainty whether we shall go to heaven or hell, whether we shall be the companions of angels, or associates with blaspheming devils to all eternity! Nothing, therefore, can be more salutary, than that you make an impartial search into your present character and state. If you have ground to conclude that you are at peace with God, what an unspeakable source of joy and consolation? If otherwise, there is no time to lose in hastening from the brink of the pit. Be persuaded then, to set apart some time for the duty of self-examination. Let every one, without exception, take up or renew this grand inquiry, "Am I in Christ? That is, Am I a new creature, or not? Am I a child of God? or do I still continue an heir of hell?"

Let me repeat in your ears this solemn truth, and may God Almighty, by his Spirit, carry it to your hearts: "Except a man be born again, he cannot enter into the kingdom of God." And remember this is a *great*, a *universal*, an *inward*, a *divine* change. It is far more than mere outward reformation. It is far more than Baptism, or any outward ordinance. Every child of Adam is, by nature, at enmity with God; and must either be renewed in the spirit of his mind, or perish eternally. It is of no consequence what you are as to outward station, if you are not reconciled to God: it is of no consequence what you are as to outward professions, if you are not inwardly changed. God is no respecter of persons; and, therefore, whether you are high or low, rich or poor, whether you are of one denomination of Christians, or another, if you have not been the subjects of a renewing and sanctifying work of the Holy Spirit, you are children of wrath; and if you die in that condition, must " go away into everlasting punishment."

But is there *now* no relief? Yes, there is: Jesus is "able to save to the uttermost, all that come to God by him." Fly to him for refuge. There is no sin of so deep a dye, but the blood of Christ is sufficient to wash it out. There is not any slave of Satan so loaded with chains, but he is able to set him free. If you perish, it is of yourselves. I have given you warning, from a sincere and ardent concern for your everlasting interest; and may God himself, for Christ's sake, by his Holy Spirit, effectually persuade you to comply with it.

THE

BENEFITS

OF

Sanctified Afflictions.

He replied to the bitter reproaches of his wife, "What! shall we receive good at the hand of God, and shall we not receive evil?"

See page 4.

PUBLISHED BY THE

AMERICAN TRACT SOCIETY,

AND SOLD AT THEIR DEPOSITORY, NO. 150 NASSAU-STREET, NEAR
THE CITY-HALL, NEW-YORK; AND BY AGENTS OF THE
SOCIETY, ITS BRANCHES, AND AUXILIARIES,
IN THE PRINCIPAL CITIES AND TOWNS
IN THE UNITED STATES.

Vol. 4.

THE BENEFITS OF
SANCTIFIED AFFLICTIONS.

APOSTATE man is born unto trouble, as the sparks fly upward. This is the language of inspiration, and it is the language of experience. While God is daily conferring favours upon us, he is at the same time bearing constant testimony against our sins, by giving to us the cup of sorrow. Disappointed hopes, losses, pains, and natural death, must be endured by man. Roses, scattered by the side of his path through life, are found to grow on thorns. His present state is every way suited to be a state of disappointment and trial.

It ought to be our constant endeavour to derive benefit from our afflictions. If they be sanctified to us, as they are to all God's people, we shall be enabled to say, with the Psalmist, " It is good for me that I have been afflicted, that I might learn thy statutes." This pious man found his troubles operating for his spiritual and everlasting good. He was excited by them to learn God's statutes, or to study and obey his revealed will. Divine truth became sweeter than honey to his taste. His love to God's character, law, government, and grace was increased, and he was engaged to run the way of his commandments with the greater delight.

It is the design of this Tract to point out some of the EVIDENCES AND BENEFITS OF SANCTIFIED AFFLICTIONS; and if it shall be the means of imparting true consolation to any afflicted soul, the writer will have an abundant reward. The subject is one in which *all* are interested, for all are exposed to afflictions; but it is especially interesting to the *children of sorrow*, now suffering under the rod of their heavenly Father; for it is a subject which occupies their thoughts, and furnishes matter for daily self-examination.

1. Our afflictions promote our best good when we *acknowledge and adore the hand of God in bringing them upon us.*

God is the universal Creator. All creatures and events, both in the natural and moral world, are, and for ever must remain under his government. If creatures could hold their existence of themselves, they would become independent of God, and might control his designs.

To suppose any part of the creation to be freed from the divine government, would be attended with the same absurd consequences. If any part of the creation could govern itself, that part might set up a claim in opposition to the designs of Jehovah, and defeat his purposes, in giving birth to creatures. Some contend that God maintains a general providence, but not a particular one, over the works of his hand; and represent it as beneath the dignity of the Infinite Mind to regard the minute parts of creation. But let such persons consider, that a general providence implies the government of all the particular things of which it is composed, and that all parts of the divine plan are connected, and therefore a denial of a particular providence goes to a denial that God governs the world. There may be a connexion, which is discerned in the divine mind, between the opening of a flower and the rise of a nation; the direction of a mote, and the fall of an empire. Though such knowledge is too high for us, it is not too high for the mind of Jehovah, and heightens the idea of his infinite greatness. When we consider him as governing all creatures and events, both great and small, we may discover something of that glory which demands our admiration and praise.

It is abundantly revealed in the Holy Scriptures, that the evils which men endure are inflicted by Divine Providence. " Shall there be evil in a city, and the Lord hath not done it?" Amos, iii. 6. " Out of the mouth of the Most High proceedeth not evil and good?" Lam. iii. 38. It is unnecessary to spend time in proving a doctrine which is abundantly revealed in the inspired volume. If it were a fact that our troubles were the fruit of accident or chance, or blind fate, we must be inconsolable under them. But we are certain that " affliction cometh not forth of the dust, neither doth trouble spring out of the ground."

We may be rationally convinced, that the evils which we endure proceed from the hand of God; and yet we may practically refuse to acknowledge and adore his agency. There is a wide difference, in the present case, between acknowledging and *murmuring*, and acknowledging and *adoring*. The former conduct characterizes the wicked; the latter characterizes the righteous. What a vast difference was there between the acknowledgment which Pharaoh paid to Jehovah, and that which was paid by Moses? Pharaoh was compelled to acknowledge the hand of Jehovah in bringing the plagues upon Egypt; but while he made this confession, his heart rose up against the church of Israel and their God. Moses acknowledged the divine hand in bringing judgments upon the Egyptians and the Israelites, and at the same time he adored or reverenced him who was revealing his wrath against the disobedient. The devils acknowledge the existence of the only living and true God; but in the moment of the confession, they tremble with horror, and are filled with pain. All the godly have a pleasing belief in the divine government, in the most trying seasons, and rejoice, in a higher or lower degree, in the dominion of infinite wisdom and love. They see the hand which is stretched out in a way of correction, as well as in a way of mercy.

When Job's substance and children were taken from him in one day, he said, " the Lord gave, and the Lord hath taken away, blessed be the name of the Lord." And when the Lord smote him with " sore biles, from the sole of his foot unto his crown, and he took him a potsherd to scrape himself withal, and sat down among the ashes," he replied to the bitter reproaches of his wife, " What! shall we receive good at the hand of God, and shall we not receive evil ? In all this did not Job sin with his lips." The Apostle saith, (Heb. xii. 9.) " Furthermore, we have had fathers of our flesh which corrected us, and we gave them reverence ; shall we not rather be in subjection to the Father of spirits and live ?" From these instances, with many more which might be adduced, it is evident that pious men acknowledge and adore the divine hand, in laying the load upon them. If, when we are afflicted, we eventually find our minds driven further from God and a cheerful acknowledgment of his chastising hand, we have just cause to be alarmed with ourselves. But let us not conclude in a moment, when we first enter into the furnace of affliction, that God hath forsaken us, because we have not that lively sense of his perfection and his providence which we may have had heretofore. If we find within ourselves, that amidst all the tumult and darkness of our minds, we have a fixed determination to trust in God though he slay us, we shall find some encouragement to hope that hereafter light will break in upon our minds, and that the present scourge will yield the peaceable fruit of righteousness.

So long as we look no higher than second causes to find the author of our troubles, we shall pay no homage to God, and shall murmur at his dealings. Let the heart be placed upon the perfect character and government of the Most High, and we shall be stilled from complaining of our lot, and shall, with Moses, Job, David, and other saints, both in the Old Testament and in the New, feel a holy reverence towards him who is pleased to chastise us. No affliction for the present is joyous, but grievous; but when it is sanctified, it produces a peace and a joy, to which the men of this world are strangers. All things work together for the good of them that love God, and the light and momentary afflictions of this life will work for them a far more exceeding and eternal weight of glory in the world to come.

2. It is good for us to have been under the rod, when we *are led to a clear discovery of our sins, and a cordial acknowledgment of the divine justice and wisdom in our chastisement.* "I know, O Lord, that thy judgments are right, and that thou, in faithfulness, hast afflicted me." The eyes of the pious Psalmist were opened more clearly than ever upon his sins, and he felt that God was perfectly just in the present affliction.

Job says, in his address to the Lord, near the close of his long and heavy trials, "I have heard of thee by the hearing of the ear, but now mine eye seeth thee; wherefore I abhor myself, and repent in dust and ashes." Observe the language of the faithful, while Jerusalem lay in ruins, and its inhabitants were either slain by the sword, or gone into captivity. "Wherefore doth a living man complain, a man for the punishment of his sins? Let us search and try our ways, and turn again to the Lord." The penitent Jews, after their return from Babylon, confessed that God was just in all that he had brought upon them: that he had done right, and that they had done wickedly.

The primitive christians, while they were in bonds and

imprisonment, and were exposed to meet death in its most dreadful forms, had a deep impression that they were among the chief of sinners, and thought themselves honoured by being accounted worthy to suffer shame for Christ's name.

Even christians have but a small degree of knowledge of the depravity of their hearts, and the sins of their lives, until they are called to pass through some painful trials. Prosperity is apt to lull the mind to sleep, to abate its devotion, to slacken its watchfulness, and to throw a languor over all its exertions. How natural is it for us to say, when our mountain seemeth to stand strong, that we shall never be moved, or that adversity will never overtake us ! When christians are indulging this frame, they are preparing the way to meet with some disappointment, worldly loss or bereavement, or to be scourged in their own persons. When God is pleased to afflict them, they will be roused to self-examination and prayer. They will not pretend to the knowledge of all the reasons why God is now contending with them, but they will see enough in themselves to discover to them the fitness, the necessity, and the justice of the present rod.

Instead of wondering that they are taken in hand by the present correction, they will rather wonder that they have escaped so long, and have enjoyed so much prosperity. Saith the patient christian in his afflictions, " I am convinced that I am a great sinner; and that I deserve all the expressions of divine wrath against the wicked, in time and in eternity. How have I 'forsaken God which made me?' 'how have I lightly esteemed the Rock of my salvation !' I have refused to give God the throne in my heart, and have been setting up idols there. I have shamefully neglected to reverence God's name and day, and have attended the ordinances of his house with coldness and indifference. I have not placed a just value on the faith once delivered to the saints, and have not been valiant for the truth upon the earth. How unfaithful have I been in the discharge of the duties which I owe to my family, to the church, and to the commonwealth ! I have neglected to instruct, counsel, and warn those to whom I have had near access; and have said to them, by my example, that religion is of no importance, and that worldly glory constitutes the happiness of man. What abundant

cause have I to mourn before God, that I have indulged
so much malice towards my fellow men! that I have
been so unwilling to forgive my enemies? and have been
so ready to rejoice at their overthrow! What impure
thoughts have I indulged, and how much have I done to
encourage the licentious in their conduct! I have not
maintained the justice, the mercy, or the truth, which the
divine law and the Gospel require. I have coveted my
neighbour's substance and enjoyments; I have envied his
superior prosperity and gifts, and have been discontented
with the place assigned me in the world.

"How often have I despised the only Saviour of sinful
men! And since I have been numbered among his followers, how unfaithful have I been to the duties of my holy
profession! I have solemnly engaged to view myself as
my own no more, and to be wholly devoted to the Redeemer, in life and in death. How cold have been my affections towards him, who is the great Immanuel, God
with us! In how many ways have I sought to shun the
cross, and to enjoy the smiles of an ungodly world! Christ's
kingdom is of infinite worth, but I have refused to promote
its interest as became me, and have symbolized with the
god of this world. I have abundant cause for deep humiliation, that I have abused my mercies, and have been so in-
corrigible under afflictions. Many promises of amendment
have I broken, and I have paid little regard to my covenant bonds. I might justly be crushed by the present rod,
and become a monument of God's everlasting wrath. I
should have no just cause of complaint, were I deprived
of all hope, and doomed to dwell in the regions of eternal
despair. But, O thou God of grace! save me, I beseech
thee! Correct me in measure and in mercy. Let it be the
fruit of this affliction to take away sin, and to prepare me
for the service and enjoyment of thyself for ever!" When
such are the breathings of the heart, in a time of trouble,
affliction is not sent in vain. .

When God's children are under the rod, they will be
convinced of the wisdom as well as the justice of the present chastisement. O christian, is thy worldly substance
taken from thee? Thou wilt be led to inquire, whether
thy heart has not been too much placed upon it, and whether this extraordinary attachment has not rendered it necessary that thy present loss should be sustained?

Set thy affections more abundantly on things which are above, and be more engaged than ever in laying up a treasure in heaven. Hast thou met with ingratitude and unkindness from one of thy fellow-creatures, on whom thou hast conferred many benefits? Let this requital of evil for good serve to teach thee the folly of trusting in an arm of flesh, and engage thee to trust in the living God. Hast thou not fondly doated on the person who now seeks to pierce thee to thy heart? Let the reception of evil for good bring thy benevolence to the trial, and engage thee to imitate thy Saviour in the forgiveness of enemies. Hath God taken from thee, by death, thy bosom friend, or the child of thy love? Ask thyself whether the deceased had not taken the place of God in thy heart, and rendered the present blow a necessary one for thy best good. Be assured that thou must be divorced from thy idols, or from God. And as thou art one of his children, he will take from thee the object of thy idolatrous love. Thy case would be deplorable indeed, if under thy bereavement thou couldst justly say, with Micah, " Ye have taken away my gods, and what have I more ?"

Art thou in a state of languishment, or pain of body, and hast thou wearisome days and wearisome nights appointed unto thee? Inquire whether thou wast not too confident of the continuance of health in former days, and whether thou wast not unthankful to him who was the health of thy countenance. Perhaps thou hadst some favourite plan to accomplish, and wast confident that thy strength and vigour would be continued until thou hadst realized thy strong hopes. Is it not just and wise in God to convince thee of thy arrogant presumption, by making thee to feel that thy breath is in thy nostrils, and that thou must soon be laid in the grave? Hast thou not cause to bless God, that he is now teaching thee the vanity of this world, and preparing thee for the joys of a glorious immortality?

We are inclined to say, that some other affliction would be better suited to promote our best good, than the present: and that some other time would be a more fit time than the period that was chosen. But how incompetent judges are we, what is wisest and best to be done ! If we were to be our own judges in the present case, we would strive to itch upon a trial, and a time of suffering, which woul lead us to avoid the cross, and leave us strangers to our own hearts. We might, indeed, by planning for ourselves, be involved in far greater difficulty than the present, and sink into despair. God, who knoweth our particular frame and temper, best knoweth when and how to try us, and how long to continue us under the rod. If we derive spiritual benefit from the afflictions which we endure, we shall be humbled for our sins, and we shall be still and know that the Lord he is God. We shall no longer say, any other trouble rather than the present, and any other time to endure it rather than the present; but we shall say, "O Lord, thy will be done, both as to the kind and continuance of affliction. Oh, cause me to adore thy justice and thy wisdom, and humbly to implore thy mercy."

Those who make the knowledge of their hearts their study, will not pass through days of adversity, without discovering, more than ever before, their sins, nor without viewing them in new points of aggravation. Sins which had been forgotten will be called to remembrance, and the aggravating circumstances which attended them will rush upon the mind. In the view of them, the humble penitent will feel that the divine justice would have shone with distinguished brightness in his eternal condemnation, and will be excited with great and earnest importunity to implore the divine mercy.

3. The subjects of sanctified afflictions will *find the grace of the Gospel peculiarly endeared to them.*

"Before I was afflicted," saith the Psalmist, "I went astray; but now have I kept thy word." Here we may observe, that the pious Psalmist was led, by means of his afflictions, to love more than ever the book of God's grace, and to conform to it in his practice. "We glory in tribulation; knowing that tribulation worketh patience, and patience experience, and experience hope, and hope maketh not ashamed; because the love of God is shed abroad in our hearts by the Holy Ghost, which is given unto us." Rom. v. 3—5. "For as the sufferings of Christ abound in us, so our consolation also aboundeth by Christ. We had the sentence of death in ourselves, that we should not trust in ourselves, but in God which raiseth the dead." 2 Cor. i. 5. 9.

The more deeply any are impressed with a sense of their sins, and of the divine justice in their punishment, the more

fully are they convinced of the necessity of Gospel grace,
and the more clearly do they see the glory of the Gospel
plan of salvation. Seasons of suffering have often proved
seasons of high enjoyment to the people of God. The patriarchs, prophets, apostles, and the primitive christians
in general, under their trials, were favoured with abundant
communications of divine grace, and rejoiced in hope of
the glory of God. We may observe, at the present time,
that those who appear to be true christians shine brightest
when in the furnace. To them Christ appears peculiarly
precious, and they appear, at times, to be cheerful in giving up all things for his sake. They discover that they
count not their lives dear unto themselves, that they may
finish their course with joy.

Christians, when under the rod, read the Holy Scriptures with special attention and uncommon engagedness,
and manifest a strong relish for the truths contained in the
inspired volume. They now feel that God's word is a light
unto their feet and a lamp unto their path, while passing
through the darkness and temptations of the present world.

"This is my comfort," says the Psalmist, "in my affliction, for thy word hath quickened me. Thy statutes have
been my songs in the house of my pilgrimage. The law
of thy mouth is better unto me than thousands of gold and
silver. How sweet are thy words unto my taste! Yea,
sweeter than honey to my mouth." Afflictions are necessary to lead persons to understand many parts of the Bible,
particularly those which relate to sufferings and the divine support under them. Who understandeth, like the
good man under the rod, how tribulation worketh patience,
and patience experience, and experience hope? Who understandeth, like the patient sufferer, how consolation
aboundeth by Christ, as the fruit of chastisement? The best
of men do not know how much they trust in themselves
and in the world, until their attachment is tried, and broken
by the rod. Now they see more fully than ever their own
folly in placing such confidence in the things which perish. They will bless God for ever for that discipline
which hath opened to them the pride and deceitfulness of
their hearts, and hath brought them to discern the worth
and glory of that kingdom which cannot be moved. True
christians have rarely so clear evidence of their adoption,
as when their earthly hopes are dashed in pieces.

4. Sanctified afflictions lead men to be more attentive to the *duties which they owe more immediately to God.* What a wide difference is there, in ordinary cases, between the prayers which are made in a day of adversity, and those which are made in prosperous seasons! Those who feel themselves to be burdened with guilt and sorrow, and are convinced that God is a rewarder of those who diligently seek him, will feel themselves engaged to go to the throne of grace, and to seek for mercy.

Prayer is not to them an unwelcome task, but is the delight of their souls. When they find Satan and their wicked hearts striving to throw hinderances in the way of the performance of this duty, they will not rest until they have in some degree obtained the victory, and can fervently pour out their hearts to God. He is pleased sometimes remarkably to fill their mouths with arguments, when all worldly appearances are against them, while they are bowing at his footstool. They are uncommonly assisted in praying for themselves, for their families and friends, for enemies, for the whole human race, and especially for the peace and prosperity of Zion.

It is painful to those who derive benefit from their afflictions, to be deprived, by ill health or other means, of attending on the worship and ordinances of God's house. These are objects for which they find an increasing relish, as they are emptied from vessel to vessel, by their trying changes. Hence, when they are excluded from the place they love, they can adopt the language of David, when he was wandering in the wilderness of Judea, by the persecutions of Saul: "O God, thou art my God; early will I seek thee. My soul thirsteth for thee, in a dry and thirsty land, where no water is; to see thy power, and thy glory, as I have seen thee in the sanctuary." Psalm lxiii. 1, 2.

5. Sanctified afflictions are instrumental in *stirring up persons to a faithful discharge of the duties of the second table of the law.* There are two in particular which I shall name. The first is the duty of administering just reproof. A mind solemnized by prayer, and communion with God in other duties; a mind which seeth the exceeding sinfulness of sin, and is brought to the footstool by the rod, is prepared to administer reproof, without being overwhelmed

with a slavish dread of the wrath of the offender, and to do it in a manner which is best suited to work a reformation. Nothing has a happier tendency to lead persons to discharge this duty, and to come home to the conscience, than enduring chastisement from the hand of our heavenly Father. His glory appears to them of such worth, and the souls of men are so tenderly loved, that they dare not be silent, when called to speak in a way of warning and reproof.

The other duty, which I shall mention in this place, is compassion and kindness to those who are afflicted. We are commanded to bear one another's burthens, to live as brethren, to be pitiful, and to be courteous. There are men whose inward thought is, that their houses shall continue for ever, and their dwelling places to all generations. They are intoxicated with their prosperity, and presume that no painful changes await them. They look with contempt upon the needy and afflicted, and are disposed to charge them with bringing their troubles on themselves, or continuing them by their imprudence or timidity. But christianity speaks a very different language. " Remember them that are in bonds, as bound with them, and them which suffer adversity, as being yourselves also in the body." Heb. viii. 3. Nothing teaches persons to feel for the children of sorrow, like experience in the school of adversity. This eminently qualifies the followers of the compassionate Saviour to sympathize with the afflicted, and to strive to lighten their woes. They extend their compassionate feelings to all who are under trouble, and especially to those who are the friends of the great Redeemer. They will strive to relieve the wants of those who are needy, and to bind up the broken spirit. " Who comforteth us in all our tribulation, that we may be able to comfort them which are in any trouble, by the comfort wherewith we ourselves are comforted of God." 2 Cor. i. 4. They labour to turn the attention of their afflicted fellow-mortals to the only source of consolation, and to prepare them for deliverance in the present world, and immortal glory in the world to come. They can cheerfully welcome to their bosoms the humble and patient disciples of the blessed Saviour, however much they are despised by the ungodly world. Knowing these to be the excellent of the earth, they are compassionate and kind to them for their Lord and Master's sake, and rejoice in the blessed prospect of meeting them in the paradise above, where all sorrow and crying shall be done away.

The enemies of the primitive christians remarked concerning them, when they saw their strong mutual affection under their fiery trials, " Behold, how these christians love one another!" The disciples of Christ sometimes, in the present world, fall out with each other, and give mutual wounds. But joint sufferings have always been found to check their animosities, and to unite them in the closer bonds of affection. When such are the fruits of our afflictions, we have not been smitten in vain, but shall derive peace and comfort from them in this world, and shall receive a far more exceeding and eternal weight of glory in the world to come.

6. Sanctified afflictions are instrumental in *weaning men from earthly attachments, and in ripening them for death and heaven.* The pious patriarchs confessed themselves, amidst their troubles, to be pilgrims and strangers on the earth, and to be looking for a city which hath foundations, whose builder and maker is God. The primitive christians took joyfully the spoiling of their goods, knowing that they had in heaven a better and an enduring substance.

Pious persons, who have suffered many pains, and endured many outward losses and bereavements, look upon this world as a very empty place, and not by any means worthy to be sought as a portion. While they give thanks to God for the innumerable temporal blessings they have received, they dare not rest their hope of support and enjoyment on any thing beneath the skies.

They can discern no earthly prospect which has unadulterated charms; but every thing around them wears the appearance of decay and dissolution. They watch and they pray that they may not be ensnared by earthly allurements, and that they may be in constant readiness for the approaching change by death. The eternal world grows more and more familiar to their minds, and their thoughts are much employed on that state into which they are soon to enter. Many of their meditations are employed on death and on the future judgment. Although they cannot determine what their views will be when they shall be called to walk through the dark valley, yet they believe that the end of the upright man will be peace. They are much in prayer to God, that he would not forsake them in the hour of death ; and believe that the only way in which divine consolation is then to be expected, is in a humble walk with God, and in the faithful discharge of every duty, while life is continued. What a firm hope, and what animating prospects were enjoyed by the apostle, when he could declare, " For we know that if our earthly house of this tabernacle were dissolved, we have a building of God, a house not made with hands, eternal in the heavens. For in this we groan, earnestly desiring to be clothed upon with our house which is from heaven. We are confident, I say, and willing rather to be absent from the body, and to be present with the Lord !" 2 Cor. v. 1, 2. 8. How earnestly desirous was our apostle, that Christ might be magnified in his body, whether by life or by death ? He could say, " For me to live is Christ, and to die is gain. But if I live in the flesh, this is the fruit of my labour, yet what I shall choose, I wot (or know) not. For I am in a strait betwixt two, having a desire to depart, and to be with Christ, which is far better." Phil. i. 21—23.

Let not christians in general be discouraged because they have not risen to the attainments of the apostle Paul. He was raised up for eminent usefulness in the church of God, and he did more to propagate christianity than any other mere man who hath ever lived. He suffered much in his labours to advance and defend the religion of the blessed Saviour. To use his own language, he was " in deaths oft," while travelling round the world, to proclaim the glad tidings of peace and salvation through a crucified Saviour. The followers of Christ, at large have not been called to such services as was the apostle, nor to endure such trials as he endured, and therefore it is not strange that their consolations should fall far below his. But remember, ye patient sufferers, that God is not unmindful of your labour of love, and that he is training you up to serve him better on earth, and to enjoy a brighter crown in heaven. God will not break the bruised reed, and the smoking flax he will not quench He heareth every sigh, and every breathing of the contrite heart, and will give you grace to persevere to the end of your days, and to come off conquerors, yea, more than conquerors, through him who hath loved you, and given himself to die for you.

We always find the most heavenly-minded christians among those who have smarted most by the rod. To them, meditations have become familiar on that glorious state in which the redeemed will be brought into the immediate presence of God and the Lamb, and will unite with the spirits of just men made perfect, and with the holy angels in everlasting songs of praise. However far they may fall short of rapturous enjoyments in religion, while they see through a glass darkly, they discover a solidity and firmness in their exercises, which manifest that their light is shining with increasing brightness unto the perfect day.

I have now endeavoured to collect and bring into view some of the principal evidences of sanctified afflictions. Can we say, in a review of our troubles, as the Psalmist did, in a review of his, "It is good for me that I have been afflicted; that I might learn thy statutes." Our afflictions have certainly had some effect upon us; either in rendering our hearts tender, and our lives obedient, or in hardening our hearts, and occasioning us to become more obstinate and open in the practice of wickedness than ever. If the last be the effect, our case is alarming indeed, and we have much cause to fear, that to us is reserved the blackness of darkness for ever.

Let us recollect the marks or evidences of sanctified afflictions, which have been brought into view; and impartially compare ourselves with them.

When any derive benefit from their afflictions, they acknowledge the hand of God in them; and they feel satisfied with the perfect government of the Most High. The subjects of sanctified afflictions are led to a clear discovery of their sins, and an unreserved confession of the divine justice and wisdom in their chastisement. They examine their hearts and their past lives, and abhor themselves, as being very vile in the eyes of infinite purity. They, who are afflicted in covenant faithfulness, will find the grace of the Gospel peculiarly endeared to them, and will strive to obey God's will in all things. They will prize and seek after communion with God in the various

exercises of private and public worship. They will endeavour to conform to the law of benevolence towards
men; and in particular, will be emboldened to reprove
sin, and be engaged to exercise compassion and kindness
towards the afflicted. Sanctified afflictions are instrumental in weaning men from earthly attachments, and in
ripening them for death and heaven.

These are very plain rules of trial, and such as must
commend themselves to our minds. If we have sought
to regard them in our practice, when we have been in
tribulation, we have found true peace, and can say with
the Psalmist, that "it is good for us that we have been afflicted." Are there not some who can adopt this language, and find evidence that they are heirs of heaven?
And may say, in some happy moments, with the Apostle,
"I reckon that the sufferings of this present time are not
worthy to be compared with the glory which shall be revealed in us." Rom. viii. 18. Let such maintain, at all
times, a patient and a devout, and a watchful and a heavenly temper. Their days of mourning will soon be ended, and they will soon be admitted into the world of everlasting light and glory.

How awful is the state of those who have become
hardened in all their afflictions! What can such expect,
in the course which they are pursuing, but everlasting
misery? "He that being often reproved, hardeneth his
neck, shall suddenly be destroyed, and that without remedy." Prov. xxix. 1. What cause is there to fear that
all the evils which they have felt, in the present world,
are but so many presages of endless, vindictive wrath, in
the world to come! Let them be warned—let them be
entreated, to search and try their ways, and turn unto the
Lord!

END.

ADVICE

FROM

A MASTER

TO

𝕳𝖎𝖘 𝕬𝖕𝖕𝖗𝖊𝖓𝖙𝖎𝖈𝖊,

WHEN LEAVING HIS SERVICE, AND ENTERING ON LIFE
FOR HIMSELF.

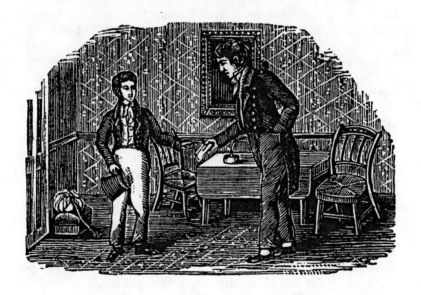

PUBLISHED BY THE

AMERICAN TRACT SOCIETY,

AND SOLD AT THEIR DEPOSITORY, NO. 150 NASSAU-STREET, NEAR
THE CITY-HALL, NEW-YORK; AND BY AGENTS OF THE
SOCIETY, ITS BRANCHES, AND AUXILIARIES, IN
THE PRINCIPAL CITIES AND TOWNS
IN THE UNITED STATES.

Vol. 4

ADVICE FROM A MASTER

TO

HIS APPRENTICE.

———

It has been my endeavour, from the time you were first committed to my care, to guard you against those evils to which your inexperienced age was exposed, and to direct and encourage you in the principles of religion and practices of virtue, that so you might lay the foundation for a happy and useful life. I would now, with great affection, fulfil the last part of my trust, by giving you some important counsels and cautions at your entrance on a new stage of life, wherein you will meet with temptations and difficulties which you never yet experienced, and will need all the assistance you can receive from God and man, for your wise and happy conduct.

1. See that the foundation of religion be well laid, in a sincere conversion, an entire and willing resignation of your soul to God, as your sovereign Lord and Ruler and supreme and satisfying Good; living by faith on Christ Jesus as the Saviour and Hope of sinners, through whose mercy and mediation you are to seek for, and receive, every blessing from God, for time and eternity. If sometimes you faintly hope that you have already advanced thus far, my advice is, that you never rest satisfied till you have, in your own conscience, a full evidence of the important and delightful fact. It is a dreadful thing for an immortal spirit to hang in a state of suspense, by the slender thread of life, between two such amazing extremes as an eternal Heaven or an eternal Hell. Satisfaction may be had; and, believe a friend, it is worth all the prayers, pains, and vigilance, you can use to obtain it.

2. As you are entering into a world wherein a variety of examples, methods of conduct, and maxims in religion will be presented to you, some plausible, some pernicious, and many destructive; if you value your conscience or your comfort, make the sacred word of God, which is to be the rule of your future judgment, the invariable rule of your

disposition and practice.   You will never find a more faithful counsellor, a more advantageous guide, or a more cordial and constant friend, than in those sacred oracles of
wisdom and truth, if you closely study and practise them.
Let no day, therefore, pass over without some serious perusal of them, joined with humble, earnest prayer to God
for wisdom to understand them, and power to conform to
them.   Study the inimitable rules of wisdom and prudence
in the Proverbs of Solomon, to direct your practice ; the
Psalms of David, to inspire your devotion ; and the whole
word of God, especially the New Testament, to form your
faith, your hope, and your temper.   Particularly, treasure
up in your mind some passages relating to each revealed
doctrine, each commanded duty, and each forbidden temper ; that your belief may be directed by the wisdom, and
your conscience awed by the authority of God, in every
season of duty and temptation.   " Bind them continually
upon thy heart, and tie them about thy neck.   When thou
goest, it shall lead thee ; when thou sleepest, it shall keep
thee ; and when thou awakest, it shall talk with thee ; for
the commandment is a lamp; and the law is a light ; and
the reproofs of instruction are the way of life."   Proverbs
vi. 21—23.

3. If you would enjoy the pleasures of a rational, religious being, let your actions not only be lawful for the matter of them, but laudable as to the ends for which you perform them ; that is, let it be the chief view, and highest
end, in all you do, to please God and glorify him.   It is
the great prerogative of the most high God, and the proper
homage that is due to him from all his reasonable creatures,
that as he is their Creator and absolute Owner, so he is
their chief End in all things ; and this end should be habitually regarded by them in all their actions.   It is the
great condescension of God, and consolation of religion,
that God hath not only permitted us to enjoy the comforts,
and perform the offices of life, but hath made it part of
our duty so to do : so that there is not a minute of our
lives but we may be doing the work of God while we are
serving ourselves, and may convert the common actions of
life into the services of religion, by directing them to his
glory.   Study noble views, in all you do : devote yourself entirely to God, and he will return you to yourself

wiser and better than he found you; study to glorify him
by a life of holiness and beneficence, and he will honour
and bless you. So much as is done for God, he will accept and reward as the expression of your duty and affection; but what is done from low and selfish views, is lost
from your account. " Whatsoever you do, therefore, do it
in singleness of heart, as unto Christ; with good-will, doing service as to the Lord."   Eph. vi. 5—7.

4. Be very watchful against an inordinate affection for
the present world. Use it with sober cheerfulness and
gratitude to Heaven, as far as is necessary to your present
comfortable existence; but suffer it not to engage your ·
heart. An earthly, sensual mind, is the basest perversion
of the noble faculties of the soul of man, and the highest
dishonour reflected on that glorious and good being who
created and redeemed it, and proposes himself to be its
full felicity and eternal joy. The predominant degree of
this evil and sordid disposition is ever inconsistent with
sincerity in religion; and the inordinate degrees of it in
good men are the foundation of many sorrows and divine
rebukes. Very just is the observation which I remember
to have seen, " That whatever we make an idol of, will
be a cross to us, if we belong to Christ; and a curse to us,
if we do not." The interests of the soul, in sincere Christians, more frequently suffer from the unhallowed love of
lawful objects than from the love of unlawful ones. Watch
carefully, therefore, over your affections ; and when any
temporal good appears unusually delightful, see that your
inclinations to God do not grow feeble and languid thereby,
and your affections to spiritual concerns more cold and indifferent : remembering " that to be carnally minded is
death ; but to be spiritually minded is life and peace."

5. Labour to possess, and constantly to cherish, a meek
and humble spirit, which is of high estimation in the
sight of God and man. This will make you easy to be
pleased, difficult to be offended, calm and serene in every
circumstance of life. This will cause you to be courteous
and affable to inferiors, respectful to superiors, and will
procure honour and esteem from others, far beyond all the
assuming airs of pride, arrogance, and self-applause. Especially let this disposition be cherished in all your religious concerns; a condescending God, a humble Redeemer,

and a proud sinner, are the most astonishing scenes that can
present themselves to the mind of man. Labour to be
sensible how little knowledge and goodness you possess,
compared with the rule of your duty and the attainments
of others ; and never measure yourself but by your superiors in wisdom and goodness, except to excite your gratitude to Heaven for its greater favours to yourself.

6. Watch over the natural appetites of the body, lest
those senses, which were designed to administer innocent
pleasures, become the incentive to sin. The sensitive affections have so far overpowered reason and conscience in
man, that the Scripture can find no word more fit to describe his fallen state, than *flesh ;* and I can assure you
that it requires all the assistance which reason and religion afford, to keep them in due subordination. Be chaste
and virtuous, not only in your discourse and behaviour,
but in the dispositions of your mind; indulge no wanton
thoughts or looks, and carefully avoid every sort of temptation; for you know not how great a flame the spark of
lust, when indulged, may kindle. Observe the injunctions,
which our Lord and Saviour has given concerning the
government of the eyes; (Matt. v. 28.) and recollect that
the unclean shall not enter into the kingdom of our God.
Be sober and temperate in the use of diet and drink ; every
degree is excessive herein, which renders you indisposed
to action and exercise of body and mind : particularly, let
no company engage you to exceed the bounds of reason ;
a peremptory refusal or two, at first, will ever after free
you from their solicitations; but easy compliance will encourage their repeated assaults.

7. Be very cautious in your choice of company and
friends, for we insensibly grow like those whom we frequently and familiarly converse with. Be rude and un-
civil to none, but intimate only with few ; and let those
few be well chosen, such as you may improve by in virtue
and goodness. Especially let this advice be attended to in
the choice of a relation for life. Affection is often blind,
and makes fatal mistakes both as to persons and things ; if
therefore you would consult your true happiness, never
enter into an engagement of this nature, without seriously
considering the importance of christian character, and ad-
vising with your elder and more judicious friends, whose

knowledge of human nature will assist you to form a proper judgment on one of the most interesting subjects which can come before the human mind. Be careful daily to worship God in secret, according to the direction of our Saviour, Matt. vi. 1. And should you be placed at the head of a family, worship Him morning and evening, with your household. Be constant also in your attendance on public worship ; and see that all under your care do the same. Let the Sabbath be observed from beginning to end, as a day of holy rest. In all your ways acknowledge God, and he will direct your paths.

8. I cannot conclude this letter of advice without strongly recommending benevolence, as the noblest disposition, and as an inlet to the richest enjoyment. Consider yourself as a member of the universe, whose proper disposition is to feel the sorrows, and rejoice in the happiness of all the beings that surround you; and permit me to assure you that the sensual, the covetous, the ambitious, in the highest gratification of their desires, never felt a joy comparable to that of doing good. Watch, therefore, against a contracted, selfish spirit, as no less injurious to yourself than to others; and be diligent, prudent, and frugal, in all your management, that you may have the privilege of being a great blessing to others ; especially endeavour to promote their best interests, by all possible means, whereby you may be an everlasting blessing unto them.

May the God of all grace inspire your heart with heavenly wisdom, preserve you from the evils of life, grant you prosperity, and make you a blessing in every relation thereof ; may he give you to feel the power, and enjoy the pleasures of religion in this world, and in due time grant you to receive the rewards of it in a better. This is the hearty prayer and desire of

YOUR SINCERE FRIEND AND

AFFECTIONATE MASTER.

KNOW THOU THE GOD OF THY FATHERS, AND SERVE HIM
WITH A PERFECT HEART, AND WITH A WILLING MIND. FOR THE
LORD SEARCHETH ALL HEARTS, AND UNDERSTANDETH ALL THE
IMAGINATIONS OF THE THOUGHTS ; IF THOU SEEK HIM HE WILL
BE FOUND OF THEE ; BUT IF THOU FORSAKE HIM, HE WILL CAST
THEE OFF FOR EVER.

BREATHING AFTER HOLINESS.

Oh ! that the Lord would guide my ways
   To keep his statutes still !
Oh ! that my God would grant me grace
   To know and do his will.

Oh ! send thy Spirit down to write
   Thy law upon my heart !
Nor let my tongue indulge deceit,
   Nor act the liar's part.

From vanity turn off mine eyes ;
   Let no corrupt design,
Nor covetous desire arise
   Within this soul of mine.

Order my footsteps by thy word,
   And make my heart sincere ;
Let sin have no dominion, Lord,
   But keep my conscience clear.

My soul hath gone too far astray,
   My feet too often slip,
Yet since I've not forgot thy way,
   Restore thy wand'ring sheep.

Make me to walk in thy commands ;
   'Tis a delightful road ;
Nor let my head, or heart, or hands,
   Offend against my God.

INSTRUCTIONS FROM SCRIPTURE.

How shall the young secure their hearts,
     And guard their lives from sin ?
Thy word the choicest rules imparts,
     To keep the conscience clean.

When once it enters to the mind,
     It spreads such light abroad,
The meanest souls instruction find,
     And raise their thoughts to God.

'Tis like the sun, a heavenly light,
     That guides us all the day ;
And through the dangers of the night,
     A lamp to lead our way.

The men that keep thy law with care,
     And meditate thy word,
Grow wiser than their teachers are,
     And better know the Lord.

Thy precepts make me truly wise ;
     I hate the sinner's road :
I hate my own vain thoughts that rise,
     But love thy law, my God.

The starry heavens thy rule obey,
     The earth maintains her place ;
And these thy servants night and day,
     Thy skill and power express.

But still thy law and Gospel, Lord,
     Have lessons more divine ;
Not earth stands firmer than thy word,
     Nor stars so nobly shine.

Thy word is everlasting truth,
     How pure is every page !
That holy book shall guide our youth,
     And well support our age.

END.

TRUE BELIEVER BOUNTIFUL.

—◦◦◦—

YE disciples of the Lord Jesus Christ, your Saviour has
set up a church in this world, has promised that the gates
of hell shall not prevail against it, and that it shall one
day embrace all nations; and calls upon you to consecrate
your property to the diffusion of that Gospel, by which he
brings men into his kingdom, and makes them happy.
Will you hear me, while I offer a few arguments to induce
you to obey him in this reasonable requisition? I will
enter upon the point without detaining you a moment, and
when I have done, you must act as you think proper.

The *first* argument is, that " the *earth is the Lord's, and
the fullness thereof,*" *and hence he has a right to make this
draft upon you.* If I fail of establishing this point, you
may lay down the book, and not read another line. You
acknowledge God as the Creator of all things. Here I
found his claim: it is prior to all others. He who built
all worlds, and peopled them, and gave that people all
their good things, may make a demand upon them, to any
amount, with the certainty that it cannot be protested. His
are all the "beasts of the forest," "and the cattle upon a
thousand hills." The same is true of your silver, your
merchandise, your children, your servants, and all you
have. If not, then name the good thing that you can be
sure will be yours to-morrow. Begin, if you please, at
the bottom of the catalogue of your comforts, and ascend
through the whole series, to the wife of your bosom, your
health, and your life, and tell me which of the whole will
be yours to-morrow. Dare you name nothing? Then
whosoever they are, they surely are not yours. For he
who has nothing that he can hold a day, has nothing but
what is borrowed. And if the good things you possess
are not yours, they are the Lord's; or whose are they?
And what was the Lord's at first, because he made it, he
has carefully watched over and preserved. Not merely
could we have *had* nothing, if God had not made it; but
we could have *kept* nothing, if God had not preserved it.

There is no kind of independence about us; we should

have been beggars if God had not cared for us. There was an eye that watched more narrowly than we did or could, or our wealth had long since taken to itself wings, and had flown away. It was the blessed God that watered our fields, and gave success to our commerce, and health to our children; that guarded our house from fire, and our lives from danger; else we should have been beggars, or should, years ago, have perished. How many, once as wealthy as you, are now poor; or as healthy as you, are now in the grave; had a home as you have, but it burned down; had children, as perhaps you have, but the cold blast came over them, and they died. And was it not the kindness of God that saved to you what you have? May he not then claim as much of your wealth as he pleases?

But I am not through the argument. God has never *alienated* his rights. He has suffered Satan to be styled the God of this world, the prince of the power of the air; but *he* owns nothing. The territories that he promised the Lord Jesus, if he would fall down and worship him, were not a foot of them his. And though men are permitted to hold under God certain rights, and which they sometimes term unalienable, still God never has renounced his right to dispose at pleasure of all that we term ours, and he never will. In a moment, if he pleases, day or night, he puts us out of our possessions, and the places that knew us, know us no more, for ever. Thus the voluptuary in the Gospel, just when about to pull down his barns and build greater, that he might have room to deposit his good things, and when about to say to his soul, " thou hast good things laid up for many years," heard from heaven the unwelcome tidings, " this night thy soul shall be required of thee." In a few hours more his life-lease would be out, when all he had must revert to its original and rightful owner."

Hence, we can serve God only with what is his already; what he has never alienated. " Of thine own, we give thee." Now, that which God has put into our hands, and the right to which he has never relinquished, we may not, without the charge of fraud, appropriate otherwise than as he shall command us.

But I have not done. God has often *asserted* his claim

to what we term ours. This he does by his *mercies*. Every shower he sends, and every sun that rises, witnesses a God riding upon the heavens and making the clouds his chariot, that he may pay a friendly visit to his own territories, and distil blessings upon the fields, whose fee, and all whose fruits are his; and every breeze, and every dew that falls, but set forth their morning and their evening claim to their Master's right. Thus "day unto day uttereth speech" of him, and "night unto night" repeats again and again the story of his kindness to his own creations, and his care of his own territory. When was any one thus careful for another's interest, and thus intent upon rendering fertile a soil whose increase he might neither appropriate to himself nor call his own? and when he heals our sicknesses, and holds us back from the grave, and purifies our atmosphere with his lightnings, and bids the autumnal frosts to cure the fevers and the plagues of our cities, of whom does he take all this care, but of his children and his servants? and when he heals the broken bone and restores the weary and the faint, has he no claim upon the existence he prolongs, and the health and life he gives? and when he feeds us daily at his table, and regales us at his fountains, and rests us upon the works he built, and furnishes the eye with light, and gladdens every sense with its appropriate delights, does he not assert his claim to be served and honoured by the beings he thus indefatigably protects, and feeds, and heals, and nourishes? Is there a star that twinkles in the firmament, or a moon that lights up night, or a bow that spreads its beauties on the cloud, and God is not seen in them, giving light and promise to the subjects of his own kingdom? Is there a flower of May, or a dew-drop of morning, or a lineament in the human face, in which God is not seen penciling out beauties upon his own works? And who will deny that God has a paramount claim to a world where he expends so much of his wisdom and his care? Where is the individual who will not acknowledge the rights of God?"

And he asserts his claim again in the *severities* of his providence. Once he claimed the whole world, and, by a sudden and fearful dispensation, displaced every tenant that had ever occupied its soil, providing afterward, timely and amply, for the single family he loved, and whom by covenant he had adopted as his own. And none will say that God went without his own dominions, to lay a world waste that was the property of *another*. When he burned the cities of the plain, he only asserted, though loudly and fearfully, his rights ; and pressed home to the bosom and the conscience, of foe and friend, his claim to be served and honoured, in every valley that he had made fertile, and by every people whom his kindness had made prosperous.

In the ruin of all the ancient monarchies, God is seen in the attitude of asserting his claim to the kingdoms of men, as sections of his own empire, to which he will send other rulers, and other subjects, whenever he shall please. The desolating pestilences by which he has dispeopled towns and cities, and the thousand nameless sweeps of death written in our gloomy history, had all their commissions from heaven, to take back the life, and health, and comforts he had loaned to men. There was one kingdom we read of, whose whole population went seventy years into bondage, because their land had not been allowed to keep its Sabbaths, and they had not paid their tithes, and emancipated their servants at the appointed jubilee.

The storms that have wrecked our merchandise, and the fires that have devoured our cities, and all the *misnamed* casualties that have ruined our fortunes, have been so many claims put in, by the rightful owner of all things, to what we had appropriated too exclusively to our own use. And the occurrences of every day are of the same character.

I know this is not the world of retribution, and that "no man knoweth either good or evil, by any thing that is done under the sun;" but let us not deny, that God is "known by the judgment that he executeth." Will he not, by repeated demands, keep men in mind that they cultivate his territory, and feed on his bounty, and are happy under his auspices? In thus asserting his claim to be served with the talents that he loans, he shows that one unchangeable law of his kingdom is, that he never alienates what was once his own.

I shall not offend the good man, when I claim, that this has been a *disastrous*, because a *disobedient* world. Perhaps the aggregate of property lost by the various calamities that God has sent upon this world, would have exactly met the claims he had upon its charity. Had that wealth been expended as he directed, it would have made the world wise and happy. "Bring ye all the tithes into the storehouse, that there may be meat in mine house, and prove me now herewith, saith the Lord of Hosts, if I will not open you the windows of heaven, and pour you out a blessing, that there shall not be room enough to receive it." We read again, "There is that withholdeth more than is meet, but it tendeth to poverty."

It is impossible to say how much more prosperous this world might have been, if men had expended their wealth as God would have them; how much more frequently the showers had fallen, or more genial our sun, or more gentle our breezes, or mild our winters, or fertile our soil, or healthful our population, if we had been a better people, and had served the Lord with our substance. His promise must have failed, or he would have "filled our barns with plenty," and caused our "presses to burst out with new wine."

As the churches shall wake to their duty, and give the world the Gospel, I hope, and if infidelity scoffs, still I will hope, that much of the curse will be removed from this ill-fated world, and God kindly "stay his rough wind, in the day of his east wind." How many of its plagues will be cured, its wars prevented, its heaths made fertile, and its earthquakes stilled; and what the amount of blessings bestowed upon this world, when it shall become more loyal and more benevolent, none but God can know. I cannot believe, that when we shall do as he bids us, he will so often rebuke us. When we cease to waste his goods, he will allow us to continue longer in the stewardship; when we shall be faithful in the few things, he will make us rulers over many things.

If you will now consider me as having established the divine claim to you, and all that you have, I will proceed to offer the *second* argument; which is, that Christians, who have the means, should contribute to disseminate the Gospel, *because they are heirs of God, and joint heirs with Jesus Christ.* They belong to that kingdom which the Gospel was intended to establish. This fact is quite enough to give the cause I plead a strong hold upon every pious heart. Ye disciples of the Lord Jesus, read once more the charter of your hopes; and while it warms your heart, tell me if you have done half your duty. "All things are yours; whether Paul, or Apollos, or Cephas, or the world, or life, or death, or things present, or things to come; all are yours, and ye are Christ's, and Christ is God's." Then it seems God and his people have but one interest. Hence, when he commands them to spread the Gospel, he but bids them buy themselves blessings, bids them foster their own interest, and make their own kingdom happy. The Christian has by his own act identified his whole interest with that of the church of our Lord Jesus Christ. If God is honoured, he is happy; and God is honoured in the salvation of sinners, and in the joy of his people. Hence God can command his people to do nothing but that which will bless themselves.

Now, when did you know of a king's son who would not joyfully expend his father's treasures to enlarge, and strengthen, and beautify the kingdom to which he was heir? He thus polishes his own crown, and blesses his own future reign. What believer has not the same interest that God has, in lengthening the cords and strengthening the stakes of Zion! He is one of the little flock, to whom it is his Father's good pleasure to give the kingdom. He is to be a king and a priest to God and the Lamb for ever; and has he still an interest distinct from his heavenly Father? If not, he will hold all he has at the control of God. He will need only to know his duty, and will perform it most cheerfully.

The *third* reason why Christians, who have the means, should contribute to disseminate the Gospel, is, that *they are merciful, as their Father in heaven is merciful.* Over that mass of misery which the apostacy has produced, their pious hearts have long bled in sympathy. And their charity is not of that kind that it can content itself with saying, "Be ye warmed, and be ye filled." They have read, and have strongly felt, that cutting interrogation of the apostle, "Whosoever hath this world's goods, and seeth his brother have need, and shutteth up his bowels of compassion from him, how dwelleth the love of God in him?" And there is no man so needy as he who has not the bread of life. The *good man* would render all men happy. His charity is warm, like that which beats in the heart of the Son of God; and to do his duty is his meat and his drink. This makes him like his Master; and to this he aspires. He cannot hope to rejoice eternally in the achievements of redemption, unless, moved by the same pity for the miserable that *he* felt, he is prepared to come up promptly, and offer the Saviour any service he requires.

Oh, it fills me with shame, when I must goad up my own heart, or must urge my Christian brother to be kind; for it is acknowledged, that we owe all we have, and all we hope for, to the loving kindness of the Lord Jesus Christ. Our reprieve from hell, we owe to his mercy; and the food we eat, and the raiment we put on, and the friends who succour us, and the tenement we dwell in, and the bed we rest on. He is the Saviour of all men; ah, and more yet *we* owe him, for he is especially the Saviour of them that believe. It is through him we have that pardon we speak of, that sanctification which we hope is begun, that adoption which placed us in his family, that peace of God which passeth all understanding, and that hope which we have cast within the vail. We had never discovered that we were sinners, but for his loving kindness; nor had mourned for sin, had the discovery been made; nor had taken any hold on the atonement; nor had looked complacently upon the attributes of God; but had lived and died aliens from the commonwealth of Israel, and strangers to the covenant of promise; nor had joined hereafter the redeemed of the Lord, or raised to his honour one anthem of praise. " God so loved the world, that he gave his only begotten Son, that whosoever believeth in him, should not perish, but have everlasting life." And says an apostle, " Ye know the grace of our Lord Jesus Christ, that, though he was rich, yet for your sakes he became poor, that ye through his poverty might be rich." And can it still be true, and must it be told in Gath, and published in the streets of Askelon, that any of his people will not diminish their wealth a little for him who bought all their riches with his poverty. Should there chance to be a covetous Christian among all the disciples of the Lord Jesus that will not spend his money to save men from hell, pray let his history be a secret, let him lodge in some wilderness, where his example may not cast a reproach upon his Master and his brethren; and let him find a grave in some dark glen, and sleep in solitude, and rise alone, and come alone to the judgment. Still, when that brother shall die, and be reckoned with, it must remain a doubt whether, having showed no mercy, he must not expect judgment without mercy.

I appeal then, ye disciples of Jesus Christ, to the kindness of your hearts, when I ask you to contribute of your wealth, to render the world happy. Would you not cure some of the plagues that sin has generated, and that have so long preyed upon the blessedness of man? Would you not quench the funeral pile, and save the young and beautiful, but infatuated widow, that she may nurse her imploring infant, and live to rear it up to life? Would you not free one half of the human family, the female sex, from that servitude to which paganism has subjected them? Would you not snatch ten thousand infants from the altars of devils, where they now lie, bound and weeping, waiting till you speak a word of mercy for them! Would you not teach the vast herd of idolaters, that there is a kinder, and more merciful God, than those they worship? Would you not break in upon the delusions of the False Prophet, and tell his misguided followers, that you have read of a holier heaven than they hope for? Would you not file off the chains that have been fastened, so many centuries, upon poor afflicted Africa? Would you not stay the progress of war, and save the thousands that are marching, warm and weary, toward the field of death? Oh, would you not, were it possible, bring back this base world to its home and its Maker? Have you then a purse, into which God may not thrust his hand, and take thence what he has there deposited, with a view to make this wretched world happy?

Bear with me, ye followers of the Lamb, a little longer, and I will say that you have *covenanted to be workers together with God* in achieving the purposes of redemption, and must now employ your energies to widen the boundaries of his holy empire, or forfeit your promise. It was in you a voluntary compact; and you pledged in that hour your prayers, your influence, your farm, your merchandise, your purse, your children, and all that you have. And

Heaven has recorded that vow, to be brought up against you, if it be violated, in the day of retribution. It was wholly at your option, whether you would enter into that sweeping covenant, whether you would swear; but you have entered, you have sworn, and cannot go back. You then relinquished for ever your personal rights, and have had, ever since, but a community of interest with God and his people. Now, God is employed in doing good, and his people too, if they are like him. How then will it correspond with your oath, to stand aloof from the calls of the church? and disregard the command of God? and let the waste places lie desolate? and let the heathen die in their pollution? and let the captives perish in their chains? and let almost the whole of that territory, purchased with the blood of the Lord Jesus Christ, lie under the usurped dominion of the prince of hell? and let a whole condemned world go to the judgment, with all this blood upon it, unsanctified? Oh, how will your broken vows rise and haunt you, in that day when the wealth you have saved shall be weighed in the balance with the souls it might have been the instrument of redeeming!

Who would venture upon the experiment of being convicted of covenant-breaking before a congregated world? of having embezzled the wealth God created purposely for the use of his church? of having squandered upon his person, or his children, (perhaps to their ruin,) what might have been used in turning the fertilizing stream of the Gospel into some parched territory, where, ever since the apostacy, there has been only desolation, and famine, and pestilence? Oh, who, for all the gold that has ever been counted, would go to the altar of God, and there swear that he would renounce the pomp and vanities of the world, and then go and stand impeached, before angels and devils, at the judgment seat, of having loved the world more than God, more than the souls of men, more than the kingdom of our Lord Jesus Christ?

I offer you one reason more. You have been sanctified, as you hope, through the truth; and hence have *some experience of the value* of that Gospel which we urge you to promulgate. Once you were ignorant of God, and were unhappy. You were in somewhat the same forlorn condition with those whose cause I plead; you had forsaken

God, the fountain of living water, and had hewn out to yourselves broken cisterns, that could hold no water. And you remember that dark period. Your mind travelled from object to object, through all the round of created good, and, in search of blessedness, found no end, in wandering mazes lost.

And there is a world of intelligent, immortal beings, seen panting and weary in the same fruitless chase. It was the blessed Gospel that arrested you, and saved you. Your heedless steps it guided; your dark mind it enlightened; your erring conscience it rectified; your insensibility it aroused; your hard heart it softened; your selfishness it expanded; your pride it humbled; your wayward course it changed; your covenant with death, and your agreement with hell, it disannulled. And here you stand, redeemed, regenerated, your whole character changed, and your final destiny altered, through the influence of the blessed Gospel. The curse is removed; you are a child of God, and an heir of glory, and shall one day see the King in his beauty : *and the Gospel has done it.* It has given you peace of conscience, joy in the Holy Ghost, a firm hope of heaven, and the soul-reviving assurance that all things shall work together for your good, till you rise to be where Christ is, behold his beauty, and rejoice in his love for ever.

Now the question is, whether you will contribute of your wealth, to save those who are perishing, as you so lately were? I now plead with you by all that religion has been worth to you, by all the joys it has brought you, by all the woes it has cured, by all the hopes it has raised, and by all the transformation it has wrought in your character and your condition. For what price would you return into the darkened, and dreary, and hopeless condition in which the Gospel found you? For what would you barter away all the delightful prospects that open before you, and calculate on no more precious sacramental seasons; no more communion of saints; no more delightful hours in your closet; nor Pisgah views of the field of promise; nor fellowship with the Father, and with his Son Jesus Christ? At no price would you part with these? Then how great are the blessings which you have it in your power to confer on those who are perishing for lack of vision.

May we be permitted to learn what estimate you put
upon religion by the pains you take to communicate its
joys to others? This is the only rule God has given us.
Weighed in this balance, how will you appear in the sight
of God? Have you foregone the gratification of your taste,
that you might send salvation to some destitute territory
of this ruined world? Have you denied yourself any article of luxury, rode in a less splendid carriage, or reclined
upon a humbler couch, or mounted a plainer staircase, or
seated yourself at a less costly table, or spent an hour
more at business, that you might have at command the
means of doing good, of enlightening the benighted or
reclaiming the vicious, or of bringing to hope and to heaven
the wayward and the lost? Or was no such economy necessary? Then, I ask, Have you allowed God and his
kingdom to put in their claim along with yours? When
you bought a luxury, did you buy a Bible for the poor?
When you enlarged and beautified your habitation, and
added another house or another field to your possessions,
did you enlarge your annual subscription to the Benevolent Institutions of the age? Did you, when you had paid
your thousands for some conveniences, pay a tithe of that
sum to enlarge, and beautify, and strengthen the kingdom
of your Master? Did you feel none the less able and the
more obligated to do good, because God allowed you to
make large appropriations for your own comfort? The
divine precept is, and it binds every Christian conscience,
" Do good to all men as you have opportunity, but especially to those who are of the household of faith;" and in
their obedience to this precept, they show exactly the
price they put upon piety. Dear as a Gospel temper, and
a Gospel hope, and a Gospel heaven are to us, proportionably high will rise our zeal to generate that temper and
that hope in every bosom, and prepare for that heaven a
whole world of benighted and perishing sinners. And as
our zeal is, such will be the promptitude with which we
shall bestow our substance to rescue the lost from the
perdition that awaits them.

Do you say, that they can purchase the privileges of the
Gospel, as you have? No, they will not. They know not
their value; and will die in their sins, ere they will give
a shilling for the light of the Gospel. Not the whole of

India, if it would save them all from hell, would be willing to support a single missionary.

If we persuade them to let our missionaries live in their territories, and to refrain from their blood, we shall rejoice. If they will allow their children to read the Bible, when we have taught them, and supported them while they were taught, we shall be happy. If they will hear us when we have come on our knees to them, and will be entreated when we have worn out our health, and even life, for them, it will be all we can expect. But, "how shall they hear without a preacher? and how shall he preach except he be sent?" and how can he be sent, unless the wealthy will feed him and clothe him? And if missionaries can be found, who will encounter a sultry clime, and die pleading with men to be willing to live for ever, need we plead long with wealthy believers to induce them to sustain these missionaries? What then will the world think of us, who march up so promptly in every enterprise dear to their hearts?

Will God send them the Gospel by miracle? No, he once did thus send it to the lost, blessed be his name! but he now commands us to send it to those who are perishing for lack of vision. We know our duty, and God will require it of us. Can we meet the heathen in the judgment, if we have done nothing to promote their salvation?

I will plead no longer. But let me tell you, in parting, that when you shall see the world on fire, your wealth all melting down, and those who have perished through your neglect calling upon the " rocks and mountains to fall on them, and hide them from the face of him that sitteth upon the throne, and from the wrath of the Lamb," and shall know that you might have been instrumental in saving them, there will be strong sensations. If you are saved yourself, and you cannot be if you remain indifferent to the salvation of others, you will wish a place to weep over your past neglects, before you begin your everlasting song; and if lost yourself, then indeed there will be weeping, and wailing, and gnashing of teeth.

NOTE.—A premium of fifty dollars, proposed by a generous individual, was awarded to the author of this Tract

PAY-NIGHT.

A DIALOGUE ON SATURDAY EVENING.

William. Come, Robert, let's call over across the common, and take a glass of grog. We have done a good week's work, and wages are fair now.

Robert. No, I am bound for home; and as for the glass of grog, it's what does all the mischief. Think of poor Sam's wife and children. A better workman never entered the shop; but he must have his grog, and last week we laid the poor fellow in his grave.

Wm. Yes, yes; but there's no harm in taking a little to refresh one's spirits after a hard day's work. It's only just past nine, and we can lie an hour longer in the morning.

Rob. Ah, it's this taking a little to refresh one's spirits that leads on to a little more, and then a little more, till we

are ruined. Just take none at all, and you are safe. Poor
Sam used to take a little, but he took it oftener and oftener,
till he had an appetite like a horse-leech. He drank up all
his wages, and you see how the matter ended. For my part,
I wish we were paid some other night besides Saturday, and
a little earlier too. It is more than one can do, at this late
hour, to get home and be ready for Sunday; besides, many of
our shopmates squander a great part of their week's wages before the day is over.

Wm. "Ready for Sunday!" I thought Sunday was intended as a day of rest and recreation. I was just going
to ask you to join a party, and take a sail with us to-morrow; but I suppose, from what you say about Sunday, that
it's of no use to ask you.

Rob. To be sure I would not like to violate and profane the Lord's day.

Wm. Violate and profane the Lord's day! What! to take
a little innocent recreation after slaving hard all the week,
do you call this violating and profaning the Lord's day?

Rob. I don't know how any one can call it otherwise.

Wm. I should like to hear what mighty reason you can
give, why a man should not take a little pleasure, only because it happens to be on Sunday.

Rob. Well, then, you must know, first of all, that the Sabbath was intended by the Almighty to be a day of rest and
cessation from labor. We read that "God blessed the seventh
day, and hallowed it; because that in it he had rested from
all his work." Now what you propose as recreation, is
harder than any of our work; and for my part, I have no
notion of volunteering to row a boat for hours together, like
a galley slave, for the sake of rest and recreation, after working hard all the week. It was but yesterday that I read
in the paper of two parties who were launched into eternity
while taking their pleasure on the water on Sunday. A bad
preparation surely for such a change. Besides, you know
it is not more than three years ago when a party of fifteen

young men and women were drowned, and the minister of our town preached a most affecting discourse on the evil and danger of Sabbath-breaking. He spoke in such a manner as made the tear trickle down from every eye; and the sighs and sobs of the people sometimes almost stopped him in his sermon. I shall not forget it as long as I live. And then, such sport cannot be had without money; and a man spends as much in this way on a Sunday, as would keep his family half the week; so he comes home at night with weary bones, a guilty conscience, and an empty pocket into the bargain.

Wm. Well, I see 'tis of no use arguing with you. I shall go and see if they have spoken for the boat, and get all things ready; for we mean to start early in the morning.

Rob. Nay, but stay a minute or two longer, shopmate, for I have another reason stronger than all the rest put together; and that is, you have the commandments of God against you. He has said, "Remember the Sabbath day to keep it holy; six days shalt thou labor and do all thy work; but the seventh is the Sabbath of the Lord thy God:" you may read more of it in Exodus, chap. 20. And in another place Jehovah speaks thus: "Ye shall keep my Sabbath, for it is holy unto you; every one that defileth it shall be put to death." And this law was actually put in force among the Israelites. While they were in the wilderness, they found a man that gathered sticks upon the Sabbath day; "and the Lord said unto Moses, The man shall surely be put to death, and all the congregation shall stone him with stones without the camp; and all the congregation brought him without the camp, and stoned him with stones, and he died." Num. 15:32–16. Well might the Apostle say, "It is a fearful thing to fall into the hands of the living God." Now as to the manner of keeping the Sabbath, I will just mention one text of Scripture more; and this, as well as all the rest, is point blank against you: "If thou turn away thy foot from the Sabbath, from doing thy pleasure on my holy day; and call the Sabbath a delight, the holy of the Lord, honorable ; and shalt honor him, not doing *thine own ways*, nor finding *thine own pleasures*, nor speaking *thine own words*, then shalt thou delight thyself in the Lord, and I will cause thee to ride upon the high places of the earth, and feed thee with the heritage of Jacob, thy father ; for the mouth of the Lord hath spoken it." Isa. 58 : 13, 14. Now, if these reasons are not enough to satisfy you, I will add another.

Wm. Another ! no, no ; I don't want any more reasons. But give over this sort of preaching, and say you will go. I'll warrant you it will be a fine day, and we shall enjoy it well.

Rob. No, William, I cannot go with you, for sure I am there is no happiness where the blessing of God is not ; much less is happiness to be found in the way of transgression; for the Bible says, " The way of transgressors is hard." But as I dare not spend the Sabbath in your way, let me invite you to come and enjoy it with me: I will say, as Moses of old, " Come thou with us, and we will do thee good ; and it shall be, if thou go with us, yea, it shall be that what goodness the Lord shall do unto us, the same will we do unto thee."

Wm. I begin to think, indeed I have thought so ever since my good old mother died, that it is not quite right to neglect church on Sunday; and I must honestly tell you, I have, more than once or twice, had some stings of conscience, when, in spite of all my endeavors to forget it, I have thought upon the foolish manner in which I have spent the past day ; and then, on Monday morning, I feel as if every thing was wrong about me. I come to work with a heavy heart, while you appear as blithe as a lark, and as happy as a prince. Tell me, Robert, how is it you pass your Sundays ?

Rob. I'll do that with pleasure ; and if you can produce but half as many good reasons against my way of spending the Sabbath, as I have against yours, then I'll say no more.

Well, then, you must know, that when Saturday evening
comes——

Wm. Saturday evening!—Why, shopmate, I asked you
how you employed the Sunday, and not what you do on
Saturday. Does your Sunday begin on Saturday? This is
making a long Sunday of it, indeed.

Rob. I always consider Saturday evening as the preparation for the Sabbath; and as to the length of it, it always
flies too fast for me—

> " The gladness of that happy day,
> " My soul would wish it long to stay."

Wm. Well, then, on Saturday evening—what then ?
Rob. Why, then my wife and little ones are all as busy
as if they were getting ready to go to court the next morning: indeed, I always count the Sabbath as the grand court-
day of the King of kings; for, as the hymn says—

> " The King himself comes near,
> " And feasts his saints to-day;
> " Here we may sit and see him here,
> " And love, and praise, and pray."

The children's play-things are all put away—shoes all
cleaned, their clothes all aired and laid ready for the morning, house made tidy, and my wife waiting till I come home
with my wages; and I must be going soon, else she will begin to think something has happened.

Wm. Yes; I always thought your wife one of a thousand.
I wish every other man's wife was as good as she is; however, I will not complain.

Rob. Well, then, as I said, all things being ready on Saturday night, we offer up our praises to Almighty God for
the mercies of the past week, and pray that, with the light
of the coming day, the light of his countenance may shine
upon our souls—

Vol. 4.

> "Safely through another week,
> "God has brought us on our way;
> "Let us now a blessing seek
> "On th' approaching Sabbath day
>   "Day of all the week the best,
>   "Emblem of eternal rest."

Then we go to bed, rest our weary limbs, and always welcome the opening of another Sabbath day.

Wm. Why, this is making the most of a good thing; but don't you lie an hour or two longer in the morning, after the labor of the week?

Rob. As to that, I'll tell you. I rise at my usual hour, read the Bible alone, and pray to the Lord that we may "begin, continue, and end" the sacred day in the fear of God.

Wm. I am afraid you have got too much religion for me; I shall not much like your way. I always thought if I went to church once on a Sunday, I did my duty quite well enough.

Rob. Too much religion! That is impossible, if a man's heart is right. If he has tasted that the Lord is gracious, he will be coming to him; and as a new-born babe, "desire the sincere milk of the word, that he may grow thereby," as the Apostle Peter speaks. Too much religion! Why, religion is happiness; and you never yet knew any one have too much happiness.

Wm. Well, after the morning prayer and reading the Bible, what then?

Rob. Why, then I come down, and find the children all clean, wife ready with the breakfast; and as soon as that is over, we prepare for family worship, which we begin with a hymn; the little ones all join, I set the tune, and my Sarah has got a pretty voice. We often begin the Sabbath with—

> "Welcome, sweet day of rest,
> "That saw the Lord arise,
> "Welcome to this reviving breast,
> "And these rejoicing eyes."

Then we all kneel down and pray for a Sabbath-day's blessing, never forgetting to commend our minister to the grace of God; that he may be aided by the Holy Spirit to speak a word in season to him that is weary.

Wm. I should think you have had praying and singing enough for one day. I should be prayed and sung to death with so much religion.

Rob. Enough! William; the best of it is not yet begun. There is the public worship of the sanctuary; and, when the hour arrives, my heart is ready to cry out with David, " I was glad when they said unto me, let us go unto the house of the Lord. How amiable are thy tabernacles, O Lord of hosts, my King and my God! A day in thy courts is better than a thousand." It would do your heart good to see our good minister; he looks like a man that is pleading with God on behalf of his people. He looks round upon the congregation with so much affection, that you would think we were all his own children. He is always upon the one grand subject, as he calls it—*Jesus Christ, and him crucified.* This was his first text when he first came to us : " I am determined not to know any thing among you, save Jesus Christ, and him crucified." 1 Cor. 2 : 2. And he has kept good his determination ever since.

Wm. I think I should not much like your minister. According to your account, he is always harping upon one string.

Rob. Harping upon one string ! Yes, truly; but it is a string on which he plays a thousand delightful tunes. Christ and him crucified ! Why, William, this is the music of heaven, and no wonder it should gladden the hearts of sinners upon earth. I could listen to it for ever. Let me tell you, William, you and I are sinners, and we stand in need of a Savior ; we are great sinners, and we need a great Savior : now, just such a Savior is Jesus Christ, as St. Paul says—" This is a faithful saying, and worthy of all acceptation, that Christ Jesus came into the world to save sinners, of whom I am chief." 1 Tim. 1 : 15. It is the blood of Christ that takes away our sins; it is the righteousness of Christ that justifies us before God; it is the Spirit of Christ that makes us holy; it is the consolation of Christ that gives comfort in affliction; it is the grace of Christ that supports us when we come to die; it is the smile of Christ that gives boldness in the day of judgment; and it is the presence of Christ that makes heaven the blessed place it is. In short, "Christ is all and in all," as the Apostle has it in another place.

Wm. I confess I never heard so much about Christ before. I always thought that if a man did as well as he could, he need not concern himself so much about Christ and religion.

Rob. I thought so once, until I heard our good minister preach from this text, "For as many as are of the works of the law are under the curse; for it is written, Cursed is every one that continueth not in all things which are written in the book of the law, to do them." Gal. 3 : 10. I then found myself to be a guilty condemned sinner; and saw there was salvation only through the atoning blood of Christ! I cried to him for mercy; and he says, "Him that cometh unto me, I will in no wise cast out."

Wm. I think I should like to hear your minister preach; but surely you don't think there can be any harm in taking a walk into the fields in the afternoon, after going to church in the morning.

Rob. Why as to that—Now suppose you come to the shop on Monday morning, and work till twelve o'clock, and then go off and lounge about the rest of the day—would this be doing your duty to our employer? Would you not justly fall short in your reckoning when Saturday night came? So our blessed Lord says, "No man can serve two masters: for either he will hate the one and love the other, or else he will hold to the one and despise the other. Ye cannot serve God and Mammon." Matt. 4 : 24.

Now I love my Divine Master, and never think I can do enough for him. I love his service also; it is "perfect freedom."

Wm. Well, I think I should like to spend a Sunday with you, but I can't to-morrow; the party is all made up except *you ;* and as you won't go, we must either get somebody else, or go as we are.

Rob. My dear fellow, let me persuade you not to go; you seem to be somewhat convinced of the evil of Sabbath-breaking, and I am sure you will not be happy. Your conscience has often warned and checked you; and you will be sinning against light, and against this friendly caution. What if God should take you away with a stroke; you have no security against it, and especially in the way of disobedience; for "he that, being often reproved, hardeneth his neck, shall suddenly be destroyed, and that without remedy." Prov. 29 : 1.

Wm. Why, you seem to have all the argument on your side. Well, if I thought they would not laugh at me, and call me a Methodist, I would give it up, and go along with you.

Rob. Laugh at you, and call you a Methodist! Why let them laugh, and let them call. So the gay pleasure-takers might have laughed at Noah while he was preparing the ark; but the flood came and drowned them all; and their laughter was turned into bitter crying, when they found themselves shut out. This may have been the case, also, with the scoffers that dwelt in guilty Sodom; but the same day that Lot left the place, it rained fire and brimstone from heaven, and destroyed them all.

Wm. Well, I'll consider of it.

Rob. I hope you will, and may the Holy Spirit incline you to determine on the side of Christ and your immortal soul; this is true wisdom; and you will find her ways "are ways of pleasantness, and all her paths are paths of peace." But I must be going; I have told you but half the delightful work of the Sabbath-day; come, and prove the rest. I will only just say, the other half of the day becomes sweeter and sweeter, as one enters into the spirit of it; and I sometimes think, if there is so much comfort in the worship of God on earth, then what must heaven be!

> " O the delights, the heavenly joys,
> " The transports of the place,
> " Where Jesus sheds the brightest beams
> " Of his o'erflowing grace!"

Now, compare your way of spending the Sabbath with mine, and let any man of common sense be the judge, and I'll venture to say he will give it in my favor. You come home, half worn out with recreation, as you call it—money all spent—wife perhaps out of humor—the children cross and sleepy—and when you lie down at night, you cannot ask God's blessing on the past day, but are obliged to skulk to bed like a thief that is afraid of being taken before his judge. But in my way of spending the Sabbath, our bodies are rested from the toils of the past week, our spirits are refreshed by the blessing of God; it makes rich, and adds no sorrow therewith; and we can lie down at night with a cheerful heart, expressing our gratitude to our Heavenly Father in devout adoration and songs of praise.

> " Come, bless the Lord, whose love assigns
> " So sweet a rest to wearied minds;
> " Provides an antepast of heaven,
> " And gives this day the food of seven.
>
> " O that our thoughts and thanks may rise
> " As grateful incense to the skies;
> " And draw from heaven that sweet repose,
> " Which none, but he that feels it, knows.
>
> " This heavenly calm within the breast,
> " Is the dear pledge of glorious rest,
> " Which for the church of God remains,
> " The end of cares, the end of pains.

" In holy duties let the day
" In holy pleasures pass away ;
" How sweet a Sabbath thus to spend,
" In hope of one that ne'er shall end !"

EVILS OF PROFANING THE SABBATH.

1. It dishonors God. He has appointed the Sabbath, and commanded men to keep it holy. To profane it by worldly business, amusement, or in any other way, is disobedience to God; and is greatly to his dishonor.

2. It ensures his wrath. The Sabbath is God's day, he requires it to be set apart for himself. If men profane it, God is angry, and will visit them with his curse. They will be cursed in the city and in the field, in their basket and in their store ; in their going out and in their coming in.

3. It is dangerous. Not unfrequently are persons called into eternity in the very act of transgression, to appear before God, where there is no more space for repentance.

4. To profane the Sabbath exposes a man to the loss of his soul. This is an evil, great beyond description. For what can a man give in exchange for his soul ? A man may lose his property, his reputation, his health, and even his life, and yet be happy : but if he lose his soul, he must be eternally wretched. To profane the Sabbath, then, is a tremendous evil. If continued, it will shut the soul out of heaven, and sink it into everlasting darkness and despair.

5. The person who profanes the Sabbath, does much, by his example, to destroy the souls of others. One such sinner destroys much good. He will lead all those who follow him, down to the pit of wo.

Reader, remember the Sabbath-day, and keep it holy. If sinners entice you to profane it, consent not : for if you do profane it, you will dishonor God. You will incur his wrath. You will be in danger of immediate judgments. You will expose your own soul to destruction; and you will do *much* to destroy the souls of others.

DIRECTIONS FOR THE OBSERVANCE OF THE LORD'S DAY.

1. ORDER all your weekly business so wisely beforehand, that you may have no unnecessary work on God's day; that your hands may be as free as possible from business, and your head from worldly cares and thoughts.

2. Think seriously: what a weighty work am I going about! My week affairs are but toys and trifles to this. What are sheep and oxen, or shops and goods, to grace, Christ, and heaven? Can I be too careful and serious in God's work? in the work of salvation? Surely no. How holy should my thoughts be, how heavenly my discourse, how earnest my endeavors all the day long!

3. Therefore prepare with all your might; search your heart and life: find out

What your sins are, to confess, mourn over, and pray against.

What the mercies are you want for soul or body; for your friends, family, and nation.

What blessings you have received, and what thanks should be returned.

EVERY MAN

THE FRIEND OR THE ENEMY

OF

CHRIST.

" When we were all fallen to the earth, I heard a voice, saying, Saul,
Saul."—*See Acts*, 26 : 13—23 ; *Gal.* 1 : 23.

PUBLISHED BY THE

AMERICAN TRACT SOCIETY,

NO. 150 NASSAU-STREET, NEW-YORK.

D. Fanshaw, Printer.

Vol. 4.

EVERY MAN

THE FRIEND OR THE ENEMY

OF CHRIST.

In some contests, they who are immediately concerned, are at liberty, or rather it is their duty, to take neither part, because the thing contended for is indifferent in itself, or because both sides are in the wrong. There are others, wherein every man is obliged to favour, at least, if not to join himself to, one of the parties engaged, because one of them is evidently in the right; and no man ought to be wholly disinterested, when the cause of truth, justice, or virtue, is debated. In the cause of religious truth, every man is a party. If this be a fact, as no doubt it is, then the happiness of every man is inseparably connected, not only with his thinking rightly in religious matters, but in some measure also with his endeavouring to make others do the same. Happiness is the effect of true religion.

The chief among these, or rather that wherein the rest are comprised, is the great contest between Christ, the fountain of true religion, of pure virtue, and real happiness, on the one side; and the author of spiritual darkness, wickedness, and misery, on the other.

What then is it to be *for Christ*, and what to be *against him*?

A man cannot be truly said to be for Christ, who only carries his name, and declares for him; since the Scriptures assure us, that not only they are *against Christ* "who deny him before men, *in words*," but they also "who profess that they know, but in *works* deny him, being abominable, and disobedient, and unto every good work reprobate;" of whom St. Paul tells us, "even weeping, that they are the enemies of the cross of Christ."

Who then are *for him*? They, no doubt, of whom he says to the Father, "I have given unto them the words that thou gavest me; and they have received them, and have known hereby that I came out from thee; and they have believed that thou didst send me. Thine they were, and thou gavest them me, and they have kept my word." " They that are Christ's," says St. Paul, " have crucified the flesh with the affections and lusts."

But are there not a third or middle sort of men, who, in the strictness of these expressions, are neither for our Saviour, nor against him? No! Christ, who best knows his own, absolutely denies this. It is true, of good men some are better, and of bad men some are worse, than others. The good are not all equally the friends, nor the wicked all equally the enemies of Christ; and for these inequalities different degrees of reward and punishment are reserved in the determination of our Judge. It is also true, that the best of men sometimes fall into sin, and the worst sometimes rise to external acts of piety and goodness. But, then, he who is to pass sentence on us, knows perfectly well where frailty ends and presumption and perverseness begin; knows who in heart and life is a good, and who a bad man, that is, who is on his part, and who against him.

Thus it appears, that, from the throne of God down to the nethermost hell, there is not, there cannot possibly be, one moral being, who is not either the friend, or the enemy of Christ. In the one or other of these lights he must regard every man, and every man must regard himself, at the final judgment. On that great occasion, the Judge will pronounce but two sentences: to the good, " Come, ye blessed of my Father, inherit the kingdom prepared for you from the foundation of the world;" and to the wicked, " Depart from me, ye cursed, into everlasting fire, prepared for the devil and his angels." At that day, there will be no man found, who will not tremble under the one, or triumph in the other of these sentences · none who will not be a fit object of either. Here is no middle judgment between *Come* and *Depart*, nor a middle region between heaven and hell, for the reception of him who is neither called as a friend, nor rejected as an enemy to Christ.

Now, will it not be a great comfort and consolation to every good man to perceive, by an infallible rule, that Christ regards him as his friend? What can so effectually

encourage him to a steady perseverance, as thus beforehand to enjoy the happy judgment of the last day? Will
it not be also as great a terror to every bad man to know,
by the same infallible rule, that he himself is the enemy
of Christ? What is so likely to lead him to repentance, as
the bitter foretaste of his future condemnation?

You who did not know this, or knew it only in the spirit
of slumber, you are the ungrateful, and hereafter, if you
do not awake in time, must be the miserable enemy of
that Saviour who laid down his life for your soul. You
may have all along professed christianity, but contented
yourself with such a kind or degree of it as the vain and
senseless world esteems sufficient; that is, you go sometimes to church, give something to the poor, and now and
then, perhaps, attend to devotional exercises. You keep
within the verge of the laws, to preserve a tolerable character; and so pass in your own, and the judgment of others
like yourself, for a moderate christian. But, in the mean-
time, you scruple not to take God's name in vain, to talk
obscenely, to get drunk sometimes, and to mingle, in your
dealings with the world, a certain degree of cunning, ex
tortion, or oppression. If you have observed this, or somewhat like it, to be the general practice, the unhappy example serves you for a law, to which all the laws of God
must give way in you, who set not up truly for a saint, but
sneer at those who are more scrupulous, as hypocritical
pretenders to that character. All this while it is with you
a matter of little moment whether you are *with Christ or
against him*, as is evident by your never, in any material
instance, preferring his service or honour to the ordinary
calls of worldly interest or pleasure.

If you are on Christ's part, what passion have you sub-
dued, what appetite denied, what view of temporal profit
or honour, though ever so inconsiderable, have you set
aside, purely to please him? Or rather, what sense of his
goodness, and your past ingratitude do you even now feel,
to prove to you that you are not wholly indifferent about
him, his religion, or your place among his followers? You
may " honour him with your lips;" but your " heart is far
from him." Full well he knows it, for he is a searcher
of hearts, and clearly sees where all the ardour of yours
is placed, while he hath only the worthless compliment of

your professions. This you may be experimentally convinced of, by an impartial consideration of your prayers,
your faith, and the general tenour of your whole life.

Your prayers are but seldom offered up to the absolute
Disposer of all things; and offered with such an unaccountable coldness of heart as testifies no affection, scarcely,
indeed, a bare dependence.

Your faith, for want of a thorough conviction, or that
close attention which the great things it sets before you
demand, amounts to little more than a mere opinion as to
either the past or future facts suggested in your creed.
Such an opinion is too weak to have any material effect on
your practice, too feeble by far to bring futurity even into
competition with the present objects of sense and appetite.
Indeed, in so great a degree of dimness and confusion does
the eye of your faith present you with a view of things to
come, that heaven hardly looks like happiness, or hell like
misery, or either like a reality.

How unlike is your faith to that of a real christian! His
faith draws his very senses into its service. He believes,
and therefore hears God speaking in his word; feels God
moving in his heart; sees the judgment-seat of Christ, with
the glories of heaven, and the horrors of hell, almost as
clearly as if they were displayed just before his eyes.
Nay, he suffers the anguish of his Saviour's wounds with
not much less pain than if the nails and spear had pierced
his own flesh; and triumphs over sin and death in the
resurrection of Christ, with a high degree of that joy he
hopes to feel when he shall arise from the grave himself.

As to the general cast and tenour of your life, an insen-
sible stupidity damps and flattens all you think, or do, in
relation to religion. Here you know nothing! Here you
feel nothing! But, in regard to this world, you are all
alive. How deeply read is your understanding here!
How warmly engaged is your heart! And for the truth
of these observations, I appeal to your own breast.

You are ready, it may be, to declare, with an affected
humility, that it is the height of your ambition, in religious
matters, to be an ordinary or middling christian. Let others,
you say, set up for singularity in holiness; for your part,
you wish to be found even among the lowest class of christians, and aspire only to a bare acquittal. And yet you

want not your share of ambition and pride too. Misguided
man! How miserably you mistake that for humility, which
is but lukewarmness and indifference! But where is the
humility of vilifying that religious warmth in others, which
you never had either the sense or goodness to feel in yourself? Know, unhappy man, that there is, there can be,
no such mortal as a middling christian. Neither the exalted joys promised, nor the shocking torments threatened,
will suffer a thinking mind to be indifferent.

If your eyes are now open, look about you, and tell us
where you are: surely not with Christ, but against him;
with reprobates and wicked spirits, who, in their lusts, and
in the pride of their hearts, have preferred rebellion to
gratitude, infamy to glory, and hell to heaven.

Reflect feelingly on what Christ hath done for you, and
as impartially on what you have done to him; and then
see your ingratitude.

He, the Son of God, hath died to save you, a poor, unworthy criminal, from endless infamy and misery: think
how great that infamy and misery! and to bring you to
endless glory and happiness: consider how high that glory!
how infinite that happiness! How coolly you hear it! As
coolly you return it, by your formal professions, your dry
thanksgivings, your unwilling services, through which
scarcely any footsteps of either your understanding or affections are to be traced. On the other side are found all
your positive sins; your vile thoughts; your false, profane,
or seducing discourse; your abominable actions; all imagined, uttered, committed directly against him who died
for you.

Know, mistaken man, that you are in a state of rebellion against the sovereign of the world, and at war with
the Almighty. If your forces are sufficient to maintain
this war, and your armour proof against this two-edged
sword, go on: but no longer say you are a christian.
There is not less sense, and more consistency, in directly
contending with God, than in pretending to be his servant,
and yet fighting against him.

Your case then will not admit a moment's delay; neither is there any medium between being " for Christ, and
against him." Salvation is found only in being for him,
condemnation only in being against him. Awake, consider

this, ere it is too late, and choose your side; BUT CONSIDER IT WITH YOUR WHOLE UNDERSTANDING, AND CHOOSE WITH YOUR WHOLE HEART, FOR REMEMBER—YOU CHOOSE FOR ALL ETERNITY.

PRAYER FOR GRACE AND ZEAL IN THE SERVICE OF CHRIST.

THOU, O my Saviour, art the only satisfying portion of our souls, in whom they can find that rest which the world cannot give. But, alas! I am sensible that the world and the things of it have engaged too much of my thoughts and my heart. I have been remiss in my duty, and cold in my love toward thee, my Saviour. I have been eager in the pursuit of the vanities of this present time, and neglectful of the concerns of eternity: intent upon this world, as if it would never end; and forgetful of the next, as if it would never begin. Justly, O Lord, mightest thou leave me to my own wretched choice, to have my reward (where I have sought it) in *this* life; and in the rewards of the next to have no part nor lot. But, O gracious Saviour, forgive me; and so moderate my desires after these inferior goods, that I may seek *first* thy kingdom, and the righteousness thereof, and prefer the peace and joys of thy service to the greatest happiness this world can give. O let me no more debase my soul by devotion to the world, the flesh, and the devil; but choose the duties of thy religion as my chief and most delightful employ; and even its cross as my welcome portion, infinitely more to be desired than all the pleasures of sin.

O holy Saviour, grant me grace faithfully to fulfil the resolution I now make, to turn unto thee with all my heart, with all my mind, and with all my strength. To thy glory and praise I would humbly devote all the powers of my soul; in the way of thy commandments I would humbly walk; to the sacrifices thy service may require, I would cheerfully submit; the temptations and difficulties I must encounter, I would resolutely oppose; to thy disposal I would entirely resign myself. O save me from a presumptuous dependence on my own strength. Teach me evermore to rely on the succours of thy grace. Excite me diligently to use all the means thou hast appointed for its conveyance. In the use of humble and earnest prayer, and in diligent attendance on the ordinances of the Gospel, may I be blessed with the influences of thy Holy Spirit, to renew my corrupt nature, to strengthen me, and enable me to devote myself to thy service; to carry me safely through all the trials of my faith; and at last to bring me, through thy merits, O blessed Jesus, to celebrate thy redeeming love in the strains of the church triumphant! *Amen.*

PRAYER FOR THE GRACE OF PERSEVERANCE.

Eternal God, thou knowest the weakness of my nature, how unable I am, of myself, to persevere in thy service, and resist the temptations that assail me. Have pity on my infirmities, pardon my past remissness, preserve me from falling away from any degree of holiness to which, by thy grace, I may have attained. Make me so firmly thine, that nothing may be able to separate between me and my God. Make me so resolute in thy duty and service, that nothing may interrupt me therein, or call me off from the way that leadeth unto life. Leave me not, nor forsake me, O God of my salvation, for on thee is stayed all my hope. Hold thou me up, and I shall be safe. Stablish, strengthen, and settle me. Preserve me by thy free Spirit. Keep me by thy power, through faith, unto salvation. Make me so constant unto death, that I may receive the crown of life; so resolutely persevering to the last, in thy service, tha I may receive the end of my faith, the salvation of my soul; through thy tender mercies, O my God, and my Saviour's all-sufficient merits. *Amen.*

> Jesus, lover of my soul,
>   Let me to thy bosom fly,
> While the billows near me roll,
>   While the tempest still is nigh!
>
> Hide me, O my Saviour, hide,
>   Till the storm of life be past,
> Safe into the haven guide,
>   O receive my soul at last!

END.

USEFULNESS OF TRACTS.

THE AMERICAN TRACT SOCIETY was formed in the city of New-York, May, 1825, by a Convention of Delegates from Tract Societies and friends of religion, of several Evangelical denominations, and from different parts of the country.*   Its sole object is to promote the great design of the Savior's mediation and death, by diffusing the truths and doctrines of his Gospel.   It was founded in prayer, and dependence on the blessing of the Holy Spirit; and the facts related in the following pages, of the authenticity of which the Committee have the most satisfactory evidence, will show to some extent how rich-

---

* The Publishing Committee of this Society embraces no two members from the same denomination, and no Tract is published unless unanimously approved.   All the other concerns of the Society are conducted under the direction of an Executive Committee, elected annually by the Board.   The labors of all the Society's Committees, and of its President and Treasurer, are performed without any pecuniary compensation.

ly that blessing has been bestowed, to the praise and glory of Divine grace.

The large public meeting, at which the Society was formed, was one of deep solemnity. The last words which the lamented Rev. JOHN SUMMERFIELD ever addressed to a public audience, were delivered at the close of that meeting. "In all the anniversaries," said he, " which I have ever attended, in Europe or America, I have never been so conscious of the presence of the Holy Spirit and christian love pervading every heart. Again and again I could not refrain from weeping. The very atmosphere we breathe is the atmosphere of heaven; one which angels come down to inhale, and in which God himself delights to dwell."

At the Society's first Anniversary, its character, design, and the evidences of the Divine approbation upon its work were presented as follows, in an

ADDRESS OF REV. JUSTIN EDWARDS, D. D.,
One of the Members of the Publishing Committee.

The object of this Society is to deliver immortal souls from a course of eternal sinning and eternal suffering; to transform them into the perfect image of God, and raise them to a state of eternal holiness and bliss in heaven.

The means by which we are to accomplish this, is the dissemination of the truths which God has revealed, in the form of interesting and impressive Religious Tracts. I say, *the truths which God has revealed;* for no other truths will accomplish this glorious end : such truths, for instance, as the utterly lost condition of sinners, and their indispensable duty, without delay, to love God with all their heart, and soul, and strength, and mind ; the necessity of being born again, not of blood, nor of the will of the flesh, nor of the will of man, but of God ; the infinite dignity, divine beauty, excellence and glory of Him on whom their help is laid ; his amazing condescension in becoming a servant, and having not where to lay his head ; his unparalleled kindness in bearing their sins in his own body on the tree, and having laid on him the iniquity of them all ; the necessity of believing on him in order to be interested in the blessings of his salvation ;

that every person to whom he is made known is under immediate obligation to embrace him, repent of sin, and live not unto himself, but unto him that died for sinners and rose again; that a day is coming when " all that are in their graves shall hear his voice, and shall come forth ; they that have done good unto the resurrection of life, and they that have done evil unto the resurrection of damnation ;" that the wicked will go away into eternal punishment, and the righteous into eternal life. These are the truths, with kindred truths, in their divinely inspired aspect and connection, stamped in bold relief on the face of Religious Tracts, and extended to every city, and town, and village, and family, and soul; by which this Society is to aid in renovating a world, and preparing a " multitude that no man can number," to shine in the beauty of holiness, and shout the triumphs of grace to everlasting ages.

These are the truths which were proclaimed on the hills and in the vales of Judea; by which the fishermen of Galilee, and men of like spirit, went out, and unarmed, in the face of an opposing world, planted the standard of the Cross on the throne of the Cæsars. These are the truths which blazed at the reformation, scattered the darkness of papal midnight, and kindled a light that will " grow brighter and brighter, even to the perfect day." These truths as they go forth, " proclaiming deliverance to captives, the opening of the prison to them that are bound," and pointing them to " the Lamb of God, that taketh away the sin of the world," will cause tears of contrition to drop down from ten thousand eyes, and ten thousand hearts to pour forth their strains of gratitude in hallelujahs to the Redeemer.

These truths it is our duty to extend, not merely because we have associated for this purpose, but because God has revealed them, and commanded us to extend them to every creature. And, if I do not mistake, Sir, there are some peculiar reasons why we, in this country, should extend them by means of Religious Tracts.

We are a great people, and if not blasted by our sins, shall become greater and greater, till the light of revealed truth, and the light of human science, the light of true religion, and the light of civil and religious freedom, shall blaze from one end of this continent to the other, and with a brightness that shall illumine the world. We are called by the God of heaven to make an experiment; and one of the most momentous that was ever entrusted to mortals.

Blessed with a country of almost unparalleled extent; settled by a people of invincible energy, of ceaseless action, and untiring perseverance; enjoying civil and religious liberty to a greater extent than any other people on the globe; holding property of every description, and to any amount, in pure fee-simple, with the strongest motives bearing upon the mass of minds, to the highest possible effort, we must make a development of character, such as creation never witnessed; and rise to a height of goodness and greatness, from which we shall be the benefactors of the world, and instruments in bearing its millions to glory, or, from which we shall sink, under a load of guilt, such as earth never bore, to endless perdition. Ah, then there would be shouting through all the world of darkness, and among all the sons of darkness through the universe; ages of darkness, which the Gospel has heaved away, would roll backward, and cover millions and millions in deep and everlasting gloom.

And are we in no danger of this? We are a republic; with no government but that which rests on the will of the people; and which cannot be perpetuated without holiness among the people. Some may say, it cannot without *public virtue*. But public virtue never did exist, sufficient to perpetuate a republican government over such an extent of country as ours, without holiness, and it never will. This holiness is not the natural growth of a single heart in the land. No means will produce it, but the means of God's appointment. Of these means a vast portion of our countrymen are now destitute. Millions and millions increasing every day, are destitute of that influence which is so essential to the preservation of all our social, civil, and religious blessings. Nor is this all: but each individual of these millions has a soul worth a thousand worlds. And without holiness they had better had no existence; for they will spend it in weeping, and wailing, and gnashing of teeth. While I speak it, I see them borne onward toward the close of their probation,

destitute of that holiness without which no one can see
the Lord, and destitute of the means of holiness which
God has appointed.

What, then, shall be done? Send them living preachers? You have not got them. Thousands, with the ardor
of Paul, with the eloquence and might in the Scriptures
of Apollos, are needed to-day, in order fully to supply
this country. Do you say, "Encourage Education Societies, and train up pious young men for the ministry?"
By all means. Let these efforts be vastly increased, and
prosecuted with all possible vigor, and generation after
generation will pass away before they can all have the
regular and stated ministrations of the Gospel. Do you
say, "Send them the Bible?" By all means. Let efforts
to extend it be increased and increased, till there shall
not be a family, from one end of the land to the other,
that has not the Sacred Volume. But then multitudes will
not read it; and multitudes more will act directly against
its holy dictates.

What then shall be done? Take the truths of the Bible,
and, in "thoughts that breathe, and words that burn,"
stamp them on the pages of Religious Tracts; multiply
these Tracts by thousands and millions; send them forth,
attended, in answer to prayer, by the Holy Ghost sent
down from heaven, to every city, and town, and neighborhood, and family, till all shall see Him who was rich,
for their sakes becoming poor, that they, through his
poverty, might be rich. And as they see him "bearing
their sins in his own body on the tree," and hear him
cry, "My God, my God, why hast thou forsaken me?"
and the sun shrinks away, the rocks break asunder, and
the dead start from their graves, there will be mourning;
yes, there will be a *very great* mourning, and there will
be a great turning unto the Lord our God.

Does any one say that many parts of the land have
the Gospel, and therefore it is not needful to send Tracts
to them! A town in the very centre of one of the most
favored states in the Union had the Gospel; they had
a minister of Christ; but, like many of his brethren, he
was ready to say, "I have labored in vain, and spent my
strength for nought," till he obtained a Religious Tract,
and under the reading of that, *eight* persons were con-

vinced of sin, and found no rest till, as it is hoped, they embraced the Savior; and when he who was watching for their souls related this account, they were all members of the church, and adorning their profession by a godly example.

Another town had the Gospel. Sermon after sermon was preached, but passed away unheeded, till a religious Tract was read, when a revival of religion commenced, which issued in the hopeful conversion of more than *forty* persons.

Another town had the Gospel, and the ordinary means of grace; but the people grew stupid, and still more stupid, till a Tract was read, and no less than twelve persons were made to feel that, "without holiness," they could not " see the Lord ;" and they obtained no rest till, as they hope, they became the sincere followers of Christ. Others became alarmed, the conviction spread to others, and to others, till it issued in the hopeful conversion of *more than one hundred persons.*

Ministers of the Gospel, whose praise is in all the churches, have testified, that they have often found the distribution of Tracts, apparently, as useful as all their other labors. A president of one of our distinguished colleges informed me, that, during a revival of religion in college, religious Tracts were circulated among the students, which were read with great eagerness, and with the most manifest advantage.

Are not, then, Tracts needful for such places? Yes, for *all* places. A man in the habit of distributing them among those who have not the Gospel, once called at a cottage on the side of a mountain, and, as usual, asked the inmates if they loved the Lord Jesus Christ? "O yes," the woman replied, "he is precious to my soul, altogether lovely." He asked her what were the means of leading her to Christ. " A man," said she, " once left here a small Tract. When he was gone, my child read it aloud, and it made me feel as if I was lost for ever." Her impressions deepened and deepened, till she discovered the way of salvation through a crucified Redeemer, hopefully embraced him, and found rest to her soul. Her husband, too, said, " He gave me a Tract, and since then I hope the Lord has showed mercy to my soul." " O,"

said the woman, "that I could see that man again."
" Well," said the man, " I am he."   -

Another man who had been in the habit of distributing
Bibles and Tracts among the destitute, was afterward informed by letter, that more than *thirty* individuals in
one town, beside the writer of the letter and his wife,
were all now rejoicing in hope, through his instrumentality.

I know the man, Sir, who has had evidence of more
than one hopeful conversion from a Tract, in a family
which had not the Gospel, and *had never seen a Bible.*
Tracts are useful every where, and we must send them
to every family throughout the country.

Does any one say, " This is impossible ?"   No; it is
not impossible. A single individual has been known to
circulate 70,000 Tracts in a year. Suppose that each
went into a family, and was read by three persons beside
him who received it; this single individual may have
been the means, through the instrumentality of Tracts,
of preaching the unsearchable riches of Christ to 280,000
souls. Let this be continued for ten years, and this single
individual might speak to 2,800,000, and tell them words
by which they and those around them may be saved.

This Society may, with the blessing of God, establish
Depositories in every county of every state in the Union,
form Auxiliary Societies around every Depository, and
soon put in circulation 12,000,000 of Tracts, equal to one
for every man, woman, and child, in the country ; and if,
in this distant world, and while looking through a glass
darkly, we may see distinctly the reading of one Tract
connected with the hopeful conversion of eight persons,
and another of forty, and another of one hundred, what
may we not hope to see, in the light of eternity, from
the reading of 12,000,000, which this Society in a few
years may put in circulation. An amazing price, Sir, is
put into the hands of this Society, and if improved, will,
through grace, be instrumental in preparing multitudes
for glory.

" No doubt," says one, " they may be exceedingly useful ; but to circulate so many will *cost too much.*" How
much, then, will it cost? $10,000 will put in circulation
1,000,000 Tracts, or of Tracts of four pages, nearly

2,500,000; equal to one for every family in the country. And if the expense were borne by every family, it would be for each not more than one half cent in a year; and the avails of these, if sold at cost, may put in circulation as many more, and the avails of those, as many more, and so on, down to the end of the world. Is this too much for the purpose of putting in circulation 2,500,000 Tracts; 6,000 of which may be furnished for $20, and one of which has, in more than twenty cases, been the means of the hopeful conversion of a soul worth a million of worlds? Ten times this sum has been expended, in this country, upon a single horse-race! A million of dollars can be raised in a single city, or town, at almost any time, for a single manufactory! $7,000,000 can be raised, in a single state, for a canal!

"This," says one, " is a great and noble object. It promotes improvements, opens communications, and facilitates intercourse between one part of the country and another." I acknowledge it is a great and noble object. And is there nothing great, nothing noble, in the everlasting improvement of 12,000,000 minds? in snowing a path, and facilitating their progress on their way to glory, and onward, from glory to glory, to everlasting ages? More than 3,000 times what it would cost to put in circulation annually a million of Tracts, is expended in this country, every year, for a single article, not of living, but of dying; an article which costs the country annually, 30,000 lives, and renders utterly wretched 200,000 more. Let us not hesitate a moment about the expense of putting in circulation annually a few millions of Tracts; but raise the money, and expend it most cheerfully for the Lord of Hosts.

But can the money be raised? I answer, it can. I know the individual who once asked a poor man if he would not give something to make his minister a life member of the Tract Society; and he answered, " Yes, I will give a dollar: for one of those Tracts has saved me from ruin."

I know the individual who has worked for one dollar a week, and worked hard too, for nearly twenty years, who, on hearing the effects of a Tract, said, without being asked, I will give $20 to print it, and to keep it in perpetual circulation; for I have no doubt that it has been the means of saving multitudes.

I know the individual who, when asked by an agent of the Tract Society to give something, said, " Who sent you here?" he answered, " The Lord, I trust." " Well," said the person, " I believe he did; for I have had $20 laid up a long time for the Tract Society, and have been waiting for some one to come and take it."

Money can be raised; and the country can never be considered as supplied till half the families have a single copy of at least half the Tracts. And it would be exceedingly useful, if every family of children could have access to a set of the whole. No books, except the Bible, would be more likely to promote their salvation. I know the man who, when a boy, had access to a set of Tracts, and became interested in reading them, and impressions were fastened upon his mind that will never be effaced; and the effect of his conversion is already felt through this land.

I know a man who, when a boy, had access to similar Tracts, whose mind was arrested, whose heart was softened, and hopefully renewed, through their instrumentality; and, I was going to say, all Africa will one day bless God for his conversion. But I see him rise upward, leaving this revolted world and taking possession of that " rest which remains for the people of God." Lately, he was here. I saw him go from place to place, pleading the cause of Africa, taking her sons and her daughters, and gathering them into a church of Christ. I saw the big tear trickle down their sable cheeks as they experienced his kindness; I saw him collect the furniture of their communion-table, gather for them a church library, obtain a printing press, and go, with his little flock, embracing all the elements of a civilized and Christian community, and plant them, with their brethren, in the land of their fathers. I heard Africa begin to sing—when the Lord had need of him, and he winged his way to glory. But his mantle will fall, his prayers be answered, and all Africa will yet bless God for his conversion.

I know the man, Sir, who, when a boy, through the kindness of a relative, had access to a parcel of Tracts; the very same which you are now publishing and circu-

Vol. 4.

lating; and he was led to think of the kindness of Christ, to feel his obligations to him, and resolve, in his strength, that he would henceforward " live not unto himself, but unto him that died for him and rose again." And he has ever since been experiencing that " it is more blessed to give than to receive." Numerous destitute settlements, all along our frontiers, the savages in our Western wilderness, the pagans in the islands of the seas, and throughout Asia, will one day bless God for his conversion.

And we must do vastly more than merely to supply our own country. The Canadas, Mexico, and all South America, are calling upon us to help them; many are now able to read among our Western Indians; thousands at the Sandwich Islands; and more than 10,000,000 in countries around the Mediterranean. Said a gentleman who visited those countries, to men who, before he left home, had furnished him with Tracts for distribution, " I thank you, gentlemen, a thousand times, for the Tracts. I had been told that it was of no use to think of offering Tracts to Italians, Greeks, Portuguese, and Spaniards; they would not read them. But, gentlemen, I know better. You have no idea how welcome the Tracts were in all the ports at which we touched, around the Mediterranean. The people ran after me in the streets, and pulled me into their houses, in order to obtain them; and that, too, after I had distributed all that I had. I could hardly pacify them, but by telling them that when I came again I would bring them more."

Printing presses are now in operation in connection with the American mission at Malta. Give them the means, and Tracts, as cheap as they can be furnished in this country, may be printed in Greek, and Italian, and French, and Arabic, and Armenian, and extended to 10,000,000 people, multitudes of whom are almost entirely destitute of the means of grace. $1,000 may put in circulation 100,000 Tracts. Here, then, is a way in which men may, from love to Christ and to souls, through the medium of this Society, employ property in a manner which, while it does not make them poor, will make many rich, and secure an inheritance incorruptible, undefiled, and that fadeth not away.

Thousands and thousands are now perishing, for the

want of Tracts, on the Island of Ceylon. " We visit," said a missionary, " from two to eight families in a day; sometimes we take long journeys, and are out six or eight days. At such times we take a number of boys from the schools, and we exceedingly need Tracts. As we pass from village to village, where the Gospel was never preached, we find hundreds, who can, and would read, had we Bibles or Tracts to give them : but, alas! we have none : no Bible, no Tract to show the poor heathen how to flee from the wrath to come. Oh that we could get a supply printed. Into how many villages might the Gospel be sent by means of Tracts : and how many souls, by a single Tract, might be saved from endless misery."

And shall the missionary, who has left his father's house, his native land, and gone 13,000 miles to tell the dying Pagans of a Savior, cry in the ears of a thousand churches, abounding in wealth, " Oh that we could get a supply of Tracts printed. Into how many villages might the Gospel be sent by means of Tracts, and how many souls might be saved by a single Tract from endless misery"—and yet cry in vain ? Let those churches answer.

At Bombay is a printing press, in the midst of a population speaking the same tongue, of 11,000,000 of people; nearly all of whom are destitute of the Gospel, and among whom Tracts might be circulated to the utmost advantage. A strong feeling of doubt and uncertainty exists in the minds of multitudes throughout that country with regard to their own religion. Numbers have come to the conclusion that it is false. Multitudes are halting between two opinions, and all are becoming impressed with the expectation that a great change is approaching. In this state, they greatly need Tracts, and many strongly desire them. Individuals have come twenty miles, and in some cases thirty and forty miles, to obtain a Tract. And, writes a missionary, " Tracts may be printed at Bombay as cheap as in America; and in no part of the world can they be distributed to greater advantage. Many of the people would be likely to receive more instruction from a little Tract, which they could read in five minutes, than from the whole of the New Testament; because they would be so much more likely to read it."

Writes another missionary, " The distribution of Tracts

is the only possible way in which we can exhibit any portion of the Gospel to *vast multitudes of the present generation* of India. Ministers enough to go and preach to them the Gospel cannot be obtained. We must print and circulate Tracts, or millions and millions of the present and future generations must go down without the Gospel, in unbroken succession, to the grave."

And these millions, Mr. President, exceedingly need Tracts; for they are exceedingly wretched, even for this life. A man who has resided among them twenty years for the purpose of investigating their spiritual condition, told me that he knew of a numerous class with whom it was an article of religion not to suffer a single female child to live. One of them, however, on the birth of a daughter, being overcome by natural affection, resolved to preserve her life. He secreted her, and intended, unknown to his countrymen, to preserve her to mature years. He succeeded without its being known, till she was, I think, seven years old. Then it became known that he had in his house a daughter. And being abroad one day, he was so overcome with the scoffs of his countrymen, and with the obloquy which they cast upon him, that he returned, and with an axe hewed her in pieces.

And not only are they miserable in this life, but in death. A Hindoo of a thoughtful, reflecting turn of mind, but devoted to idolatry, lay on his death-bed. As he saw himself about to plunge into that boundless unknown, he cried out, " What will become of me?" " O," said a Brahmin who stood by, " You will inhabit another body." " And where," said he, " shall I go then?" " Into another." " And where then?" " Into another, and so on, through thousands of millions." Darting across this whole period, as though it were but an instant, he cried, " Where shall I go then?" And paganism could not answer. And he died, agonizing under the inquiry, " Where shall I go last of all?"

Another Hindoo lay on his death-bed; he, however, had seen a religious Tract, and had read it. It had led him to religious teachers, and to Christ. His friend, hearing of his sickness, came to see him, and found him in the last stage of disease, and as he bore up his languishing head, watching to see him breathe his last, the

dying man broke out in ecstacy, " Sing, brother, sing."
" What," said he, " shall I sing?"   " Salvation," said he;
" salvation, by the death of Jesus"—and winged his way
to bow with ransomed millions before the throne.

Let us send Tracts to those sinners, and all other sinners on the globe : Tracts blazing with the effulgence of
the *truths which God has revealed, in the aspect and connection* in which he has revealed them, and attended, in
answer to the prayers of God's people, by the Holy Ghost
sent down from heaven ; and multitudes out of every nation, and kindred, and people, and tongue, will assemble
on Mount Zion, and open an everlasting anthem " unto
him that loved us, and washed us from our sins in his
blood; and every holy creature in the universe will cry,
" Unto him be glory for ever, and ever."

INFLUENCE OF TRACTS UPON INFIDELS.

As a respectable physician, who had long been an
avowed infidel, was reading the Tract entitled *The Praying Negro*, he was led to reflect that he possessed a very
different temper from that there exhibited.   When *he* was
injured, he was disposed to seek revenge ; but this *pious
person*, when injured, found relief in prayer to God.
This produced a conviction of his sinfulness, guilt, and
danger.   He saw no hope of salvation by his own works ;
but felt himself a lost sinner.   What then could he do,
but look to that Savior whom he had so long rejected
as not worthy his regard.   By faith in him, he obtained
peace and comfort.   He then collected his deistical books
at home, and those which he had lent to his neighbors,
and committed them to the flames.   He found the Bible
infinitely better.   Recollecting one night that one of these
books was lent to his minister, he knew not how to sleep
till it was burned ; but as the night was dark and stormy
he concluded to wait till morning.   Then neither the
severity of the storm, nor the infirmities of his age, prevented the execution of his purpose.   When he asked for
the book, the minister was fearful that he might still
doubt the truth and inspiration of the Scriptures, and so
wish to read this book again.   This had been his favorite
author.   But no sooner was it returned, than with much

emphasis, he said, "In the presence of the Lord Jesus Christ and these witnesses, I now solemnly renounce all the errors contained in this book." He then cast it into the fire. He since warns, with much affection and faithfulness, those whom he had before led astray, and intreats them to renounce their errors and embrace the Savior. His exertions are not in vain, Christians are animated, and sinners alarmed.

An eminent Lawyer in Alabama.

A volume of Tracts was presented in a school to the son of a Lawyer of eminence in Alabama, who denied the authenticity of the Bible. As it lay on the mantel, he took it up one day, and his eye fell on the history of the *African Servant*, by Rev. Legh Richmond. His first impression was that it must be a benevolent religion which should induce that eminent man thus kindly to regard the welfare of a poor Negro; and as he read the narrative he could not restrain the conviction, that the same religion which was necessary for the salvation of the soul of the Negro, was necessary also for himself. "This," says a christian friend, "occurred about four months since; and at our communion, two weeks ago, he and his wife unitedly made a public profession of religion. He is a gentleman of fine talents and a highly cultivated mind; who was well acquainted with the Bible as a history; but had read it with strong prejudices against it, in consequence of reading most of the works opposed to it. He is now an active and useful member of the church. One of his first acts, after his conversion, was to appropriate a sum of money for the distribution of Tracts." Two or three years after, when the Agent of the American Tract Society visited the place of his residence, he was called to preside at a public meeting in behalf of the Tract cause, delivered a very animated Address, and headed the subscription with $20 for himself, and $10 for his children.

A young Infidel in North-Carolina.

A Baptist clergyman of North-Carolina says, that a young infidel in that state was walking by the side of a

pond, when he discovered two leaves of a book partly in
the water, which he took up, and soon perceived another
fragment of a book lying at a little distance before him,
and still farther on a third. He took up the whole, and
putting them together, they composed an entire Tract.
The perusal of it so arrested his attention, that he read
it again and again; and such were the impressions created in his mind, that he felt an unconquerable desire to
read the Bible. He was ashamed that this wish should
be known to any one; and devised a plan for *procuring
a Bible by stealth.* He recollected a little pocket Bible
in his grandmother's book case; went and made her a
visit, and while looking at, and praising her library, secured the Bible under the folds of his coat, went home
and read it in his retired chamber—embraced the Lord
Jesus Christ, there set forth as crucified for a lost world,
as his Savior and Redeemer—and is now a member of
the church, and an active Christian.

INFLUENCE OF TRACTS UPON THE PROFANE.

At the time of a revival of religion in a village in Vermont, a young man had become so profane that he would
spend the silence of the night to invent blasphemies more
horrid than he had heard or before conceived, and com-
mitting them to memory, would repeat them the next
day in the presence of those who were laboring under
the weight of conscious guilt. His father, having become a member of an Auxiliary Tract Society, brought
home a parcel of Tracts, and addressing his son, said,
" here are some Tracts for you; I wish you would read
them." The son replied, with an oath too shocking to
repeat, " you may read them yourself." But passing the
table on which they were placed, the title " *Swearer's
Prayer*" caught his eye, and thinking it would help him
to be still more profane, he read it, and addressing his
mother, said, " Mother, do you believe that Tract to be
true?" " No doubt that he who wrote it, had reason to
believe every word of it true," was the reply. " Then,"
said he, " I shall never swear again." He has since been
received to the bosom of the church, as is believed, a
humble and penitent Christian.

A Scoffer and Blasphemer.

An Agent of the American Tract Society in Connecticut, says, I became acquainted with a man who, a few months ago, was a *Scoffer and a Blasphemer;* and so bitterly opposed to religion, in all its forms, that he actually prohibited his little daughter from attending the Sabbath school. She continued incessant in pleading with him for permission to go, till at length he yielded to her entreaties. She went—received a Tract—carried it home—her father's curiosity was excited to know its contents—he read it—by the power of Divine Grace it fastened convictions on his mind—he was for some time almost in despair—till at length the Savior was pleased to manifest himself to him—and he appears now to be a humble devoted Christian.

Travels and Conquests of the "Swearer's Prayer."

An Agent of the American Tract Society in Missouri, says, *The Swearer's Prayer* was given to a man who had awfully abandoned himself to blaspheme the name of God, but whose regard for the individual by whom it was presented induced him to read it. It wounded, but to heal. He is now restored from a debased, despicable standing in society, to an honorable and useful standing in the church. The identical Tract traveled nearly a hundred miles. It fell into the hands of *three other individuals* of a similar character; and all the four have, in the judgment of enlightened charity, by means of this Tract, obtained a gracious claim to a standing at God's right hand.

A Swearer and Gambler.

A minister of the Gospel informed me, says an Agent in Alabama, that about two years ago he had a neighbor who was a profane Swearer and Gambler. The minister conversed with him as he had opportunity, and at length put into his hand *The Swearer's Prayer.* He at first determined to throw the Tract away without reading it; but influenced by curiosity, when he was alone he began to read it. When he had read the first page he paused and reflected thus: " This is the prayer which I have been offering nearly all my days!" He now saw the dreadful import of his oft repeated prayer, and trembled with apprehension, lest God should grant his impious request. He read the Tract through, and stood still for some time reflecting what he should do. At first he resolved to go home, take his horse, and dissipate his serious impressions among a club of gamblers. But on reaching home he relinquished that resolution, and resorted to his Bible; he read it, but the more he read the more clearly he saw himself ruined by sin. In a few days he was rejoicing in hope of pardon. Two or three months afterward he united with the church at ——, and he has since given good evidence of being a true convert.

INFLUENCE OF TRACTS ON THE INTEMPERATE.
A Father in New-York City.

A benevolent lady in the city of New-York says, in 1825, when visiting for a Bible Association, I became acquainted with a family who by industry and frugality obtained a comfortable subsistence. Early in 1827 the mother's health declined; expenses were increased; and to complete their wretchedness, *the father exhausted his earnings at the dram-shop;* and, as might be expected, often personally abused the family. The little furniture they had got by honest industry was taken from them for rent; and on leaving the city the succeeding April, the family were reduced to wretchedness. I called to take leave of them, and left for the father, as a parting present, *The Rewards of Drunkenness.* On my return to New-York I ascertained where they had moved, and expected to find a scene of misery. But, on entering the room, I should have thought myself mistaken in the place, had I not seen and recognized my old friends. Neatness and comfort characterized the dwelling, and peace smiled on every countenance. It was Saturday evening, and evident to me, that the sacred rest of the Sabbath had been anticipated in the arrangements of the family. The mother discovered my pleasing surprise, and exclaimed, " O! the Tract—the Tract—the Tract has got all these nice things! My husband never drank

after you gave him the Tract. He seems to be a reform-
ed man; and says the Tract has made him happy, and
brought peace and plenty into his house."

An intoxicated Man saved from suicide.

A Report of the New-York City Tract Society says,
a gentleman of respectable family and genteel appearance, while traveling on Long-Island, near this city, indulged repeatedly in drinking ardent spirits, contrary, it
would seem, to his usual practice; and before he was
aware, became intoxicated. Deeply mortified at finding
himself in this situation, he resolved, in a rash moment,
to destroy himself, and for this purpose retired to the
woods. After finding a suitable place he took from his
hat the handkerchief with which he intended to execute
his dreadful purpose; but providentially, with the handkerchief he drew out from his hat a little Tract, which
arrested his attention. It had on the title page, *A Word
in Season.* He perused it—it struck conviction to his
heart—he instantly fell on his knees, and cried to God to
have mercy on him—and after continuing for some time
in earnest prayer, arose, and made his way to a neighboring house, where, happily, dwelt a pious Christian. Here
he gave no sleep to his eyes, but spent the whole night,
like Jacob, wrestling with God—and we trust he did not
wrestle in vain. In the morning he returned to the city,
thanking God for deliverance, effected through the instrumentality of the *Word in Season.*

The Tract and the Peach Orchard.

A gentleman formerly a member of my church, says a
clergyman, being on a visit to a friend, expressed much
anxiety to return home within a given time, as he had a
large orchard of peaches which he wished to gather for
the distillery. His friend remonstrated with him; but it
availed nothing; he must go and gather his peaches for
the distillery. "Well, if you must go," said his friend,
"I will give you a Tract to read," and presented him
Kittredge's Address. He accepted it, and read it; and
soon after sent word to his friend, that instead of carry-

ing his peaches to the distillery he had given them to his hogs, and further, that he had resolved never again to *suffer his mill to be used to prepare grain for the distillery.*

The Drunkard's Home.

Some unknown person, says the Secretary of a Tract Society in Virginia, left in a tavern at S——, the Tract, *To Distillers.* On looking into it, the landlord observed on the cover an article entitled, " *The Drunkard's Home,*" which drew his attention. He read it, and became considerably out of humor, wondering who could have left *that* in *his* house. The result, however, was, that *he took down his sign*, declaring that his house should never again be called " *The Drunkard's Home.*"

INFLUENCE OF TRACTS ON REVIVALS OF RELIGION.

I knew, says a gentleman of New-Hampshire, a circle of ladies who had been in the habit for more than a year of meeting almost every week for the purpose of religious reading. There was not among them one professor of religion. They had, however, read Baxter, and Doddridge, and many other works of a similar character; but, as yet, the ball chamber and the party of pleasure presented attractions much more powerful, and much more congenial to their hearts. But on a certain evening—an evening ever memorable in the annals of that community—an evening on which the Holy Spirit designed to change the current of their moral feelings—a religious Tract was selected as the subject of their contemplations. It was put into the hands of a gay and thoughtless young lady, whose turn it was to read. She looked at the title; it was the *End of Time*, (by Dr. Watts.) She began to read—she paused—she attempted to proceed, but her heart was too full. She resigned her seat to a companion. The Tract was read. And the end of time, and the realities of eternity, were brought into close connection with the scenes of that evening. The influence extended from heart to heart, from family to family, from neighborhood to neighborhood, and in the short space of a few weeks, most of the individuals who first listened to the reading of the Tract, with *more than sixty others*, were led to place their hopes of salvation on Jesus Christ. That people had once been favored with the ordinances of the Gospel. A faithful and holy man had been their minister more than forty years. He had labored, he had prayed, he had plead with earnestness the cause of his Redeemer. But he had wept and mourned all his days over the hardness of impenitent sinners, and had gone down to his grave without ever witnessing a revival of religion. I well remember his prayers—I have often witnessed his tears—and I remember also when the pious few followed his remains to the tomb, and with him buried all their hopes of enjoying a preached Gospel: and though years passed away, their hopes never revived till the reading of that Tract.

The Tract " Poor Sarah," in a Destitute Settlement.

A very striking instance of the usefulness of Tracts, writes a Missionary, has occurred in the family of an aged and godly father and mother, residing some miles distant from me, in Ohio. These parents had seven sons and daughters, all married, and resident in their own immediate vicinity. In February last the aged father, anxious that the ordinances of the Gospel should be enjoyed by the families of his children and others, called on me, desiring my advice and assistance in obtaining for them a preacher of the Gospel. I could not aid him in this respect, but, as I bade him farewell, I put into his hand a few Tracts to read to his children and neighbors, among which was *Poor Sarah, or the Indian Woman.* The reading of this Tract was the apparent means of deeply convicting one of his married daughters, who shortly after was filled with joy and peace in believing. This circumstance, in connection with the reading of the same Tract, was the means of awakening another; others still, soon became deeply interested in the subject of religion; the aged father was urged to establish religious meetings on the Sabbath himself; and one and another of his children, by birth and by marriage, became seriously impressed, until, on my visiting them lately, I found twelve of the fourteen indulging (most of them rejoicing in) a hope in Christ. One of the remaining two was in great distress of mind—one only of the fourteen remained careless.

How Tracts were used in a Revival.

During an extensive revival, says a Clergyman in Massachusetts, we have had opportunity to observe the effect of Tracts, and feel that they have been rendered powerful instruments in bringing sinners to Christ. This has been especially the case when they have been distributed with *particular reference to the feelings and character of individuals.* We have endeavored to distribute them discreetly, but have not hesitated to give, *to any one,* Tracts which inculcate the duty of immediate submission to God, repentance, and faith. When we have found an impenitent man who knew his guilt and felt his danger, and given those directions or warnings which, in our judgment, his condition required, it has been found important, in some instances, to leave with him a Tract *exactly adapted* to the state of his soul. The Tract which is given under such circumstances, is read with care—with tears. It is often the last thing an anxious soul reads before the eyes are closed in sleep. It probably lies on his pillow, and it may be, directs his earliest thoughts when he awakes. It may be instrumental in giving form to the character, and shape to the destiny, of an immortal being. The proper selection of a Tract for such an individual is vastly important. When we have found those who supposed they were reconciled to God, we have thought it important, that, to personal instruction and counsel, we should add something which the babe in Christ might carry with him, and from which he might obtain the means of growing in grace, of examining his heart, and of deciding respecting his religious character In this respect, those Tracts which relate to Christian character and experience have been found exceedingly useful.

The summer past, writes a lady, we have been blessed with the gentle droppings of that grace which purifies

the heart; and not unfrequently have I heard those who
were inquiring the way to Zion, refer to some sentence
which they have observed *in a Tract*, as one that filled
them with astonishing solemnity. Again, those who felt
the joys of sins forgiven, and could exclaim, " None but
Christ; he is the chiefest among ten thousand, and altogether lovely," have often quoted some Tract which
they delighted to peruse, because it expressed so entirely the language of their hearts.

One thousand Tracts in Alleghany county, N. York.

An Agent in New-York says, a young man in L——,
being about to remove to Alleghany county, called at the
Depository in Utica, and obtained about one thousand
Tracts. These he caused to be faithfully distributed in
the town where he had fixed his abode. Their distribution was soon followed by a general revival of religion.
Between fifty and sixty professed converts to Jesus Christ
were the fruits of this revival; and *nearly thirty of them
traced their first serious impressions to the Tracts which
had been put into their hands.*

Work of Grace in the American Tract Society House.

The Committee in their Third Report say, an interesting work of Divine grace has, for several months, been
apparent among the females employed in printing, folding, and stitching Tracts in the Society's House. An
unusual seriousness was observed among them in February of the last year, and at no time have the influences
of the Spirit seemed to be entirely withdrawn. Songs of
praise have often ascended from their lips, while their
hands have been active in folding those messages of truth;
and many a Tract has been wet with tears of sorrow for
sin, and, it is hoped, of real penitence, before it has gone
forth on its errand of mercy. Since the commencement
of the work, 41 different individuals have been employed
in these departments of the Society's operations, 15 of
whom were previously members of the church. Of the
remaining 26, 18 have, since the period above mentioned, professed faith in Christ, and most of them have con-

nected themselves with churches of different Evangelical denominations in the city.

A work of similar character, and simultaneous in its progress, has also been witnessed among the females engaged in the house of the American Bible Society.

USEFULNESS OF TRACTS AMONG THE HEATHEN.

Great, says the departed Rev. Dr. Milne, whose loss is lamented by every friend of China, great are our obligations to the Tract Society; and great is the necessity that exists in these pagan lands for the exercise of its beneficence. Tracts are soon read through, and easily carried about with one. They may be circulated more widely than the sacred Scriptures can. If we calculate either the price, or the persons capable of deriving profit from religious books among the Chinese, we shall find that *fifty* Tracts may be given away for the expense of *one* New Testament. A missionary among the Heathen can carry a hundred Tracts in his hand; and he will ever find great satisfaction in leaving an appropriate one in the house where he has been visiting; or in putting one into the hands of those with whom he has been conversing; or dropping one in the highway, where it is likely to be taken up by some passing stranger; or in reading and explaining one to those who are inclined to hear. The Tract Society is a most important Auxiliary in the work of converting the Heathen to Christ; and though, in comparison with Missionary and Bible Societies, it holds, in some respects, a lower place; in other respects its utility is more immediate, more extensive, and more apparent.

A Brahmin in India.

We are informed by Dr. Carey, that a distinguished Brahmin, who had, for four years, observed a vow of perpetual silence, in the temple of Kalee, and was worshipped as a god, and whose case was apparently the most hopeless of all the human family, was converted to Christianity by the reading of a Tract.

Converts in Ceylon.

Dr. J. Scudder, missionary at Ceylon, after urging the claims of that benighted country upon the American churches, says, " Glad tidings from this place have already reached you; and we number among those who have been rescued from heathenish darkness, *two, whose attention to the religion of the only true God was first awakened by religous Tracts.* One of them was a youth of high rank in Changane, who now rejoices in Jesus as his Savior, and is almost daily, from house to house, and in other ways, making known this salvation to others. The other, a young man who resides near us, was led, from the attentive reading of the Tract, " *The Heavenly Way,*" to forsake his idols, and now stands a candidate for baptism and admission to the church. In the great day of account you will meet a number from among this people whose robes have, as I trust, already been washed and made white in the blood of the Lamb; and what rapture will find your breast, should you see this one and that one pointing to you in that day, and hear them saying, *Behold, there stands the friend who was instrumental in sending me a Tract, through which, under God, I, who was once a poor benighted heathen, have been brought to know Jesus. Blessing, and honor, and glory, and praise, be unto Him that sitteth on the throne, and unto the Lamb, for ever and ever.*

A communication from the mission here, relates the striking conversion of a young native by reading a Tract, and says, " *No method of doing good in Ceylon, or India, is so promising, with the same sacrifice, as the distribution of Tracts.* They are better adapted for general circulation than even the Scriptures, among such a population as we find here, who read but little; and they *feel not the sun, and sink not under the climate, as does the living missionary.*"

Testimony of Dr. Marshman.

" Of the *value of Tracts in missionary labor,*" says Rev. Dr. Marshman, a most zealous missionary in India, " it is needless to speak. *Portions of Scripture, or*

Tracts, have had something to do in the conversion of almost every individual who has joined the Christian church in India."

Letter from Rev. Dr. Judson, in Burmah.

I can spare time to write a few lines only, having a constant press of missionary work on hand : add to which, that the weather is dreadfully oppressive at this season. Poor Boardman has just died under it, and Mrs. Wade is nearly dead. Brother Wade and I are now the only men in the mission that can speak and write the language, and we have a population of above ten millions of perishing souls before us. The great annual festival is just past. During this festival I have given away nearly 10,000 Tracts, *giving to none but those who ask.* I presume there have been six thousand applicants at the house ! Some come two or three months' journey, from the borders of Siam and China—" Sir, we hear that there is an eternal hell. We are afraid of it. Dr. give us a writing that will tell us how to escape it." Others come from the frontiers of Cassay, a hundred miles north of Ava—" Sir, we have seen a writing that tells us about an eternal God. Are you the man that gives away such writings? If so. pray give us one, for we want to know the truth before we die." Others come from the interior of the country, where the name of Jesus Christ is a little known—" Are you Jesus Christ's man? Give us a writing that tells about Jesus Christ." Brother Bennett works day and night at the press; but he is unable to supply us; for the call is great at Maulmein and Tavoy, as well as here, and his types are very poor, and he has no efficient help. The fact is, that we are very weak, and have to complain, that hitherto we have not been well supported from home. It is most distressing to find, when we are almost worn out, and are sinking, one after another, into the grave, that many of our brethren in Christ at home are just as hard and immovable as rocks; just as cold and repulsive as the mountains of ice in the polar seas. But whatever they do, we cannot sit still and see the dear Burmans, flesh and blood like ourselves, and like ourselves possessed of immortal souls that will shine

for ever in heaven, or burn for ever in hell—we cannot
see them go down to perdition without doing our very
utmost to save them.   And thanks be to God, our labors
are not in vain.   We have three lovely churches, and
about two hundred baptized converts, and some are in
glory.   A spirit of religious inquiry is extensively spread-
ing throughout the country, and the signs of the times
indicate that the great renovation of Burmah is drawing
near.   O, if we had about twenty more, versed in the language, and means to spread schools, and Tracts, and Bibles, to any extent, how happy I should be.   But those
rocks, and those icy mountains, have crushed us down
for many years.   However, I must not leave my work
to write letters.   It is seldom that I write a letter home,
except my journal, and that I am obliged to do."

MISCELLANEOUS EVIDENCES OF USEFULNESS.

Influence of two Tracts in a Military Academy.

The late Professor of Ethics and Chaplain of the Mili-
tary Academy at West Point, presented four Tracts to a
student who called on him, two of which he requested
him to read for his own personal benefit, and the other
two, one of which was, *The Last Hours of the Hon.
Francis Newport*, to drop where some of his skeptical
fellow students would be likely to find them.   One week
afterward, on Saturday afternoon, another student called
on him and said, "You do not know me, Sir, my name
is ——;" and then burst into tears.   For some time he
could not utter a word.   The professor, convinced what
was the cause of his distress, said to him, "My friend,
if, as I trust, your grief is connected with religion—if you
desire to become a servant of God, be encouraged to open
your heart to me, whose heart is already open to you."
"I do desire to become a servant of God," said he.   Deep
emotion prevented his further utterance for a few moments.   Being then asked what were the circumstances
of his case, he replied, "A Tract was lying in my room
last Saturday.   I cannot imagine how it got there; but I
took it up, read it, and it made a powerful impression
upon my mind.   It was *an account of the death of an Infidel.*"   On being requested to give some account of the

previous state of his mind he said he had not actually considered himself an Infidel, but had been very profane, and in the habit of speaking lightly of religion, and nothing had effectually arrested his attention till he read the Tract. He, not long after, gave evidence that he had been born of God, and united himself to the communion of the church. He soon manifested much anxiety for the student through whose instrumentality he had received the Tract. "To him, under God," said he to the professor, "next to you, Sir, I owe an immeasurable debt; and, by the help of God, I will not let him alone till we have him among us." A few days after, he called upon the professor, with this very young man from whom he had received the Tract, leaning on his arm: "Here he is, Sir," said he, "the Lord has brought him." Unable to restrain his emotions at beholding what he hoped the Lord was doing for him, the professor threw his arms around his neck, and blessed him. "I can hold out no longer," said he; "this is not the first time; I have been often called. I can hold out no longer. I will be a servant of God, henceforth, for ever." It was in reading *The Shepherd of Salisbury Plain*, that he first felt his heart expanded with love to God, and bursting with the spirit of prayer.—"Behold, how great a matter a little fire kindleth." These two young men are now active members of the Church of Christ; they have distributed thousands of Tracts among the destitute, the ignorant, and the perishing: they are both zealously engaged in the cause of Sabbath schools: by one of them a school of a hundred children has been raised up, where, in a population of a thousand, the Gospel has scarcely ever been preached: by one, among a people destitute of the regular means of grace, social meetings for prayer and instruction are held every week: by the instrumentality of one of them, as many as *ten*, who just now were dreadfully wicked, have been hopefully converted, and are so altered as to astonish their former companions. Both have made up their minds to consecrate their lives to the ministry of the Gospel, and will be, we trust, through many years, continually gathering new fruits in testimony of the unspeakable blessings which may flow to the church and to the world *through the instrumentality of one religious Tract.*

A Tract encountered by a Literary Gentleman.

An Officer of a College, says the Report of the Tract Society at Boston, called one morning on a neighboring clergyman, and being seated in a room alone, took up the Tract *Sixteen Short Sermons.* His attention was powerfully arrested. He read it through, and saw and felt himself to be a condemned sinner. At the same time he saw the sinner's only refuge—A CRUCIFIED REDEEMER. The reading of that Tract was the means, under God, to which he now attributes his first conviction of sin and his hope of pardon.

Testimony of a Clergyman at the West.

Tract Societies, writes a Clergyman at the West, are, under God, *the hope of this land;* and will be for years The inhabitants are so mixed and multiform in their religions, that, except in a comparatively few favored spots, there are scarcely enough active Christians, of any one denomination, to support the preached Gospel. Nor are they a reading people. A book is too voluminous to be read. Tracts meet precisely our wants. They preach without pay—and they preach without fear—and they preach by day and at night—and they preach to parents and children—they preach short sermons and plain, and they can be changed frequently, and at small expense— and they stop while the hearer is sleeping, or when he grows impatient, and begin again when he is ready to hear—and they can bear insults without repining, and favor without becoming vain—contempt, and scorn, and poverty, present to them no terrors—they rest as comfortably in the unthatched cabin as in citizens' palaces, and live as happily with the poor as those who fare sumptuously—they have no ears to hearken to terrible reports of fevers and pestilences in the wilds of the West— their sympathies are not confined to them that can best pay them, nor their efforts in saving, to those who best entertain them. No. They go forth in the spirit of Gospel preachers—to the broken-hearted—to the lost—those wandering upon the mountains and in the wilderness— they go—*to preach the Gospel to the poor.*

THE END.

THE

HAPPY WATERMAN,

OR

HONESTY THE BEST POLICY.

A GENTLEMAN who was one day a passenger on the river Thames, observed on the stern of the boat these words: "HONESTY THE BEST POLICY." Taking notic of it, he determined to enter into conversation with the Waterman; and, inquiring into his situation in life, found that he had a wife and five children, and supported also an old father and mother-in-law by his own labour. The Gentleman upon this was still more desirous to know why he had given such a title to his boat, and asked him the reason of it. "I can easily explain this to your satisfaction," answered the young man, "if you will give me leave;" and being desired to proceed, he spoke as follows:

"My father and mother died a few years ago, and left a large family; my father was a waterman, and I was his assistant in the management of a ferry-boat, by which he supported his family; on his death it was necessary (in order to pay his just debts) to sell our boat. I parted from it even with tears: but the distress that I felt spurred me on to industry, for I said I will use every kind of diligence to purchase my boat back again. I went to the person who had bought it, and told him my design; he had given five *guineas* for it, but told me, as I was once the owner, that I should have it whenever I could raise five *pounds* 'Shall the boat be mine again ?' said I; my heart bounded at the thought, and I resolved to do my utmost in an honest and fair way to obtain my object.

" I was at this time married to a good young woman, and we lived in a small cottage. She was healthy, industrious, and careful. We loved one another dearly, and, united in our affections and our efforts, what might we not undertake ? My father used to say to me. ' Always do what is right; labour diligently, and spend your money carefully ; and God will bless your store.' We treasured up these rules, and determined to try the truth of them. My wife had long chiefly supported two aged parents: I loved them as my own—and the desire of contributing to their support, was an additional spur to my endeavours to re-purchase the boat. I entered myself as a day-labourer, in the garden of our squire; and my wife was called occasionally to perform some services at the house; and employed herself in needle-work, spinning, or knitting at home : not a moment in the day was suffered to pass unemployed. We lived sparingly, not a shilling was spent at the ale-house, nor on any improper object; and by these means we were enabled to contribute a little both to the support of religion, and to real objects of charity; and also to drop, every week, a little overplus into a fairing-box, to buy the boat. If any accident or charity brought us an additional shilling, we did not enlarge our expense, but kept it for the boat ! The more careful we were, the more comfortable we felt, for we were more independent, and daily approached nearer to the object of our wishes. Our family indeed increased, but with it our friends increased also; for the cleanliness and frugality which furnished our cottage, and the content and cheerfulness that appeared in it, drew the notice of our rich neighbours; of my master and mistress particularly, whose rule was to assist the industrious, but not to encourage the idle.

They did not approve of giving money to the poor; but in cold winters, or dear times, allowed us to buy things at a cheaper rate; this was *money to us*, for when we counted our little cash for the week's marketing, all that was saved to us by our tickets to purchase things at reduced prices, went into our 'little box.' If our children got a penny at school for a reward, or a present from a neighbour for any little service done, instead of buying gingerbread with it, they brought it home and gave it to their mother, saying it would help to buy the boat. I felt it my duty to teach them, from their infancy, to be obliging, industrious, and careful; recollecting that early habits are most lasting; and when we 'train up a child in the way he should go,' we have the assurance of God's promise, that 'when he is old, he will not depart from it.'

"Thus our little store insensibly increased from time to time, till one pound only was wanting of the sum so much desired; and often my dear wife and I used to remark, that the blessing of heaven was very observable in the success of our honest endeavours.

"But the following accident seemed to disappoint our hopes. Coming home one evening from my work, I saw in the road a small pocket-book; and on opening it, I found a bank note of *ten pounds*, which plainly enough belonged to my master, for his name was upon it, and I had also seen him passing that way in the evening : it being too late, however, to return to the house, I went on my way. When I told my family of the incident, the little ones were thrown into a transport of joy. 'My dears,' said I, 'what is the matter?' 'O daddy, the BOAT! the BOAT! we may now have two or three boats!' I checked them by my looks, and asked them if they recollected whose money that was? They said, 'Yours, as you found it.' I reminded them that I was not the real owner, and bade them think how they would all feel, supposing a stranger was to take our box of money, if I should happen to drop it on the day I went to buy back the boat. This thought had the effect on their young minds that I desired : they were silent and pale with the representation of such a disaster, and I begged it might be a lesson to them never to forget the golden rule of ' doing as they would wish others to do to them ;' and never to turn aside from what God had made their duty. I also took this opportunity to explain to them, that the possession of the boat by dishonest means would never answer, since we could not expect the blessing of GoD upon *bad deeds.* Nothing, I think, Sir, is of greater consequence than to embrace such opportunities for warning children against what is wrong; and for earnestly pressing upon their tender minds these principles of religion and morality, which are the means appointed by heaven for guiding their youthful minds to what is right. Early religious instruction has been an unspeakable blessing to me.

" To go on with my story :—The next morning I put the pocket-book into my bosom, and went to my work, intending as soon as the family arose, to give it to my master ; but what were my feelings, when, on searching in my bosom, it was nowhere to be found ! I hasted back along the road I came, looking diligently all the way, but in vain ! there were no traces of any such thing. I would not return into my cottage, because I wished to save my family the pain I felt : and in the hope of still recovering the book, I went to my work, following another path which I recollected I had also gone by. On my return to the garden-gate, I was accosted by the gardener, who in a threatening tone told me, I was suspected ; that our master had lost a pocket-book, describing what I had found, and that I being the only man absent from the garden at the hour of work, the rest of the men also denying that they had seen any such thing, there was every reason to conclude that I must have got it. Before I could answer, my distressed countenance confirmed the suspicion; and another servant coming up, said I was detected, for that a person had been sent to my house, and that my wife and family had owned it all, and had described the pocket-book. I told them the real fact, but it seemed to every one unlikely to be true; every circumstance was against me, and (my heart trembles to look back upon it) I was arrested, and hurried away to prison ! I protested my innocence, but I did not wonder that I gained no credit. Great grief now oppressed my heart; my poor wife, my dear children, and my gray-headed parents, were all at once plunged into want and misery : instead of the ease and happiness which we were expecting, all our hopes were blasted at the very time when we were just arriving at the height of our earthly wishes; and what was worse, my character was tarnished, and all my ungodly fellow-servants, whose practices I had often condemned, were triumphing, and reviling religion on my account.

"My misery seemed almost complete; and under these accumulated sufferings I should certainly have sunk, if the consolations of religion had not borne me up. I knew, however, I was innocent; and in frequent and fervent prayer endeavoured to 'commit my way unto the Lord, and trust in him.'

"I resolved that, having been the cause (though without any design) of the second loss of the property, I would offer the whole of our little store to make it good, as far as in my power; and accordingly sent for my dear wife, to give her this sad commission. But alas! when she came, I found this sacrifice could be of no avail, 'for,' said she, 'my master has been at the cottage, when I told him freely how you had found the note, but unfortunately had lost it again; and I added, that I was sure both I and my husband would make the best return in our power; after which I produced our little fairing-box, and begged him to accept the contents, which had been so long raising, as all we had to offer: but, Sir," said the Waterman, "conceive my agony, when she added, that my master angrily refused, saying, that our being in possession of all that money, was of itself the clearest proof of my guilt; for it was impossible, with my large family, and no greater opportunities than my neighbours, that I could come honestly by such a sum; therefore he was determined to keep me in jail till I should pay the whole. My unhappiness was very great; however, my mind by degrees began to be more easy, for I grew confident that I should not trust in God and my own innocence in vain : and so it happened : one of my fellow-labourers proved to be the person who had picked up the note after I had dropt it, having come a few minutes after me along the same road to his work, and hearing that the suspicion had fallen altogether upon me, he was tempted to turn the accident to his own advantage, and conceal the property; which having kept in his own box for a few weeks, till he thought no suspicion would rest upon him, he went and offered the note for change, and being then suspected, my master had him taken up, and I was released.

" The second change from so much misery to happiness, was almost too much for us. My master sent for me, and with many expressions of concern for what had passed, made me give him an account of the means by which I had collected the little fund that fixed his suspicions so strongly upon me. I accordingly related the history of it, as I have now done; and when I came to that part, where I checked my children for their inconsiderate joy, on their finding the note, he arose with much kindness in his looks, and putting the bank bill into my hand, he said, ' Take it: the bank note shall be theirs. It is the best and only return I can make you, as a just reward of your honesty: and it will be a substantial proof to your children of the goodness of your instructions; for they will thus early see and feel the benefit of honesty and virtue !'

" This kind and worthy gentleman interested himself much in the purchase of my boat, which, in less than a week, I had in my possession. The remainder of my master's bounty, and the additional advantage of the ferry, have placed me in comfortable circumstances, which I humbly trust God will continue to us, as long as we continue our labour and honest diligence; and I can say from my long experience, that the fruit of our own industry is always sweetest. I have now also the pleasure of being able to help others; for when a rich passenger takes my ferry, as my story is well known in the neighbourhood, he often gives me more than my fare, which enables me to let the next poor person go over for half price.

" My employment in this way has become also a pleasure. I see the blessing of God on my honest and lawful industry; and when I go home to my family at night with my little earnings, I find it a paradise of domestic enjoyment. My wife, according as our slender circumstances will permit, is always contriving how she can make me happier at home than anywhere else. My children are waiting to share a father's smiles, and tell me all their little tales of what has passed during the day. And my little cottage, though poor, is always neat and clean, and orderly, and the habitation of peace. By never frequenting the ale-house, I save daily from sixpence to a shilling more than many others in my employment; and this, put into one of the *Savings Banks* lately instituted for the benefit of the poor, has amounted, last year, to twelve pounds. Vice and extravagance, Sir, are the fruitful parents of misery; but godliness, as the Scripture says, ' is profitable unto all things, having the promise of the life that now is, and of that which is to come.' "

The Gentleman was exceedingly pleased with the Waterman's story, and the piety of his remarks; and from this time, becoming acquainted with his family, he did him every service in his power, giving books and schooling to the little ones, and such things as would make the aged parents comfortable, as long as they survived. He was very desirous of knowing what became of the unfortunate fellow-labourer, who had so dreadfully gone aside from the principles of honesty; and he learnt that he was, after a short imprisonment, set at liberty by his master, at the earnest entreaty of the honest Waterman; as he said it was partly through his carelessness in losing the note, that the temptation had fallen in his fellow-labourer's way : he had moreover a very large family, his master also was so good as to consider that he was a man who had not been blessed with a good education in his youth, so that having little fear of God before his eyes, and having a great temptation in his way, he had been the more easily led to commit this very wicked action, by which he would have enriched himself at the expense of an innocent man. I have great pleasure in adding, that the thought of what he had done, together with the generosity of the Waterman, had so strong an effect upon this poor fellow that he afterwards, had it written upon his cottage door, Do as you would be done unto. And he has resolved to follow this rule himself in future, and has also taught it to all his children : indeed, it became a rule well known over the whole parish; for every little child, having been informed of this story, was told that he ought to consider, before he did any action, whether he would like his brother, or sister, or school-fellow, to do the same by him; and if not, that the action was wrong, and not to be done, let the profit be ever so great. Surely, then, those who have lived long, and seen much of life, and have had much religious instruction also, should never depart from this simple and certain rule. It is the same to all ranks; it is the sum of the second table of the law; and the man who does not

act under its influence, shows too plainly that he has never
been changed by the renewing of his mind. For the Scriptures assure us that every man is by nature " dead in tres-
passes and sins ;" (Eph. ii. 1.) but when he becomes a new
man, and is "created in Christ Jesus unto good
works," the dispositions and affections of his mind are
changed; and his devout, and regular, and honest conduct
are the most certain evidences which we can have, that he
is a christian.

Christianity is not that empty and notional thing which
many take it to be. It is not a mere name; a Sabbath cere-
mony; a compliance with the customs of a country. It
changes a man's character and conduct; makes him contented, industrious, and useful, like this honest Waterman.
And if it does not this, it wants the signature of heaven;
and the man who professes it, while he maintains not a
conversation becoming the Gospel, is only deceiving his
own soul.

———

WHO shall ascend thy heavenly place,
Great God, and dwell before thy face?
The man who minds religion now,
And humbly walks with God below.

Whose hands are pure, whose heart is clean ;
Whose lips still speak the thing they mean ;
No slanders dwell upon his tongue :
He hates to do his neighbour wrong.

Firm to his word he ever stood,
And always makes his promise good :,
Nor dares to change the thing he swears,
Whatever pain or loss he bears.

He never deals in bribing gold,
And mourns that justice should be sold ;
While others gripe and grind the poor,
Sweet charity attends his door.

PAUSE AND THINK,

AM I A CHRISTIAN?

BY REV. J. ALLEINE.

"EXCEPT YE BE CONVERTED,—YE SHALL NOT ENTER INTO THE KINGDOM OF HEAVEN."—Matt. xviii. 3.

DEAR READER,

AS you may not understand properly what Conversion is, I will first endeavour, by the help and blessing of God, to show you the *nature* of it.—As it may be your case, that you expect mercy and favour with God, though you continue in your natural state, I would next prove the *necessity* of Conversion; and lest you should make a most dangerous and destructive mistake, and imagine that you are converted when you are not, I would also lay before you the *marks of the unconverted.*—But lest you should fear no harm, because you see none, and so continue satisfied in your present condition, I would show you the *misery of the unconverted.*—To stir you up to seek the Conversion of your heart, I would offer you some *motives* to it.—And lastly, if you are convinced of your need of Conversion, and are become anxious for it, I would direct you to some *means in order to your obtaining it,* and therewith your present and eternal Salvation.

I. I would show you the *nature of Conversion,* both what it *is not,* and what it *is.*

Your *profession of Christianity* is not conversion. St. Paul says, it lies not in word, but in power. 1 Cor. iv. 20. There were persons in Sardis and Laodicea that were Christians by profession, and had a name to live, yet because they had but a name, they were condemned by Christ.

Your *Baptism* is not conversion. Many a person has been baptized, and yet been destitute of holiness. Wicked Ananias and Sapphira had both been baptized, a yet were both suddenly struck dead in their sins. Simon Magus was baptized, and yet continued in the gall of bitterness and in the bond of iniquity. Where Christianity is the professed religion of any country, very many who are called by the name of Christ, have only the name, and not the disposition of Christ.

A good education is not conversion. Education may render you decent in your behaviour, but cannot change your heart. Joash appeared very devout while his uncle Jehoiada lived, but after his good tutor was taken out of the way, he soon showed what spirit he was of, by his suddenly giving way to idolatry.

A strict performance of all the outward duties of religion, and a diligent attendance upon all the means of grace, is not conversion. Paul, even when he was unconverted, could say that he lived after the strictest sect, and in all good conscience, and that touching the righteousness of the law, he was blameless. The Pharisees in general were so remarkably strict in outward things, that it passed for a common proverb among the Jews, that if but two persons went to heaven, one would be a Pharisee : and yet our Lord, instead of commending them, said unto them, wo, wo, wo, unto you.

A turning from former immorality and profaneness to sobriety and regularity, is not conversion. Lead may be cast into many different shapes, and yet it remains but a base metal still. And so men may be greatly changed, and be reformed from all gross outward acts of sin, and escape the pollutions of the world, and yet be unrenewed in their hearts. Herod heard John the Baptist gladly, and honoured him, and did many things; and yet rested short of conversion.

Deep convictions of sin, and sharp and sore pangs of conscience, if the person go no farther, are not conversion. Pharaoh, Ahab, Felix, and Simon Magus, and even Judas, were under great terrors of conscience. These distresses often come to nothing, and prove only so many foretastes of hell.

Strong movings of the affections under the powerful preaching of the word, or under some peculiar dispensations of Providence, may not end in conversion. There may be very strong desires after good things, and likewise great delight in them, even in the unconverted, as was the case with those of whom the Lord said, they seek me early, and delight to know my ways, and take delight in approaching to God. Is. lviii. 2. And there may be great flashes of joy, as in the case of the hearers our Lord speaks of, who received the word with joy, but had no root in themselves, and so in time of tribulation and persecution withered away.

As you would not be deceived in a matter of the greatest importance, examine what you ground your hopes of heaven and salvation upon.

Is it your profession of Christianity—your baptism—your religious education—your sobriety—your diligence in your business—your justice and honesty in your dealings—your performance of religious duties—or the trouble of mind you have sometimes had for your sins? I do assure you, from the word of the Lord, these pleas will not be accepted at God's bar. All these, however good, will not prove that you are converted, and so will not be sufficient to your salvation.

But if those who can say thus much of themselves, come short of conversion, what must be the case of the open, outward sinner? If you, alas! are such a one, you are to know that you are far, very far, from the kingdom of God. May a man be civilized, and yet not be converted? Where then shall the outwardly ungodly and the gross sinner appear? May a man keep company with the wise virgins, and yet be shut out? And shall not a companion of fools, that is, of sinners, much more be destroyed? May a man be true and just in all his dealings towards his fellow creatures, and yet not be justified before God? What then will become of you? Oh, bethink yourself of turning to the Lord speedily and thoroughly, or else iniquity will be your ruin. Seek to the Saviour for his pardoning and renewing grace, and rest not until God has made a thorough change upon you, for you must be another man, a new man in Christ, or else you will be a lost man for ever.

But I am now to show you positively what *is* conversion. *It is a universal change in your heart, and also in your life.* It goes throughout a man, throughout his mind, and his whole conduct. The old man is put off, the new man is put on, and all things are become new.

1. In conversion *the understanding is enlightened*, so that he why was sometime darkness is become light in the Lord. *He is enlightened with the knowledge of God.* His spotless purity, his perfect hatred and abhorrence of sin, his infinite justice to punish it, his infinite knowledge and power and goodness, his all-sufficiency, and his other glorious perfections, as revealed in the word, are powerfully perceived in his mind. Now he sees what he only heard of before.

His understanding is also enlightened into the knowledge of *sin*. Now the sinner sees it, in some measure in its proper colours, as the worst of evils, exceeding sinful, though he could see but little evil in it before. Oh, what deformed monsters do his formerly beloved lusts appear! If they were right eyes, he would pluck them out; or if they were right hands, he would consent to their being cut off. He sees the unreasonableness, the unrighteousness, and the abominableness there is in sin, how odious and offensive it is to God, and how hurtful and destructive to his own soul; so that he is affrighted at it, loathes it, flees from it, and looks upon himself as the greatest fool for fighting so long against the Lord, and harbouring such a destroyer in his breast.

His understanding is illuminated with the knowledge of *himself.* The prodigal is now come to himself, and is made, as it were, full of eyes within; sees that his inward parts are very wickedness, and knows and feels the plague of his own heart. He sees how desperately corrupt his fallen nature is, what enmity against the holy God and his holy law has lodged there all his life; so that he abhors himself. He that could see little sin before in himself, and could find no matter of confession before God, except some few gross evils, now sees the deep and universal corruption of his whole soul, feels that his heart is deceitful above all things, and desperately wicked; and he is made to cry out, "Unclean, unclean! O Lord, wash me thoroughly from my sin, and create in me a clean heart." He writes. *Unclean,* upon all his performances; he sees the blasphemy, and the theft, and murder and adultery, that are in his heart, of which before he was ignorant. Though he saw no danger before, he now concludes himself lost for ever. unless renewed by the power of grace.

Farther, his understanding is enlightened with the knowledge of *Christ.* Heretofore he saw no form nor comeliness in Christ, nor any beauty in him, that he should desire him ; but now he discovers a superlative worth, and
a transcendent glory and excellency in the Lord Jesus
Christ, which darkens all created excellencies, as the rising
sun makes the stars to hide their heads ; he sees an infinite
fulness in him, sufficient for the supply of all his wants,
enough to satisfy the boundless desires of his immortal
soul, and this makes him determined to believe in Christ
and him alone, as his portion for ever.

Now, my dear Reader, examine yourself here ; try your
own heart. Is your understanding thus enlightened ? Are
you made acquainted with the things I have been speaking
of ?

2. In conversion *the will is renewed and brought into subjection to the will of God.* It is cured of its utter *disincli-
nation* to do any thing good. A fixed aversion to evil, and
an inclination and propensity to good is implanted in it.
Now the man has new ends and designs ; owns his intention
is to glorify God in all things. He chooses Jesus as his
Lord; and his choice is not merely a choice made in a
fright, as with a dying sinner, that only would believe in
Christ rather than go to hell, when he does not really hate
sin, nor wish to be delivered from it. Again, he takes the
ways of holiness for his path. He takes God's testimonies,
not as his bondage, but his heritage, his heritage for ever.
He does not only bear, but take up with pleasure Christ's
yoke. No time passes so agreeably, as that which he
spends in the exercises of religion.

Now put your conscience to this, my friend, as you go ·
on, whether you really are thus renewed. You are truly
a happy person if this be your case ; but see that you are
faithful in examining yourself.

3. In conversion *the exercise of the affections is changed.*
The convert's great desire is not after riches, but grace.
He hungers and thirsts after it ; he had rather be gracious
than great; he had rather be the holiest man upon earth,
than the most learned, the most famous, and the most prosperous. Once perhaps he was ready to say, "Oh ! if I was but
in great esteem, if I rolled in wealth. and swam in pleasure,

if my debts were paid, and I and mine provided for, then I should be a happy man." But now his language is altered. "Oh!" says he, "if I were but a real Christian, though poor and despised, I should reckon myself a happy man." Reader, is this the language of your heart?—The converted man rejoices in the way of God's testimonies more than in all manner of riches. He delights in the law of the Lord, for which he once had no relish. He has no such joy now, as in the thoughts of Christ, and in the company of his people.

His *cares* are altered. They were before chiefly about the world ; nor would he allow the least time for the concerns of his soul ; but now his cry is, " What must I do to be saved ?"—His *fears* are different. Once he was afraid of nothing so much as suffering the loss of his earthly goods, or the esteem of the world and of his friends ; nothing seemed so terrible to him as pain, poverty, or disgrace. But now, in his view, these are not to be compared with the dishonour of God, or his displeasure. He walks circumspectly and cautiously, lest he should be overtaken with sin. It fills his heart with grief to think of losing God's favour : this he dreads as his only undoing. No thought in the world pains him so much, as to think of parting with Christ.

Reader, is your will determinately fixed for God in Christ ; and are your affections agreeable to that choice ?

The change wrought upon a man in conversion has an effect upon *all his powers.* These that were before the instruments of sin, are now become the instruments of righteousness. He who before abused his *body,* now possesseth his vessel in sanctification and honour, in temperance, chastity, and sobriety, and dedicateth it to the Lord alone.

Conversion has an effect upon a man's *whole life and practice.* He takes a new course. His conversation is in heaven. When once God has given him a new heart, and written his law upon his mind, immediately he walks in his statutes, and keeps his judgment. Though sin may dwell in him, yet it has no more the dominion over him. He has his fruit unto holiness, he has an unfeigned respect to all God's commandments, and makes conscience of what some may think little sins and little duties. And now, my dear Reader, examine well your own heart and life, and ask your own conscience, whether, while I have been representing the nature of conversion, I have been describing your case, and your experience, or not?

As I have not the least hope of seeing your face in heaven, unless you are converted here on earth, (See Matt. xviii. 3.) and as there is very great danger of your resting satisfied in your natural state, and expecting mercy and favour with God, without being altogether changed and renewed by his grace and Spirit, I proceed to prove,

II. *The absolute necessity of Conversion.*

1. Without this your *existence is a blank ;* for you cannot answer the end of your being. Did not God make you, body and soul, entirely for his service? But without conversion you live to no purpose, yea, rather to a very bad purpose ; all your powers and faculties are so entirely corrupted by the fall, that except you are purified from dead works, you cannot serve the living God. An unsanctified person cannot possibly work the work of God ; for he has no skill in it, and no inclination at all to it. Without conversion you live to a very bad purpose : the unrenewed soul is " a cage of unclean birds," " a sepulchre" full of corruption. All your members and powers are instruments of unrighteousness, and the servants of Satan. You are dishonouring God, and fighting against him continually. Oh! awful abuse of God's workmanship.

2. Without Conversion, your *religious duties and performances will be all of them utterly in vain ;* for they can neither please God nor save your soul.

3. *Your hopes are all in vain.* Your hopes of any solid comfort here ; for you may as well expect ease when all your bones are out of joint, as true happiness while you are in your sins. And your hopes of salvation hereafter are vain. Perhaps you are ready to say, " I hope in Christ ; I put my whole trust in God, and therefore I doubt not but I shall be saved." But to hope to get to heaven without being born again, is to hope that Christ will prove a false teacher. John iii. 3. David's plea was, 'I hope in thy word ;' but your hope is against the word. You cannot show me any word of Christ to give you hope of hea-

ven, while you go on still in your wickedness. God rejects such hope with abhorrence. Isaiah xlviii. 1, 2. You will ask. " Would you have me then despair ?" Yes : you ought absolutely to reject all hope of getting to heaven in an unconverted state. You must despair of ever being happy without being holy. But you must by no means despair of finding mercy, if you repent and turn to God; neither must you despair of obtaining repentance and conversion, if you use the means which God hath appointed in order to your obtaining them.

4. Without conversion *all that Christ hath done will be to you in vain;* (John xiii. 8. Titus ii. 14.) it will not avail to your salvation. Without the application of the Spirit in regeneration, you can have no interest in the benefits of Christ's redemption. To suppose you might, would overturn his designs, which are, that men should be brought through sanctification to salvation. Christ will save none in a way contrary to his Father's will; and this is the will of God, even our sanctification. 1 Thes. iv. 3.

5. To save you in your sins would *oppose the attributes of God.* (1.) His *justice,* for the righteousness of God's judgment consists in rendering to all according to their work. But if men were to sow to the flesh, and yet reap everlasting life, where would be the glory of God's justice; since it would be giving to the wicked according to the work of the righteous ? (2.) His *holiness.* If God should not only save sinners, but save them in their sins, his holiness would be defaced. It would be offering violence to the infinite purity of his nature to have such to dwell with him. If David would not endure such in his house nor in his sight, (Psalm ci. 3—7.) can you think that God will endure such in his presence? (3.) His *truth:* for God hath declared from heaven, that if any shall say, " I shall have peace, though I walk in the imagination of my heart, the Lord will not spare him, but his anger and his jealousy shall smoke against that man, and all the curses that are written in this book shall lie upon him, and the Lord shall blot out his name from under heaven." God further declares that he who shall " ascend into his hill, must be of clean hands and a pure heart." How could God be true, then, if notwithstanding all this, he should take men to heaven with-

out conversion? (4.) His *wisdom:* for this would be to throw away the greatest of his mercies upon those that would not value them. The unsanctified sinner puts very little price upon God's great Salvation. And it would not be at all consistent with God's infinite wisdom to force spiritual blessings upon those that would not be exceedingly thankful for them. It would also be a reflection upon his wisdom, as sinners are not prepared to receive his mercy. The wisdom of God is seen in suiting things to each other, the means to the end, and the quality of the gift to the capacity of the receiver. Now if Christ should take an unconverted person to heaven, he could not possibly, in the very nature of things, be in the least degree happy there. If the entertainments of the heavenly world consisted in those things in which sinners delight here; if its enjoyments were earthly riches, pleasures, and honours; if its employments were the amusements of this present life; then they might have some sort of delight there, though still no real solid happiness; but these things have no place in heaven. The felicity of that state consists in the contemplation of God's perfections, and the displays of them in the works of creation, of providence, and especially of redemption. Hence it is described by " seeing the Lord;" as a state of knowledge, of complacency in God, and in perpetually serving and praising him. Hence adoration is generally mentioned as the employment of the host of heaven. These are the entertainments of the future world, and those who cannot find supreme happiness in these, cannot find it in heaven. But these things could afford no true satisfaction to an unholy person; a holy God would be an object of horror, rather than delight to him; and his service a weariness, as it is now. If *now* your conversation is on earth, and not in heaven—If *now* you are living in the enjoyment of the pleasures of sense—If *now* you are serving foolish and hurtful lusts, instead of presenting your body, soul, and spirit, a living sacrifice, holy and acceptable to God—If *now* you are seeking happiness in the vanities of time—If *now* you disrelish and avoid the company of God's people—If *now* earthly, sensual tempers reign in you, instead of the pure, holy, heavenly dispositions of the true Christian; you may be assured there is no entrance

for you into the blissful presence of God ; you are under
an absolute incapacity of drawing near to him, you can
have no idea of the happiness of real Christians, you can
be no more sensible of it, than the blind to the beauties of
sight, or the deaf to the pleasures of harmony.   (5.) The
admission of unconverted sinners into heaven would be contrary to God's *omniscience, omnipotence, immutability :* it is
the determination of heaven, that none but " the pure in
heart shall see God."   Matt. v. 8.   Now if Christ were to
take the unconverted to heaven, he must do it without
God's knowledge—where would then be his omniscience ?
Or against his will—where would then be his omnipotence?   Or else he must change his will—and then where
would be his immutability ?   O how vain and foolish, how
unreasonable and absurd, how wicked and blasphemous,
then, is your hope of going to heaven without being regenerated and converted here on earth?

 6.   For Christ to save you in your sins, would be against
/his *word*.   He, who is truth itself, hath declared, " Except
ye be converted, ye shall not enter into the kingdom of
heaven."   Matt. xviii. 3.   And again, " Except ye repent,
ye shall perish."   Luke xiii. 3.   One would think that a
single word from Christ should be enough, but how often
and how earnestly does he repeat it !   " Verily, verily, I
say unto thee, except a man be born again, he cannot enter into the kingdom of God.   Marvel not that I said unto
thee, Ye must be born again."   John iii. 3, 5, 7.   And will
you yet hold fast your vain hope, and your presumptuous
confidence, directly against Christ's own words?

 But he must not only go quite against the law of his
kingdom, to save you in this state, but against his *Oath*.
He hath sworn that those that continue ignorant and unbelieving, impenitent and disobedient, shall not enter into his
rest.   Heb. iii. 18.   The covenant of grace is confirmed
by an oath, and sealed by blood.   Heb. vi. 17. Matt. xxvi.
28.   But all must be made void, if you be saved, living
and dying unsanctified.

 God will certainly show *his hatred of sin, at the same time
that he shows his mercy to the penitent sinner.*   Therefore, he
that rightly nameth the name of Christ, departs from iniquity, and denies all ungodliness; and he that hopes for

life through Christ, purifies himself, even as he is pure: otherwise Christ would be thought a favourer of sin. But he will make all men know that though he pardons sin, he will not cherish it.

But it would be also against *all the offices which Christ sustains in the economy of salvation :* God hath exalted him to be a Prince and a Saviour, to give repentance and remission of sins; and he would act against both if he were to save men in their sins. It is the office of a Prince or a King, to be a terror to evil doers, and a praise to them that do well. He is a minister of God, a revenger to execute wrath upon him that doeth evil. Now if Christ was to favour the ungodly, continuing so, and take those to *reign with him* that would not that he should *reign over them*, this would be quite against his office. What king would take rebels in a state of open hostility, into his court? And as Christ would not be a Prince, so neither would he be a Saviour, if he was to do this; for his salvation is divine : he is called " Jesus, because he saves his people from their sins :" so that if he were to save them in their sins, he would neither be a **King** nor a Saviour.

Oh! then ; what meanest thou, O sleeper? Arise, call upon God, that thou perish not. Awake, O secure sinner ; lest you be consumed in your iniquities. Say as the lepers, " If we sit here, we die." Verily, it is **not more** certain, that you are now out of hell, than that you will very soon be in it, except you repent and be converted. You must either turn, or perish. How wilful will your destruction be, if you should yet harden yourself in your sinful state! If you are a man, and not a senseless creature, stand still and consider whither you are going If you have the reason and understanding of a human being, dare not run into the flames of hell with your eyes open, but bethink yourself, and seek to the Lord for repentance What, a man, and yet go wilfully into the pit, when beasts must be forced into danger! What, endowed with reason, and yet trifle with death, and hell, and the vengeance of the Almighty! Will you not hasten to escape from everlasting torments? Let reason prevail with you. Is it a reasonable thing to contend with the infinitely great God, to harden yourself against his word? Is it reasonable for the potsherds of the earth to strive with their Maker? Reader, will you sit still, till the tide of God's wrath come upon you, and drown you in the ocean of everlasting misery?—Is it good for you to try whether God will be as good as his word, and harden your heart, in vain conceit that all will be well with you, while you remain unsanctified?—O distracted sinners! What will they do in the day of visitation? and to whom will they flee for help? Isaiah x. 3. How powerfully hath sin bewitched them! How effectually hath the god of this world blinded them! How strong is the delusion! How obdurate their hearts! Sometimes I think the mercies of God will melt them, and his winning invitations will overcome them; but I leave them as they were: sometimes, that the terrors of the Lord will prevail on them; yet neither will these do the work. O Lord God, send help from above. For thy mercy's sake, and for thy dear Son's sake, have compassion on the souls of those that read these lines, and save them from everlasting burnings.

Lest you should make a most dangerous and destructive mistake, and imagine that you are converted, when you are not, I would now lay before you,

III. *The marks of the unconverted.*

St. Paul gives us a dreadful calendar of sinners, to which I beseech you to attend with all diligence: " For this ye know, that no whoremonger, nor unclean person, nor covetous man, who is an idolater, hath any inheritance in the kingdom of Christ and of God. Let no man deceive you with vain words; for because of these things cometh the wrath of God upon the children of disobedience." Eph. v. 5, 6. " But the fearful and unbelieving, and the abominable, and murderers, and whoremongers, and sorcerers, and idolaters, and all liars, shall have their part in the lake which burneth with fire and brimstone; which is the second death." Rev. xxi. 8. " Know ye not that the unrighteous shall not inherit the kingdom of God? Be not deceived; neither fornicators, nor idolaters, nor adulterers, nor effeminate, nor abusers of themselves with man kind, nor thieves, nor covetous, nor drunkards, nor revil-

ers, nor extortioners, shall inherit the kingdom of God.'
1 Cor. vi. 9, 10.

There are other unconverted unholy persons, that do
not carry their marks thus openly in their foreheads, but
secretly in their hands. These often deceive themselves
and others, and pass for christians and good people, when
they are still unsound at heart. And many pass undiscov-
ered, till death and judgment bring all to light. Remember, my friend, many perish by some sin, that is not only
hid from others, but even from themselves, owing to their
not observing their own hearts. *Some of the secret sins, by
which persons are ruined, are these that follow :*

1. *Ignorance* is one of these sins. Oh! how very many
doth this sin kill in the dark! while they think they have
good hearts, and are in the way to heaven. Whatever excuses you may make for your ignorance, know that it is a
soul-ruining evil.—The God of truth declares that some,
who called themselves his people, " were destroyed for
lack of knowledge." Hos. iv. 6. " For it is a people of
no understanding, therefore he that made them will not
have mercy on them, and he that formed them will show
them no favour." Isaiah xxvii. 11. Beware that this be
not you case, and no longer make excuses for your ignorance.

2. *Secret reserves in giving the heart to Christ.* Some will
do much, but they will not be entirely devoted to him.
They must have some sweet sin ; they have secret exceptions, for life, or liberty, or possessions.

3. *Formality.* Many rest in the outside of religion,
in the external performance of duties ; and this often does
most effectually deceive them, and more certainly ruin
them, than open wickedness ; as it was in the Pharisees'
case. They hear, they fast, they pray, they give alms,
and therefore will not believe but their state is good.
Luke xviii. 11, 12. Whereas, resting in these outward
things, and coming short of the power of religion, all their
flattering hopes and confident persuasions of being in the
way to heaven will fail them after death. Matt. vii.
22, 23. O dreadful case, when a man's religion shall
serve only to harden him, and effectually to deceive his
soul.

4. *Self-righteousness.* When persons trust in their own righteousness, they do thereby reject Jesus for their Saviour. O my dear friend, you had need be very watchful here, for not only your sins, but a dependance upon your duties may ruin you: for your trusting in your fancied righteousness to satisfy God's infinite justice and thus obtain pardon, is putting Christ out of his office, and making a Saviour of your own duties and performances.

5. *The reigning love of the world* is a sure evidence of an unconverted heart. Mark x. 22. John ii. 15. This sin often lurks under a fair covert of forward profession. Such a power of deceit is there in it, that oftentimes when every one else can see the man's worldly-mindedness, he sees it not himself; but has so many excuses and pretences for his eagerness after the world, that he blinds his own eyes, and perishes in his self-deceit.

6. *Resentment against those who are thought to have injured them.* Too many, that would wish to be esteemed religious, bear malice in their hearts, and return evil for evil, directly against the rule of the Gospel, the pattern of Christ, and the nature of God. Such persons are in the gall of bitterness, and a state of misery.

Reader, doth nothing of this touch you? Oh! search and search again; take your heart solemnly to task. Wo is from God against you, if you be found under the power of wilful ignorance, resting in formality, trusting in yourself, drowned in worldly mindedness, or envenomed with malice : if either of these is your case, you are verily an unconverted person.

7. *Pride.* If you love the praise of men more than the praise of God, it is certain that you are yet in your sins. If you have never seen and groaned under the pride of your heart, you are a rebel against God, instead of being converted to him. This sin reigns in the hearts of many that know it not, and are utter strangers to themselves. John ix. 40.

8. *The prevailing love of pleasure.* 2 Tim. iii. 4. The person that liveth in pleasure is dead to God while he liveth, saith the Lord. This therefore is a very black mark. If you will give the flesh its liberty, if you will pamper and please it, instead of denying and restraining it;

if your delight is in gratifying your senses, whatever appearance you may have of religion, you serve not the Lord
Jesus, but are certainly an unconverted person. Rom. xvi.
18. Rom. viii. 8. They that are Christ's have crucified
the flesh, and are careful to keep it under as their enemy.
Gal. v. 24.

Carnal security, or a presumptuous hope that you are in
a safe state already, is very dangerous. Many cry peace
and safety, when destruction is coming suddenly upon
them. Many are willing, and even resolved upon the
slightest grounds, to cherish in themselves a hope that their
condition is good, and therefore do not seek for any change,
and so perish in their sins. Are you at peace? Upon
what grounds? Is it a scripture peace? Do you bear upon your soul, in your temper, in your conversation, and
your course of life, the distinguishing marks of a true believer? If not, fear this peace more than any trouble ;
and know, that a carnal peace does generally prove the
most mortal enemy of the soul.

And now, conscience, do thine office. Speak out, and
speak home to him that heareth or readeth these lines.
If thou findest any of these marks upon him, thou must
pronounce him utterly unclean, utterly unholy. Take not
a lie into thy mouth, speak not peace to him, to whom
God speaketh no peace. Let not lust bribe thee, let not
self-love nor carnal prejudice blind thee. Is the man
converted, or is he not? Does he allow himself in any
way of sin, or does he not? Does he truly love, and prize,
and please, and delight in God above all things, or not?
Has he been thoroughly convinced of sin, been taken off
from all dependance on himself, and brought off from his
sins to give himself up entirely to the Lord Jesus Christ?
Or dost thou find him to this day under the power of ignorance, or in the mire of profaneness, or a stranger to prayer,
a stranger to God, a neglecter of the word, and a lover of
this present world? Dost thou find his heart fermented
with malice, or burning with lust, or going after his covet-
ousness? Then set him aside; his portion is not with the
saints ; he must be born again, he must be converted, and
made a new creature in Christ Jesus, or else he cannot enter heaven.

So unspeakably dreadful is the case of every unconverted soul, that it might well be thought, if one could but get
men convinced that they are yet unregenerate, the work
were done. But such a spirit of sloth and slumber possesses the unsanctified, that though they are convinced that
they are unconverted, yet they are still careless, and,
through worldly cares and business, or through sensual
pleasures, corrupt lusts, and inordinate affections, the voice
of conscience is drowned, and sinners go no farther than
some cold wishes and general purposes of repenting and
amending. I would therefore endeavour to show you,

IV. *The misery of an unconverted state.*

1. *The infinite God* is against you while you are unregenerate and unrenewed. And, believe it, it will be
found a most dreadful thing to fall into the hands of the
living God, when his wrath is justly incensed against you.
There is no friend like God, and there is no enemy like
God. As much as heaven is above the earth, so much
more dreadful will it be to fall into the hands of the living,
angry God, than into any earthly trouble. God himself
will ere long be your tormentor; your destruction shall
come from the presence of the Lord. Tophet, the place
of punishment, is deep and large; the pile thereof is fire
and much wood; and the wrath of the Lord like a river
of brimstone doth kindle it. Isaiah xxx. 33. And if God
be against you, who shall be for you? If a man sin against
the Lord, who shall entreat for him? 1 Sam. ii. 25. Sinner, does it not go like a dagger to thine heart, to hear that
God is thine enemy? Oh! whither wilt thou go? Where
wilt thou shelter thyself? There is no hope for thee, unless thou layest down thy weapons, and suest for pardon,
and gettest Christ to stand thy friend, and make thy peace.
Mercy and salvation are now offered to you through him.
But if thou wilt not forsake thy sins, and turn thoroughly
unto the Lord, the wrath of God abideth on thee, and he
proclaims himself to be against thee by Ezekiel, "Therefore, thus saith the Lord God, behold I, even I, am against
thee."

2. *All his attributes are against thee.* His *Justice* is like a
flaming sword unsheathed against thee. "If I whet my
glittering sword, and my hand take hold on judgment, I

will render vengeance to mine adversaries, and will reward them that hate me ; I will make mine arrows drunk
with blood." Deut. xxxii. 41, 42. Divine justice is very
strict ; it must have satisfaction to the utmost farthing ; it
denounces indignation and wrath, tribulation and anguish,
upon every soul that doeth evil. It curses "every one
that continueth not in all things which are written in the
book of the Law to do them." Gal. iii. 10. The justice
of God to the unpardoned sinner, that hath a sense of his
misery, is more terrible than the sight of the Judge and
bench to the robber, or of the irons and gibbet to the guilty murderer. When infinite Justice sits upon life or death,
Oh ! what dreadful work does it make with the wretched
sinner ! "Bind him hand and foot, and cast him into outer
darkness, there shall be weeping and gnashing of teeth."
Matt. xxii. 13. "Depart from me, depart, ye cursed,
into everlasting fire." Matt. xxv. 41. Think of it, by
this severe justice thou must be tried; and as the Lord
God liveth, this killing sentence thou shalt hear denounced
against thyself, unless thou be speedily converted, and
born again.

The *Power* of the infinitely great God is against thee.
The glory of his power will be displayed in the wonderful
"destruction of them that know not God, and that obey not
the Gospel." 2 Thes. i. 8, 9. He will make his power
known in them, by the greatness of the sufferings he will
inflict upon them. Rom. ix. 22. It were better thou hadst
all the world up in arms against thee, than to have the almighty power of God engaged against thee. There is no
escaping his hands, no breaking his prison. The thunder
of his power who can understand ! Unhappy man that
shall understand it by feeling it ! "If he will contend with
him, he cannot answer him one of a thousand." "He is
mighty in strength." "Who hath hardened himself against
him, and hath prospered ?" And wilt thou rise in opposition to such an almighty enemy ? O consider this, "ye that
forget God, lest he tear you in pieces and there be none to
deliver you." Psalm l. 22. "Wo to him that striveth
with his Maker." Isaiah xlv. 9.

Know, O sinner, to thy terror, that all the attributes of
the infinite God are bound together, as in an oath, to de-

2 *

stroy thee Heb. iii. 18. And what wilt thou do? Whither wilt thou flee? If the all seeing God can find thee out, thou shalt not escape. If the true and faithful God will save his oath, thou must perish; and if the almighty God hath power to torment thee, thou shalt be perfectly miserable both in body and soul, to all eternity, unless thou dost turn to the Lord with full purpose of heart.

The *guilt* of all your sins lies like a mountain upon you. You feel it not, yet this it is which seals your misery upon you. However light you may make of sin now, you will one day find that the guilt of unpardoned sin is an intolerably heavy burden. Oh! what work did it make with the God-Man Christ Jesus. It pressed the very blood out of his veins, and made his heart in the midst of his body even like melting wax. And if it did this in the green tree, in the holy and innocent Saviour, what will it do in the dry, in you, a sinful, guilty rebel against God, who are like dry stubble, fit fuel for the devouring fire? Oh! consider your case in time. Can you think of that threat without trembling, "Ye shall die in your sins?" John viii. 21. Oh! it were better for you to die in a jail, or a dungeon, than to die in your sins. If death, as it will certainly take away all your comforts, would but take away all your sins too, it would be a great relief—But your sins will all follow you, when all your friends leave you, and all your worldly enjoyments are taken from you. Your sins will not die with you, as a prisoner's other debts will; but they will all go to judgment with you, there to be your accusers; and they will all go to hell with you, there to be your tormentors. Oh! look over your debts in time, then; how much you are in the books of every one of God's commandments; how every one of his holy laws is ready to arrest you. Consider, then, what will you do, when they shall altogether fall upon you? Hold open the eyes of your conscience to think deeply of this, until you despair of yourself, and are driven to Christ, and made to fly for refuge to lay hold of the hope set before you.

Your raging *lusts* do miserably enslave you. While you are unconverted you are the very servants of sin, it reigns over you, and holds you under its dominion, till you are brought within the bonds of God's covenant Now there is no tyrant so cruel as sin. Would it not pierce a man's heart, to see a number of poor creatures drudging and toiling, and all to carry faggots and fuel for their own burning? Yet this is the employment of the drudges of sin. Even when they bless themselves in their unrighteous gains ; while they sing and swell in pleasures, they are but treasuring up wrath and vengeance for themselves, and, as it were, casting in oil, to make the flame rage the more fiercely. Who would serve such a master, whose work is drudgery, and whose wages is death and destruction? Rom. vi. 23.

Though *conscience* is now asleep, yet when death and judgment shall bring you to your right senses, then you will feel the raging smart and anguish of every wound. The convinced sinner is a sensible instance of the miserable bondage of sin. Conscience flies upon him, and tells him what the end of these things will be, and yet such a slave is he to his lusts, that he still goes on headlong, with his eyes open, till he falls into infinite and everlasting destruction. What thinkest thou, O man, O woman, of being in hell to all eternity? "Can thy heart endure, or can thy hands be strong, in the day that I shall deal with thee, saith the Lord of Hosts?" Canst thou dwell with the devouring fire ? when thy whole body and soul shall be as perfectly possessed by God's burning vengeance, as the fiery sparkling iron when heated in the fiercest forge? Thou art even crushed and ready to wish thyself dead, under the weight of his finger ; how then wilt thou bear the weight of his Almighty arm? How wilt thou endure, when immortality shall be thy misery, and to die the death of a brute, and be swallowed up in the gulf of annihilation, would be such a happiness as a whole eternity of wishes and an ocean of tears shall never purchase ? Now thou canst put off the evil day, and canst laugh and be merry, and forget the terrors of the Lord ; but how wilt thou endure when God shall cast thee into torments, and make thee lie down in endless sorrow? In a word, when " the smoke of thy torments shall ascend up for ever and ever," and thou shalt have no rest, day nor night, no peace in thy conscience, no ease in thy bones ; but thou shalt be an execration, and an astonishment, and a curse, and a reproach for evermore.

O sinner! stop immediately, and consider this dreadfu condition. Do not blind thine own eyes; do not wilfully deceive thyself; see thy deplorable misery, while thou mayest prevent it : think what it is to be a vessel of wrath, into which the Lord will be pouring out his tormenting fury while he has a being.

And is this true indeed ? Is this thy misery ? Yes, it is as true as that there is a God. It is better to open thine eyes and see it now, while thou mayest remedy it, than to blind and harden thyself, till (to thy eternal sorrow) thou shalt feel what thou wouldst not believe. And since it is true, dost thou mean to loiter and linger in such a case as this ? O let me knock up, and awaken this sleeper. Who dwells within the walls of this flesh? Is there a soul here, a rational understanding? Art thou a reasonable soul, and yet so far brutified as to forget thyself to be immortal, and fancy thyself to be as the beasts that perish? O unhappy soul, that wast the glory of man, the companion of angels, and the image of God? that wast God's representative in the world, and hadst the supremacy among all the creatures upon earth, and the dominion over thy Maker's works here ! Art thou now become a slave to sense, a servant to so base an idol as thine appetites, for no higher felicity than to heap together a little earth, no more suitable to thy spiritual, immortal nature, than sticks and dirt ? O why dost thou not think where thou shalt be for ever ? Death is at hand, the Judge is even at the door. Yet a very little while, and time shall be no longer. And wilt thou run the hazard of continuing in such a state, in which if thou shouldst be overtaken, thou wilt be irrecoverably miserable ?

Arise at once and take thy flight; there is but one door that thou mayest flee by, and that is the strait door of conversion. Unless thou dost unfeignedly turn from all thy sins, and come unto Jesus Christ, and take him for thy Prophet, Priest, and King, and walk in him in holiness and newness of life, as the Lord liveth it is not more certain that thou art now out of hell, than that thou shalt without fail be in it, but a few days or nights hence. O do not then contend with God. Repent and be converted, so none of this shall come upon thee. "Seek the Lord while he may be found, and call upon him while he is near. Let the wicked forsake his way, and the unrighteous man his thoughts, and let him return unto the Lord, and he will have mercy upon him : and to our God, for he will abundantly pardon." Isaiah lv. 6, 7.

Although what has been already said of the necessity of conversion, and of the miseries of the unconverted, might be thought sufficient to induce any considerate person to resolve upon immediately turning to God, yet knowing that the heart of fallen man is deceitful above all things, and desperately wicked, I find it necessary to add thereto,

V. Some farther *Motives to Conversion.*

The God that made you, does most graciously invite you. His most kind and merciful *nature* encourages you to come to him. He is full of compassion, and gracious, long suffering and plenteous in mercy. Psalm lxxxvi 15. This is a great argument to persuade sinners to return : "Turn to the Lord your God ; for he is gracious and merciful, slow to anger, and of great kindness." His encouraging *calls and promises* do invite you. Oh, what an earnest suitor is mercy to you ? How lovingly does it call after you ! "Return, backsliding sinner, saith the Lord, and I will not cause mine anger to fall upon you, for I am merciful, saith the Lord, and I will not keep anger for ever, only acknowledge thine iniquity. Turn, O backsliding soul, and I will heal your backslidings." O melting, gracious words ! And is not your heart broken by them ? O that to-day you would hear and obey his voice !

It is to be added for your encouragement ; if you will now return to the Lord, he will immediately settle unspeakable *privileges* upon you. He will redeem you from the power of all your most inveterate sins, from the power of the Devil, and deliver you from this present evil world. Prosperity shall not hurt you, and adversity shall work for your good. He will in due time redeem you from the power of the grave, and make the king of terrors a messenger of peace to you. He will save you from the arrest of the law, and turn the curse into a blessing to you. He will not only deliver you from misery, but bestow upon you the richest blessings. He will bestow himself upon you : he will be a friend and a father unto you ; he will be a sun

and a shield; in a word, he will be a God unto you. And
what can be said more ? As to your body, he will with-
hold from you no manner of thing that is good, that is necessary and expedient for you. And as to your soul, he will
pardon your sins, accept your person and services, hear
and answer your prayers, give you a title to glory, and
make you meet for it by his grace and Spirit.

VI. If you are now made sensible of your need of Conversion, and are become anxious for it, I conclude all with
adding some *Directions* in order to your obtaining it.

1. *Get a proper sense of your sins.* Till you are weary
and heavy laden, and sick of sin, you will not come to
Christ for ease and cure. Meditate then upon the number
of your sins. David's heart failed him when he thought
of this. Look backward . where was ever the place, when
was ever the time, in which you have not sinned ? Look
inward : what part or power can you find in body or soul,
but what is poisoned with sin ? What duty did you ever
perform, which was not corrupted with iniquity ? O how
great is the number of your sins ! For your soul's sake,
my friend, no longer make light of sin ; O study the nature
of sin, till your heart is inclined to fear and loathe it. Meditate on the aggravations of your particular sins, how you
have sinned against all God's warnings, and corrections,
and mercies ; against all your own prayers and promises,
and resolutions, and vows, and covenants of duty and obedience. Charge your heart home with these things, till
it blushes for shame, and you no longer think well of yourself. Meditate on what your sin deserves. It cries to heaven for vengeance against you.—Its due wages is death.
It brings the curse of God upon your soul and body The
least sinful word or thought lays you under the infinite
wrath of the Almighty God. O then what a load of wrath,
what a weight of curses, what a horrible store of vengeance have all the millions of your sins deserved ? Above
all sins, fix your mind upon the sin of your nature Study
how deep, how lasting, how universal your original pollution is. It is this which makes you backward to all good,
and prone to all evil. This hath brought blindness and
pride, prejudice and unbelief, into your heart ; enmity, in
constancy and obstinacy into your will ; disorder and ir

regularity into your affections; and insensibility and unfaithfulness into your conscience : in a word, this hath put every power of your soul out of order; and has made it, instead of a habitation of holiness, a very sink of iniquity. This has defiled and perverted all your members, and turned them into instruments of unrighteousness and servants of sin. And will you any longer talk of your good heart? O never leave meditating on the desperate contagion of your original corruption, till with the deepest shame and sorrow you smite upon your breast, and with Job, abhor yourself, and repent in dust and ashes

2. *Strive to affect your heart with a deep sense of your present misery.* Remember when you lie down, for ought you know, you may awake in torments; and remember when you rise up, that perhaps before the next night you may make your bed in hell. And are you willing to continue in such a fearful case? to stand tottering upon the brink of the bottomless pit, and to live at the mercy of every accident and disease that may send you into everlasting misery?—Suppose you saw a condemned person hanging over Nebuchadnezzar's burning fiery furnace by nothing but a thread, which was ready to break every moment, would not your heart tremble for him? Thou art the man. This is your very case, if you are yet unconverted. And what if the thread of your life should break? (and you know not but it may the next night, or the next moment) where would you be then? whither would you drop? O study then your misery, till your heart cries out for Christ, as earnestly as ever a drowning man did for help, or a wounded man for a surgeon.

3. Settle it deeply in your mind, that *you cannot possibly recover yourself.* Think not that your praying, reading, hearing, confessing, or even amending will work the cure. You must indeed *attend* upon these, but if you *depend* on them you will perish. You are lost and ruined for ever, if you continue hoping to escape by any other than Christ, who is "the way, the truth, and the life."

4. In the strength of the Lord immediately *renounce all your sins.* If you will yield yourself to the practice of any sin, you will be undone. It is in vain that you hope for salvation from Christ, except you depart from iniquity

Forsake your sins, or else you cannot possibly find mercy. Prov. xxviii. 13. Give up the traitor, or you can have no peace with God. Keep not Delilah on your lap ; you must either part with your sins, or with your soul ; spare but one sin, and God will not spare you. Never make excuses ; your sins must die, or you must die for them. If you allow of one sin, though but a little, a secret one ; though you plead necessity ; and have many excuses for it ; the life of your soul must go for the life of that sin—and will it not be dearly bought ?

5. Receive the Lord Jesus Christ, as your Prophet, Priest, and King, as proposed to you in the Gospel. O my friend, you have by sin destroyed yourself, but Jesus is able, and willing, and ready, even now, to help you. He freely offers to save you. I testify unto you therefore this day, that if you perish, it is not because there was not a Saviour provided for you, nor salvation offered to you, but because, like the Jews, you preferred a murderer before your Saviour, and your lusts before the Lord Jesus Christ. Though your sins be ever so many, and ever so great, and of ever so long continuance, yet if you do not wretchedly neglect the offer of God now made to you, you shall be pardoned. you shall be saved ; for the mouth of the Lord God hath spoken it. If you perish, it is because you would not come to Christ for salvation. But Oh ! for your soul's sake, be wise at length, and be prevailed on to accept him as your All, your Saviour from sin and from misery. In the name of the Lord, and in the strength of his Spirit, renouncing all confidence in the flesh, yield yourself up to him unreservedly ; solemnly join yourself unto the Lord in covenant to be wholly his, and glorify him in your body, and in your spirit, which are his ; so shall it be well with you in time, and well with you to all eternity, through the same Jesus Christ, our only Lord and Saviour. Amen and Amen.

LITTLE HENRY

AND

HIS BEARER.

BY MRS. SHERWOOD.

When he was only ten months old, he used to put his arms round his neck, and kiss him.—*See page* 3.

PUBLISHED BY THE

AMERICAN TRACT SOCIETY,

NO. 150 NASSAU-STREET, NEW-YORK.

D. Fanshaw, *Printer.*

LITTLE HENRY

AND

HIS BEARER.

——◆——

HENRY L——— was born at Dinapore in the East
Indies. His father was an officer in the company's service,
and was killed in attacking a mud fort belonging to a petty
Rajah, a few months after the birth of his son. His mother
also died before he was a year old. Thus little Henry was
left an orphan when he was a very little babe; but his
dying mother, when taking her last farewell of him, lifted
up her eyes to heaven, and said, "O God, I leave my
fatherless child with thee, claiming thy promise in all
humility, yet in full confidence that my babe will never be
left destitute; for in thee the fatherless find mercy." The
promise to which she alluded is to be found in Jeremiah,
xlix. 11. "Leave thy fatherless children, I will preserve
them alive; and let thy widows trust in me."

As soon as Henry's mamma was dead, a lady, who lived
at that time in a large brick house near the river between
Patna and Dinapore, came and took little Henry, and gave
him a room in her house, giving strict orders to her servants
to provide him with every thing that he wanted. But as
she was one of those fine ladies who will give their money
(when they have any to spare) for the relief of distress,
but have no idea how it is possible for any one to bestow
all his goods to feed the poor, and yet want *charity*; she
thought that when she had received the child, and given
her orders to her servants, she had done all that was necessary for him. She would not afterwards suffer Henry to
give her the least trouble, nor would she endure the smallest
inconvenience on his account; and thus the poor child,
being very small and unable to make known his wants,
might have been cruelly neglected, had it not been for the

attention of a *bearer*,* who had lived many years with his papa, and had taken care of Henry, from the day that he was born.

When he was a very little babe, Boosy (for that was the *bearer's* name) attended him night and day, warmed his pap, rocked his cot, dressed and undressed and washed him, and did every thing for him as tenderly as if he had been his own child. The first word that little Henry tried to say, was *Boosy;* and when he was only ten months old he used to put his arms round his neck and kiss him, or stroke his swarthy cheek with his little delicate hand.

When Henry was carried to the lady's house, Boosy went with him; and for some years the little child had no other friend than his *bearer.* Boosy never left his little master, except for two hours in the twenty-four, when he went to get his food. At night he slept on his mat at the foot of the child's cot; and whenever Henry called, he was up in a moment, and had milk or toast-and-water ready to give him to drink. Early in the morning, before sunrise, he took him out in a little carriage which was provided for him, or carried him in his arms round the garden. When he brought him in, he bathed him and dressed him, and gave him his breakfast, and put him in his cot to sleep: and all the day long he played with him; sometimes carrying him in his arms, or on his back, and sometimes letting him walk, or roll upon the carpet. Every body who came to the house noticed the kindness of Boosy to the child, and he got a present from many people for his goodness to Henry.

When Henry was two years old, he had a dreadful illness; so alarming indeed was it, that for many days it was thought he would die. He had afterwards a very severe illness when he was four years old, for he was never a very healthy child. During the height of these sicknesses, his *bearer* never left him; nor would he take any rest, even by the side of his bed, till he thought the danger was over.

These things considered, it cannot be a matter of wonder that this little boy, as he grew older, should love his *bearer* more than all the world besides; for his *bearer* was his

* A servant whose work it is to assist in carrying a palanquin, in which persons in India ride, as in a carriage; but who is frequently employed to take care of children

best friend, no one else taking any thought about him. He
could not speak English, but he could talk with Boosy in
his language as fast as possible ; and he knew every word,
good or bad, which the natives spoke. He used to sit
in the *varandah** between his *bearer's* knees and chew
paun† and eat *bazar*‡ sweetmeats. He wore no shoes nor
stockings ; but was dressed in *pangammahs*,§ and had silver
bangles‖ on his ancles. No one could have told by his
behaviour or manner of speaking that he was not a native ;
but his pretty light hair and blue eyes at once showed his
parentage.

Thus his life passed till he was five years and a half
old : for the lady in whose house he lived (although he
was taught to call her mamma) paid him no kind of attention ; and it never occurred to her that it was right to give
him any religious instructions. He used to see his *bearer*
and the other natives performing worship, and carrying
about their wooden gods ; and he knew that his mamma
sometimes went to church at Dinapore : so he believed
that there were a great many gods, and that the God that
his mamma went to pray to at Dinapore was no better than
the gods of wood and stone and clay which his *bearer*
worshipped. He also believed that the River Ganges was
a goddess, and called Gunga ; and that the water of the
river would take away sins. He believed, too, that the
Mussulmans were as good as Christians, for his mamma's
servant had told him so. Besides these, he was taught by
the servants many other things which a little boy should
not know : but the servants, being Heathen, could not be
expected to teach him any thing better ; and therefore they
were not so much to be blamed as the lady who had undertaken the charge of Henry, who might have been ashamed
to leave the child of christian parents under the care of
such persons.

When Henry was five years old, a young lady, who was
just arrived from England, came to reside for a while with
his mamma. She was the daughter of a worthy clergyman
in England, and had received from him a religious education. She had brought with her from home, a box of

---

* An open gallery or passage.　† An intoxicating mixture of
opium, sugar, &c.　‡ A market.　§ Trowsers.　‖ Ornaments
generally worn around the wrists and ancles.

Bibles, and some pretty little children's books and pictures.
When she saw poor little Henry sitting in the passage-way,
as his custom was, between his *bearer's* knees, with many
other native servants surrounding him, she loved him, and
was very sorry for him; for, indeed, it is a dreadful thing
for little children to be left among people who know not
God. So she took some of the prettiest coloured pictures
she had and spread them on the floor of the room, the
door of which happened to open into the passage-way
near the place where the little boy usually sat. When
Henry peeped in and saw the pictures, he was tempted by
them to come into the room; but at first he would not
venture in without his *bearer*. Afterwards, when he got
more accustomed to the lady, he was contented that his
bearer should sit at the door, while he went in. And at
last he quite lost all fear, and would go in by himself:
nay, he never was more happy than when he was with
this lady; for she tried every means to gain his love, in
order that she might lead him to receive such instructions
as the time of her intended stay with his mamma would
allow her to give him.

She was very sorry when she found that he could not
speak English; however, she was resolved not to be
checked by this difficulty. She taught him many English
words by showing him things represented in the coloured
pictures, telling him their English names; so that in a
short time he could ask for any thing he wanted in English.
She then taught him his letters in one of the little books
she had brought from home, and from his letters she proceeded to spelling: and so diligent was she, that before
he was six years old he could spell any words, however
difficult, and could speak English quite readily.

While this young lady was taking pains, from day to day,
to teach little Henry to read, she endeavoured by word of
mouth to make him acquainted with such parts of the
christian religion as even the youngest ought to know; and
without the knowledge of which no one can be a christian;
and she did not like to wait until Henry could read his
Bible, before she would instruct him in subjects of so
much importance.

The first lesson of this kind which she strove to teach
him, was, that there was only *one true God*, and that he

made all things, namely, the glorious heaven, to which
those persons go who have been made the children of
God on earth; and the dreadful hell, prepared for those
who die in their sins; the world, and all things in it; the
sun, the moon, the stars, and all the heavenly bodies. And
she was going to teach him the following words from
Colossians, i. 16. "For by him were all things created,
that are in heaven and that are in earth"—but no sooner
did little Henry understand that she meant to teach him
that there is but *one* God, than he got very angry, and told
her that she did not speak *a true word;* for his mamma had
a God, and his *bearer* had a god, and there were a great
many gods: and he ran out into the passage-way and told
his *bearer* what the young lady had said; and down he sat
between his *bearer's* knees, and would not come to her
again that day, although she brought out her finest pictures
and a new book, on purpose to tempt him.

The young lady did not fail to pray very earnestly for
little Henry that night, when she was withdrawn to her
room, and her door shut. And her Father, on whom she
called in secret, heard her prayer: for the next day little
Henry came smiling into the room, having quite forgotten
his fit of ill-humour; and she was now enabled to talk to
him with advantage on the same subject. And she made
him kneel down, and pray to God to give him sense to
understand the truth. She had also provided herself with
one of the Hindoo gods made of baked earth; and she
bade him look at it, and examine it well: she then threw
it down upon the floor, and it was broken into an hundred
pieces. Then she said, "Henry, what can this god do
for you? it cannot help itself. Call to it, and ask it to get
up. You see it cannot move."—And that day the little
boy was convinced by her arguments.

The next discourse which the young lady had with
Henry was upon the nature of God. She taught him that
God is a Spirit: that he is every where; that he can do
every thing; that he can see every thing; that he can
hear every thing; that he knows even the inmost thoughts
of our hearts; that he loves that which is good, and hates
that which is evil; that he never had a beginning, and
never would have an end.

Henry now began to take pleasure in hearing of God,

and asked many questions about him. He next learned that God made the world in six days, and rested from his work on the seventh : and that he made man and woman innocent at first. He then was taught how our fore-father Adam was tempted, with Eve his wife, to eat the forbidden fruit : and how by this means sin entering into the world, and the nature of Adam becoming sinful, all we his children, being born in his likeness, are sinful also.

Henry here asked what sin is ?

" Sin, my child," answered the lady, " is whatever displeases God. If your mamma were to esire you to come into her room, or to do something for her, and you were to refuse, would she not have reason to be displeased with you ?"

" Yes ; I suppose so."

" Or if you ask Boosy to fan you, or to carry you in your palanquin, and Boosy does something quite different; or if you desire him to carry you one way, and he carries you another; would he not do wrong ?"

" Yes, to be sure."

" Well, then; whatever you do contrary to the commands of God displeases him, and is sin."

But the lady still found great difficulty in making Henry understand the nature of sin : for he had been so neglected, that he did not know right from wrong. He did not consider a lie as sinful : nor feel ashamed of stealing, unless it was found out. He thought also, that if any body hurt him, it was right to hurt them in return. After several days, however, she made the subject clear to him; and then further explained how sin has corrupted all our hearts : and she made him repeat the following words till he could say them quite well : " The Lord looked down from heaven upon the children of men, to see if there were any that did understand, and seek God. They are all gone aside, they are altogether become filthy; there is none that doeth good, no, not one." Psalm xiv. 2, 3.

She next made the little boy understand that eternal · death, or everlasting punishment, is the consequence of sin ; and he soon could repeat two or three verses to prove this : one was, " The unrighteous shall not inherit the kingdom of God; (1 Cor. vi. 9.) and another, " They shall look upon the carcasses of the men that have transgressed against me; for their worm shall not die, neither shall their fire be quenched; and they shall be an abhorring unto all flesh." Isaiah, lxvi. 24.

And now the lady had brought Henry to know that he and all the world were sinners, and that the punishment of sin is eternal death; and that it was not in his power to save himself, nor of any thing on the earth to wash him from his sins; and she had brought him several times to ask her with great earnestness what he must do to be saved, and how his sins could be forgiven, and his heart freed from evil tempers—her next lesson, therefore, was to explain to him what the Lord Jesus Christ had done for him; how "God was manifest in the flesh, justified in the Spirit, seen of angels, preached unto the Gentiles, believed on in the world, received up into glory;" (1 Tim. iii. 16.) and how "we have redemption through his blood, he having made peace for us through the blood of his cross." Colossians, i. 14. 20.

Little Henry was particularly pleased whenever he heard of our Saviour: and, by divine grace, his heart seemed to be wonderfully filled with love for his Redeemer; and he was so afraid of offending him, that he became careful of every word he said, and of every thing he did; and he was always asking the young lady if *this* was right? and if *that* was right? and if God would be angry with him if he did *this* or *that*? so that in a short time his whole behaviour was altered. He never said a bad word, and was vexed when he heard any other person do it. He spoke mildly and civilly to every body. He would return the *salam** of the poorest *coolie*† in the market. If any body had given him a *rupee*,‡ he would not spend it in sweetmeats or play-things; but he would change it into *pice*‖ and give it to the *fakeers*§ who were blind or lame, or such as seemed to be in real distress, as far as it would go.

One day Henry came into the lady's room, and found her opening a box of books. "Come," said she, "Henry, help me to unpack these books, and to carry them to my bookcase." Now while they were thus busy, and little Henry much pleased to think that he could make himself

---

* Health; Salutation.   † A kind of low cast of men, who have no trade, but work at any kind of employment.   ‡ A coin.   ‖ Pence.
§ Beggars; a religious order of men, something like monks or dervises.

useful, the lady said, "These books have different kinds of covers, and some are larger than others, but they all contain the same words, and are the book of God. If you read one of these books, and keep the sayings written in it, it will bring you to heaven; it will bring you to where your beloved Redeemer is; to the throne of the Lamb of God, who was slain for your sins."

"O! I wish," said Henry, "that I had one of these books! I will give you all my playthings, ma'am, and my little carriage, for one of them."

The lady smiled, and said, "No, my dear, keep your playthings, and your little carriage too: you shall have any one of these books you like best."

Henry thanked the lady with all his heart, and called Boosy in to give his advice whether he should choose a book with a purple morocco cover, or one with a red one. When he had fixed upon one, he begged a bit of silk of the lady, and carried it to the tailor to make him a bag for his new Bible: and that same evening he came to the lady to beg her to teach him to read it.

So that day he began: and he was several days over the first chapter of Genesis; but the next chapter was easier, and the next easier still; till very soon he was able to read any part of the Bible without hesitation.

With what joy and gratitude to God did the young lady see the effect of her pious labours! She had, in the space of a year and a half, brought a little orphan from the grossest state of heathen darkness and ignorance to a competent knowledge of those doctrines of the christian religion, which are chiefly necessary to salvation. She had put into his hand the book of God, and had taught him to read it: and God had, in an especial manner, answered all her prayers for the dear child.

The time was now coming on very fast, when she must leave little Henry; and the thoughts of this parting were very painful to her. Some days before she set out on her journey, she called him into her room, and questioned him concerning the things which she had taught him; directing him, as often as he could, to give his answers from the Bible. Her first question was, "How many Gods are there?"

HENRY. "There is one God; and there is none other but he." Mark, xii. 32.

LADY. Do we not believe that there are three Persons in this one God?

HENRY. "There are three that bear record in heaven; the Father, the Word, and the Holy Ghost: and these three are one." 1 John, v. 7.

LADY. What do you mean by the Word?

HENRY. The Word is the Lord Jesus Christ.

LADY. Do you know that from the Bible?

HENRY. Yes; for St. John says, in the first chapter of his Gospel, "In the beginning was the Word, and the Word was with God, and the Word was God. He was in the world, and the world was made by him, and the world knew him not."

LADY. Did God make man good at first?

HENRY. Yes; for in the first chapter of the Bible, the last verse, it is written, "God saw every thing that he had made, and behold, it was very good."

LADY. Are men very good now? Can you find me one person who deserves to be called good?

HENRY. I need not look into the Bible to answer that question. I need but just get into the *palanquin*, and go into the market, and show you the people there: I am sure I could not find one good person in all the market.

LADY. But I think, Henry, you might spare yourself the trouble of going into the market to see how bad human creatures are; could you not find proofs of that nearer home?

HENRY. What, our servants, you mean? Or, perhaps, the ladies in the hall with my mamma? They laughed at the Bible, at breakfast; I knew what they meant very well; and my mamma laughed, too: I am sure nobody can say that they are good.

LADY. No, my dear; those poor ladies are not good: it would be misleading you to say they are. But as we cannot make them better by speaking ill of them in their absence, it would be better not to mention them at all, unless it were in prayer to God that he would turn their hearts. But to return to my question—You need not go so far as the hall for an answer to it. There is a little boy in this very room, called Henry: can he be said to be a good boy? A very few months ago, that little boy used to tell lies every day: and only yesterday I saw him in a passion, because the coachman would not let him get on the back of one of the coach-horses; and I think, but I am not sure, that he gave the coachman a blow with his hand.

HENRY. I know it was very wicked: but I had no stick in my hand, and therefore I hope I did not hurt him. I hope God will give me grace never to do so again. I gave the coachman all that I had left of my *rupee*, this morning; and I told him I was very sorry.

LADY. I mentioned it, my dear, that you might know where to look for an answer to my question.

HENRY. Oh! I know that I am not good. I have done many, many naughty things, which nobody knows of; no, not even Boosy. And God only can know the naughtiness of my heart.

LADY. Then you think yourself a great sinner.

HENRY. A very great one.

LADY. Where do sinners go when they die?

HENRY. "The wicked shall be turned into hell, and all the nations that forget God." Psalm ix. 17.

LADY. If all the wicked people are turned into hell, how can you escape?

HENRY. If I believe on the Lord Jesus Christ, I shall be saved. Stay one moment and I will show the verse. "Believe on the Lord Jesus Christ, and thou shalt be saved." Acts, xvi. 31.

LADY. What! if you believe in the Lord Jesus Christ, shall you go to heaven with all your sins? Can sinful creatures be in heaven?

HENRY. No; to be sure not. God cannot live with sinners. He is "of purer eyes than to behold evil." Habakkuk, i. 13. But if I believe in the Lord Jesus Christ, He will take away my sin; for His "blood cleanseth from all sin;" (1 John, i. 7.) and he will give me a new heart, and make me a new creature, and I shall purify myself, as he is pure. 1 John, iii. 3.

Now the lady was pleased with little Henry's answers: and she thanked God in her heart for having so blessed her labours with the poor little boy. But she did not praise him, lest he should become proud: and she well knew that "God resisteth the proud, but giveth grace to the humble." James, iv. 6. So she refrained from commending him; but she said, "What do you mean, my dear, by being made quite new again?"

HENRY. Before I knew the Lord Jesus Christ, I used to think of nothing but naughty things. I loved myself more than anybody else. I loved eating fruit and sweetmeats; and was so greedy of them, that I would have told a hundred lies, I do think, for one mouthful of them. Then I was passionate and proud. I used to be so pleased when anybody bowed to me, and said, "Little master." And you cannot think how cruel I was to all kinds of little creatures I could get hold of, even the poor cock-roaches: I used to kill them just for my own pleasure. But now I do think my heart is beginning to change a little, I mean a very little, for I gave all my last sweetmeats to the sweeper's boy. But still I know that my heart is far from being clean yet; but God can make it white and clean when he pleases.

LADY. You must pray every day, and oftentimes in the day, and in the night, when you are awake, my dear child; that God will send his Holy Spirit into your heart, to make it clean and pure, and to lead and direct you in all you do. Blessed are those, my dear child, who love the Lord Jesus Christ: for unto them "the Spirit of truth" shall be revealed; and it "shall dwell with them, and be in them." John, xiv. 17.

She then shut the door of the room; and she and the little boy knelt down together, and prayed to God, that he would, for his dear Son's sake, "create a clean heart in" the child, "and renew a right spirit within him." Psalm li. 10. When the young lady arose from her knees, she kissed little Henry, and told him, not without many tears, that she must soon go away from him.

When Henry heard this news, for some moments he could not speak; at length he cried out, "What shall I do, when you are gone! I shall have nobody to speak to but my *bearer*, for my mamma does not love me; and I shall spend all my time with the natives. I shall never more hear anybody talk of God. Oh! I very much fear that I shall become wicked again."

"My poor child," said the lady, "do not doubt the power of God. When our Saviour was going to leave his disciples, he said, 'I will not leave you orphans;* I will

* The word is *orphans* in the original.

come to you.' John, xiv. 18. And do you think, my child, that after the blessed Lord God has made himself known unto you as a dear son, that he will leave you comfortless ? Think how good he was to call you from the paths of destruction, and from the way of hell. You knew not so much as his holy name, and were living altogether among the Heathen. It was by his providence that I came here ; that I remained here so long : that I loved you, and endeavoured to teach you ; and that I had a Bible to give you. 'Faithful is he,' my beloved child, 'who called you. He will preserve your whole spirit and soul and body blameless unto the coming of the Lord Jesus.' 1 Thess. v. 23, 24. She then sung a verse of a hymn to him ; which he often repeated, and would try to sing when she was far away from him.

> Jesus sought me when a stranger,
>   Wandering from the fold of God ;
> He, to save my soul from danger,
>   Interpos'd his precious blood.*

Now it would take more time than I have to spare, to repeat the several conversations which this young lady had with little Henry before she went away. He cried sadly the day she went. He followed her down to the river-side ; for she was going to Berhampore, where she was soon afterwards married to a very pious young man of the name of Baron.

Henry went on board the boat, to take leave of her. She kissed him many times before they parted ; and gave Boosy, who was with him, four pieces of money, that he might continue to behave well to his little master. The last words almost that she said to Henry were these, "You must try, my dear child, with the grace of God, to make Boosy a christian ; that he may be no longer numbered among the Heathen, but may be counted among the sons of God."

When the boat was ready to sail, little Henry took his last leave of the lady, and came on shore ; where he stood under the shade of a braminee fig-tree,† watching the boat

---

* Sung ♭ the tune of the Sicilian Mariner's Hymn.   † A tree that takes root downward from its branches.

as it sailed down the broad stream of the Ganges, till it was hidden by the winding shore. Then Boosy, taking him up in his arms, brought him back to his mamma's house: and from that time he was as much neglected as he had been before this good young lady came; with this difference only, (and that indeed was a blessing for which I doubt not he will thank God to all eternity,) that he was now able to read the book of God; whereas, before, he knew not even God's holy name.

Sometimes his mamma would let him eat his luncheon with her; but, as she always employed herself at table (when not actually eating) in smoking her *hookah,** and as most of her visiters did the same, the luncheon time was very stupid to the little boy; for instead of pleasant and useful discourse, there was in general nothing to be heard at these meals but the rattling of plates and knives and forks, the creaking of a large fan suspended from the ceiling; and the guggling of water in the pipe; except his mamma (which not unseldom happened) occasioned a little variety, by scolding the servants, and calling them names in their own language.

So poor little Henry found no better companion than his *bearer;* and he never was more pleased than when he was sitting by him in the gallery, reading his Bible to himself.

And now the young lady's last words returned to his mind, namely, "You must try to make Boosy a christian." But he did not know how to begin this work: it seemed to him, that the heart of poor Boosy could only be changed by the immediate interference of God; so fond was he of his wooden gods and foolish ceremonies, and so much was he afraid of offending his Confessor. And in this respect Henry judged rightly; for no one can come to God without the help of God; yet he has pointed out the means by which we must endeavour to bring our fellow-creatures to him; and we must, in faith and humility, use these means, praying for the divine blessing to render them effectual.

The first step which Henry took toward this work, was to pray for Boosy. After some thought, he made a prayer, which was much to this purpose: 'O Lord God, hear the

---

* A kind of pipe, the smoke of which is drawn through water, and the motion of the air through the water causes a bubbling noise.

humble prayer of a poor little sinful child. Give me power,
O God, for thy dear Son's sake, who died for us upon the
cross, to turn the heart of my poor *bearer* from his wooden
gods, and to lead him to the cross of Jesus Christ.' This
prayer he never failed to repeat every night, and many
times a day: and from time to time he used to talk to
Boosy, and repeat to him many things which the young
lady had taught him. But although Boosy heard him with
good humour, yet he did not seem to pay much heed to
what the child said, for he would argue to this purpose:
" There are many brooks and rivers of water, but they all
run into the sea at last; so there are a great many religions, but they all lead to heaven: there is the Mussul-
man's way to heaven, and the Hindoo's way, and the
Christian's way: and one way is as good as another." He
asserted also, that if he were to commit the greatest sin,
and were to go immediately afterwards and wash in the
Ganges, he should be quite innocent. And a great many
other foolish things he had to say to the same purpose, so
that he sometimes quite out-talked the child. But Henry
was so earnest in the cause he had undertaken, that
although he might be silenced at one time, yet he would
often, after having said his prayer, and consulted his Bible,
begin the attack again. He would sometimes get close to
him, and look in his face, and say, " Poor Boosy! Poor
Boosy! you are going the wrong way, and will not let me
set you right: there is but one way to heaven; our Saviour,
the Lord Jesus Christ, is *the way* to heaven, and " no man
cometh unto God but by him." John, xiv. 6. Then he
would try to explain who the Lord Jesus Christ is: how
he came down to the earth; that he took man's nature
upon him; suffered and died upon the cross for the sins of
men; was buried and rose again on the third day, and
ascended into heaven; and is now sitting at the right
hand of God, from whence he will come to judge the
quick and the dead.

In this manner the little boy proceeded from day to day,
but Boosy seemed to pay him little or no attention; nay,
he would sometimes laugh at him, and ask him why he
was so earnest about a thing of so little consequence!
However, to do Boosy justice, he never was ill-humoured
or disrespectful to his little master.

Now it happened, about this time, that Henry's mamma had occasion to go to Calcutta; and, as she went by water, she took Henry and his *bearer* in the boat with her. Henry had not been well, and she thought the change of air might do him good. It was at the end of the rains; at that season of the year when India is most green and beautiful, although not most healthy. When the boat came to anchor in the evening, Henry used to take a walk with his *bearer;* and sometimes they would ramble among the fields and villages for more than a mile from the river. Henry had all his life been confined to one spot; so, you may be sure, he was well pleased to see so many different countries, and asked many questions about the things which he saw. And often during these rambles, he used to have an argument with Boosy concerning the great Creator of all things : and Henry would say to his *bearer*, that the Great God, who made all things, could not be like the gods which he believed in, which, according to his accounts of them, were more wicked and foolish than the worst men.

Once, in particular; it was in one of those lovely places near the Rajamahal hills ; Henry and his *bearer* went to walk. Henry's mamma had during the day been very cross to him, and the poor little fellow did not feel well, although he did not complain; but he was glad when he got out of the boat. The sun was just setting, and a cool breeze blew over the water, with which the little boy being refreshed, climbed without difficulty to the top of a little hill where was a tomb. Here they sat down : and Henry could not but admire the beautiful prospect which was before them. On their left hand was the broad stream of the Ganges, winding round the curved shore, till it was lost behind the Rajamahal hills. The boat, gaily painted, anchored just below them, and with it many smaller boats, with thatched and sloping roofs. The boatmen and native servants, having finished their day's work, were preparing their food, in distinct parties, according to their several *casts,* upon the banks of the river; some grinding their spices, some lighting their little fires, some washing their brass vessels, and others sitting in a circle upon the ground smoking their cocoa-nut pipes. Before them, on the right hand, was a beautiful country abounding with corn-fields, *topes* of trees, thatched cottages with their little bamboo porches, plantain, and palm-trees; beyond which the Rajamahal hills were seen, some bare to their summits, and others covered with brush-wood, which even now afford a shelter to tigers, rhinoceroses and wild hogs.

Henry sat silent a long time. At last he said, "Boosy, this is a good country: that is, it would be a very good country, if the people were Christians. Then they would not be so idle as they now are; and they would agree together, and clear the brush-wood and build churches to worship God in. It will be pleasant to see the people, when they are Christians, all going on a Sabbath morning to some pretty church, built among those hills, and to see them in an evening sitting at the door of their houses reading the *shaster**—I do not mean *your* shaster, but *our* shaster—God's book."

Boosy answered, that he knew there would be a time when all the world would be of one religion, and when there would be no *cast;* but he did not know when that would be, and he was sure he should not live to see it.

"There is a country now," said Henry, "where there are no *casts;* and where we all shall be like dear brothers. It is a better country than this; there are no evil beasts; there is no more hunger, no more thirst; there the waters are sure; there the sun does not scorch by day, nor the moon smite by night. It is a country to which I sometimes think and hope I shall go very soon; I wish, Boosy, you would be persuaded either to go with me, or to follow me."

"What!" said Boosy, "is *little master* going to *England?*" And then he said he hoped not; for he could never follow him.

Henry then explained to him, that he did not mean England, but heaven. "Sometimes I think," said he, "when I feel the pain which I did this morning, that I shall not live long; I think I shall die soon, Boosy. O, I wish! I wish I could persuade you to love the Lord Jesus Christ!" And then Henry, getting up, went to Boosy, and sat down upon his knee, and begged him to be a christian. "Dear Boosy," said he, "good Boosy, do try

---

* The Hindoo religious books.

to be a christian." But poor little Henry's attempts were yet quite ineffectual.

In little more than a month's time from their leaving Dinapore, they reached Calcutta, and were received into the house of a worthy gentleman of the name of Smith.

When Henry's mamma was settled in Mr. Smith's house she found less inclination, if possible, than ever, to pay any attention to Henry. According to the custom of India, she must pay the first visit to all her acquaintance in Calcutta. Her dresses, too, having all been made at Dinapore, did not agree with the last European fashions which were come out: these were all to be altered, and new ones bought; and it was a good deal of trouble to direct the tailor to do this properly. Her hair was not dressed in the fashion: and her *ajah** was very stupid; it was many days before she could forget the old way and learn the new one. So poor Henry was quite forgotten in all this bustle; and although he was for several days very ill, and complained to his *bearer* that his side gave him great pain, yet his mamma never knew it.

Mr. and Mrs. Smith once or twice remarked, when they looked at Henry, that the child was very pale, and that his eyes were heavy: but his mamma answered, " O, it's nothing; the child is well enough; children in India, you know, have that look."

It happened one afternoon, as Mr. and Mrs. Smith and Henry's mamma were in the drawing-room after *luncheon*, while the ladies were giving their opinion upon a magazine which contained an account of the last European fashion of carriages and dresses, &c. (for I am sorry to say that Mrs. Smith, although she had the best example in her husband, had still to learn not to love the world,) Mr. Smith, half angry with them, and yet not knowing whether he should presume to give them a check, was walking up and down the room with rather a hasty step; when his eye, as he passed the door, caught little Henry sitting on the mat at the head of the stairs, between his *bearer's* knees, with his Bible in his hand. His back being turned towards the drawing-room door, Mr. Smith had an opportunity of observing what he was about, with-

*A waiting-maid.

out being seen : he accordingly stood still, and listened : and he heard the gentle voice of Henry, as he tried to interpret the sacred book to his *bearer* in the *bearer's* own language!

Mr. Smith at first could scarcely believe what he saw and heard; but, at last, being quite sure he was not dreaming, he turned hastily towards the ladies, exclaiming, "Twenty-five years have I been in India, and never have I seen anything like this.   Heaven be praised! truly it is written, 'Out of the mouths of babes and sucklings thou hast perfected praise.' Matt. xxi. 16.   For shame! for shame! Mrs. Smith, will you never lay aside your toys and gewgaws?   Do give me that book, and I will let the cook have it to light his fire with.—Here are two persons, who have been nearly fifty years in the world, sitting together talking of their finery and painted toys; while a little creature, who eight years ago had not breathed the breath of life, is endeavouring to impart divine knowledge to the heathen.   'But God hath chosen the foolish things of the world to confound the wise; and God hath chosen the weak things of the world to confound the things which are mighty'." 1 Cor. i. 27.

"My dear," cried Mrs. Smith, "surely you forget yourself!   What can you mean?   Toys and finery,—my dear, my dear, you are very rude!"

"Rude!" said Henry's mamma, "rude indeed!   Mr. Smith,—and pray, Sir, what do you mean by saying, 'Fifty years?'   Do you suppose that I am fifty years old? —Extraordinary indeed!"

"I beg pardon," said Mr. Smith.   "I did not mean to offend—but there is that little boy trying to explain the Bible to his *bearer*."

"But, surely," said Henry's mamma, "you do not think that I am fifty years of age?—you are mistaken by twenty years."

Mrs. Smith. O! my dear madam, you must excuse my husband—Whenever he is a little angry with me, he tells *me* that I am getting old.   But I am so used to it that I never mind it.

Mr. Smith. Well, my dear; leave me, if you please, to speak for myself.   I am not a man that disguises the truth.   Whether I speak or not, time runs on, death and eternity approach. I do not see why it should be a matter of politeness to throw dust into each other's eyes.—But enough of this, and too much. I want to know the meaning of what I but now saw; a little English child, seven years of age, endeavouring to explain the Bible to his bearer. I did not even know that the child could read.

"O," said Henry's mamma, "this matter is easily explained. I had a young lady at my house at Patna, some time since, who taught the child to read: for this I was obliged to her. But she was not satisfied with that alone! she made an enthusiast, a downright canting enthusiast of the boy. I never knew it till it was too late.

MR. SMITH. An enthusiast? What do you mean, madam?

"Indeed," said Henry's mamma, "the child has never been himself since.—Captain D—— of the —— native infantry, when they were quartered at Dinapore, used to have such sport with him! He taught him, when he was but two years old, to call the dogs and the horses, and to swear at the servants in English—But I shall offend Mr. Smith again," she added; "I suspect him a little of being a religious enthusiast himself. Am I right, Mrs. Smith?" and she laughed at her own wit. But Mrs. Smith looked grave; and Mr. Smith lifted up his eyes to heaven, saying, "May God Almighty turn your heart!"

"O, Mr. Smith," said Henry's mamma, "you take the matter too seriously: I was only speaking in jest."

"I shall put that to the trial, madam," said Mr. Smith. "If you really feel no ill-will against religion, and people who call themselves religious, you will not refuse to let me consider Henry as my pupil while you remain in my house, which I hope will be as long as you can make it convenient. You have known me some years, (I will not say how many, lest you should be angry again,) and you will make allowances for my plain dealing."

"Well," said Henry's mamma, "we know you are an oddity; take your own way, and let me take mine." So she got up to dress for the evening airing on the course: and thus this strange conversation ended in good humour; for she was not, upon the whole, an ill-tempered woman.

The same evening, his mamma being gone out, Mr. Smith called Henry into his own room; and learned from him all that he could tell of his own history, and of the young lady who taught him to read his Bible, and had advised him to try to make Boosy a christian. I will relate to you the last part of this discourse which passed between Mr. Smith and Henry.

MR. SMITH. Do you think that Boosy's heart is at all turned toward God?

HENRY. No, I do not think that it is; although for the last half year I have been constantly talking to him about God; but he still will have it that his own idols are true gods.

MR. SMITH. It is almost dangerous, my dear little boy, for a child like you to dispute with a heathen: for although you are in the right, and he in the wrong, yet Satan, who is the father of lies, may put words into his mouth which may puzzle you; so that your faith may be shaken, while his remains unchanged.

HENRY. Oh! Sir, must I give up the hope of Boosy's being made a christian? Poor Boosy! he has taken care of me ever since I was born.

MR. SMITH. But suppose, my dear boy, that I could put you in a better way of converting Boosy: a safe way to yourself, and a better for him? Can Boosy read?

HENRY. Only a very little, I believe.

MR. SMITH. Then you must learn to read for him.

HENRY. How, Sir?

MR. SMITH. If I could get for you some of the most important chapters in the Bible, such as the first chapters of Genesis, which speak of the creation of the world and the fall of man, with the first promise of the Saviour, and some parts of the Gospel, translated into Boosy's language, would you try to learn to read them to him? I will teach you the letters, or characters as they are called, in which they will be written.

HENRY. O! I will learn them with joy.

MR. SMITH. Well, my boy; come every morning into my study, and I will teach you the Persian characters; for those are what will be used in the copy of the chapters I shall put into your hands. Sometime or other, the whole Bible will be translated in this manner.

HENRY. Will the words be Persian, Sir? I know Boosy does not understand Persian.

MR. SMITH. No, my dear; the words will be the same

as those you speak every day with the natives. When you
have as much of the Bible as I can get prepared for you
in this manner, you must read it to your bearer every day;
praying continually, that God will bless his holy word to
him. And never fear, my dear, but that the word of God
will do its work; 'for as the rain cometh down, and the
snow from heaven, and returneth not thither, but watereth
the earth, and maketh it bring forth and bud, that it may
give seed to the sower, and bread to the eater; so shall
my word be that goeth forth out of my mouth : it shall not
return unto me void; but it shall accomplish that which I
please, and it shall prosper in the thing whereto I sent it.'
Isaiah, lv. 10, 11. "But do not, my dear boy," added Mr.
Smith, "argue and dispute with your *bearer* about religion; you are not able.   Only read the Bible to him, and
pray for him continually; leaving the rest with God."

But not to make my story too long; while Henry's
mamma remained at Calcutta, which was more than a
year, Henry received a lesson every day from Mr. Smith
in his study; and Mr. Smith taught him the Persian characters, and provided him with so many chapters in the
Bible in Hindostanee as he could get properly prepared in
so short a time : these he had bound in red morocco, and
presented them to Henry, not without asking the blessing
of God upon them.

How delighted was Henry, when he received the book,
and found that he could read it easily!   He was in his
place on the mat between Boosy's knees in a minute, and
you might have heard him reading from one end of the
house to the other, for he could not contain himself for
joy.   Nor was he contented with reading himself, he must
make Boosy learn to read it too.   And this was brought
about much sooner than you would have supposed it possible : for as Henry learned the Persian letters from day to
day of Mr. Smith, he had been accustomed afterwards to
write them on a slate, and make Boosy copy them as they
sat together; and so by degrees he taught them all to his
bearer before he was in possession of the Hindostanee
copy of the chapters.

"Now, my boy," said Mr. Smith, "you are in the safe
way of giving instruction in an ancient path cast up by
God. Jeremiah, xviii. 15. Do not trust to the words of

your own wisdom, but to the word of God. Hold fast to
the Scripture, dear boy, and you will be safe. And be not
impatient, if the seed you sow should not spring up immediately : something tells me I shall see Boosy a christian
before I die : or if I do not see that day, he that outlives
me will."

Now the time arrived, when Henry's mamma was to
leave Calcutta. Indeed, she had stayed much longer there
than she had at first proposed; but there were so many
amusements going forward; so much gay company; so
many fashionable dresses to purchase; that she could not
find in her heart to leave them, although she was heartily
tired of Mr. Smith's company. She respected him indeed,
as an old friend and worthy man; but he had such particular ways, she said, that sometimes she had difficulty to
put up with them.

She proposed, as she went up the country, to stop at
Berhampore, to see Mrs. Baron. When Henry heard of
this, he was greatly pleased; yet when he came to take
leave of Mr. Smith, he cried very much.

As they went up the river, Henry took every opportunity of reading his chapters to his bearer, when his mamma
could not hear him: and he had many opportunities early
in the morning, and in the afternoon when his mamma was
asleep, as she always slept for an hour after luncheon.
And he proceeded very well indeed, Boosy daily improving, at least in the knowledge of the Bible, till the
weather suddenly becoming excessively hot, Henry was
seized with a return of violent pain in his side, and other
very bad symptoms. He became paler and thinner, and
could not eat. His mamma, having no company to divert
her, soon took notice of the change in the child, and began
to be frightened; and so was his *bearer.* So they made all
the haste they could to Berhampore, that they might procure advice from the doctors there, and get into a cool
house; for the boat was excessively hot : but notwithstanding all the haste which they made, there was a
great change in the poor little boy before they reached
Berhampore.

When they were come within a day's journey of the
place, they sent a servant forward to Mrs. Baron's; so
that, when the boat anchored next day near the canton-

ments, Mrs. Baron herself was waiting on the shore with *palanquins* ready to carry them to her house. As soon as the board was fixed from the boat to the bank of the river, she jumped out of her *palanquin*, and was in the boat in a minute, with little Henry in her arms. "O my dear boy!" she said, "my dear, dear boy!" She could say no more, so great was her joy; but when she looked at him and saw how very ill he appeared, her joy was presently damped; and she said, in her haste, to his mamma, "Dear madam, what is the matter with Henry? he looks very ill."

"Yes," said his mamma, "I am sorry to say that he is very ill: we must lose no time in getting advice for him."

"Do not cry, dear Mrs. Baron," said little Henry, seeing the tears running down her cheeks; "we must all die, you know we must, and death is very sweet to those who love the Lord Jesus Christ."

"O my child," said his mamma, "why do you talk of dying? You will live to be a judge yet, and we shall see you with seven silver sticks before your *palanquin*."

"I do not wish it, mamma," said Henry.

The more Mrs. Baron looked at Henry, the more she was affected. For some moments she could not speak, or command her feelings at all: but after having drank a little water she became more composed; and proposed that they should all immediatbly remove to her house. And when she found herself shut up in her *palanquin*, she prayed earnestly to God, that whether the sweet babe lived or died, he might not be taken from her in this sickness: but that she might, with the help of God, administer holy nourishment to his immortal soul, and comfort to his little weak body.

When they were arrived at Mrs. Baron's house, she caused Henry to be laid on a sofa by day in the sitting-room, and at night in a room close by her own. The chief surgeon of the station was immediately sent for, and every thing was done for little Henry that the tenderest love could suggest.

Berhampore happened at that time to be very full; and Henry's mamma, finding many of her old acquaintance there, was presently so deeply engaged in paying and receiving visits, that she seemed again almost entirely to forget Henry, and all her concern about him: comforting herself, when she was going to a great dinner or ball, that Mrs. Baron would be with him, and he would be well taken care of. But it is a poor excuse to make for our neglect of duty, and one that I fear will not stand at the day of judgment, to say that there are others that will do it as well for us.

Notwithstanding all the surgeon could do, and all the care of Mrs. Baron, Henry's illness increased upon him; and every one had reason to think that the dear little fellow's time on earth would soon come to an end. Mr. and Mrs. Baron were by turns his almost constant nurses: when one left him, the other generally took the place by his couch. It was very interesting to see a fine lively young man, like Mr. Baron, attending a little sick child; sometimes administering to him his food or medicine, and sometimes reading the Bible to him—but Mr. Baron feared God.

When Henry first came to Berhampore, he was able to take the air in an evening in a *palanquin,* and could walk about the house; and two or three times he read a chapter in the Hindostanee Bible to Boosy: but he was soon too weak to read, and his airings became shorter and shorter! He was at last obliged to give them quite up, and to take entirely to his couch and bed, where he remained until his death.

When Boosy saw that his little master's end was drawing on, he was very sorrowful, and could hardly be persuaded to leave him night or day, even to get his food. He did every thing he could think of to please him, and more, as he afterwards said, to please his dying master, than his God: he began to read his chapters with some diligence; and little Henry would lie on his couch, listening to Boosy as he read (imperfectly indeed) the word of God in Hindostanee. Often he would stop him to explain to him what he was reading; and very beautiful sometimes were the remarks which he made, and better suited to the understanding of his *bearer* than those of an older or more learned person would have been.

The last time that his *bearer* read to him, Mrs. Baron sitting by him, he suddenly stopped him, saying, " Ah, Boosy, if I had never read the Bible, and did not believe in it, what an unhappy creature should I now be! for in a

very short time I shall 'go down to the grave to come up
no more;' Job, vii. 9. that is, until my body is raised at the
last day. When I was out last, I saw a very pretty burying
ground with many trees about it. I knew that I should
soon lie there; I mean that my body would : but I was
not afraid, because I love my Lord Jesus Christ, and I know
that he will go down with me unto the grave; I shall sleep
with him, and 'I shall be satisfied when I awake with his
likeness'." Psalm, xvii. 15. He then turned to Mrs. Baron,
and said, "'I know that my Redeemer liveth, and that he
shall stand at the latter day upon the earth; and though
after my skin, worms destroy this body, yet in my flesh
shall I see God'. Job, xix. 25, 26. O kind Mrs. Baron!
who, when I was a poor sinful child, brought me to the
knowledge of my dear Redeemer; anointing me with sweet
ointment (even his precious blood) for my burial, which
was soon to follow."

"Dear child!" said Mrs. Baron, hardly able to preserve
her composure, "dear child! give the glory to God."

"Yes, I will glorify him for ever and ever," cried the
poor little boy; and raised himself up in his couch, joining
his small and taper fingers together: "yes, I will praise
him, I will love him. I was a grievous sinner; every imagination of the thought of my heart was evil continually!
I hated all good things; I hated even my Maker : but he
sought me out; he washed me from my sins in his own
blood; he gave me a new heart; he has clothed me with
the garments of salvation, and hath put on me the robe of
righteousness; he 'hath abolished death, and brought life
and immortality to light'." 2 Timothy, i. 10. Then turning
to his *bearer*, he said, "O my poor *bearer!* what will become
of you, 'if you neglect so great salvation'?" Hebrews, ii. 3.
"O Lord Jesus Christ," he added, "turn the heart of my
poor *bearer!*" This short prayer, which little Henry made
in Hindostanee, his *bearer* repeated, scarcely knowing what
he was doing. And this, as he afterwards told Mr. Smith,
was the first prayer he had ever made to the true God—
the first time he had ever called upon his holy name.

Having done speaking, little Henry laid his head down
on his pillow, and closed his eyes. His spirit was full of
joy indeed, but his flesh was weak; and he lay some hours
in a kind of slumber. When he awoke, he called Mrs.

Baron, and begged her to sing the verse of the hymn he loved so much,

"Jesus sought me," &c.

which she had taught him at Dinapore. He smiled while she was singing, but did not speak.

That same evening, Boosy being left alone with his little master, and seeing that he was wakeful and inclined to talk, said, " I have been thinking all day that I am a sinner, and always have been one; and I begin to believe that my sins are such as Gunga cannot wash away. I wish I could believe in the Lord Jesus Christ !"

When Henry heard this he strove to raise himself up, but was unable, on account of his extreme weakness; yet his eyes sparkled with joy : he endeavoured to speak, but could not; and at last he burst into tears. He soon, however, became more composed, and pointing to his *bearer* to sit down on the floor by his couch, he said, " Boosy, what you have now said makes me very happy : I am very, very happy to hear you call yourself a sinner, and such an one as Gunga cannot make clean. It is Jesus Christ who has made this known to you: he has called you to come unto him. Faithful is he that calleth you. I shall yet see you, my poor *bearer*, ' in the general assembly and church of the first born.' Hebrews, xii. 23. You were kind to me, when my own father and mother were dead. The first thing I can remember, is being carried by you to the *Mangoe tope*, near my mamma's house at Patna. Nobody loved me then but you : and could I go to heaven, and leave you behind me in the way to hell ? I could not bear to think of it ! Thank God ! I knew he would hear my prayer : but I thought that perhaps you would not begin to become a christian till I was gone. When I am dead, Boosy," added the little boy, " do you go to Mr. Smith at Calcutta. I cannot write to him, or else I would; but you shall take him one lock of my hair (I will get Mrs. Baron to cut it off and put it in a paper) and tell him that I sent it. You must say that Henry L———, that died at Berhampore, sent it with this request, that good Mr. Smith would take care of his poor *bearer*, when he has lost *cast* for becoming a christian." Boosy would have told Henry that he was not quite determined to be a christian, and that he could not think of losing *cast ;* but Henry, guessing what he was going to say, put his hand upon his mouth. " Stop ! stop !" he said : " do not say words which will make God angry, and which you will be sorry for by and by : for I know you will die a christian. God has begun a good work in you, and I am certain that he will finish it."

While Henry was talking to his *bearer* Mrs. Baron had come into the room : but, not wishing to interrupt him, she had stood behind his couch ; but now she came forward. As soon as he saw her, he begged her to take off his cap, and cut off some of his hair, as several of his friends wished for some. She thought that she would endeavour to comply with his request. But when she took off his cap, and his beautiful hair fell about his pale, sweet face ; when she considered how soon the time would be when the eye that hath seen him shall see him no more ; she could not restrain her feelings ; but throwing down the scissors, and putting her arm round him, " O my child ! my dear, dear child !" she said, " I cannot bear it ! I cannot part with you yet !"

The poor little boy was affected : but he gently reproved her, saying, " ' If you love me you will rejoice because I go to my Father'." John, xiv. 28.

There was a considerable change in the child during the night : and all the next day till evening he lay in a kind of slumber : and when he was roused to take his medicine or nourishment, he seemed not to know where he was, or who was with him. In the evening he suddenly revived, and asked for his mamma. He had seldom asked for her before. She was in the house, for she was not so hardhearted (thoughtless as she was) as to go into gay company at this time, when the child's death might be hourly expected. She trembled much when she heard that he asked for her. She was conscious, perhaps, that she had not fulfilled her duty to him. He received her affectionately when she went up to his bedside, and begged that every body would go out of the room, saying that he had something very particular to speak about. He talked to her for some time, but nobody knows the particulars of their conversation : though it is believed that the care of her immortal soul was the subject of the last discourse which this dear little boy held with her. She came out of his room with her eyes swelled with crying, and his little well-worn Bible in her hand, (which he had probably given her, as it always lay on the bed by him,) and shutting herself in her room, she remained without seeing any one, till the news was brought that all was over. From that time she never gave her mind so entirely to the world as she had formerly done; but became a more serious character, and daily read little Henry's Bible.

But now to return to little Henry. As there are but few persons who love to meditate upon the scenes of death, and too many are only able to view the gloomy side of them, instead of following, by the eye of faith, the glorious progress of the departing saint; I will hasten to the end of my story. The next day, at twelve o'clock, being Sunday, he was delivered from this evil world, and received into glory. His passage was calm, although not without some mortal pangs. "May we die the death of the righteous, and may our last end be like his." Num. xxiii. 10.

Mr. and Mrs. Baron and his *bearer* attended him to the last moment, and Mr. Baron followed him to the grave.

Sometime after his death his mamma caused a monument to be built over his grave, on which was inscribed his name, Henry L******, and his age, which at the time of his death was eight years and seven months. Underneath was a part of his favourite verse, from 1st Thessalonians, v. altering only one word; "faithful is he that called *me*." And afterwards was added, by desire of Mr. Smith, this verse, from James, v. 20. "He which converteth a sinner from the error of his way, shall save a soul from death, and shall hide a multitude of sins."

When I first visited Berhampore, I went to see little Henry's monument. It was then white and fair, and the inscription very plain; but I am told that the damp of the climate has so defaced the inscription, and blackened the whole monument, that it cannot be distinguished from the tombs which surround it. But this is of little consequence, as all who remember Henry L——— have long ago left Berhampore; and we are assured, that this dear child has himself received "an inheritance that fadeth not away." 1 Pet. i. 4. "The world passeth away, and the lust thereof: but he that doeth the will of God abideth for ever." 1 John, ii. 17.

Every person who reads this story will, I think, be anxious to know what became of Boosy. Immediately after the funeral of his little *master*, having received his wages, with a handsome present, he carried the lock of hair, which Mrs. Baron sealed up carefully, with a letter from her to Mr. Smith. He was received into Mr. Smith's family, and removed with him to a distant part of India; where shortly after, he renounced *cast*, and declared himself a christian. After due examination, he was baptized; and continued till his death (which happened not long after) a sincere christian. It was on the occasion of the baptism of Boosy, to whom the christian name of *John* was given, that the last verse was added to the monument of little Henry.

From Mrs. Baron and Mr. Smith I gathered most of the anecdotes relative to the history of Henry L———.

Little children in India, remember Henry L———, and "go, and do likewise." Luke, x. 37. For "they that be wise shall shine as the brightness of the firmament: and they that turn many to righteousness, as the stars for ever and ever." Daniel, xii. 3.

LITTLE CHILDREN IN AMERICA,

Think on Henry L———, and *go and do likewise.* He was born among ignorant heathen, those who worshipped the rivers, the stones, and the images they had made. You live in a christian land, where the true God, He who dwells in the heavens, and who knows every thing you say and do, is adored. Little Henry was an orphan; he had a kind friend to watch over and protect him; a compassionate stranger informed him about religion and the way to heaven, and gave him a Bible, the book of God. You have parents and instructers to tell you of right and wrong, how to love God and keep his commandments, and you are early taught to read his word. Did then this little child hearken to what was told him, and read God's holy book? Did he strive also to cause his poor bearer to leave his false gods and turn from them to love and serve the one only true God? When therefore your parents and friends would restrain you from what is wrong, and prompt you to the exercise of what is right; when they would urge upon you the necessity of religion, and of reading that book which contains the words of eternal life; or whensoever you yourselves have an opportunity of reproving others around you, who are living without God in the world, and who regard not his holy commandments, think how Henry L——— would have done, and *go and do likewise.*

My young friends, Henry was only one of the many destitute children in that heathen land. Thousands are there now, who have no kind lady to instruct them, and who I fear will never be thus favoured, and hear of Christ and God. You perceive what pleasure it gave him to be told of these things, and how glad he was to receive a Bible. Think what he would have done, and how dreadful must have been his situation, when sick and dying, had he not met with the compassionate lady.

Now you have heard of *Missionaries.* These are pious and benevolent persons, who leave their beloved friends and their native shores to go to those distant countries, and carry Bibles to such poor children as little Henry, and tell them about religion. Should you not like to send a Bible to those destitute children? or to do something to let them know that there is a God? Suppose you were in little Henry's country, and some kind persons should send one to instruct you and bring you good books; would you not feel very grateful to them?

You are small now, and much is not to be expected of you. But remember, should every one do but little, yet, in the whole, much would be done. There are those who are willing to leave their country to make known to the heathen the existence of God, and the way of salvation by his Son Jesus Christ, and convey to them his holy word; and they wait only for means to enable them to go. Let then every one, who, in reading this little Tract, felt pity toward Henry in his forsaken state, and rejoiced when he found a friend to instruct and comfort him, do something toward sending them.

Remember also, dear children, that although you are now young and dependant upon others, you are daily growing older. Your parents and friends will soon be gone, and you will stand in their places; property will be at your own disposal, and you will have the direction of whatever concerns the church and your country. In after life, therefore, whenever any measure is proposed for the benefit of the heathen; whenever your assistance is asked to promote in any way this important cause; think how little Henry L——— of Dinapore would have done, and *go and do likewise.* Verily, I say unto you, you shall not lose your reward.

☞ An incidental confirmation of this narrative, from Mr. Money, an English gentleman, late a resident in India, may be found on the cover.

TRUE PROPHECIES.

See page 9

EVERY person is eager to know what shall happen to himself and to his connexions in future, and what events shall occur in the world; and there are many events of a most interesting and important nature, which any wise man may foretell. I shall therefore endeavour to look into futurity, for the purpose of stating what shall befall some of the readers of this Tract.

I see a person whom God in his providence has blest with a good constitution, good health, and a comfortable subsistence in life. Such a person's circumstances are almost enviable; for he is exempted from the cares of riches and the troubles of poverty. But I see that this person is thankless for the good which he enjoys; he seldom bows his knees before God, morning or evening; he never thinks it worth his while to reverence God's Sabbath, or to obey his commands, by attending on public religious worship. Providence has blest him with a kind of independence in the world, and he foolishly and wickedly lives as if he were independent of God himself.

I have, therefore, to prophesy to thee, O man, that safe, quiet, easy and independent as thy circumstances seem to be, if thou livest and actest as thou hast done, thou mayest expect a sad reverse, when it shall please God to deal righteously with thee. What saith the Scriptures? "Man knoweth not his time; as the fishes are taken in an evil net, and as the birds are caught in the snare, so are the sons of men snared in an evil time, when it falleth suddenly upon them." Eccles. ix. 12. *Thy* evil time may soon come. Thou art ensnaring thyself by thine ingratitude and disobedience to God, who hath given thee so many blessings; and if thou goest on to provoke him, he may even "curse thy blessings;"—thy change may be sudden, and thy destruction terrible! "Give glory, therefore, to the Lord thy God," by fearing and serving him, "before he cause darkness, and before thy feet stumble upon the dark mountains; and while thou lookest for light, he turn it into the shadow of death." Jeremiah, xiii. 16.

Who is this that I see coming out of the ale-house, with his face red, not as it ought to be, with shame, but with drunkenness? His confused head is utterly unfit for any business; his tottering steps are directed toward another ale-house; and hour after hour will pass, before he enters his own habitation, that he may there sleep away his intemperance! Poor man! his pockets are empty; he will be unable to work to-morrow, and his habit of drinking will make him more and more averse to honest labour!

Without any hazard of mistake, I have a prophecy concerning this man : That if he continue in this shameful and awful course, he will soon bring his family to poverty, and himself to the grave! Ah! has the sight of his wife and children in tears for his misconduct, no effect on him? Have their sad forebodings, and their fears of speedy ruin, often, very often expressed, made no impression on his mind? Does the prospect of a jail and of an opening grave for himself, and of the workhouse for his wife and children, bring upon him no misgivings that his case is desperate, no repentance, no reformation of conduct? Let him hear, therefore, what the Scriptures say: "The drunkard and

the glutton *shall* come to poverty." "At the last," drunkenness "biteth like a serpent, and stingeth like an adder !"
Prov. xxiii. 21—32. "Be not deceived, drunkards shall
not inherit the kingdom of God." 1 Cor. vi. 9, 10. This
is a description of thy case; and this must be thy portion,
O drunkard, unless thou repent.

This is the Sabbath. The laws of God and the laws of
the land ordain that it be kept holy ; and various places
are opened for the worship of God, and the instruction
and gratification of all who love his service and obey his
commands. But, with great pain, I see a number of children playing in the streets and in the fields, and hear them
shouting and revelling, in a manner disgraceful to themselves and their parents, and dishonourable to Jesus Christ,
who is "Lord of the Sabbath."

I have a prophecy that concerns both them and their parents. If these children be not restrained from such evil
courses ; if their parents do not set them a pious example;
if they be not sent, or do not accompany their parents, to
public worship ; and if they attend no Sabbath-school that
may be in the neighbourhood, I see nothing but guilt and
misery before them in the present life : and oh, what must
be their portion in the life to come ! *That child*, it is likely,
will be a drunken, idle fellow, and will bring his father and
his mother to shame. *That other* may be a thief; and his
parents may live to see him come to the gallows ! "He
may be the grief of his father, and bitterness to the mother
who bare him." Prov. xvii. 25. Another of them may provoke the special anger of God, for the daring abuse of his
own day, and the neglect of his own worship. For, " God
is angry with the wicked every day ;" (Psalm vii. 11.) but if
on his own day, his special and merciful commands are slighted and despised, it may be expected that he will "break
such rebels with a rod of iron, and dash them in pieces like
a potter's vessel." Psalm ii. 9. Be wise and obedient,
therefore, ye children, and repent, lest God suddenly take
you away with a stroke ; lest ye live not out half your days;
lest ye be destroyed for the iniquity of your childhood and
youth ! And ye parents, instruct your children, and set before them a good example, and they shall give you rest.
Prov. xxix. 17. Otherwise, " your eyes shall see their destruction, when they drink of the wrath of the Almighty."

That man and that woman are greatly alarmed at the idea of spirits and apparitions; they dread to be alone, or to go through the church-yard, in the dark; the whispering of the evening breeze, and the rustling of the shaking leaf, startle them with terror.

Ah! I can prophesy to these, respecting what they should fear; though, with regard to spirits and apparitions, they have nothing to fear. They have reason to be afraid; for God is not in all their thoughts, nor acknowledged in all their ways; they never think of being disembodied spirits themselves, and how they will be able to stand before him who is the "God of the spirits of all flesh;" they are afraid of hearing or seeing any thing from the world of spirits; because they know it would bring nothing but terror to them. A spirit from the place of torment might tell them, "Soon thou must become like one of us!" And a spirit from heaven might say, "Between us and you there will be a great gulf fixed." I therefore counsel thee to dismiss all groundless fears and apprehensions, and to reverence and fear Him "who is able to destroy both body and soul in hell." Matt. x. 28. Endeavour to obtain just thoughts of his majesty, power, and glory. Betake thyself to his favour and mercy, through Jesus Christ; commit thy body and soul into his gracious hands; consider thyself always in his presence "who compasseth thy path and thy lying down, and is acquainted with all thy ways." Pslam cxxxix. 3. Love, serve, and glorify him; and he will give his angels charge to keep thee in all thy ways; and when thy body shall return to the dust, they will bear thy spirit to the innumerable company of angels, and to the spirits of the just made perfect, in the heavenly world, where thou wilt be happy with them for ever.

I see in that man's house a Bible covered with dust; and which, I fear, has not been used for a great length of time.

I have a prophecy concerning thee, O man, from that Book which thou treatest with so much contempt. "Whoso despiseth *the word* shall be destroyed." Prov. xii. 13. "He that turneth away his ear from hearing the law, even his prayer shall be abomination." Prov. xxviii. 9. God has written *to thee* the wondrous things of his law, and the gracious declarations and promises of his Gospel. He has spoken to thee by Patriarchs, Prophets, and Apostles; and directly from heaven by his Son. He has counselled thee, reproved thee, warned thee, and invited thee; but all in vain. By thy conduct thou "puttest all these things from thee, and judgest thyself unworthy of eternal life." There remaineth, therefore, for thee, while thou continuest thus to think and act, nothing but eternal death! For, God's word shall not return unto him void; it shall not be frustrated by thy contempt and disobedience; thou shalt be judged by it at the last day; and every threatening contained in it will be executed upon thy guilty and miserable soul for ever! Oh then, search the Scriptures; for they contain the words of eternal life; they testify of Jesus, the Saviour of sinners; they point out the way of mercy through him, and they are able to make thee wise unto salvation.

But who is that person with such a demure countenance, and, in appearance, of a very different character from any I have yet described? He says his prayers every morning and evening, and goes to church, or meeting, every Sabbath. This *is well;* and he takes care to let every body know it : this *were well* too, if **he** intended to excite others to do good by his example; but he does it that he may obtain the praise of men, and that he may gratify his spiritual pride, by setting himself so much above the level of his neighbours. He thanks God that he is not as other men are: his meaning is, that he is not *naturally* so bad as other men; and also, that he has made himself a great deal better than they are. He has no confessions to make to God of the depravity of his nature, the deceitfulness of his heart, or any wickedness of his life. He does not feel it necessary to do this; and is even above doing it: this would make him appear to be no better than some of his neighbours, who, in his estimation, are notorious sinners. It suits his views and dispositions better, to tell God how good he is, and what good he does; and thus to make it an act of justice in God to notice and reward such a righteous and meritorious person as he thinks himself to be.

For this person I have a sure prophecy! "Thine heart is not right in the sight of God!" Thy sentiments, the pride of thy heart, and the self-righteousness of thy soul, oppose themselves to the free "grace of God," by which alone thou

canst be saved, and to the very purpose for which Christ
came into the world; for he came "to seek and to save those
that are lost." "Except thy righteousness exceed that of
the Scribes and Pharisees, thou canst, in no wise, enter into the kingdom of heaven." Matt. v. 20. I tell thee, from
the mouth of our Saviour himself, that the poor sinner,
whose sense of depravity and guilt was so great "that he
would not lift up so much as his eyes unto heaven, but
smote upon his breast, saying, God be merciful to me a sinner,"—even this man returned from prayer, to his house,
justified, rather than the self-righteous Pharisee : such as
thou seemest to be. "For every one that exalteth himself,
shall be abased; and he that humbleth himself, shall be exalted." Luke, xviii. 9—14. Except, therefore, thou come
to God as a poor, guilty, miserable, but repenting sinner,
to be saved by his grace and mercy alone, through Jesus
Christ, and to be sanctified by the Holy Spirit, thou wilt
finally fall into dreadful and eternal condemnation. Consider this; and may God give thee understanding in all things!

I see a man, who, although he possesses a rational, intelligent, accountable and immortal spirit, and is endowed
with powers and capacities for exercising himself in love
and obedience to God in the present state, and for perfect
holiness and happiness in the world to come; yet he is in-
sensible of the infinite value of his soul; of the condition
into which it has been brought by depravity and guilt; of
the tender mercy of God in the gift of Jesus Christ, for the
redemption and salvation of sinners; and of the necessity
of conversion to God, by the influence of the Holy Spirit.
I see him active and intelligent in all concerns of a worldly
nature; but ignorant, indolent, and even dead, with regard
to the knowledge of God revealed in his word; to the life
of God, to be enjoyed in the soul; and to that cheerful and
constant obedience which should be exhibited in his conduct. In this man it is spiritually, "as if the pulse of life
stood still;" but 'tis an "awful pause—prophetic of an end!"

How long it may please God to permit such a person to
live on the bounty of his providence, while he is both in-
sensible and ungrateful; to have the word of God in his
hands, and the means and ordinances of grace to enjoy,
while he derives no true knowledge from the former, and

utterly neglects the latter; or how long this fatal stillness of
soul may continue, unattended by evident tokens of divine
displeasure—I cannot say. But I can truly prophesy, that,
sooner or later, the time *will come*, when, unless this person is mercifully alarmed, and effectually quickened, by the
Word and Spirit of God, he will experience a most awful
change; and, instead of apparent ease, comfort, and enjoyment, will feel exquisite pain, sorrow, and anguish. The
immortality of his soul; his accountableness to God, as his
Maker and Judge; the depravity and guilt of his nature;
the mercy of God, in the redemption of sinners by Jesus
Christ; the gracious invitations and the awful threatenings of the word of God, and the necessity of conversion to
God by the influence of the Holy Spirit—all these, and
many more essential and eternal truths, will be impressed
on his mind, with a conviction which it will not be possible to evade, and with terror which he will not be able to endure. The providence of God may also begin to frown upon
him: God may look at him, and trouble him; so that he
may be forced to say, Let me flee from the face of the Lord,
for he is fighting against me. Exod. xiv. 25. Let such a
man, therefore, remember his ways and his doings, wherein
he hath sinned, and loathe himself in his own sight, for all
the evils which he hath committed. Ezek. xx. 43. And
when, by self-examination, by reading the word of God, and
by humble and earnest prayer, he is enlightened to see his
danger, and influenced to seek for an interest in the salvation of Christ, let him present himself as "a living sacrifice, holy and acceptable to God." Let him be no longer
" conformed to this world, but be transformed by the renewing of his mind; that he may prove what is that good, and
acceptable, and perfect will of God." Rom. xii. 1, 2.

Look at that man: with what self-complacency and confidence he is giving his opinion to the company who are
listening to him, on a sermon which they have just heard
respecting *conversion* and *the new birth*. How full he is of
levity and profane ridicule; and how earnestly he is endeavouring to excite these unsuitable and unholy dispositions in those who are hearing him! I pity and am shocked at this person in my very heart. He is throwing about
fire-brands, arrows, and death, quite in sport. He is deceiv-

ed himself, in a concern on which his eternal happiness depends; and he is endeavouring to seal this awful deception on others.

I have, therefore, a most awful prophecy concerning such a deluded and wicked man. "Verily, verily," saith Jesus Christ himself, "except a man *be born again*, he cannot see the kingdom of God." John, iii. 3. "If a man," saith St. Paul, "be in Christ, he is a *new creature*." 1 Cor. v. 17. If thou be a man that believest the word of God, here is surely enough to satisfy thee, that thou must be either converted or condemned; that thou must be born again, or be excluded from the kingdom of heaven; and these sacred declarations ought to excite thee to the most earnest and serious examination of thy state in the sight of God. But, I can truly tell thee, that the reason why thou wilt not believe, with thy heart, these declarations of Scripture, is, that thy depraved and sinful dispositions are utterly averse to the holiness of the state which conversion and regeneration plainly describe; and thou art thinking of God as if he were such a one as thyself; as if he had no greater hatred to sin, or love to holiness, than thou hast; and as if he would punish the guilty no further than they themselves would pronounce reasonable. I prophesy to thee, that thou art calling thy Maker to the bar of thine own judgment; that thou art presuming thyself to be wiser and more righteous than he is; that thou art disbelieving the truth of God's word, which plainly shows thee thy depravity and guilt; that thou art despising and rejecting the only means of thy recovery to the favour and image of God, and for the salvation of thy soul. I assuredly tell thee, that in *misunderstanding and misrepresenting* the doctrines which Jesus Christ taught, when he said, "except ye be converted, and be born again, ye cannot see or enter into the kingdom of God," thou art awfully deceiving thyself; that, in *disbelieving* these momentous truths, thou art rejecting his divine authority; sinning greatly against God; and ruining thy own soul. I therefore earnestly advise thee to lay these things to heart; to read God's holy word, with ardent prayer for the teaching of his blessed Spirit, to humble thyself before him; and to desist from the levity and ridicule which thou art so fond of exercising on subjects connected with Divine truth, and with the salvation of thy soul; lest thou be numbered with those miserable victims to whom it will be said, " Behold, ye despisers, and wonder, and perish!" Acts, xiii. 41.

At the door of that mansion I perceive the carriages are waiting, which have brought physicians to consult on the diseased and dangerous case of its rich but dying inhabitant! I have formerly seen the door, and even the street, crowded with the equipage of visiters, who have assembled in this house to partake of the splendid entertainment; to surround the fascinating card-table; and to enjoy the festive dance. But, ah! what a reverse! The noise of the tabret and harp hath ceased, and where luxury and festivity lately revelled, all is now silent, gloomy, and sorrowful! This man had long tried what health and riches would procure, without religion : now he is to experience whether sickness and pain can be borne without it. He has lived without God, and without **hope**; now he is about to learn what it is to die without Divine support and consolation. I see him on his bed, restless, turning from side to side; earnestly soliciting the utmost efforts of medical skill; anxiously watching the countenances of his attendants; and, in the trembling balance of hope and fear, weighing every expression that falls from their lips! Ah! he has had his good things; but he has neither received them gratefully, nor used them wisely. He has walked in the ways of his heart, and in the sight of his eyes; and for all these things God is bringing him into judgment. He now would think it comparative happiness to be dispossessed of his wealth, if he could but obtain a continuance in life; but as *riches* have been misapplied and abused, and *life* has been forfeited by depravity and guilt, *both*, as to himself, will terminate together.

I prophesy of this state, that it is the most deplorable and awful into which a human being can possibly fall; that it is attended with feelings of agony which the heart of man cannot support; and that it is connected with forebodings of everlasting destruction, which implant in the conscience the never-dying worm, and enkindle in the soul the inextinguishable flame. " The Lord of this servant has come in a day when he looked not for him, and at an hour when he was not aware!" Luke, xii. 46. There has been no use of the means of grace; no prayer; no watchfulness; no holy obedience! The world has been his treasure, and has had his heart. He has put religion away from him, and has thus counted himself unworthy of eternal life. And now nothing remains but a " certain fearful looking for of judgment and fiery indignation." Heb. x. 27. Ah! that deep groan was the last effort of expiring agony! He has given up the ghost, and where is he! " O my soul, come not thou into their secret; unto their assembly, mine honour, be not thou united."

Another scene opens, a far different scene, in which the bitterness of domestic sorrow is corrected by the consolations of the Gospel. Around that bed stand the sorrowing wife and the weeping children of a poor, industrious, and pious cottager; who, while life is just expiring, has a smile of sweet serenity on his countenance, the language of humble confidence on his lips, and the sure hope and anticipation of heaven in his heart. The providence of God toward him, hardly ever exceeded, although it never fell short of, that promise, "Bread shall be given thee, and thy water shall be sure;"(Isa. xxxiii. 16.) but the grace of God made him rich in faith, and an heir of eternal glory. The world has scarcely looked upon him, or known him; but the eyes of the Lord, which are ever on the righteous, have been constantly fixed on him, and his ears have been opened to this poor man's prayer. Many have been the privations and afflictions which he has endured; and he has *appeared* to struggle with them, without any human interference to assist and support him, but He who hath said, " Blessed is the man that endureth temptation," hath laid underneath him everlasting arms; these have secretly, but effectually, strengthened and comforted him; and he is now brought to the very close of every mortal suffering. O what a contrast must there be between the *apparent* condition of this poor men, and his real state, in the sight of angels, " who are sent forth to minister to the heirs of salvation !"

I can, without any presumption, prophesy, that, as soon as his heart shall have heaved its last sigh, sorrow will have fled away for ever, and death will be swallowed up in victory! In the light of Divine truth, I see this poor, but pious man passing through the valley and shadow of death, under the guardian care of the great and good Shepherd, whose rod repels every enemy, and whose staff affords all needful comfort and support. I see him anxiously, but hopefully, standing on the verge of dissolution ; and, as the light of heaven breaks through the dark clouds of mortality, he beholds Jesus " standing at the right hand of God," ready to receive his departing soul. I see the afflicted widow, and the fatherless children, the only witnesses of the last struggle and the expiring sigh ;—but beyond this, I behold the immortal and happy spirit carried by angels into Abraham's bosom. I see the late humble, and almost unknown inhabitant of earth, recognised and welcomed by the spirits of the just made perfect, as a brother, and by angels as a friend. And, above all, I behold him entered into the eternal joy of his Divine Lord and Saviour !

" Let me die the death of the righteous ; and let my last end be like his."

I pass from the consideration of some of the various states and pursuits of mankind, to the earth itself, and to the whole of its inhabitants. I place myself, in imagination, on an eminence, from which I see all its beauty and glory, and all its vanity and guilt. I see the natural world exhibiting wonderful proofs of the wisdom, the power, and the goodness of God. The sun enlightens and invigorates it ; the rain refreshes and fertilizes it ; the cattle are grazing on a thousand hills ; the pastures are clothed with flocks ; the vallies are covered over with corn ; the great and wide sea is filled with things innumerable, both small and great ; and all is subservient to the support, the comfort, and the benefit of man. But, while with admiration I perceive all this goodness and glory, I am constrained to deplore the curse that sin hath entailed upon the whole creation, which evidently " groaneth and travaileth in pain, waiting to be delivered from this bondage of corruption." Rom. viii. 21, 22. I see the irrational creation suffering, in innumerable ways, by the exercise of man's wanton pleasures, or his merciless cruelty. I see storms and tempests bursting on the world, laying waste its fertility, and destroying its beauty. I see earthquakes, with dreadful convulsions, tearing the earth in pieces, and ingulphing its

inhabitants in sudden and awful ruin. I behold thou
sands of the human race hourly starting into life, and thousands hourly subjected to the just and immutable decree
of that glorious Being "who turneth man to destruction."
I see the world lying in darkness and in the shadow of
death, notwithstanding the light of truth, immortality, and
glory, which is revealed in the Gospel. I hear the joyful
sound of salvation by grace, proclaimed by the ambassadors of Christ; but I perceive men turning a deaf ear to
it; refusing all its merciful invitations, and despising all
its tremendous warnings. With such scenes before me,
my soul is affected and sorrowful ; yet I am revived at the
consideration, that God has a people in the world, whom
he hath called by his grace, and renewed by his Spirit;
and the language of my heart is, "Remember me, O Lord,
with the favour which thou bearest unto thy people; oh
visit me with thy salvation." Ps. cvi. 4. But what shall the
end of all these things be ? Will the earth endure for ever ?
Will day and night, seed-time and harvest, summer and
winter, never cease their gracious successions ? Will the
judgments of God on his rebellious creatures be always
confined to their present state of existence ? Are there no
gracious rewards for the righteous, and no just punishments
for the wicked, beyond the grave, to which they all are
hastening ?

 Hear, O Reader, my last and sure *prophecy !* It is taken
from the records of *inspired* truth ; it concerns thee inti-
mately and eternally ; lay it therefore to thine heart. "The
day of the Lord will come as a thief in the night; in
the which the heavens shall pass away with a great noise,
and the elements shall melt with fervent heat ; the earth
also, and the works that are therein, shall be burnt up."
2 Pet. iii. 10. "The hour is coming, in which all that are
in the graves shall hear his voice and shall come forth ;
they that have done good unto the resurrection of life, and
they that have done evil to the resurrection of damnation."
John, v. 28, 29. "And these shall go away into everlast
ing punishment, but the righteous into life eternal." Matt
xxv. 46.

BRAVERY AND HAPPY DEATH

OF

JAMES COVEY.

BY REV. JOHN GRIFFIN, OF PORTSEA, ENG.

MR. PRATT relates an affecting anecdote of a sailor on board the Venerable, the ship in which Admiral Duncan commanded the fleet in the action against the Dutch, off Camperdown. He received the account from Dr. Duncan, lord Duncan's chaplain and relative, who, in the action, assisted the surgeon and his mate in binding up the wounds, and amputating the limbs of the unfortunate sufferers. "A mariner," says the doctor, "of the name of Covey, was brought down to the surgery, deprived of both his legs: and it was necessary, some hours after, to amputate still higher." "I suppose," said Covey, with an oath, "these scissors will finish the business of the ball, master mate?" "Indeed, my brave fellow," cried the surgeon, "there is some fear of it." "Well, never mind," said Covey, "I have lost my legs, to be sure, and mayhap lose my life; but," continued he, with a dreadful oath, "we have beat the Dutch! we have beat the Dutch! so, I'll e'en have another cheer for it; Huzza! Huzza!"

K

Covey was a good seaman, and noticed among his shipmates for his intrepidity; but he was pre-eminent in sin, as
well as in courageous actions. About a fortnight before
the English fell in with the Dutch fleet, he was alarmed
by a dream, which made him tremble, and sometimes attempt to pray; but, not liking to retain God in his thoughts,
he endeavoured to obliterate these impressions by drinking, and blasphemous intercourse with the ship's company.
His efforts, however, were in vain. The thoughts of his
sins of God, and of death, harassed his mind day and night,
and filled him with gloomy forebodings of what awaited
him in this world and the next, till the sight of the Dutch
fleet, and their conversation with each other concerning
the heroic achievements they should perform, dispelled
the gloomy subject from his mind. As the two fleets were
coming into action, the noble Admiral, to save the lives of
his men, ordered them to lie flat on the deck, till, being
nearer the enemy, their firing might do the more execution. The Dutch ships at this time were pouring their
broadsides into the Venerable, as she passed down part of
the Dutch fleet, in order to break their line. Covey, having lost all the impressions of his former reflections, heap-
ed in rapid succession the most dreadful imprecations on
the eyes and limbs, and souls, of what he called his cow-
ardly shipmates, for lying down to avoid the balls of the
Dutch. He refused to obey the order, till, fearing the
authority of an officer not far from him, he in part complied,
by leaning over a cask which stood near, till the word of
command was given to fire. At the moment of rising, a
bar shot carried away one of his legs, and the greater part
of the other; but, so instantaneous was the stroke, though
he was sensible of something like a jar in his limbs, he
knew not that he had lost a leg till his stump came to the
deck, and he fell. His legs were amputated; and he was
soon put into Haslar Hospital, from which he at length
came out, capable of walking by means of two wooden
legs and two crutches; but his spirits were sorely dejected, from fearing that, as his sins had brought upon him the
judgments of God in the loss of his limbs, they would bring
it upon him in the loss of his reason and the loss of his soul.

Having heard of Orange-Street Chapel, Portsea, he
came on the first Sabbath evening after his leaving the
hospital. The text that evening was, "And they come to

Jesus, and see him that was possessed with the devil, and had the legion, sitting, and clothed, and in his right mind." Mark, v. 15. The minister represented this demoniac as a fit emblem of sinners in general, especially of those who live without rule and order, drunkards, blasphemers, and injurious to themselves and others; but his sitting at the feet of Jesus, clothed, and in his right mind, as an engaging representation of the sinner converted to God by the Gospel, made sensible of the evil of sin, the value of his soul, and the necessity of salvation through a crucified Redeemer; enjoying peace of mind, having fellowship with Christ and his people, submitting to the authority of the Scriptures, and receiving instructions from Christ, the friend of sinners. Covey listened with attention and surprise; wondered how the minister should know him among so many hundred people; or who could have told him his character and state of mind. His astonishment was still more increased, when he found him describe, as he thought, the whole of his life, and even his secret sins. He could not account for it, why a minister should make a sermon all about him, a poor, wooden-legged sailor. His sins being brought afresh to his mind, filled him with horrors tenfold more gloomy than before. Despair for some minutes took a firm hold on his spirits; and he thought he was now going out of his mind, should die, and be lost; till the minister declared Jesus Christ was as willing to save the vilest of sinners, as he was to relieve this poor creature possessed of the devil; and that a man was restored to his right mind, when he believed in him. He now began to think he had been out of his mind all his life, and that to love and serve Jesus Christ would be a restoration to his right senses again. He was now almost overwhelmed with pleasure. While hearing of the astonishing love of Jesus Christ to sinners, hope took the place of despair, and joy of grief and horror! Those eyes which had never shed a tear when he lost his legs, nor when the shattered parts of his limbs were amputated, now wept in copious streams, flowing from strong sensations of mingled joy and sorrow!

Some weeks after this, he called and related to me the whole of his history and experience; and, something more than twelve months after, he was received a member of our church, having given satisfactory evidence of being a genuine and consistent christian. A few weeks since, hearing he was ill, I went to visit him. When I entered his room, he said, "Come in, thou man of God! I have been longing to see you and tell you the happy state of my mind. I believe I shall soon die; but death has now no terrors in it. The sting of death is sin, but thanks be to God, he has given me the victory through Jesus Christ. I am going to heaven! O! what has Jesus done for me, one of the vilest sinners of the human race!" A little before he died, when he thought himself within a few hours of dissolution, he said, "I have often thought it was a hard thing to die, but now I find it a very easy thing to die. The presence of Christ makes it easy. The joy I feel from a sense of the love of God to sinners, from the thought of being with the Saviour, of being free from a sinful heart, and of enjoying the presence of God for ever, is more than I can express! O how different my thoughts of God, and of myself, and of another world, from what they were when I lost my limbs on board the Venerable! It was a precious loss to me! If I had not lost my legs, I should perhaps have lost my soul!" With elevated and clasped hands, and with eyes glistening with earnestness, through the tears which flowed down his face, he said, "O, my dear minister, I pray you, when I am dead, to preach a funeral sermon for a poor sailor; and tell others, especially sailors, who are as ignorant and wicked as I was, that since poor blaspheming Covey found mercy with God, through faith in the blood of Christ, none that seek it need to despair! You know better than I do what to say to them! But, O be in earnest with them: and may the Lord grant that my wicked neighbours and fellow sailors may find mercy, as well as Covey!" He said much more; but his last words were, "Hallelujah! Hallelujah!" If the anecdote of his fortitude and courage is worthy of being recorded, I think it due to Covey, and to the honour of Divine Grace, to relate his dying testimony in favour of the religion of Jesus Christ. I wish Dr. Duncan and Mr. Pratt had witnessed the last dying hours of this once ignorant and blasphemous sinner: they would have seen what a pleasing change was effected by the meek and efficacious grace of our compassionate Redeemer.

PUBLISHED BY THE AMERICAN TRACT SOCIETY.

TO THE SICK,

WHO ARE WITHOUT HOPE IN CHRIST.

———

MY DEAR FRIEND,

IF you are in Christ, and his Spirit is in you, I have nothing but peace to speak to you. But if it be otherwise; if you are yet in a carnal state, and were never born again, give me leave to speak plainly, though affectionately, while I set before you at once your sin and your remedy, and tell you what you must do to be saved.

Alas! did not you know, while in health, that you have an immortal soul, which must live in joy or misery for ever? Did not you know, that you were made to love and serve your Maker? That the short term of your life was given you to prepare for an endless state? If you doubted the truth of these things, why did you not take pains to be satisfied about them? If you did believe them, how could you forget them? Could you believe in a heaven and a hell, and not regard them, or regard any worldly vanity above them? Did not you know what you had to do in the world; and yet is it all undone till now? Were you never warned of this day of sickness? Did no preacher, no friend, no Scripture, no book, nor yet conscience, admonish you of your end? Did none of these tell you what would be the fruit of sin, and of your contempt of Christ? Did you know that you must believe in Christ, and love God above all, if ever you would be saved; and that for this purpose, you must be born of the Spirit; and yet would you keep setting your heart upon the world, indulging the lusts of the flesh, and never seeking after Christ?

Do you not think it would have been better to seek first the kingdom of God and his righteousness, than to neglect them for the vanities of this world? What have you got by all your sinful love of the world? Where now are all your pleasures? Will they save you from death, or the wrath of God? Or do you think it will comfort a soul in hell, to remember the wealth he got and left behind him on earth, or the pleasures he enjoyed in sin?

Would it not be more comfortable to you, if you could say, " My days were spent in the love and service of my dear Redeemer. My work was to know and do his will. While I followed my lawful calling, my eye was fixed on eternal life; and now I am going to enjoy the God I loved and the happiness I sought!" Would not this be far more comfortable for you now, than to look back on your time spent in a worldly, carnal life? If you had cleaved to Christ, he would not have forsaken you in this time of extremity. You little know what peace and comfort you would have found in a holy life, as well as in the near approach of death. How dear would the word of Christ have been to you! How delightful prayer and meditation! How excellent would the loving-kindness of God have been esteemed! How animating to believers, to read the promises of eternal life; to think and talk of that blessed state in which they shall dwell with God for ever! Do you not now wish that this had been your course? But that which is done cannot be undone, and time which is past can never be recalled!

Allow me, as a friend, who feels for your present situation, and is alarmed for your future prospects, to expostulate with you on the necessity of an immediate attention to the things that belong to your eternal peace. Take a retrospect of your past course. Let conscience say, if it has not been a course of sin and folly. What has by far the greater part of your life been, but a series of provocations against that good and gracious Being from whom all your mercies have been derived. Call into review your multiplied transgressions. Let not self-love cast a deceptive veil over your numerous violations of God's holy law. Attempt no extenuation or excuse of the aggravated sins which a reflection on the events of past years cannot fail, in appalling colours, to exhibit to your view. Take no consolation from the recollection of a few supposed virtues, which the enemy may lead you to think will lessen the deep shade in which sin has involved your hopes. If the declaration of God's word be true, " Cursed is every one who continueth not in all things written in the book of the law, to do them," then the brightest catalogue of seeming virtues cannot save your soul from the condemnation sealed upon it by the commission of one sin. Alas! how innumerable a multitude of sins, both of omission and commission, stand registered against you in the book of God! What heartfelt sorrow and contrition should they excite! Into what deep humiliation should they bring you before that God whom they have offended, and at whose bar you may soon be called to render a dread account! How hopeless your case, if mercy do not intervene to save. You can make no satisfaction to your offended Maker for one of your transgressions, and without an atonement to his justice, you are ruined and undone for ever.

But there is a remedy, if you have a heart to receive and use it. Hear this good news from heaven : " God so loved the world, that he gave his only begotten Son, that whosoever believeth in him might not perish, but have everlasting life. This is a faithful saying, and worthy of all acceptation, that Jesus Christ came into the world to save sinners, even the chief. God was in Christ, reconciling the world unto himself. Jesus Christ was made sin for us, that we might be made the righteousness of God in him. Behold the Lamb of God, which taketh away the sin of the world! The blood of Jesus Christ cleanseth from all sin. Be it known unto you, therefore, that through him is preached unto you the forgiveness of sins."

This is the glorious Gospel of the blessed God. What do you think of it? Is it not good news? Is it not glad tidings of great joy? Yes, it is the record of God, it is the testimony of heaven, " God hath given to us eternal life, and this life is in his Son." Is not this Gospel worthy to be received with all your heart? There is no other way for your relief. Beware of false hopes! Say not within yourself, " I have not been so bad as others." You have been a sinner, and as such you need a Saviour. Say not, you hope to make amends by your future life. Alas! you may not live to prove this; and if you should, you must not *depend* upon a good life, for this would be to reject Christ. Jesus Christ is the Saviour. He alone has made peace by the blood of his cross, and your enjoyment of this peace can be secured only by believing.

Beware, then, of hardening your heart any longer! You have too long neglected this great salvation. Yet such is the wonderful patience and goodness of God, that Christ is still set before you, able and willing to save. The great danger is, your not feeling your need of him; your not seeing yourself to be a sinner, and such a one as God might justly destroy. If, indeed, God is now granting you repentance, you will be more ready to fear than to presume. Perhaps you are beginning to fear that it is too late; that Jesus will not receive you; since no heart can conceive, no tongue can express, what a sinner you are. Blessed be God if it is thus with you! if indeed your soul longs to be saved from sin and sanctified by grace. Jesus Christ is both able and willing to save the greatest sinners.

Does not this revive your heart, that, after all your sin, after a life of folly and vanity which it may well give you pain to think of, yet such is the astonishing grace of God in Christ, that he will still-receive you and pardon your sins? Beg of God, then, to take away your heart of stone, and give you a heart of flesh, to save you from your sins, and prepare you for the blessedness of heaven. Let your reflections be such as these:

"O my soul, look forward a little with seriousness and attention, and 'learn wisdom, by the consideration of thy latter end.' To-morrow's sun may not enlighten mine eyes, but only shine around a senseless corpse, which may lie in the place of this animated body.

"And now, O my soul, answer as in the sight of God, Art thou ready? Art thou ready? Is there no sin unforsaken, and unrepented of, to fill me with anguish in my departing moments, and to make me tremble on the brink of eternity? Dread to remain under the guilt of it, and this moment make thy most earnest applications to the mercy of God, and the blood of a Redeemer, for deliverance from it.

"If thou dost cordially repent, and sincerely commit thyself, by faith, into the hands of the blessed Jesus, then start not at the thoughts of a separation: it is not in the power of death to hurt a soul devoted to God, and united to the great Redeemer."

PUBLISHED BY THE
AMERICAN TRACT SOCIETY,
And sold at their Depository, No. 150 Nassau-street, near the City-Hall, New-York; and by Agents of the Society, its Branches, and Auxiliaries, in the principal cities and towns in the United States.

THE SINNER

DIRECTED TO THE SAVIOR

BY REV. JOHN FLAVEL

"Behold the Lamb of God, which taketh away the sin of the world !"
John, i. 29

THESE are the words of John the Baptist; and they were spoken in consequence of the question which was asked of him by the Jews, " Who art thou ?" The humble prophet confessed, " I am not the Christ ;" and on the next day, seeing Jesus coming to him, he exclaimed, " Behold the Lamb of God, which taketh away the sin of the world !" ·

Since the Redeemer left the world, he is not to be seen with an eye of flesh; but believing on him is seeing him by the eye of faith ; and every one who thus seeth the Son, and believeth on him, shall have everlasting life. John vi. 40.

Jesus Christ himself hath pronounced a blessing on those "who have not seen, and yet have believed." John, xx. 29. And this blessedness is well described by the Apostle Peter, when he saith, "Whom having not seen, ye love; in whom, though now ye see him not, yet, believing, ye rejoice with joy unspeakable, and full of glory." 1 Pet. i. 8. It is a disparagement to so glorious an object as Christ, to behold him, and not wonder; to see, and not love him. Certainly, the admiration, love, delight, and joy of our hearts are all at the command of faith: let us therefore consider what excellencies are in Christ, for the eye of the believer to behold and admire.

1. "*God was in Christ.*" 2 Cor. v. 19. He was "God manifest in the flesh." 1 Tim. iii. 16. A God incarnate is the world's wonder. Here are infinite and finite joined in one. The Creator and creature united in one person. It is an argument of weakness to admire little things; and of stupidity, not to admire great things. Many miracles were wrought by Christ in the flesh; but the greatest of all miracles was, that he "was made flesh, and dwelt among men." John, i. 14.

2. "Christ is *the wisdom of God;*" (1 Cor. i. 24.) yea, "in Him are hid all the treasures of wisdom and knowledge." Coloss. ii. 3. Never did the Divine wisdom display its glorious beams in the eyes of men and angels, in any work since the beginning of time, as it hath done in the appointment of Christ to be the Lamb of God, a sacrifice for sin. *Behold the Lamb of God!* and in him behold the unsearchable wisdom of God, in recovering sinners who believe in him, from all the danger of sin; and yet making sin more dreadful to them, by way of their recovery from it, than ever it could be made by any other consideration. Behold the depth of infinite wisdom, in suiting the sinner's remedy to the cause of his disease. The disease was the pride of man; the remedy was the humiliation of the Son of God. Man affected to be as God—that ruined him: God was manifested in the flesh, and found in fashion as a man—that saved him. O, profound wisdom! which, from the loss and ruin of our primitive glory, (which was the undoing of us, soul and body,) takes the occasion of raising us up to a far better state, and settles us in it, with much better security than the former.

3. *The love of God* is in Christ. Behold the Lamb of God! and in him behold the love of God, in the highest and most triumphant discovery that ever was, or can be, made in this world. "Herein is love, not that we loved God, but that he loved us, and sent his Son to be the propitiation for our sins." 1 John iv. 10. O here, here is the love of God to sinners! God manifests love to us, in our daily provisions, protections, deliverances, and comforts. That we have health, when others groan under pains; therein is love: that we have bread to eat, when others are ready to perish; therein is love: O! but to have Christ to be a propitiation for us, when the angels that fell were left in their fallen state; therein was love indeed! All the love that breaks out in the variety of providences in this world, in our healths and estates, in our relations and comforts, is nothing, compared with this love: herein is love indeed!

4. *The tender mercies of God over poor sinners*, are in Christ. As Christ is the mercy promised, (Luke, i. 72.) —the capital mercy—so he is the channel, through which all the streams of God's mercy flow freely to the sons of men, Jude, 21. The mercy of God to eternal life, or his saving mercies, are only dispensed to us through Jesus Christ. Behold the Lamb of God! a Lamb prepared by the astonishing mercy of God, a sacrifice for us when no sacrifice was appointed for fallen angels. This is the Lamb of God, to which, under the Jewish dispensation, all legal sacrifices had respect, and from which they derived all their virtue and value. The paschal lamb, and the lamb for daily sacrifice, were but the types and shadows of this Lamb of God. Behold the Person appointed by God for a sacrifice to take away sin! Jesus Christ, the Son of God, was crucified for us. He shed his precious blood and offered up his life, a sacrifice to God, of a sweet-smelling savour, "that whosoever believeth in him should not perish, but have everlasting life." John, iii. 16. Look! as the sprinkling of the blood of the paschal Lamb upon the door-posts of the Israelites was that which preserved them from the destroying angel; so the blood of Christ, the Lamb of God, typified by that blood, saves all who believe on him, from the wrath to come. Thus Christ, the Son of God, prevents the destroying angel from executing the fierceness of his Father's anger, and preserves them as his peo-

ple, that they may enter into the land of Canaan, the everlasting rest. But who can open the unsearchable riches of Christ, or recount his wonderful excellencies? Angels and the spirits of just men made perfect, behold and admire him for evermore! Heaven would be no heaven for them, if they could not behold Christ there, sitting as a King, in his perfect beauty, on his holy hill of Zion.

But let us rather proceed to IMPROVE this subject, than endeavour further to unfold it; for new wonders will appear in Christ, if we behold him, through the countless ages of eternity.

1. O sinner! if you are sensible of a stony, hard heart, which cannot relent and mourn for all the wrong done to Jesus Christ by sin; if your affections are benumbed and stupified so that no considerations you can urge upon your own heart, are able to cause a relenting pang for sin; to you I would direct the words which we have now been contemplating, as the most effectual means to melt your heart. Look hither: *Behold the Lamb of God!* Consider, believe, and apply what is here represented; and thy heart is hard indeed, if it relent not upon such a view of Christ. It is said, (Zech. xii. 10.) "They shall look upon me whom they have pierced, and they shall mourn for Him, as one mourneth for his only son, and shall be in bitterness for him, as one that is in bitterness for his first born." Behold the Son of God, brought "as a lamb to the slaughter" for thee, a vile, polluted sinner: Behold the invaluable blood of this sacrifice shed for thee! Bring thy thoughts close to this subject; think who it is that was made a Lamb for sacrifice; for whom he endured all his unspeakable sufferings; how meekly and willingly he endured all the wrath of God and men, standing in his perfect innocency, to be slain for thee. Behold! he was made sin for thee, who had no sin, that thou, who hadst no righteousness, mightest be made the righteousness of God in him! 2 Cor. v. 21. Oh! who ever loved thee as Christ hath done? Who would endure that misery that Christ endured for thy sake? Would thy father, or the wife of thy bosom, or thy friend, that is as thy own soul, be content to feel that for thee, though but for one hour, which Christ felt when "his sweat was, as it were, great drops of blood falling down to the ground?" Luke, xxii. 44. Nay, thou

wouldest thyself never taste such a cup, for the saving of
thy own child, as Christ drank off to the very last dregs,
when he cried, " My God ! My God ! Why hast thou forsaken me ?" Behold how he loved thee ! Surely, if the
rocks rent asunder at his sufferings, thy heart is harder
than a rock, if it melt not at such a sight as this. Fix thine
eyes awhile here, and thine eye will affect thine heart.

2. O sinner ! Are you making too light of sin, and are
you easily overcome by every temptation to the commission of it ? O ! come hither : *Behold the Lamb of God* and
you cannot possibly have slight thoughts of sin after such
a sight of Christ. See here the price of sin ! Behold what
it cost the Son of God to atone for it ! Did he come into
the world as a Lamb, bound with the band of an irreversible decree, to die for sin ? Did he come from the bosom
of his Father to be thy Ransom, and that at the price of
his own life ? Did the hand of Divine Justice shed the
heart-blood of this immaculate Lamb, to satisfy for the
wrongs thy sins have done to God; and yet canst thou
look upon sin as a light matter ? God forbid ! Thy sin actually cost the blood of Christ ; one drop whereof is more
valuable than all human blood ; and yet, wilt thou not deny thy lusts, nor resist a temptation for His sake ? Behold the Lamb of God slain for thy sin, and thou canst
never have slight thoughts of sin any more.

3. Are you drooping and discouraged in your spirits, because of your manifold and aggravated iniquities ; and
sinking into despair from being overwhelmed with the burden and weight of your sins ? These words are a sovereign cordial to revive your hearts and hopes : *Behold the
Lamb of God,* that taketh away the sin of the world ! If
the blood of the Lamb can take away the sin of the world,
it can take away thy sin, though there be a world of sin in
thee. For do but consider Christ, as appointed, from eternity, to be our propitiation : " Him hath God the Father sealed." Consider him as sacrificed in our room in the fulness
of time : " Christ our passover is sacrificed for us." 1 Cor. v.
7. Consider him as accepted by the Father with the greatest
content and pleasure, even " as a sweet-smelling savour."
Ephes. v. 2. Consider him as publickly justified and dis-
charged by God, the creditor, at his resurrection. 1 Tim.
iii. 16. and John xvi. 10. And, lastly, consider him as

L

now in heaven, where he appears in the presence of God for
us, as a Lamb that had been slain, (Rev. v. 6.) bearing the
very marks of his death, and presenting them before God,
as the most effectual and moving plea to procure pardon and mercy for his people.   Let these things, I say,
be duly pondered, and nothing will be found more effectual to relieve your mind under the desponding sense of
your sin.

4. Are you faint-hearted, and ready to shrink away from
any sufferings for Christ, as unable to bear and endure any
thing for his sake ?   *Behold the Lamb of God !*   Did Christ
suffer such grievous things for you, and cannot you suffer
small matters for him ?   Alas! what is the wrath of man,
to the wrath of the great and terrible God ?   Besides, Christ
was an innocent Lamb, and deserved not to suffer the least
degree of penal evil upon his own account ; but you have
deserved hell, and yet shrink under the suffering of a moment.   Did he suffer so much for you, and can you suffer
nothing for him ?   Surely He, in suffering for you, hath
left you an example " that ye should follow his steps."
1 Pet. ii. 21.   Are our sufferings compared, in kind or degree, to the sufferings of Christ ?   Or our blood compared,
in dignity, to the blood of Christ ?   Remember, " if you are
planted in the likeness of his death, you shall be also in the
likeness of his resurrection ;" (Rom. vi. 5.) that, like
Christ, you may endure the cross, and despise the shame,
for the joy that is set before you.

5. Are you impatient under your personal trials and
troubles, apt to grieve under common afflictions, or to swell
with revenge under injuries from the hands of men ?   *Behold the Lamb of God !*   " As a lamb before her shearers is
dumb, so he opened not his mouth." Isa. liii. 7.   And can
you bear nothing without complaining ?   How meek was
Christ the Lamb, when he suffered most vile things from
the hands of sinners ; and art thou a lion for fierceness ?
He suffered patiently, and deserved it not ; you suffer im-
patiently, and have deserved what you suffer.   O that you
would learn to be more like Christ, in all your trials and
afflictions !

6. Are you staggering at the promises, through unbelief?
Can you not rely upon the word of promise, because your
unbelieving heart fills you with unworthy suspicions of the

power, faithfulness, or willingness of God to perform it for you? *Behold the Lamb of God!* Are not " all the promises of God yea and amen in Jesus Christ, to all that believe in him?" 2 Cor. i. 20. Or is there any thing put into any promise of greater value than the blood of the Lamb, that was shed to purchase it? Or is not the giving of Christ to die for us, the accomplishment of the greatest promise that ever God made to us? And after the fulfilment thereof, what ground remains for you to doubt the fulfilling of lesser promises? For, if God spared not his own Son, but delivered nim up for us all, how shall he not with him also freely give us all things?" Rom. viii. 32.

=====

SPECIMEN OF WELCH PREACHING.

A little time ago, I heard Christmas Evans preaching on the depravity of man by sin—of his recovery by the death of Christ—and he said, " Brethren, if I were to represent to you in a figure, the condition of man as a sinner, and the means of his recovery by the cross of Jesus Christ, I should represent it something in this way. Suppose a large graveyard surrounded by a high wall, with only one entrance, which is by a large iron gate, which is *fast bolted.* Within these walls are thousands and tens of thousands of human beings, of all ages and of all classes, by one epidemic disease bending to the grave—the grave yawns to swallow them, and they must all die. There is no balm to relieve them—no physician there—they must perish. This is the condition of man as a sinner—all, all have sinned, and the soul that sinneth shall die. While man was in this deplorable state, *Mercy* came down and stood at the gate, looked at the gate, looked at the scene, and wept over it, exclaiming, 'Oh that I might enter—I would bind up their wounds —I would relieve their sorrows—I would save their souls!' While Mercy stood weeping at the gate, an embassy of angels, commissioned from the court of Heaven to some other world, passing over, paused at the sight, and Heaven forgave that pause; and seeing Mercy standing there, they cried, 'Mercy, Mercy, can you not enter? Can you look upon this scene and not pity? Can you pity and not relieve?'

Mercy replied, 'I *can* see;' and in her tears she added, 'I can pity; bu' I cannot relieve.' 'Why can you not enter?' 'Oh!' said Mercy, 'Justice has barred the gate against me, and I cannot, must not unbar it.' At this moment, Justice himself appeared, as it were, to watch the gate. The angels inquired of him, 'Why will you not let Mercy in?' Justice replied, 'My law is broken, and it must be honored. Die *they* or *Justice* must!' At this, there appeared a form among the angelic band, like unto the Son of God, who, addressing himself to Justice, said, 'What are thy demands?' Justice replied, 'My terms are stern and rigid—I must have sickness for their health—I must have ignominy for their honor —I must have death for life. *Without shedding of blood there is no remission.*' 'Justice,' said the Son of God, '*I accept thy terms.* On me be this wrong, and let Mercy enter.' 'When,' said Justice, 'will you perform this promise?' Jesus replied, 'Four thousand years hence, upon the hill of Calvary, without the gates of Jerusalem, I will perform it in my own person.' The deed was prepared and signed in the presence of the angels of God; Justice was satisfied, and Mercy entered, preaching *salvation* in the name of Jesus. The deed was committed to the patriarchs, by them to the kings of Israel and the prophets; by them it was preserved till Daniel's seventy weeks were accomplished; then, at the appointed time, Justice appeared on the hill of Calvary, and Mercy presented to him the important deed. 'Where,' said Justice, 'is the Son of God?' Mercy answered, 'Behold him at the bottom of the hill, bearing his own cross;' and then she departed, and stood aloof at the hour of trial. Jesus ascended the hill, while in his train followed his weeping church. Justice immediately presented him with the deed, saying, 'This is the day when this bond is to be executed.' When he received it, did he tear it in pieces, and give it to the winds of heaven? No, he nailed it to his cross, exclaiming, 'It is finished.' Justice called on holy fire to come down and consume the sacrifice. Holy fire descended—it swallowed up his humanity, but when it touched his Deity it expired! and there was darkness over the whole heavens; but 'glory to God in the highest; on earth peace, and good will to men.'"

HISTORY

OF

PETER AND JOHN HAY.

" Like one distracted, poor Mrs. Hay rushed to the fire to save her husband."—*See page* 10.

PUBLISHED BY THE

AMERICAN TRACT SOCIETY,

AND SOLD AT THEIR DEPOSITORY, NO. 150 NASSAU-STREET, NEAR
THE CITY-HALL, NEW-YORK: AND BY AGENTS OF THE
SOCIETY, ITS BRANCHES, AND AUXILIARIES, IN
THE PRINCIPAL CITIES AND TOWNS
IN THE UNITED STATES.

PETER AND JOHN HAY.

PETER and John Hay were brothers. John remained
single, but Peter was married, and had become the father
of a little son. Their prospects in life were highly promising. By wisely improving the fruits of their father's labours, they were growing rich; and by freely imparting
of their riches in acts of hospitality, they had rendered
themselves very dear to all their neighbours. John, the
younger and single brother, lived with his father; but
Peter and his wife, with their little son, lived by themselves. For convenience sake they had chosen different
houses to live in, yet it might well be said of them that
they lived together; for their houses were not farther
apart than just served for a pleasant walk, which was almost every day indulged, either by the old gentleman going over to see and play with his little grandson, or by his
mother fondly carrying the child over to prattle with his
grandfather. Shaded by the rustling trees, and fanned by
every breeze of summer, their houses stood on the grace-
ful ridge that bounds on the north the great valley of the
Congaree, while below, far stretching to the river, lay
their fruitful fields, covered over with bursting pods of
cotton, white as the driven snow; and on either side, a
wilderness of corn, with lusty shocks, gratefully pointing to
heaven. The silver flood that embosomed their plantation was stored with fish and wild fowl of many a savoury
sort. Their numerous herds poured them forth milk in
foaming pailsfull, while, from the flowers that perfumed
both field and forest, the ever busy bees supplied them
yearly with hives of honey-comb.

O favoured family! the reader is ready to exclaim;
thrice favoured, whose lines are cast in such pleasant
places! Sure they will improve the bounties of their God,
and secure to themselves a felicity proportionate to such
opportunities. Doubtless each morn, mild as it opens, will
attest their waking joys; and every day, bright as it rolls

along, will mark their cheerful toils; crowning with gratitude each mercy of the present life, and looking forward
with hope to the better blessings of the next. Such was
the result to have been hoped for, and such, indeed, to
have been expected, by all who beheld their distinguished
lot. But alas! what avails it to put good into the hands
of those who know not its worth? Wisdom to understand
our benefits, and gratitude to adore the Benefactor,—these
are the only essentials of happiness. But, alas! Peter and
John Hay possessed not these essentials;

> " Knowledge, to them, her ample page,
> Rich with the spoils of time, had ne'er displayed."

They considered not the many gloomy regions of the
earth bound in eternal ice and snow. How then could
they enjoy their own favoured clime, where nature crowns
the copious year with fruits and golden grain?

And still less did they consider Him, the Great Author
of all, whom, in all his wondrous works, to contemplate,
with ever admiring, ever adoring delight, constitutes our
only heaven upon earth. For lack of this, what wonder
they should have turned to the garbage of the world! And
disappointed there of true pleasure, what wonder they
should have seized the false pleasures of the intoxicating
cup!

Great was the grief of their neighbours, when they beheld these young men yielding themselves up the slaves
of intemperance, and, for so ignoble a vice, tarnishing the
lustre of their long respected names.

But greater still the grief of their aged father. Lovely
in his eyes had shone the cheeks of his boys, all reddened
over with the roses of youth. To see those dear cheeks
inflamed, though with but an innocent fever, had often
wrung his heart; then, oh! how passing the bitterness
of death, to see them swollen and ghastly red with infla-
ming liquors. Divorced from the world by his gray hairs,
he had wisely confined himself to the society of his children, fondly hoping in their affections to forget the world's
neglect; in their bloom to see his youth renewed; and in
their virtues, his own name immortalized. Ah! who bu
a parent can conceive his grief, when he saw those dear

est hopes of nature all blasted for ever! With cheeks bathed in tears, he sat in the silence of his silver locks, going down in sorrow to his grave.

But there was one whose grief was far more pungent still. I mean the young wife of Mr. Peter Hay. Wedded to her husband by the tenderest ties of love, and therefore "tremblingly alive" to his interest and honour, the first time she saw her husband deformed by intemperance, she turned pale with terror. Her fears, however, at first were soothed with hope. But when she found that, in spite of all her tears and all his own promises, he still continued, time after time, to come home stupified and staggering with drink, she yielded herself up to despair. Like a young widow by her husband's grave, she often sat by his bedside, deeply revolving her early blasted hopes, and the sad change that had passed in her late happy family.

Till of late he had always returned from *Court*, with looks brightened with the double joy of conscious integrity and love ; till of late, with her little son in her hand, she had always flown to welcome his return, and accompany him to the parlour. There, leaning on his bosom, with her boy in her lap, she was wont to listen, delighted, to his sprightly voice, as he related the pleasant occurrences of the day.

But now, alas! those happy scenes are no more. Now, whenever he comes home, it is in a reeling gait, and his face is marked with the sullen frown of conscious guilt.

Returning from court one night, rather more disguised than usual, he had not strength to gain the door, but tripping at the last step, he fell forward sprawling into the piazza. His little son was not yet put to bed, though the hour was late, but stood, heavy-eyed and nodding, at the knees of his mother, who, with an aching heart, was sitting up, waiting for her husband's return. Hearing the noise of his heavy fall, and suspecting what it was, she cried out, " *Oh! my God!*" and snatching a candle, ran to the door. Her little son followed. On reaching the door, she beheld a spectacle too painful to be presented before the fancy of the reader—What then was it for the eyes of an affectionate wife!

The next morning, red faced and snoring like an apoplectic patient, he lay till late. Poor Mrs. Hay, pale and deeply sighing, left her sleepless bed, and leading her little son by the hand, walked down stairs, sad and silent, to the parlour. The child had not yet learned to know the cause of this change, but he felt that the present morning was not joyful like the past, and he wept.

The breakfast-table was set, spread with snow-white diaper, and covered with a set of purest china, and tea-pots and sugar dishes of solid silver. On the marble hearth, before a fire of hickory, glittered a coffee-pot of the same precious metal, waiting the reception of the family.

But nothing could divert the settled melancholy of poor Mrs. Hay. With her child at her knees, and her forehead leaning on the back of the chair, like a statue, dumb with grief, she sat regardless of all but her own hapless lot—her husband's sore disgrace, and the ruin impendent over herself and child. Often, as borne along the stream of mournful thought, she would deeply groan and heave the most piercing sighs; then, stooping down to her little son, she would kiss him and press him to her bosom, watering his cheeks with her tears.

About twelve o'clock, her husband came down stairs, and in sullen silence entered the parlour; but, oh! how changed from the temperate and elegant Mr. Hay, of a few months ago! Whoever saw him then, bright in the pure robes of innocence and joy, without adoring the charm of virtue? Who could see him now, long bearded, with red eyes and carbuncled face, but must lift the pitying eye, and sighingly exclaim, " *Alas! my brother!* "

Poor Mrs. Hay! She marked the woful change, and wept. The child ran and stretched his little arms to his father, who took him up and kissed him.

" O Pa!" said the lisping angel, with his arms around his neck, " you don't know how I did cry for you last night, Pa."

" Cry for me, my baby, what made you cry for me?"

" O Pa, I did cry for you because you were so sick, Pa; what did make you so sick, Pa?"

He could make no answer to his son, but, deeply blushing and confused, looked up to his wife.

The words of the child, with the guilty looks of her husband, overcame her; with eyes rolling in tears, she gave him one melting look, and suddenly turning aside her face, burst into a loud cry.

Hearing the cries of his mother, the child slipped from his father's lap, and running to her knees, joined his artless cries with hers. The scene was too much for poor Mr. Hay; pale and silent with anguish, he got up and went to the door, and there, as he wiped the trickling tears from his face, a thousand and a thousand times did he wish he was dead. Her tears flowed afresh. Moved by her cries, he went and sat down by her side, and embraced her. But alas! it was not that fond and hearty embrace in which conscious innocence is wont to clasp its beloved object. It was the sad approach of guilt to innocence; constrained and shy.

With her face still turned away, she continued to weep. He entreated her to be composed, assuring her that this was the *last time;* for that he would never give her cause of sorrow any more. She turned towards him, and throwing her arms around his neck, with her cheek on his bosom, bathed with tears, cried aloud, "Oh, my husband! Don't promise so any more. How often have you promised me so before; and yet you go on to break my heart. You wish *you* were dead; Oh! it is *I* who should wish to die; and were it not for my child, glad should I be to die this very night. Yes, but for the pain of leaving him a poor orphan, gladly would I lie down and part with all my sorrows this night in the grave."

At this, he tenderly embraced and kissed her, repeating his assurances that he would never, *never more*, give her cause of grief. " Besides," continued he, " I am the person that ought to weep, and not you. I am the one that has played the fool, and disgraced myself; but *you*, innocent and good as you are, what cause have you of grief?"

" Oh, said she, eagerly looking at him, how little do you know of my heart! I was young when I married you; was called handsome, and thought rich; what then could have induced me to make you my husband, but affection? How then, without distraction, can I see the dishonour that you are bringing upon yourself, and also the certain ruin of myself and your poor unoffending child?"—

"O no! my dear," rejoined he, interrupting her, "that I deny. I agree I do dishonour myself, and am truly ashamed of it; but as to bringing ruin upon you and our dear child, that's all out of the question; I shall keep clear enough of that."

"Oh, my dear husband," replied she, "I pray you, don't flatter yourself any more with that hope. It is a fatal, fatal hope, that has ruined thousands, and will, I fear, ruin you and your family too. How hard is it for a man to thrive with all his industry and wits about him! Then how can it be done by one who is stupified and palsied by hard drink? You know that after a single night of intemperance you are sick for several days, an unfit for business; and even when you return to it again, is not with that delight which you formerly manifested in it. And it makes me mourn, to think what a sad change has taken place in you in that respect. Formerly you seemed never happy but at home. Myself and your little son, with your plantation and the improvement of it, seemed to make all your paradise. It appeared as though you wanted nothing more. Your looks bespoke the most perfect contentment and cheerfulness. And, O how often and how heartily did I thank God, that, while so many other husbands were not satisfied with their wives, you were so well satisfied with me; that while so many other husbands were constantly running to taverns and company for pleasure, you appeared to look for pleasure no where but in me and your little family. But now, alas! that for which I so often pitied others, is come upon me also. You seem never to be happy with us now. When you stay at home, it seems only to be that you may get well of your sickness; and as soon as you are well again, you appear wretched at home. Your vivacity is gone. Contentment has left your countenance. You sit silent, or mope about, as if you wanted something you cannot find at home. And then you order your horse, and go away, leaving me here, with my little son, to solitude and distraction. Oh, how can I bear to drag out life, weeping, and broken-hearted as I have been, ever since you took to this fatal course! Oh, when I look back to the happy days so lately past; when I think how enviable above all women was my lot;

my dear husband, young, handsome, and affectionate ; my estate ample, and still becoming more so by his virtues, and my little son daily growing up the sweet and smiling image of his father! This, but a few short months ago, was my prospect; all bright with honour and happiness. But, oh! where is it now? All overcast and darkened for ever! I have no comfort, no hope in any thing around me. If I look at you, my heart bleeds ; your face is bloated, your eyes are red, your whole air melancholy and sad. If I look at my son, it sets my heart a bleeding, he is so changed; he never plays now as he did. You, who once so delighted in him, have forsaken him. I am always weeping. He feels himself a poor forlorn child, and often comes and stands at my knees, and cries as if he would break his heart. And indeed, were he to smile and laugh, he would make me weep to think what evils are coming upon him. I see gamblers and sharpers crowding around you; pressing you to drink, getting you tipsy, winning your money, and then taking your notes. I never look at you riding away from the house, but I feel a deadly sickness at heart ; I feel a sad foreboding that I shall never see you again. A thousand times a day do I see you killed by your horse, or drowned in the deep waters, or dying of some of those deaths by which men in their cups generally perish. Then I see the creditors coming to tear every thing from us, selling all over our heads, and turning my poor boy and myself out of house and home, to starve or beg. Oh! why was I ever born ; or why did I not die before I ever came to see such woful days as these!"

Here she burst into piercing cries. Her husband, poor wretch! in the mean time stood looking on, sobbing, and promising great amendments.

For a few days he kept his promise ; which sprung a fresh dawn of hope in the bosom of this excellent woman. But, alas! all his promised reformation was but as the morning dew before the burning sun. At the very next court he was ensnared by a pack of gamblers, who getting him tipsy, won his money, horse, saddle, bridle, and great coat! Some short time afterwards, on his way from Charleston, where it was understood he had received a sum of money, he was decoyed by the same gang of sharp-

ers, who got him drunk, and won eight hundred dollars of
him. In this way he would no doubt have broken his
wife's heart, and beggared his boy, had not God in his
providence prevented it, by suddenly taking him away,
and also his brother John; and in a manner which, I pray
God, may strike terror in the hearts of all who read this
awful story.

Their fields near the river, as I have said, brought
forth plenteously, insomuch that, like the man in the Gospel, they began to be at a loss where "*to bestow their
fruits, and their goods.*" I know not that they *pulled down
their old barns,* but it is certain they built a large new
barn, in one end of which they finished an apartment for
their overseer. In this apartment they found their destruction. Fearing to get drunk at home, and yet so en-
slaved to strong drink that they could not live without it,
they came to the resolution to keep a jug of rum in their
barn. On a cold and very windy morning in March, they
went down, at an early hour, to the barn; and, using
the cold as a plea for a dram, they went on "*dramming it,
and dramming it,*" till they got perfectly drunk, and fell
down without sense or motion on the floor. In this awful
moment the building took fire! owing, as was said, to the
carelessness of an old negro woman, who had hobbled that
morning with her pipe in her mouth into the barn, which
contained a large quantity of hackled hemp. The first
thing that struck the attention of the negroes at work in
the fields, as also of old Mr. Hay and his excellent daugh-
ter-in-law, was a prodigious smoke issuing in black vol-
umes from the barn. Instantly, from all parts of the plantation, there was a violent running together of the family, white and black, to save the barn. But all, alas! too
slow; for scarcely had they got half way, before they beheld the flames bursting out from all sides of the building,
with a noise like thunder. Though aghast with horror and
despair, they still continued to run as fast as they could
towards the dreadful conflagration, and there, around the
raging element, amidst mingled shrieks and screams, nothing was to be heard but, "*Where is young masters?*"—"*Oh,
my children! my children!*"—"*My husband! Oh, my husband!*"—"*Oh, Pa! Pa! Pa!*"

Presently they were presented with a spectacle almost too shocking to relate. Through the red billowy flames, which, driven by the fury of the wind, had now completely encircled the apartment, and burst open the door, they distinctly beheld these wretched brothers lying dead-drunk and helpless on the floor, and the fire rapidly seizing on every thing around them. Like one distracted, poor Mrs. Hay rushed to the fire to save her husband. But the forbidding flames, with scorching blast on her face, struck her back, senseless and suffocated, to the ground.

The negroes, too, roused to the utmost by their strong sympathies, made many daring efforts to save their young masters, but in vain; for after getting miserably scorched, they were compelled to give them up; and, with bleeding hearts, to behold the flames kindling upon them. Built of combustible materials, the barn was quickly reduced to ashes, which being speedily swept away by the violence of the wind, left the *hapless pair* lying side by side, *pale, chalky skeletons* on the whitened earth.

Thus ends this most affecting narrative. How applicable are the words of the inspired Apostle to the wretched and awful case of these miserable men, " The end of these things is death !" The vice that destroyed them is one especially suited to the design of him " who, like a roaring lion, goeth about seeking whom he may devour." By it, the understanding is blinded, and the conscience bribed, or " seared as with a hot iron." Even the common affections of nature are deadened, and often utterly destroyed; so that, in not a few instances, men, and women too, have sunk even below brutality, and have lost all feeling and concern for their dearest relations and tender offspring ! Ah ! how many have set out on the journey of life with delightful prospects before them, who yet have been caught in this snare of the infernal fowler, out of which so few escape ! O ! who can conceive of the many dreadful consequences of drunkenness, both temporal and eternal ! It has destroyed the health, and beggared the families, and ruined the souls of thousands.

Reader, are you a *temperate drinker?* If so, remember, that whenever you apply the glass to your lips, you are forming *an unnatural appetite*, which, by a law of your nature, will increase the more it is cherished, and threatens to destroy you. Your only safety is in *total abstinence from all intoxicating drinks.* Receive the above affecting narrative as a friendly caution! Reflect on the awful condition of those who, by the insidious progress of this sin, have blasted every fair prospect for this life, and plunged themselves into a miserable eternity. Go to the Lord Jesus Christ for strength to resist this and every temptation. Commit your soul and all your ways to him. Hear his tender expostulations: "Seek ye the Lord, while he may be found, call ye upon him, while he is near." " Let the wicked forsake his way, and the unrighteous man his thoughts ; and let him return unto the Lord, and he will have mercy upon him, and to our God, for he will abundantly pardon." " *If thou art wise, thou shalt be wise for thyself ; but if thou scornest, thou alone shalt bear it.*"

MEDICATED DRINKS.

In one of the northern towns in the state of New-York considerable excitement has been occasioned by a recent development on the part of a spirit merchant, which has given the cause of temperance a new impulse, and shown to moderate drinkers, and to drunkards, that

" There may be in the cup a spider steeped ;"

and if the abhorred ingredient be not presented to the eye, a man may drink and drink again, and go from year to year with the poison rankling in his veins, unconscious of the cause which unnerves his limbs, and pollutes al.

2

his springs of happiness. The merchant alluded to observed, that after selling out a cask of spirit there remained several gallons of foul, unsightly sediment, which on examination was found to consist of various drugs, some that could be distinguished and some that could not, but all judged unfit for the use of human beings. These vile compounds had been infused in the liquor to give to a spurious article the appearance of genuineness. Such are the effects of a traffic founded in a dishonest and ungenerous disregard to the best interests of the community—a traffic whose object, end, and aim, are the aggrandizement of self, at whatever cost to the welfare of others!

Did moderate drinkers and drunkards know how often what they drink is not what it is called, but a horrible mixture of noxious ingredients, would they swallow these medicated draughts with the same reckless indifference that they now do? Investigations are going forward, which it is hoped will expose the system of frauds and adulterations, bring to light the receits for the fabrication of high-priced liquors, and the numberless abuses inseparable from a traffic in its nature *immoral*. When this development shall take place the moderate drinker, the drunkard, and the community at large, will have a better opportunity to judge of the nature of the traffic against which we feel it our duty to lift up a warning voice. Against a traffic so destructive of life, so fatal to happiness, so blighting in its influence on national and individual prosperity, our duty to our Maker, to outraged humanity, and to the cause we advocate, compels us to array ourselves, determined on an opposition which shall be unending while the evil exists in our land.

Temperance Recorder.

QUESTIONS AND COUNSEL.

BY REV. ASHBEL GREEN, D. D.

FOR THOSE WHO HOPE THAT A WORK OF SAVING GRACE
HAS BEEN WROUGHT UPON THEIR HEARTS.

QUESTIONS. 1. Have you seen yourself to be, by
nature and by practice, a lost and helpless sinner? Have
you not only seen the sinfulness of particular acts of transgression, but also that your heart is the seat and fountain
of sin?—That in you, naturally, there is no good thing?
Has a view of this led you to despair of help from yourself?
—To see that you must be altogether indebted to Christ
for salvation, and to the gracious aid of the Holy Spirit for
strength and ability rightly to perform any duty?

2. On what has your hope of acceptance with God been
founded? On your reformation? on your sorrow for your
sins? on your prayers? on your tears? on your good works
and religious observances? or has it been on Christ alone,
as your all in all? Has Christ ever appeared very precious
to you? Do you mourn that he does not appear more so?
Have you sometimes felt great freedom to commit your
soul to him? In doing this (if you have done it) has it
been, not only to be delivered from the punishment due to
your sins, but also from the power, pollution, dominion,
and existence of sin in your soul?

3. As far as you know yourself, do you hate, and desire
to be delivered from all sin—without any exception of a
favourite lust? Do you pray much to be delivered from
sin? Do you watch against it, and against temptation to
it? Do you strive against it, and in some degree get the
victory over it? Have you so repented of it as to have
your soul really set against it?

4. Have you counted the cost of following Christ, or of
being truly religious? That it will cut you off from vain
amusements, from the indulgence of your lusts, and from a
sinful conformity to the world? That it may expose you
to ridicule and contempt; possibly to more serious persecution? In the view of all these things, are you willing
to take up the cross, and to follow Christ, whithersoever
he shall lead you? Is it your solemn purpose, in reliance

on his grace and aid, to cleave to him, and to his cause and people, to the end of life?

5. Do you love holiness? Do you earnestly desire to be more and more conformed to God, and to his holy law? to bear more and more the likeness of your Redeemer? Do you seek, and sometimes find communion with your God and Saviour?

6. Are you resolved, in God's strength, to endeavour conscientiously to perform your whole duty—to God, to your neighbour, and to yourself?

7. Do you make conscience of secret prayer daily? Do you not sometimes feel a backwardness to this duty? Do you at other times feel a great delight in it? Have you a set time, and place, and order of exercises, for performing this duty?

8. Do you daily read a portion of the Holy Scriptures in a devout manner? Do you love to read the Bible? Do you ever perceive a sweetness in the truths of Holy Scripture? Do you find them adapted to your necessities, and see, at times, a wonderful beauty, excellence, and glory, in God's word? Do you make it the man of your counsel, and endeavour to have both your heart and life conformed to its doctrines and requisitions?

9. Have you ever attempted to covenant with God? To give yourself away to him, solemnly and irrevocably, hoping for acceptance through Christ alone; and taking God, in Christ, as the covenant God, and satisfying portion of your soul?

10. Does the glory of God ever appear to you as the first, greatest, and best of all objects?

11. Do you feel a love to mankind, such as you did not feel before you became religious? Have you a great desire that the souls of men should be saved, by being brought to a genuine faith and trust in the Redeemer? Do you love God's people with a peculiar attachment, because they bear their Saviour's image, and because they love and pursue the objects, and delight in the exercises, which are most pleasing and delightful to yourself?

12. Do you feel it to be very important to adorn religion by a holy, exemplary, amiable, and blameless walk and conversation? Do you fear to bring a reproach on the cause of Christ? Does this appear to you extremely dread-

ful? Are you afraid of backsliding, and of being left to return to a state of carelessness and indifference in religion?

13. Do you desire and endeavour to grow in grace, and in the knowledge of Christ your Saviour, more and more? Are you willing to sit at his feet as a little child, and to submit your reason and understanding implicitly, to his teaching; imploring his Spirit to guide you into all necessary truth, to save you from all fatal errors, to enable you to receive the truth in the love of it, and to transform you, more and more, into a likeness to himself?

COUNSEL. 1. Remember that these questions are intended to point your attention to subjects of enquiry the most important. Do not, therefore, content yourself with a careless or cursory reading of them. Read and deliberate, and examine yourself closely, on the questions under each head; and let your heart be lifted up to God, while you are considering each particular question, in earnest desire that he may show you the very truth. You cannot ordinarily go over all these questions at one time. Divide them, therefore, and take one part at one time, and another at another. But try to get over the whole in the course of a week; and do this every week for some months. When you find yourself doubtful or deficient in any point, let it not discourage you; but note down that point in writing, and bend the attention of your mind to it, and labour and pray till you shall have made the attainment which will enable you to answer clearly.

2. Remember that secret prayer, reading the word of God, watchfulness, and self-examination, are the great means of preserving comfort in religion, and of growing in grace. In proportion as you are exact and faithful in these, such, usually, will be your inward peace, and the safety of your state. Unite them all together, and never cease to practise them, while you live.

3. Besides the Bible, have constantly in reading, at your leisure hours, some author of known piety and excellence. Read Baxter's Saints' Rest, Doddridge's Works, &c.

4. Do not suppose that any evidence of a gracious state, which at present you may think you possess, will release you from the necessity of maintaining a constant vigilance in time to come; nor from repeated examinations and

trials of yourself even to the end of life. Many marks and evidences of a gracious state are set down by pious writers. But they must all come to this : to ascertain what is your *prevalent* temper and character; whether, on the whole, you are increasing in sanctification, or not? If you are, you may be comforted; if not, you have cause to be alarmed. It is only he that endureth to the end, that shall be saved.

5. I think it of very great importance to warn you not to imagine that true religion is confined to the closet, or to the church; even though you apprehend that you have great comfort and freedom there. Freedom and comfort there, are, indeed, most desirable ; but true religion reaches to every thing. It alters and sweetens the temper. It goes into every duty, relation, station, and situation of life. If you have true religion, you will have a better spirit, you will be better sons, better scholars, better friends, better members of society, and more exemplary in the discharge of every duty; as the sure consequence of this invaluable possession. And if your religion does not produce these effects, although you may talk of inward comforts, and even of raptures, you have great reason to fear that the whole is a delusion, and that the root of the matter is not in you. "Herein," said the Saviour, "is my Father glorified, that ye bear much fruit; so shall ye be my disciples."

6. Be careful to avoid a gloomy, and to cherish a cheerful temper. Be habitually cheerful; but avoid levity. Mirth and laughter are not always sinful; but let your indulgence in them be clearly innocent, not very frequent, and never of long continuance. Be very humble. Be not talkative. Before experienced christians be a hearer, rather than a talker. Try, in every way, however, to promote religion among your relatives and friends. Win them to it by your amiable temper and exemplary deportment. "Flee youthful lusts." Shun every excitement to them. Guard against dissipation : it extinguishes piety. Be not disconcerted by ridicule and reproach. Your Saviour bore much of these for you. Think of this, and be ashamed of nothing so much as of being ashamed of Him. Trust in his protection, live to his praise, and you will spend an eternity in his blissful presence.

PUBLISHED BY THE
AMERICAN TRACT SOCIETY.

SERIOUS THOUGHTS

ON

ETERNITY.

See page 6.

ETERNITY! What is it? Who can explain it? Who can comprehend it? Eternity is duration without limits. Properly speaking, that only is eternal which has neither beginning nor end. In this sense, God alone is eternal. There never was a time when He was not. His existence is not capable of being measured by any period of time, ever so often repeated and multiplied. "He is the same from everlasting to everlasting. He was, and is, and is to come: the high and lofty One, who inhabiteth eternity." There are some creatures which have both a beginning and an end: as the whole brute creation. There are others which have had a beginning, but shall have no end: such are angels, and the spirits of men. But O, how deeply does it concern a creature born to live for ever, to make himself acquainted with that future state to which he is hastening; and what subject is more suited to restrain the licentiousness of this thoughtless, luxurious age, than that of eternity! Let a few minutes, then, be devoted to the serious perusal of the following pages; and may they be read with a mind disposed to offer up to God such desires as these:

"O God, the fountain of wisdom and goodness, assist me to read this little book with a serious attentive mind; let me not satisfy myself with barely commending the important truths which it contains, but teach me to make a devout application of them. May I read them as addressed to my conscience; and, as far as they agree with thy holy word, may I receive and submit to them as an oracle of God. May they afford me present instruction and benefit; and thus tend, by thy grace, through Jesus Christ, to fit me for the enjoyment of eternal glory."

The soul of man is immortal. This is a principle on which all the divine dispensations are founded. The sacred writers do not set themselves directly to prove it, yet it is abundantly asserted in the book of God. Our Saviour maintains the future existence of the soul, from God's calling himself the God of Abraham, Isaac, and Jacob, many years after their death; "for God," saith he, "is not the God of the dead, but of the living; for all live unto him." The same Divine Teacher asserts, that though men may kill the body, they cannot kill the soul; but if the soul died with the body, or ceased to think and act after death, they might kill the soul as well as the body. The Apostles speak of being unclothed; putting off the body, or the tent in which the soul resides. They speak of giving up the ghost, (or spirit,) of the spirits of wicked men being in prison; and of the spirits of just men being made perfect.

The Scriptures also speak of two future states: a state of happiness in heaven, and a state of misery in hell; and affirm that each of these is *eternal*. Holy souls, when removed from this world, are admitted into heaven, which is undoubtedly a state of glory and happiness, and the principal stress laid on this, is, that it is an eternal state. Thus we frequently read of eternal life; eternal redemption; and eternal glory. The house to which good men shall be removed, is eternal in the heavens. The king-

dom which they shall possess, is an everlasting kingdom.
Their happiness is called an eternal weight of glory, and
it is said, they shall be for ever with the Lord.

The misery of hell is also *eternal*. Those who lived in
rebellion against God, and disobedience to the Gospel, and
died impenitent and unrenewed, are removed to a state of
misery and torment. Our Lord, speaking of it, calls it
"the fire that never shall be quenched;" and this he repeats no less than four times. St. Paul says, that the
wicked "shall be punished with everlasting destruction."
Jude speaks of the inhabitants of Sodom as "suffering the
vengeance of eternal fire." Our Lord also, describing the
day of judgment, says, "The wicked shall go away into
everlasting punishment."

How astonishing then is the folly and the madness of
mankind! One would imagine, from their conduct, that
they expect either to die like the brutes, or else that God
has no *wrath* for them to fear, and no *mercy* for them to
desire. Look into the lives of men in general, and you
will see, that visible and temporal things appear to them
the most important, unseen and eternal things the most
trifling. They are eager to provide for their frail dying
bodies, and to heap up wealth which they cannot carry
with them; but take little or no care of the nobler part
of their nature, their *never-dying* souls. They are every
day laying up for years to come, but take no thought for
eternity. They are diligent in trading, but negligent in
praying. Their shop-books are duly posted, but they seldom consult the book of God. Some, who have lived
sixty or seventy years, and know that eternity cannot be
far off, have perhaps never spent one serious hour in inquiring into the state of their souls, and what preparation
is necessary for *eternity*. There are others, less busy about
temporal concerns, but equally careless about eternal ones.
They waste that precious time in unnecessary sleep or recreation, which was given to them to improve for *eternity*.
They contrive a thousand methods to kill time, (as they
ignorantly speak,) and are thankful to any one for an expedient to pass it off. They waste God's sacred time, as
well as their own, and will not devote even the short in-
terval of a Sabbath to consider the things that make for
their eternal happiness. "The life everlasting" is indeed

an article of their creed, but is strangely forgotten and lost sight of. The warnings of conscience, the admoni-tions of friends, the addresses and prayers of ministers, have no abiding effect on their mind. Thus they go on, in a round of folly and impenitence, till their foot slippeth in some dreadful moment, and they are lost for ever!

One of the Fathers, with great beauty and propriety, calls death "the gate of *eternity*." The death of a human creature is his passing out of time into eternity; and what event can be more solemn? Yet, this is so common that we seldom make any serious reflections on it; and we talk of it with as much indifference as of any common article of news. With regard to death itself, there is one event to the righteous and to the wicked: but O! what a vast difference immediately succeeds! To each, their time of trial is ended, and their eternal state is begun. The right-eous man puts off the body with all its cares, temptations, and sorrows; his soul ascends to God, and enters upon everlasting rest, security, and joy. What a glorious and delightful change! The sinner likewise changes his tem-poral, for eternal things; but it is for torment and misery. "When a wicked man dieth," saith Solomon, "his ex-pectation shall perish, and the hope of unjust men perish-eth" His last breath and his last hope expire together. He shall never hear preaching or praying any more; never receive one more invitation of mercy. He is brought to the bar of God, to give an account of the time, the means and advantages he has enjoyed, and to receive his doom. This is the portion of a wicked man! And is it not then an awful thing to die? You will think so when the king of terrors seizes you. A man of humour, in his gay hours, wrote and published a history of those who had died jesting; but he solemnly retracted it in writing on his death-bed; for he found that death was no jesting matter. *Ah! eternity! eternity!* said a graceless wretch, when dy-ing, and looking dismally at those about him—and there he stopped: he said no more; more he could not say; more he needed not to say. Ponder upon this example; and if you dread such a death, do not lead such a life.

When you hear of the death of others, how proper and useful a reflection would this be, "They are gone into *eternity!*" When you hear the solemn sound of a tolling bell, think, "Another soul is gone into *eternity!*"   When you see the funeral of a neighbour, think, "His time is ended; he has arrived at his *eternal* home, and is fixed in an unchangeable state."   "Man giveth up the ghost," saith Job, "and where is he?" What is become of him whom, but a few days ago, we saw and conversed with? In what place, with what company, is he now?   While I am thus reflecting, what does *he see*, and feel, and think? And how soon will the same thing be said concerning me also : "He is dead!" O that solemn, awful day, that shall finish my course; that infinitely important day when I must enter upon *eternity!* Surely these just and natural reflections should make me serious, as they did a very eminent courtier and states-man in Queen Elizabeth's time, (secretary Walsingham,) whose memorable words cannot fail to make some im-pression on every reader.   This great man having retired from the busy world into the privacy of the country, some of his gay companions rallied him on his becoming reli-gious, and told him he was melancholy.   "No," said he, "I am not melancholy, but I am *serious;* and 'tis fit I should be so." Ah! my friends, while we laugh, all things are serious round about us.   God is serious, who exerciseth patience toward us : Christ is serious, who shed his blood for us : the Holy Spirit is serious, in striv-ing against the obstinacy of our hearts : the Holy Scrip-tures bring to our ears the most serious things in the world : the whole creation is serious in serving God and us : all that are in heaven or hell are serious.—How then can we be gay?

Let us then maintain a steadfast regard to eternity, wherever we are, and whatever we do. Were we deli-berately to compare temporal and eternal things, we could never imagine that providing for the present life was wor-thy so many hours' thought and labour every day, and eternity scarce worthy of half a thought in many hours, and perhaps not one fixed serious thought in many days. Proper thoughts of eternity will restrain our immoderate fondness for the things of time; they will show us that the riches, honours, and pleasures of this life, are all tem-porary, fading and deceitful.   They will teach us to fol-low even our lawful worldly business with moderation, by reminding us that we have more important affairs to attend to. They will abate our fondness for the distinctions of the world, which are so generally prized. The honours of this world cannot silence a clamorous conscience, much less can they suspend their possessor's *eternal* doom. A great man had an extraordinary mark of distinction sent him by his prince, as he lay on his death-bed. "Alas!" said he, looking coldly upon it, "this is of immense value in this country; but I am just going to a country where it will be of no service to me."

In like manner, considerations of eternity will restrain your fondness for the diversions and amusements of life. You will have better things to mind, nobler objects to pursue. A lady, who had spent the evening at cards and in gay company, returning at night, found her servant-maid reading a religious book: she looked over her shoulder, and said, "Poor melancholy soul! what pleasure can you find in poring so long over that book?" That night the lady could not sleep, but lay sighing and weeping: her servant repeatedly asked her what was the matter? At length she burst into a flood of tears, and said, "O! it was one word I saw in your book, that troubles me; there I saw that word ETERNITY! O, how happy should I be, if I were prepared for *eternity*." The consequence of this impression was, that she laid aside her cards, forsook her gay company, and set herself seriously to prepare for another world. That eminent man, Mr. Philip Henry, when he felt the most acute pain, in a fit of the stone, said, "'I am tormented,' but, blessed be God, not 'in this flame.' I am on fire, but, blessed be God, it is not the fire of hell."

A regard to eternity would make us serious and lively in all the duties of religion. A celebrated painter among the ancients, being asked why he took so much pains about his pictures, answered, "I am painting for *eternity*." This thought—"I am reading, I am hearing, for *eternity*," would put life and vigour into all our religious exercises.

Serious thoughts of eternity will render the Gospel of Jesus Christ unspeakably precious. They will lead us to receive those humbling truths which are so opposite to the pride of worldly men. Why is it that the approach of death and eternity fills the mind with fear and apprehension? It is because we are *sinners*; and therefore "judgment is come upon all men to condemnation." And indeed it is "a fearful thing to fall into the hands of the living God." When these terrors of the Lord have taken hold of the conscience, how refreshing is it to hear that the word of God reveals a free, full, and everlasting salvation! It publishes pardon and eternal life as the gift of God, through the obedience and death of his Son JESUS CHRIST; without which there could have been no forgiveness of sin, no admission into eternal happiness. It is therefore only through faith in his blood, that we can hope for the justification of our persons. It is only through the power of his grace, that we can attain a meetness for the inheritance above. Thus shall we excite and cherish the most grateful and affectionate emotions of the heart toward our Lord Jesus Christ, and God, even our Father, " who hath loved us, and given us everlasting consolation, and good hope through grace;" and, in proportion to the solidity and liveliness of that hope, it will fill us with joy unspeakable and full of glory.

And now, candid Reader, permit me to request that you would most seriously and carefully review this subject, and ask yourself: " O my soul, art thou prepared for *eternity*?" Prepared, or not, eternity is at hand. Let me entreat this small favour of you, to retire this very day, and spend a little time in thinking upon eternity. Ponder, in your mind, what it is to live for ever in a state of endless happiness, or endless misery. If you will do this, I shall have a cheerful hope that one quarter of an hour, so spent daily, may be the most profitable you ever spent in all your life; and that God will make the meditation useful to your soul, and the beginning of eternal felicity. If I thought an apology necessary for dwelling so long on *eternity*, and being so earnest in this address, that apology should be no more than the answer which a pious man once made to this question from his friend, " Why do you spend so much time in reading, meditation, and prayer?" The good man lifted up his eyes and hands to heaven, and said, with great solemnity— "*for ever! for ever! for ever*"

CHRIST COMING TO JUDGMENT

Lo he comes—the King of glory!
　With his chosen tribes to reign;
Countless hosts of saints and angels
　Swell the mighty conqueror's train :
　　Now in triumph,
　Sin and death are captive led.

See the rocks and mountains rending—
　All the nations filled with dread!
Hark! the trump of God—proclaiming
　Through the mansions of the dead!
　　" Come to judgment—
　" Stand before the Son of Man !"

Now behold the dead awaking;
　Great and small before him stand;
Not one soul forgot or missing;
　None his orders countermand :
　　All stand waiting—
　For their last decisive doom!

Hear the chief among ten thousand
　Thus address his faithful few :
" Come, ye blessed of my Father,
　" Heaven is prepared for you;
" I was hungry—I was thirsty—I was naked—
　" And ye minister'd to me."

But how awful is the sentence,
　" Go from me, ye cursed race—
" To that place of endless torment,
　" Never more to see my face :
" I was hungry—I was thirsty—I was naked—
　" Ye to me no mercy show'd."

Jesus, save a trembling sinner,
　While thy wrath o'er sinners roll;
In this general wreck of nature,
　Be the refuge of my soul :
Jesus, save me! Jesus, save me! when the light-
　　nings
　Blaze around from pole to pole.

THE DECAY OF

SPIRITUAL AFFECTIONS.

BY REV. DR. JOHN OWEN.

SOME there are, yea many, who upon the beginning of a profession of their *conversion* to God, have made a great appearance of vigorous, active spiritual affections : yea, it is so with most who are really converted.

In some, this vigour of spiritual affections is from the real power of grace exerting its efficacy on their hearts. In others it is from other causes. The change that is made, be it what it will, is most striking, when it is wrought upon persons in their younger days ; for then their spiritual affections, so far as they are connected with the natural powers, are most active, and bear the greatest sway in the soul. But many christians, as they increase in age, and grow up in worldly wisdom and in the love of earthly things, and multiply secular cares, decay in their spiritual affections. They abide in their profession, but have "lost their first love."

It is a shame and folly unutterable that it should be so with any who make profession of that religion, wherein there are so many *incomparable excellencies* to endear and engage them to it more and more. But why should we hide what experience makes manifest, and what multitudes proclaim concerning themselves? I look upon it as a great evidence of life and growth in grace, when men, as they grow up in age, grow in an *undervaluation* of present things, in contempt of the world ; and abound more in the duties of charity and love. As we have before said, usually the *entrances* upon a religious life are attended with vigorous, active affections toward spiritual things. Of them who really and sincerely believed, it is said that "they rejoiced with joy unspeakable and full of glory." And of those who only had a work of conviction on them, that they "received the word with joy," and did "many things gladly."

In this state many abide and thrive, until their affections are transformed into the image and likeness of things above. But with many it is not so : they fall into a woful decay of their spiritual affections, and consequently, in their whole profession and conversation, their moisture is changed into the drought of summer. They have no experience of the life and actings of spiritual things within them, nor any comfort or refreshment from them. They honour not the Gospel with any fruits of love, zeal, or delight; nor are they useful any way to others, by their example. Some of them have had seeming *recoveries*, and are yet again relapsed into a lifeless frame; warnings, afflictions, the word, have awakened them, but they are again fallen into a *dead sleep ;* so that they seem to be " trees whose fruit withereth, without fruit, twice dead! plucked up by the roots."

There may be *a time of temptation*, wherein a soul may apprehend in itself, not only *decay*, but an utter *loss* of all spiritual affections, when it is not so. As believers may judge that the Lord hath forsaken and forgotten them, when he hath not; so they may, under temptations, apprehend that they have forsaken God, when it is not so. A man in the night may apprehend he has lost his way, and be in great distress, when he is in his proper road. Temptation brings darkness and amazement, and leads into mistakes and a false judgment in all things. They find not grace working in love, joy and delight, as formerly, nor that activity of heart and mind in holy duties, which spiritual affections once gave them. But yet it may be, the same grace works in godly sorrow by mourning, humiliation, and self-abasement, no less effectually, nor less acceptably to God.

Again, there may be an *apparent* decay of spiritual affections when there is no *real* decay. The same inward feelings may cease to produce the same outward symptoms and effects. This may be owing to age, to weakness, or infirmity. Men in their younger days are generally more ready to express their sorrow by tears, and their joy by sensible elevation of spirits, than in riper years. But here let it be remarked, that when decay is only apparent, it will ever be a burthen to those in whom it is found. They cannot but mourn and have a godly jealousy over themselves, lest the decays they find should not be in the outward, but in the inward man. And they will labour, that in all duties, and at all times, it may be with them as in the days of old; though they cannot derive that strength and vigour of spirit from these duties, nor that life and comfort which others have found. There will be in such persons, no decays in holiness of life; no remissness in the performance of religious duties. If decay be really of grace in the affections, it will be accompanied with a proportionable decay in all other things wherein holiness of life is concerned: but if it be only as to the sensible actings of natural affections, no such decay will ensue. Grace in this case will more vigorously act itself in the various faculties of the soul. The judgment and the will will be more decidedly and uniformly in favour of spiritual things.

When men find their affections quick, active, and intent on other things, as the lawful enjoyments and comforts of life, and yet dull and inactive in the things of religion, it is in vain for them to relieve themselves by supposing that the decays they find in themselves are in natural, and not in spiritual affections. If we see a man in his old age grow more in love with the things of the world, and less in love with the things of God, it is not through the weakness of nature, but through the strength of sin.

A real decay of spiritual affections is an awful frame of heart. It is a consumption of the soul, which threatens it with death every day. Among the many and dangerous evils wherewith this state is attended, are the following.

1. *It is displeasing to the Lord Jesus Christ.* He pities professors and intercedes for them, when they are under temptations; but threatens them under spiritual decays. "Nevertheless I have somewhat against thee, because thou hast left thy first love. Remember, therefore, from whence thou art fallen, and repent, and do the first works, or else I will come unto thee quickly, and will remove thy candlestick out of its place, except thou repent. Be watchful, and strengthen the things which remain, that are ready to die; for I have not found thy works perfect before God. Remember, therefore, how thou hast received and heard, and hold fast, and repent. If, therefore, thou shalt not watch, I will come on thee as a thief, and thou shalt not know what hour I come upon thee." This state of decay, Christ, who is the head of the church, and of every believer, cannot bear with, since it both reflects dishonour on himself, and is ruinous

to those in whom it is found. Christ speaks now the same
to each one of us, that he spoke to the churches of old; for
he lives for ever and ever, and is always the same, and his
word is living and unchangeable. If any of us are under this
frame, the Lord Jesus Christ, by his word and Spirit, testi-
fieth his displeasure against us; and if he be against us, who
shall plead for us? Oh, who can stand before the dreadful
tokens of his displeasure! The Lord help us to look well
to our condition, lest He, in whom we profess to place our
only trust, be found our greatest enemy. Take heed of that
state, in which Christ himself, our only advocate, hath declared he will not save us.

2. *This state tends above all things to grieve the Holy Spirit.*
His work it is, to give an increase and progress of holiness.
He begins it, and carries it on. Can any thing be apprehended to be such a just matter of grief and complaint to
the Holy Spirit, as to see those whom he had once raised
up to holy and heavenly affections, become earthly and sensual, and have no sensible actings of spiritual things within them? This is the only case wherein God speaks to men
in the way of complaint and expostulation; and uses all
sorts of arguments to convince them of the folly of such a
state. "What," saith he, "could I have done more to my
vineyard, that I have not done in it? Wherefore, when I
looked, that it should bring forth grapes, brought it forth
wild grapes?" When the Holy Spirit has nourished and
brought us up to some growth and progress in spiritual affections, wherein all his concern in us lies, and we grow
cold, dull, and earthly-minded, and cleave to the pleasures
and sins of the world, how is he grieved, how is he pro-
voked! It may be, this consideration of *grieving the Holy
Spirit*, has no great weight with some; if so, it would be
impossible for them to give a greater evidence of a profligate hardness in sin.

3. *This state is absolutely inconsistent with all comfortable
assurance of the love of God.* Whatever assurance of God's
love persons under the power of such a frame pretend to,
their security is only a sinful security, and not a gracious
assurance of peace. It is ever the case, that when professors decay in spiritual affections, stupidity of conscience
and security of mind also grow upon them; unless, perhaps, they are for a time in trouble and distress, by being
surprised into some great sin which reflects severely on

their consciences. That peace with God, and a comfortable assurance of salvation, should be consistent with an habitual decay in grace, is contrary to the whole tenor of Scripture; and the supposition of it would be the bane of religion. I do not say that our peace and assurance of the love of God arise wholly from the actings of grace in us; there are other causes also for these; but this I say, under an habitual declension of grace in the affections, no man can maintain a gracious sense of the love of God, or of peace with him. True peace with God is a fruit that will not grow on a vain, earthly, selfish frame of mind. "Do men gather grapes of thorns, or figs of thistles?" Nothing can be so ruinous to our profession, as once to suppose it an easy matter, a thing of course, to maintain peace with God. God forbid that our utmost endeavours to thrive in every grace should not be required thereto; for the whole beauty and glory of our religion depend upon it. "To be spiritually minded is life and peace."

4. *Such a decay as we have described is a dangerous symptom of an evil state and condition, and of the most awful self-deception.* I do not say that every one in whom there is this prevalent decay in spiritual affections is deceiving himself; that he is certainly a hypocrite; I only say, that where it continues without remedy, it is such a symptom of hypocrisy as that he who is wise and hath a care of his soul will not rest until he has searched it to the bottom. It seems as if such persons had had a false or imperfect work in that conversion unto God which they have professed. Now it is the nature of such a work greatly to flourish for a season, in all the principal parts and duties of a profession; but it is its nature also gradually to decay, until it is quite withered away: in a few, it is lost by the power of some vigorous temptation; but in most the decay is gradual, until the work entirely disappears. Wherever this decay exists, it is the duty of men to examine how things stand with them, and to know whether they have even savingly closed with Christ; since there is every appearance of the work's being of another nature. A saving work thrives and grows; but a false and imperfect work, having no root, withers away.

5. *Persons in this state of decay are apt to entertain false hopes and notions, whereby the deceitfulness of sin puts forth its power to harden them to their ruin.* This pernicious

effect is produced by the prevalency of a particular sin, or by the neglect of spiritual duties and the indulgence of a vain conversation in the world. Some plead for indulgence *only in one sin*. Let me be spared in this one thing, and in others I will be exact enough. There have been persons who have lived long in the practice of some gross sins, and yet all the while used a semblance of great diligence in other duties of religion. In this way poor sinners delude their own souls. Suppose it were possible that a man should give himself up to any sin, or be under the power of it, and yet be observant of all other duties; yet this would give him no relief as to the eternal condition of his soul. One sin, willingly lived in, is as able to destroy a man's soul, as a thousand. Besides, what we have supposed is practically false. There is no man that lives in any one known sin, but he really lives in more, though that one may bear the chief sway. Let no man relieve himself with the thought that it is but *one* sin, whilst that one keeps him in a constant neglect of God. Where God is not loved supremely, he is not loved at all. Let not the light you have, nor your gifts, nor your duties, nor your profession, deceive you; if you live in sin, you love not God.

There are some who determine, that at such or such a season, after such satisfaction in sin, they will utterly give over, so as that finally iniquity shall not be their ruin. But this is a false notion also, an effectual instrument of the deceitfulness of sin. He that will not *now* give over, that will not immediately, upon the discovery of the prevalency of any sin, and warning about it, endeavour sincerely and constantly to relinquish it, say what he will, never intends to give over; nor is it probable, in an ordinary way, that he ever will.

There are many who are ready to say, that though they have some cause to mistrust themselves, yet their condition is not so bad as some may apprehend it. This arises from hence, that they have not yet been overtaken with any enormous sin, which has filled their consciences with disquiet or terror. But let such remember, that every decay is dangerous, and especially that which the mind is ready to plead for an excuse.

If any suppose their decay does not arise from themselves and the evil of their own hearts, but from their circumstances, business, and state of life, from which, when they are freed, they will return at least to their former love and delight in spiritual things; they are deceiving themselves. Let men's circumstances be what they will, all their departures from God are from an evil heart of unbelief.

Many judge it no hard matter to retrieve themselves out of this state, but that which they can easily do, when there is absolute necessity for it. But this is a false notion also. Recovery from backsliding is the hardest task in the christian religion, and which few do either comfortably or honourably.

In this state, I say, men are apt, by such false reasonings, to deceive themselves to their eternal ruin. Wherefore I add, that they who find themselves under the power of this wretched frame, who are sensible in themselves, or at least make it evident to others that they are under a decay in their spiritual condition; if they rest in that state, without groaning, labouring, and endeavouring for deliverance from it, they can have no well-grounded hope of life and immortality; yea, they are in those paths which go down to the chambers of death.

I shall close with some advice to such as find themselves in a state of spiritual decay, and are desirous of being delivered from so dangerous a situation.

Remember whence you are fallen. Call to mind former days; consider if it were not better with you then than now; when in your lying down and rising up you had many thoughts of God, and of the things of God, and they were sweet and precious to your souls; when you rejoiced at the " remembrance of his holiness;" when you had zeal for his glory, delight in his worship, and were glad when they said " Let us go up to the house of the Lord ;" when you poured forth your souls with freedom and enlarged affections before him, and were sensible of the visits and refreshments of his love. Remember what peace, what tranquillity of mind you had, while it was thus with you; and consider what you have got, since you have in any degree forsaken God. Dare to deal plainly with yourselves. Is it not true, that all wherein you have to do with God, is either from custom and selfishness, or is attended with trouble, disquiet, and fears? Do you truly know, either how to live, or how to die? Are you not sometimes a terror to themselves? It must be so, unless you are hardened through the deceitfulness of sin. What have sin and pleasure, which you have received into your hearts, in the room of God and heavenly things, done for you? Speak plainly. Have they not wounded you, weakened you, and brought you into that condition, that you know not what you are, or to whom you belong? What are your thoughts, when your eyes are most open to your danger, when you are most yourselves? Do you not sometimes pant within yourselves and say, O that it were with us as in former days? If you can be no way affected with the remembrance of former things, then one of these two great evils you are certainly under; either you have never had a real work of grace in your souls, or you are hardened through the deceitfulness of sin.

Let those to whom this frame is a burden, consider, that as there are many things dreadful, pronounced in the Scriptures against backslidings and backsliders in heart, yet also there are special calls and promises given to those in your condition, who earnestly desire to return. "Return, thou backsliding Israel, saith the Lord, and I will not cause mine anger to fall upon you; for I am merciful, saith the Lord, and I will not keep anger for ever." Again, "I will heal their backslidings, I will love them freely; for mine anger is turned away from them."

As you design to live and not die, yield obedience to these calls, plead these promises before God, doing it with faith. As you value your souls, defer not the duty to which you are called, for one moment. You know not how soon you may be beyond the reach of calls and promises.

As to those who, on these and the like considerations, do not only desire, but will endeavour also to recover themselves from this condition, I give them this advice: BE IN GOOD EARNEST. *If you will return*, RETURN, COME. Make thorough work of it; this you must do some time or other or you will perish. Why not do it now? Why is not this the best season? Who knows but it will be the only time you will have for it? O remember, that trifling endeavours, occasional resolutions and attempts, will pass away like the "morning cloud and early dew," and leave your souls to ruin. Unless there be universal diligence and perseverance in your endeavours, you are undone. "Then shall ye know, if ye follow on to know the Lord."

SABBATH OCCUPATIONS.

See page 8.

PUBLISHED BY THE

AMERICAN TRACT SOCIETY,

NO. 150 NASSAU-STREET, NEW-YORK.

D. Fanshaw, Printer

Vol. 4.

SABBATH OCCUPATIONS.

—◦◦◦—

FRIEND,

ALLOW me to ask, What are you engaged in, or whither are you going? Are you preparing to join in the public worship of God? or are you following your worldly business, or seeking for amusement on this day? If one of the latter is your object, do you not recollect that this is the day which God has marked as his own, by the fourth commandment? But lest you should have forgotten it, permit me to refresh your memory. In the 20th chapter of Exodus it is thus written:

"*Remember the Sabbath-day, to keep it holy. Six days shalt thou labour, and do all thy work; but the seventh day is the Sabbath of the Lord thy God: in it thou shalt not do any work, thou, nor thy son, nor thy daughter, thy man-servant, nor thy maid-servant, nor thy cattle, nor the stranger that is within thy gates: for in six days the Lord made heaven and earth, the sea, and all that in them is, and rested the seventh day: wherefore the Lord blessed the seventh day, and hallowed it.*"

What excuse can you now make for profaning this day, which God has pronounced holy? If you did not know it before, you can now plead ignorance no longer. But, in truth, I strongly suspect that this is not the first, nor the second time, you have broken this commandment, by working, travelling, drinking, and many other idle practices: your own conscience will tell you whether I am right in what I suspect, or not.

Perhaps you will say, "It is not often that I break this commandment." Show me any one authority from the Bible which permits you to break it at any time. I am certain you cannot. It does not appear that the man who was stoned in the wilderness, for gathering sticks on the

Sabbath-day, had ever done so before; and yet he was stoned to death, God himself being the Judge, who tried the cause, passed the sentence, and ordered Moses to see it executed. See Numb. xv. 32. Were you, and all who are at this moment breaking the Sabbath, to be struck dead by the visitation of God, what a dreadful spectacle would be exhibited! It is to be feared, there would hardly be a house, a street, or a road, where there would not be some dead! It is only by the patience and long-suffering of God that you are spared, that you may repent, and not perish; and will you despise this mercy, and continue to insult your God, Sabbath after Sabbath? If you will do so, beware lest he cut you off suddenly, and deliver you over to everlasting torments. Or, if sudden judgment should not overtake you, as you know it has others, in very awful and numerous cases, be sure your repeated and aggravated sins will find you out at death, at judgment, and in hell, where your misspent, abused Sabbath hours, will be avenged with ages of useless sorrow.

But, perhaps you will say, "I see those who are my betters, and who ought to know what is right, travelling, driving about in their carriages, and following their amusements, as much on the Sabbath as on any other day." If so, they will have to answer for it at the dreadful day of judgment; but their conduct, my friend, is no rule for you. The Bible, which ought to be your rule of life, directs you not to "follow the multitude to do evil." Exod. xxiii. 2. It declares, that "though hand join in hand, the wicked shall not be unpunished." Prov. xi. 21. Perhaps you may say, "I am a poor man, or I have a large family, and cannot afford to be idle: besides, I can make more by working, and letting my cattle work on this day, than on any other; and you know I should disoblige my employers and customers, were I to refuse their orders." Oh, friend, reflect for a moment on the folly, as well as sinfulness of these excuses; so far from excusing, they add to your sins. Can you not trust to God for such a blessing on your six days' labour, as will supply the wants of your family? By working on the Sabbath, you plainly declare that you will not trust him. And if so, how can you expect that he will bless any thing you do? Is it not God whose day you are breaking, who gives you health and ability to earn the food

that you eat, and the clothes that you wear? Can all your
wages do you good, if he puts his curse upon them? The
little that is got in the fear of God goes much further than
the rewards of sin. How many are there, who have all
their earnings poisoned by their greediness in working on
the Sabbath! God can send sickness to take away what
is sinfully gotten. Look around among your neighbours;
and if you know any one that fears God and keeps his
Sabbath, I will venture to say that you find that man
more happy and comfortable than those who work, or
take their pleasure on those days. " Godliness hath the
promise of the life that now is, as well as of that which is
to come." Poor unhappy creatures, who are toiling at
your labours, keeping open your shops, sitting at your
stalls, when you ought to be employed in worshipping
God, and seeking for the salvation of your souls by Jesus
Christ his Son, how much do I pity you, how much do I
blame you! I will suppose, that by working on the Sabbath you gained six times as much as on any other day;
but let me ask you, in the words of our Lord Jesus Christ,
" What would it profit you, if you gained the whole world,
and lost your own soul?" If you fear disobliging your
master or employers, it plainly shows that you fear man
more than God. But let me ask you, Are you to obey
God, or man? and which ought you to seek to please?
Oh, my friend, remember that Jesus Christ hath said,
" Seek ye first the kingdom of God and his righteousness,
and all these things shall be added unto you." Matt. vi. 33.

Perhaps you may say, that you do keep the Sabbath-day
holy; for you go to church, and when going on business,
or a journey, you attend prayers in the way; and you
think there is no harm in working, travelling, or enter-
taining yourself with your friends for the remainder of
the day! But be assured, my friend, whatever *you* may
think, there is *much harm* in it, though you *may have* been
at prayers: observing the day in *one part*, will no more
excuse you for profaning the remainder, than having
hitherto kept the whole law, would excuse you for com-
mitting murder. The Sabbath-day consists of as many
hours as any other day, and it is the *day*, and not a particular part of it, that God commands to be kept holy.
Suppose you hire a labourer for a day, do you not con-

sider him as bound to work for you the whole of that day, except during the time allowed for his meals? or would you pay him the day's wages, if he only worked for one hour and a half? I am very certain you would not. And do you suppose that the great God will allow you to despise his day, and put him off with a formal service of an hour or two? Be assured he will not;—he will require it of you.

Had the laws of your country enacted, that every Sabbath-breaker should lose his property and substance, and also be confined in prison for life, would you then dare to break it, when you knew the consequence? It is true, you are not subject to such punishments here; but let me tell you, that, by the laws of God, you are exposed to much more dreadful judgments hereafter. The wilful breach of any one of God's commandments subjects you to the loss of both soul and body, when they will be cast into a prison from whence there is no escape, even into that bottomless pit, " where there is weeping, and wailing, and gnashing of teeth; where the worm dieth not, and the fire is not quenched." Will you, therefore, fear the power of man, and yet pay no regard to the laws of that God who can destroy both soul and body in hell-fire? Consider that, at this moment, you are exposing yourself to his just vengeance: this very night your soul may be required of you, and you may be summoned before the bar of that dreadful Judge, whose laws you are now breaking, and whose judgments you seem at present to despise.

Ah! could one of those miserable and tormented spirits which are at this moment suffering the agonies of eternal despair, tell you what he feels, and what he would give for one hour of this sacred day which you are trampling under foot for pleasure or for gain, so as to have the offers of pardon and eternal life made to him but once more; how would you tremble to hear his language, and fear lest this Sabbath should pass away, before you were delivered from that curse under which he suffers! Be assured that, unless you repent, a few more broken Sabbaths will make you his companion, and fellow-sufferer. Some are now in hell, who were on earth breaking with you, perhaps, the last Sabbath. Do you not know some one who lately prostituted the sacred day with you at work, or in idleness, if not in the public-house, who is now dead? Be sure, that, if he did not truly repent, he is a wretched soul, in the fire that can never be quenched. And, as surely as you follow his sins, shall you suffer his punishment. You cannot tell but this may be the last warning you may ever have.

God has the same abhorrence of the sin of breaking the Sabbath now, that he had when he commanded his ancient people to put to death the person that should be guilty of it: saying, " Ye shall keep the Sabbath, for it is holy unto you: every one that defileth it, shall surely be put to death: for whosoever doeth any work therein, that soul shall be cut off from among his people. Six days may work be done, but the seventh is the Sabbath of rest; holy to the Lord. Whosoever doeth any work in the Sabbath-day, he shall surely be put to death." Exod. xxxi. 14, 15. And though God does not now require his people to put Sabbath-breakers to death, yet he often calls them into the eternal world, while in the act of transgression, to appear before him, with all their guilt upon their heads.

A few of these affecting and alarming providences I shall now mention; and may God grant that they may prove a salutary and effectual warning to every reader who provokes God to come out against him in wrath, by profaning his holy day.

A lamentable occurrence, says the London Baptist Magazine, took place on Lord's-day, July 4, 1824, which may prove an additional warning to those who spend the sacred hours of the Sabbath in folly. Six young men, belonging to the town and vicinity of Ulverstone, Lancashire, resolved on having a pleasure excursion in a boat. They set off from Ulverstone very early in the morning, and intended to proceed down the bay of Morecambe, and visit the southern extremity of the island called Walney. The evening arrived, and the night passed over, but they did not return. On Monday their friends were extremely anxious concerning their safety, and made inquiry in all directions, but to no purpose. The result has proved, alas! too plainly, that all have perished; not one having escaped to communicate to their friends the tidings of woe, or relate the particulars of the accident It is supposed a squall had upset the boat, (which has been found empty,) and precipitated all within into the deep. At the date of this, four of the bodies have been found. The writer was called on to discharge the painful duties of the funeral service at the interment of one of them. He was a young man, about thirty-one years of age, the son of religious parents, members of the Independent church at Ulverstone. They accustomed him, from his infancy, to attend the house of God; but when he arrived at manhood, he broke through the restraints of education, he associated with the profligate, and became himself a profligate character. Not long before the awful catastrophe, in conversation with a pious relative, he expressed himself to this effect: "What is there," said he, "of pleasure that I have not tried? yet I cannot obtain happiness. I know the good man is the only happy one. I would give the world to be such; but I cannot pray." His relative wished him to attend religious service at the chapel. "I would," he replied, "do any thing almost that you wish me, except attending there—that I cannot do." Such were the sentiments of his heart, and such the despairing condition into which he had brought himself by his sin. Did he find satisfaction in his iniquity? No; he confessed the contrary; he was wretched; he honestly acknowledged that: for with all his crimes, he abhorred deceit, and urged that as one reason why he could not attend the house of God: —lest he should seem, by hypocrisy, to disgrace the cause of religion. His Sabbaths, of course, were misspent; and, it is said, some former escapes from a watery grave might have taught him wisdom. Being an excellent swimmer, he thought himself always secure; but the time was come when divine forbearance grew weary. He was found a great distance from the place where it is supposed the boat was upset, and, probably, sunk, after contending with the waves for a great length of time. He was naked, and so disfigured as scarcely to be recognised by his relatives. The immortal spirit was for ever gone. Reader, reflect on the wages of iniquity! Be admonished. Art thou a barren fig-tree? Even now the axe is laid unto the root: if thou bear fruit, well; but if not, God shall speedily cut thee down. Beware, lest he take thee away with a stroke; —then a great ransom cannot deliver thee.

In a town in Connecticut, a man and his companions, on the Sabbath, went out in a boat for the purpose of fishing; but soon the boat upset, and two of them were hurried into eternity.

A number of persons appointed a certain Sabbath, as a time to play at foot-ball. And while two of them were tolling a bell, to call the company together, they were struck with lightning, and both died.

A number of young men went out, on the Sabbath, to a forest, and cut down a small tree, for a liberty-pole. And while they were bringing it home upon a cart, one of the wheels suddenly went down a low place, and the pole struck one of the young men upon his head, and killed him upon the spot. And there he lay a fearful spectacle of the wrath of God against those who profane the Sabbath.

A young man, in the State of Connecticut, went down after public worship on the Sabbath, to a pond, for the purpose of bathing. His parents supposed that he was in his chamber, engaged in reading; and they knew not his danger, till a messenger arrived and informed them that he was drowned.

A young lady, in the State of New-York, agreed with her associates to meet on the Sabbath for a party of pleasure. When the day arrived, she mounted her horse to join her companions. But she had not proceeded far, when she was thrown from the horse. Although she was not materially injured, yet conscience in some measure awoke, and she knew that she was doing wrong. She observed to her friends that she would never again visit on the Sabbath : and that she would then return, were it not for disappointing her companions. She proceeded, but was soon thrown from the horse again, and so severely injured that she shortly after died.

A man in Vermont, took up a carpenter's instrument on the Sabbath, for the purpose of doing some unnecessary business; and in using it, he gave himself a wound which soon ended his days, and sent him to the tribunal of his final Judge.

A man in the vicinity of New-Orleans set out on a Sabbath morning to cross a river, on some worldly business. As he could find no boat but one which was fastened to a tree by a lock, he attempted to get that. Some persons who were present requested him to desist from his purpose. But he replied, that he would either go to the other side of the river, or to *hell.* He therefore broke the lock and entered the boat. But he had not gone far when it upset. And the spectators were so impressed that it was a judgment from God, that they stood amazed, till it was too late to afford him any help. Thus he was launched into a boundless eternity, in the midst of his impiety.

Several young men in New-Hampshire went to the Merrimack river, on the Sabbath, to bathe. After being in the water about an hour, they came on shore. One of them boasted that he had spent many Sabbaths in this way; and said that he meant to spend many more. His companions were about to leave the river, and requested him to do it. But he refused; and said that, at any rate, he would have another good swim. He then plunged into the river, and, although one of the best swimmers, sunk to the bottom, and was raised a corpse. His spirit had returned to God, to receive its irrevocable doom.

Three young persons in Massachusetts went out, on the Sabbath, to amuse themselves by sailing on a mill-pond. The next day they were all found at the bottom of the pond, dead.

A young man in New-Hampshire, who had often profaned the Sabbath by bathing in the water, one Sabbath boasted that he had bathed that day in two ponds, and that he would yet bathe in another. At evening he was found at the bottom of the pond, and carried home a corpse.

By records which have been kept in a place near one of our large rivers, it appears that more than twice as many have been drowned there on the Sabbath, as on any other day of the week. And those who were thus drowned, were cut off as in a moment, while breaking the command of God.

Several lads in Massachusetts went out in a boat, on the Sabbath, for amusement. A tything-man saw them, and ordered them to come on shore. But they treated his orders with contempt, and while making efforts to get out of his reach, they overturned their boat, and found themselves at the bar of God.

A pious minister, in his sermon, once spoke of the man in the camp of Israel, who was stoned to death for gathering sticks upon the Sabbath. A thoughtless man present was offended. And to show his contempt, left the house, and began to gather up sticks. When the congregation came out, they found the man dead, with the bundle of sticks in his arms.

The Sabbath-breaker is exposed continually to instant death. And he is exposed to everlasting destruction in hell. He must repent and forsake his sins, or he must perish for ever. Those who were thus cut off, while breaking the command of God, were perhaps not greater sinners than many who are spared. But being exposed to sudden death, they ought to have been engaged in an employment which would have fitted them for heaven. Instead of this, they were provoking God to destroy them, by openly profaning his precious Sabbath. And what time had they to repent or obtain pardon? And where can the person go, who persists in transgression till God cuts him off, but to the world of despair!

My Friend, you are in the hands of that God who hath commanded you to " *remember the Sabbath-day to keep it holy.*" You are breaking his command. And yet without him you cannot draw a single breath. He can easily destroy you; and if you continue to profane the Sabbath, he will do it. " *He that being often reproved, and hardeneth his neck, shall suddenly be destroyed, and that without remedy.*"

Oh! I beseech you, for the sake of your never-dying soul, consider what I now lay before you: read it over and over again, till it pleases God to bring you to a sense of your guilt and your danger, and to work in you true repentance, living faith in Jesus Christ, and a firm resolution of paying respect and obedience to *all* his commandments in future.

Should you ask me how you ought to keep this day holy, I shall feel great pleasure in directing you. You are to consider the Sabbath as a day on which you are to rest from labour, not that you may be idle, or that you may have time to amuse yourself with sports, but that you may have leisure to attend to " the one thing needful," the salvation of your soul. How often have I heard persons complain, that they were so occupied by business, as to have no time for reading the Bible, or considering reli-

gious things! If such persons had considered that the
Sabbath was given for this very purpose, and had they
spent it in reading the Scriptures, in prayer, hearing the
Gospel preached, joining in public worship, and in conversation with pious persons, they would have had no
reason to complain of ignorance, and might now have been
christians in reality, as well as in profession.

Hoping that you have some desire to improve this holy
season, I will give you a few plain directions concerning it.

If you are sensible of the blessings which the Sabbath
affords, you will hail its returning dawn with praise and
thanksgiving; you will pray to God to free your heart
from worldly thoughts and cares, and enable you to profit
by the means of grace which he has afforded you. You
should employ the early part of the morning in prayer and
reading the Bible, or hearing it read, and thinking upon it.
This will prepare your mind for joining in the prayers and
praises of the congregation, and for hearing that Gospel
preached, which will direct you in the way of life, and is
able to make you wise unto salvation.

After worship, you should return home, thinking of
what you have heard, and talking with your family or
friends about it, seeking to apply it to yourself, and praying to God to make it profitable to you. If you are a husband and a father, you must be careful that all your family
attend the worship of God with you. Suffer not trifling
excuses to keep your wife and children away from the
house of God. But you must also worship God in your
own house, as well as in public. Call your family together,
in the morning and evening, read the Bible to them, pray
with them, and for them, and teach them, as far as you
are able, the things of salvation. If you cannot instruct
your children yourself, send them to a neighbouring Sabbath-school, where they may be taught to read God's word,
and to know their duty to God and man. Be careful that
no one belonging to you is suffered to mix in the company
of those who break the Sabbath, lest their example should
tempt him to do the same; nor, under pretence of needful
recreation, to loiter about the streets or fields in the hours
between and after public worship. The remainder of the
day you should seek to improve in such a way as will
be most profitable to your own soul, and the soul of each

in your family; for if you are determined to keep the Sabbath-day holy, you will no longer keep company with those who profane it.

If you have no Bible, or feel your ignorance of the truths of religion, seek out, among your neighbours, for some religious persons who observe the Sabbath: they will be glad to receive you among them: there you will hear the Bible read, and you may derive more benefit than you can conceive at present from their experience and conversation. They will perhaps tell you, that formerly they were in the same blind and unconcerned state as yourself; how they were awakened to a sense of their lost condition, and brought to seek the Lord; how they sought him by fervent prayer; how they found peace with him through the blood of his dear Son Jesus Christ, which " cleanseth from all sin ;" how he has given them not only the pardon of their sins, but the good hope of his favour; and taught them by his Holy Spirit to see that, although they are guilty in themselves, they are accounted righteous before God for the sake of Jesus; that they " shall not come into condemnation, but are passed from death unto life." They will bring you to those ministers from whom they have derived comfort and instruction in right-eousness, and they will all pray for you, which thing is a greater blessing than you may be aware of; " for the effectual fervent prayer of a righteous man availeth much."

If you will spend the Sabbath in such a manner as this, I hope you will soon find the comfort of it; you will no longer look upon it as a restraint or drudgery, but will esteem one such day better than a thousand spent in idleness and folly; and if so, you will be prepared to conclude it as you began, with prayer and thanksgiving. After such a Sabbath, you will be able to enter on the business of the following week with cheerfulness, and with a lively hope that God will abundantly bless your labours. I shall conclude this, by requesting that you will keep it by you, that you will consider it over and over again, and also lend it to those of your neighbours who have been your companions in this sinful course, recollecting that you and I must soon meet at the judgment-seat of Christ, where we must give an account of all the advice we have received and refused to attend to, and all the opportunities we have neglected to improve. Farewell.

IMPORTANT QUESTIONS.

WITH

ANSWERS FROM THE BIBLE.

"Are you aware that the Holy Scriptures are full of solemn and awakening admonitions, to induce us to consider the salvation of our souls as the first and most important concern?"

PUBLISHED BY THE

AMERICAN TRACT SOCIETY,

AND SOLD AT THEIR DEPOSITORY, NO. 150 NASSAU-STREET, NEAR
THE CITY-HALL, NEW-YORK; AND BY AGENTS OF THE
SOCIETY, ITS BRANCHES, AND AUXILIARIES,
IN THE PRINCIPAL CITIES AND TOWNS
IN THE UNITED STATES

IMPORTANT QUESTIONS,

WITH ANSWERS

FROM THE BIBLE.

I. Do you consider that you have an immortal soul, infinitely more valuable than the body?

Then shall the dust return to the earth as it was, and the spirit shall return unto God who gave it. Eccl. vii. 7.

Fear not them which kill the body, but are not able to kill the soul; but rather fear him which is able to destroy both body and soul in hell. Matt. x. 28.

II. Have you ever *seriously* considered that the human soul is in a guilty, polluted state; and, of course, in danger of eternal death?

Behold I was shapen in iniquity, and in sin did my mother conceive me. Psalm li. 5.

There is none righteous, no, not one. Rom. iii. 10.

We were by nature the children of wrath, even as others. Eph. ii. 3.

III. Are you aware that the Holy Scriptures are full of solemn and awakening admonitions, to induce us to consider the salvation of our souls as the first and most important concern?

To-day, if ye will hear his voice, harden not your hearts, as in the provocation, in the day of temptation in the wilderness. Heb. iii. 7, 8.

Be ye also ready, for in such an hour as ye think not, the Son of Man cometh. Matt. xxiv. 44.

What is a man profited, if he shall gain the whole world, and lose his own soul? or what shall a man give in exchange for his soul? Matt. xvi. 26.

IV. Are you never alarmed by the solemn apprehension, that peradventure you may be called out of time into eternity, by some sudden and unexpected stroke; and not even be allowed a moment to think or pray, or in the least degree to prepare for ETERNITY?

Boast not thyself of to-morrow; for thou knowest not what a day may bring forth. Prov. xxvii. 1.

And he said this will I do: I will pull down my barns, and build greater, and there will I bestow all my fruits and my goods. And I will say to my soul, Soul thou hast much goods laid up for many years; take thine ease, eat, drink, and be merry. But God said unto him, Thou fool, this night thy soul shall be required of thee: then whose shall those things be which thou hast provided? So is he that layeth up treasure for himself, and is not rich toward God. Luke, xii. 18—21.

V. You have broken the divine law, and offended the great God: are you brought to see the sinfulness and danger of these things; and are you humbly confessing, and truly repenting of the same?

God now commandeth all men every where to repent. Acts, xvii. 20.

Except ye repent, ye shall all likewise perish. Luke, xiii. 5.

Him hath God exalted with his right hand to be a Prince and a Saviour, for to give repentance to Israel, and forgiveness of sins. Acts, v. 31.

There is joy in the presence of the angels of God over one sinner that repenteth. Luke, xv. 10.

Godly sorrow worketh repentance to salvation, not to be repented of. 2 Cor. vii. 10.

Bring forth fruits meet for repentance. Matt. iii. 8.

VI. If you are indulging the hope of repentance in time to come, and promising future amendment, are you not awfully deceiving yourself, inasmuch as the time of sick-ness and the hour of death may suddenly overtake you? And these are not favourable seasons for repentance; and if you wilfully put it off, neither space nor grace may be granted you for the purpose, since neither are at your command.

And as he reasoned of righteousness, temperance and judgment to come, Felix trembled; and answered, Go thy way for this time; when I have a convenient season, I will call for thee. Acts, xxiv. 25.

*_** *We have no evidence that such a time ever occurred.*

For what is your life? It is even a vapour, that appear-eth for a little time, and then vanisheth away. James, iv. 4.

VII. Do you know that you are in danger of mistaking your own character, condition, and prospects? And if so, should you not examine your heart and state before God?

The heart is deceitful above all things, and desperately wicked: who can know it? Jer. xvii. 9.

And you hath he quickened, who were dead in tres-passes and sins. Eph. ii. 1.

I know you, that ye have not the love of God in you. John, v. 42.

The carnal mind is enmity against God. Rom. viii. 7.

Which shall know, every man the plague of his own heart. 1 Kings, viii. 38.

Search me, O God, and know my heart: try me, and know my thoughts: and see if there be any wicked way in me, and lead me in the way everlasting. Psalm cxxxix. 23, 24.

VIII. Have you considered the law of God, that it is holy, just, and good? Have you tried yourself by it? Do you know it is spiritual, and therefore extends to your thoughts and intentions, as well as to your words and actions; and that if you offend in one point, you are condemned.

Ye have heard that it was said by them of old time, Thou shalt not kill; and whosoever shall kill shall be in danger of the judgment. But I say unto you, that whoso-ever is angry with his brother without a cause, shall be in

danger of the judgment.   Ye have heard that it was said
by them of old time, Thou shalt not commit adultery.   But
I say unto you, That whosoever looketh on a woman to
lust after her, hath committed adultery with her already in
his heart.   Matt. v. 21, 22. 27, 28.

For I was alive without the law once; but when the
commandment came, sin revived, and I died.   And the
commandment, which was ordained to life, I found to be
unto death.   Rom. vii. 9, 10.

Whosoever shall keep the whole law, and yet offend in
one point, he is guilty of all.   James, ii. 10.

IX. Are you aware, that all your own righteousness is
as filthy rags, and is in itself utterly insufficient to justify
you: that it must in no sense be relied upon as the ground
of your acceptance with God?

And he spake this parable unto certain which trusted in
themselves that they were righteous, and despised others :
Two men went up into the temple to pray; the one a
Pharisee, and the other a publican.   The Pharisee stood,
and prayed thus with himself: God, I thank thee that I
am not as other men are, extortioners, unjust, adulterers,
or even as this publican.   I fast twice in the week, I give
tithes of all that I possess.   And the publican, standing afar
off, would not lift up so much as his eyes unto heaven, but
smote upon his breast, saying, God be merciful to me a
sinner.   I tell you, this man went down to his house justified rather than the other; for every one that exalteth
himself shall be abased, and he that humbleth himself
shall be exalted.   Luke, xviii. 9—14.

But we are all as an unclean thing, and all our righ-
teousnesses are as filthy rags; and we do all fade as a leaf;
and our iniquities, like the wind, have taken us away.   Isa.
lxiv. 6.

Not by works of righteousness, which we have done,
but according to his mercy, he saved us, by the washing
of regeneration, and renewing of the Holy Ghost.   Tit. iii. 5.

X. If you are convinced, and affected by these important truths, do you know that the Holy Ghost alone can
work an effectual change in your heart: that you must be

born of the Holy Spirit, or you cannot see the kingdom of
God?

Jesus answered, Verily, verily, I say unto thee, Except
a man be born of water, and of the Spirit, he cannot enter
into the kingdom of God. John, iii. 5.

Now we have received, not the spirit of the world, but
the Spirit which is of God ; that we might know the things
that are freely given to us of God. But the natural man receiveth not the things of the Spirit of God : for they are
foolishness unto him : neither can he know them, because
they are spiritually discerned. 1 Cor. ii. 12. 14.

XI. If you are touched with compunction : if you cry,
"What must I do to be saved?" have you considered the
love of God in giving his Son to die for the sins of the
world? Have you believed that Jesus Christ is God over
all, blessed for ever, but was made flesh, that he might be
sin for you, who knew no sin? And will you listen, poor
lost sinner, when the ministers of Christ beseech you, in
Christ's stead, to be reconciled to God? Will you come to
him? will you receive him? will you venture to cast your
poor ruined soul on him : to be redeemed, cleansed from
all sin by his blood, justified before God?

The same came for a witness, to bear witness of the
Light, that all men through him might believe. And the
Word was made flesh, and dwelt among us, (and we beheld
his glory, the glory as of the only begotten of the Father,)
full of grace and truth. John, i. 7. 14.

He that believeth on him is not condemned : but he
that believeth not is condemned already ; because he hath
not believed in the name of the only begotten Son of God.
John, iii. 18.

For all have sinned, and come short of the glory of God ;
being justified freely by his grace, through the redemption
that is in Christ Jesus ; whom God hath set forth to be a
propitiation through faith in his blood, to declare his righteousness for the remission of sins that are past, through
the forbearance of God. Rom. iii. 23—25.

XII. Are you aware that you cannot escape, if you

neglect so great salvation ? That unless you are justified by the blood of Jesus Christ, who is the end of the law for righteousness to every one that believeth, you will die in your sins ? Nay, do you know that it is the greatest of sins to despise the blood of Christ, and the atonement he has made ?

I said therefore unto you, that ye shall die in your sins ; for if ye believe not that I am he, ye shall die in your sins. John, viii. 24.

Therefore we ought to give the more earnest heed to the things which we have heard, lest at any time we should let them slip. For if the word spoken by angels was steadfast, and every transgression and disobedience received a just recompense of reward ; how shall we escape if we neglect so great salvation ? which at the first began to be spoken by the Lord, and was confirmed unto us by them that heard him. Heb. ii. 1—3.

He that despised Moses' law, died without mercy, under two or three witnesses ; of how much sorer punishment, suppose ye, shall he be thought worthy, who hath trodden under foot the Son of God, and hath counted the blood of the covenant, wherewith he was sanctified, an unholy thing, and hath done despite unto the Spirit of Grace ? Heb. x. 28, 29.

XIII. If you profess to be justified by the blood of Christ through faith ; and become a child of God, by being born of the Spirit, are you aware that the only scriptural and decisive evidence of your being in that happy state is, the real sanctification of your heart, by the Holy Spirit ; so that by the Spirit you mortify the deeds of the body, crucifying your affections and lusts, and come out from the wicked world ? While the fruits of the Spirit are in your heart, do they appear in your life and conversation, by performing your duty to God : and doing good unto all men, especially those who are of the household of faith ?

And such were some of you : but ye are washed, but ye are sanctified, but ye are justified in the name of the Lord Jesus, and by the Spirit of our God. 1 Cor. vi. 11.

And for their sakes I sanctify myself, that they also might be sanctified through the truth. John, xvii. 19.

Who gave himself for us, that he might redeem us from all iniquity, and purify unto himself a peculiar people, zealous of good works. Titus, ii. 14.

Teaching us that, denying ungodliness and worldly lusts, we should live soberly, righteously, and godly, in this present world. Titus, ii. 12.

Yea, a man may say, Thou hast faith, and I have works: show me thy faith without thy works, and I will show thee my faith by my works. James, ii. 18.

XIV. Do you keep in recollection, that while all spiritual blessings are revealed in the exceeding great and precious promises of God in Christ, yet that they must be sought for, nay, wrestled for, by earnest prayer, until you obtain them; looking unto Jesus, that by the power of his death your old man of sin may be destroyed, and you may walk in newness of life?

Ask and it shall be given you; seek, and ye shall find; knock, and it shall be opened unto you. Matt. vii. 7.

I the Lord have spoken it, and I will do it. Thus saith the Lord God; I will yet for this be inquired of by the house of Israel, to do it for them. Ezek. xxxvi. 36, 37.

Behold he prayeth. Acts, ix. 11.

Pray without ceasing. 1 Thess. v. 17.

Knowing this, that our old man is crucified with him, that the body of sin might be destroyed, that henceforth we should not serve sin. But God be thanked that ye were the servants of sin; but ye have obeyed from the heart that form of doctrine which was delivered you. Being then made free from sin, ye became the servants of righteousness. Rom. vi. 6. 17, 18.

If ye then, being evil, know how to give good gifts unto your children; how much more shall your heavenly Father give the holy Spirit to them that ask him. Luke, xi. 13.

XV. Are you diligent in using the means of grace? Do you love and prize the Lord's-day, and keep it holy? Do you not suffer it to be profaned by idleness, or taking pleasure, or doing business? Rather, do you consider it your

duty and privilege to dedicate it wholly to the concerns of
the soul and eternity, and to employ it in the peculiar service of God?

Remember the Sabbath-day to keep it holy. Six days
shalt thou labour, and do all thy work: but the seventh
day is the Sabbath of the Lord thy God; in it thou shalt
not do any work, thou, nor thy son, nor thy daughter, thy
man-servant, nor thy maid-servant, nor thy cattle, nor the
stranger that is within thy gates. For in six days the Lord
made heaven and earth, the sea, and all that in them is,
and rested the seventh day: wherefore the Lord blessed
the Sabbath-day, and hallowed it. Exod. xx. 8—11.

XVI. Do you experience, that the ways of God are ways
of pleasantness? That you are not merely obliged to walk
in the path of duty, because it is inculcated by the highest
authority, but that his service is perfect freedom; and that
while you are following holiness, your heart is both glad-
dened by the present satisfaction you feel, and cheered with
the assurance and anticipation of greater things to come?

Beloved, now are we the sons of God, and it doth not
yet appear what we shall be; but we know that when he
shall appear, we shall be like him; for we shall see him
as he is. 1 John, iii. 2.

And in that day thou shalt say, O Lord, I will praise
thee; though thou wast angry with me, thine anger is
turned away, and thou comfortedst me. Behold, God is
my salvation; I will trust and not be afraid: for the Lord
JEHOVAH is my strength and my song: he also is become my salvation. Therefore, with joy shall ye draw water out of the wells of salvation. Isa. xii. 1—3.

Her ways are ways of pleasantness, and all her paths
are peace. Prov. iii. 17.

Therefore, being justified by faith, we have peace with
God, through our Lord Jesus Christ: by whom also we
have access by faith into this grace wherein we stand, and
rejoice in hope of the glory of God. And not only so, but
we glory in tribulations also; knowing that tribulation
worketh patience; and patience, experience; and experience, hope. Rom. v. 1—4.

XVII. Do you value, and constantly attend the preaching of the Gospel? Do you diligently search the Scriptures, considering that these are the appointed means of your becoming wise unto salvation, through faith that is in Christ Jesus?

So then faith cometh by hearing, and hearing by the word of God. Rom. x. 17.

And that from a child thou hast known the Holy Scriptures, which are able to make thee wise unto salvation, through faith which is in Christ Jesus. 2 Tim. iii. 15.

O how I love thy law! It is my meditation all the day. Psalm cxix. 97.

Search the Scriptures; for in them ye think ye have eternal life, and they are they which testify of me. John, v. 39.

Open thou mine eyes, that I may behold wondrous things out of thy law. Psalm cxix. 18.

These were more noble than these in Thessalonica, in that they received the word with all readiness of mind, and searched the Scriptures daily, whether those things were so. Acts, xvii. 11.

XVIII. Are you constant, diligent, and faithful in self-examination, dreading formality and hypocrisy above all things? Do you remember that the Holy Scriptures speak of some who thought they knew God, called him Father, and professed to fear and love him, while they were resting in the name and form of religion, without any real interest in him? Do you then walk in the fear of God? Do you, by the power of the cross of Christ, strive to correct your evil tempers—your worldly lusts—your foolish imaginations—your idle and profane words; and that diligently, daily, and hourly, as they arise? Do you arouse yourself to your duty? Are the last works more than the first?

A son honoureth his father, and a servant a master: if I then be a father, where is mine honour? and if I be a master, where is my fear? saith the Lord of hosts unto you, O priests, that despise my name. And ye say wherein have we despised thy name? Malachi, i. 6.

This people draweth nigh unto me with their mouths,

and honoureth me with their lips; but their heart is far
from me. Matt. xv. 8.

They profess that they know God; but in works they
deny him, being abominable and disobedient, and to every
good work reprobate. Titus, i. 16.

Having a form of godliness, but denying the power
thereof: from such turn away. 2 Tim. iii. 5.

XIX. Should you not, my dear fellow-immortal, above
all things, remember and be affected with the thought that
nothing can support or comfort you in the hour of death,
but the saving knowledge of the Lord Jesus Christ, and a
scriptural hope of heaven through him?

O death, where is thy sting? O grave, where is thy victory? The sting of death is sin; and the strength of sin is
the law.   But thanks be to God, which giveth us the victory through our Lord Jesus Christ. 1 Cor. xv. 55—57.

Yea, though I walk through the valley of the shadow
of death, I will fear no evil; for thou art with me; thy
rod and thy staff, they comfort me. Psalm xxiii. 4.

Blessed are the dead which die in the Lord from
henceforth. Yea, saith the Spirit, that they may rest
from their labours; and their works do follow them.
Rev. xiv. 13.

XX. Finally, the writer of these plain questions earnestly entreats you to consider, that there will be a solemn
judgment of both the righteous and the wicked; that
you, and I, and the whole world, must appear at that
day, not as spectators, but as parties concerned, and
shall receive a righteous sentence from the great and
holy God.

When the Son of Man shall come in his glory, and all
the holy angels with him, then shall he sit upon the
throne of his glory; and before him shall be gathered
all nations; and he shall separate them one from another,
as a shepherd divideth his sheep from the goats.   Matt.
xxv. 31, 32.

The Lord Jesus shall be revealed from heaven, with his
holy angels, in flaming fire, taking vengeance upon them

that know not God, and obey not the Gospel of our Lord Jesus Christ: who shall be punished with everlasting destruction from the presence of the Lord, and from the glory of his power. 2 Thess. i. 7—9.

Be ye therefore ready; for in such an hour as ye think not, the Son of Man cometh. Matt. xxiv. 44.

These shall go away into everlasting punishment; but the righteous into life eternal. Matt. xxv. 46.

CONCLUSION.

Have you read these questions?—Are they not drawn from the Holy Scriptures?—Are they not infinitely important in themselves?—Do they not respect things which relate to your present and eternal interest?—Have you not neglected them, either through your hurry in business, or your fondness for the amusements and follies of the world? Oh, that you may now be wise, that you may understand these things, and seriously consider your latter end! What a mercy that you have not been cut off in your ignorance, and in your sins—that you have not been banished from the presence and kingdom of God. Attend and hear the good things of the Gospel. God waits to be gracious. The door of mercy is yet open—and yet there is room. Jesus Christ came into the world to save sinners, yea, the very chief of sinners. His blood cleanseth from all sin. Now is the accepted time, now is the day of salvation. Come, poor sinner, to this neglected Redeemer; he gives righteousness, and peace, and glory. He casts out none that come to him, by faith. May the Lord work in you, both to will and to do of his own good pleasure; and the end shall be peace and life everlasting.

FINIS.

FRIENDLY CONVERSATION.

My Dear Friend,—Will you permit one, with the best intentions, to converse with you a few moments on a very important subject? As a friend, I feel interested in your welfare: allow me, then, to inquire, What are you? What ought you to be? What must you be?

I. *What are you,* my friend?

Do not be offended at the question; it is one which each of us should be prepared to answer, and it surely deserves your serious consideration.

You are *a rational and an accountable being.* The past you can remember. You can reflect and reason on what is present—on any piece of work you are engaged in, or on the friendly Tract in your hand. And the future you can anticipate, or look forward to. Hence those alarming thoughts which you have felt when a friend has been snatched away by the iron hand of Death, or when pale sickness has threatened to bring you to "the King of

Terrors." Of all the creatures on earth, man alone is capable of doing this. This faculty you and I have received from God our Maker; and hence,

We are *accountable* to him for every thought we think, for every word we speak, and for every thing we do. Matt. xii. 36. God has not left us to do as we think proper; he has given us a law, which is exceedingly broad, extending to thought, word, and action. This law is contained in the Bible, and is holy, just, and good. Did you ever think of this, my friend?

The law of God proves that you are a *sinful* creature. Its righteous demand is, that you love God at all times, with *all your mind and strength*, and your neighbour, whether enemy or friend, *as yourself*. Now I will not suppose you are as bad as many are, who are openly and daringly " fornicators, idolaters, adulterers, thieves, covetous, drunkards, revilers, or extortioners." 1 Cor. vi. 9, 10. These are in a most alarming state indeed! They " shall not inherit the kingdom of God." Awful declaration! Where, then, shall they take up their everlasting abode? There is only one other kingdom to afford them shelter—the kingdom of Satan : and who can dwell with " everlasting burnings?" Who can take up his abode amidst " devouring fire?"

I would rejoice, my friend, if you rank not among these open enemies of God, who wear the mark of destruction in their foreheads. But, alas! if you have broken only one commandment of the law, or have ceased to love God with all your heart, for a single moment, you are a sinner: he that keepeth the whole law, and offendeth in *one* point, is guilty of all. James, ii. 10. Now this law, which you must be conscious you have broken, thunders the most dreadful curses on every soul of man that acts as you have done. Gal. iii. 8, 9. It will admit of no compromise. You must present a perfect obedience to it, or suffer all the weight of its curse for ever! How many thousands are *now* groaning under this weight, while we are speaking of it, and must continue to do so through an awful eternity! God declares your situation to be dreadful. Rem. iii. 10, &c. And yet amidst all this,

You are a *dying* creature. As many years as you have lived so many Death has been on his way toward you.

to deprive you of life. Surely, then, he can be at no great distance now. Have not his arrows, flying around, cutting off your friends and acquaintances, warned you of his approach? Perhaps now, while you read, he is setting you as his mark, and drawing to the head the arrow which will break the thread of life, and plunge you into eternity! And are you prepared to stand before the judgment-seat of Christ, to give an account of the deeds done in the body? For remember,

You are an *immortal* creature. Your soul will live for ever, either in heaven or in hell. And " as the tree falls, so it must lie" for ever. If you die unholy, you will be unholy still.

II. *What, then, ought you to be?*

You ought no longer to remain careless and unconcerned about your immortal soul. Why should you spend your precious moments in contriving how you may gather riches, or gratify the desires of the flesh, when every moment may be your last! Did God create you only that you might gather money, or that you might become expert in trade, or that you might eat and drink, and sleep and wake, like the brutes that perish?

You should diligently read the Bible. For, however you may neglect it now, you must be judged by it ere long. You should constantly attend the preaching of the Gospel, that you may be made wise unto salvation. And, above all, you should immediately flee to Jesus Christ, in earnest prayer, and a living faith, that you may be pardoned through his blood, acquitted before God, for his righteousness-sake, and be made holy by the power of the Spirit.

Now let me entreat you, (and then I have done,) seriously to inquire, for a moment,

III. *What must you be?*

You are now either the friend or the enemy of God. If you reverence and love him, because he is so holy and so just that he cannot but abhor every kind and degree of sin, and is determined to punish it in the most tremendous manner, while he pardons and saves the penitent and believing sinner, then you are the friend of God, interested in the merits of his Son, and fitted, by his Spirit, for his presence in heaven. But, if not, you are his enemy, fit only for hell: and, dying in your present state, you will, you must be banished thither.

If unholy, what would you do in heaven? What sort of company, employment and pleasure would you find there? It would be a hell to you, in your present state; and sickness and death will make no change in you for the better: they have no power at all to do this: nothing but believing on Jesus Christ, loving and obeying him, can prepare us for, or entitle us to, a place in his kingdom. Both you and I, my dear friend, must for ever dwell either with angels and just men made perfect in heaven, or with devils and damned souls in hell. There is no possible alternative; and how soon our state may be fixed, who can tell?

Here I am obliged to stop. But ah! how can I take my leave! Perhaps all this will be in vain; the snares of the world, the deceitfulness of riches, the wiles of Satan, and the depravity of my friend's heart, will cause him to throw aside this paper, and forget these infinitely important truths; he may live and die a stranger to salvation through Jesus Christ; and then—how shall I utter it! he will be for ever undone! Nay, this friendly endeavour to lead him to Christ, will then aggravate his final ruin!—But, should these truths sink down into your heart, my dear friend, and cause you to flee from the wrath to come, to a crucified Saviour, my present pain will be all forgot, while I rejoice with angels over one sinner that repenteth. Farewell.

PUBLISHED BY THE
AMERICAN TRACT SOCIETY,

And sold at their Depository, No. 150 Nassau-street, near the City-Hall, New-York; and by Agents of the Society, its Branches, and Auxiliaries, in the principal cities and towns in the United States.

A STRANGE THING.

——◆——

I FIND by conversation with my neighbours, and from
the perusal of books and pamphlets which they are frequently putting into my hands, that there is an opinion
extensively prevalent that all mankind will be saved.
Those with whose views I am best acquainted, generally
believe that there is no punishment after death. Sin, it
is thought, involves its own punishment. Consequently,
when mankind cease to sin, as it is supposed they all will
at death, there will be an end to all their sufferings. This
opinion appears to me *strange*, not because it is entirely
new, but because it is inconsistent with so many other
things which I have long considered as facts, and which,
so far as I know, have been considered as facts by others.

The *first* of these is the *solicitude* which the Apostles
manifested for the salvation of their hearers. They conversed, and preached, and prayed, and laboured, as though
they were deeply concerned for the salvation of their fellow men. Paul, in his Epistle to the Romans, thus expresses the anxiety which he felt for his brethren the
Jews: "I say the truth in Christ, I lie not, my conscience also bearing me witness in the Holy Ghost, that
I have great heaviness and continual sorrow in my heart.
For I could wish myself accursed from Christ, for my
brethren, my kinsmen according to the flesh." In the
first verse of the next chapter, he gives us the reason why
he was so anxious respecting his brethren: "My heart's
desire and prayer to God for Israel is, that they might be
saved." That the salvation of his hearers was the object
of Paul's *exertions*, as well as prayers, is more than inti-
mated in the following passage: "I am made all things
to all men, that I might by all means *save* some." Paul
was anxious, not only so to conduct *himself* as to secure
the salvation of his fellow creatures, but that *all* to whom
the treasures of the Gospel were committed, should do
the same. This is apparent from the following address
to Timothy: "Take heed unto thyself, and unto thy doc-

trine; continue in them; for in doing this thou shalt both *save* thyself and them that hear thee." Now, upon the supposition, that Paul, and the rest of the Apostles, knew that all would be saved, it appears to me *strange*, that they should manifest this *solicitude* about it. It is not natural for mankind to be anxious that an event should take place, when they know infallibly that it cannot be prevented. We see no one anxious lest the sun should not continue to rise and set, and the seasons observe their appointed successions. And the only conceivable reason is, all men are satisfied that the rising and setting of the sun, and the rotation of the seasons, will continue as they have done. Now if Paul knew, and, if it is a truth, he did unquestionably know it, that all men would be saved, he could not have had any anxiety respecting the salvation of his brethren, or any one else, any more than those who know the sun will rise to-morrow, can be anxious lest they be left in total darkness. Paul's anxiety respecting the salvation of his brethren and others, and the great exertions which he made, and endeavoured to influence others to make, in order to save them, are strange and unaccountable things, upon every other supposition, but that of his considering them in danger of perishing, and his seriously fearing that many of them actually would perish.

2. If the doctrine of universal salvation was taught by the Apostles, it appears to me strange that their hearers were so much *alarmed* at their preaching. That the preaching of the Apostles did excite great alarm and anxiety among their hearers, is a fact with which few can be unacquainted. On the day of Pentecost, three thousand were pricked in their heart, upon the hearing of Peter's sermon; and under the influence of their deep anxiety, they exclaimed, "Men and brethren, what shall we do?" It seems to have been a conviction of his guilty, perishing condition, produced by the doctrine of Paul, that influenced the jailer to inquire what he should do to be saved. When Paul stood before Felix, the Roman governor, and "reasoned of righteousness, temperance, and judgment to come, Felix *trembled.*" Now if the Apostles believed the doctrine of universal salvation, they were doubtless understood to preach it. But it appears to me

strange, that their hearers, while hearing that all will be saved, or what evidently implied this, should *tremble*, give signs of the deepest distress, and with tears entreat the Apostles to inform them what they must do to be saved. Their deep solicitude is perfectly *natural*, upon the supposition that they were taught the reality of a future judgment, and the danger in which they stood of perishing for ever, as a just punishment for their sins. We can easily see, that a firm belief in this truth, and a lively apprehension of it, would produce the very trembling, and alarm, and inquiry, which were produced. But as the opinion under consideration is inconsistent with their having been taught any such thing, it renders the fact of their deep anxiety wholly unaccountable. To get rid of the difficulty, we will for the present suppose that they were *needlessly* alarmed, as many are occasionally thought to be at the present day.

3. Admitting the fact that Christ and the Apostles taught the doctrine of universal salvation, it appears to me inexpressibly strange, that wicked men manifested so much *opposition* to their preaching. Christ and the Apostles doubtless preached the truth plainly and faithfully. Of course, if the doctrine of universal salvation is true, they preached this doctrine; they were understood to preach it; and they never preached any thing inconsistent with it. Now what there is in this doctrine so repugnant to the feelings of wicked men as to excite such opposition as Christ and the Apostles encountered from them, I never could see. That the feelings of all men in an unsanctified state are opposed to the doctrine of future and eternal punishment, is a truth which every one knows from his own experience, as well as from observation. On the supposition that Christ and his Apostles preached *this* doctrine, it would be perfectly easy to account for all the opposition which was made against them. But why all the world, as it were, should rise up against these holy men, and persecute them even unto death, only for declaring the glad tidings of the salvation of all men, is one of those unaccountable things which I acknowledge myself unable to explain.

4. Upon the supposition that all will be saved, there is something peculiarly strange in *the language, in which*

*Christ and the Apostles speak of the future state of the right-
eous and the wicked.* With the idea in his mind, that it
was the design of Christ and the Apostles to teach the
certain salvation of all men, let the reader consider for a
moment a few of their expressions, and see if there is not
something peculiarly *strange* in them. " Fear not them
which kill the body, but are not able to kill the soul; but
rather fear him which is able to destroy both soul and
body in hell." Matt. x. 28. Again, " Fear him, which,
after he hath killed, hath power to cast into hell; yea, I
say unto you, fear him." Luke xii. 5. It is not a little
surprising that Christ, who, upon the principle here assumed, wished to guard his hearers against any apprehensions of a punishment beyond this life, should here speak
of God's being able to destroy the *soul* as well as the
body; to destroy the soul in *hell, after* he had killed the
body.

Besides, I cannot see the conclusiveness of our Saviour's reasoning in this place. What if God is *able* to
destroy the *soul* as well as the body? This is no good
reason why we should fear *him*, rather than any other being, if it is known that he *will* not do it. What if God is *able*
to destroy the soul in *hell?* If it is known that there is no
such place of future punishment as hell, and if God is
such a being that he will not destroy the soul in hell, I do
not see why the circumstance that he is *able* to do it need
to frighten us. I doubt not Christ did reason conclusively. But in this case I cannot see the force of his argument, unless he meant to teach the dreadful doctrine, that
the souls of the wicked will go to hell, as a place of punishment after the decease of their bodies.

" Enter ye in at the strait gate; for wide is the gate
and broad is the way that leadeth to destruction, and many there be which go in thereat; because strait is the
gate and narrow is the way which leadeth unto life, and
few there be that find it." Matt. vii. 13, 14. Now if
Christ believed in the doctrine of universal salvation, I
should suppose, that instead of *exhorting* his hearers to enter in at the strait gate, he would have told them that
they *would* enter in at the strait gate: that instead of using
the alarming expression, " Wide is the gate and broad is
the way that leadeth to destruction, and many there be

which go in thereat," he would have told them honestly,
that there *is* no way to destruction, and of course that
none are going there; that instead of saying, in the style
of the illiberal partialists of the present day, "Strait is
the gate and narrow is the way which leadeth unto life,
and few there be that find it," he would have adopted
the more catholic language of another class, and without
hesitation declared, that the gate of Heaven is *wide*, that
the way thither is *broad*, and that *all* will find it.

"Marvel not at this, the hour cometh in which all that are
in their graves shall hear his voice and come forth, they that
have done good to the resurrection of life, and they that have
done evil to the resurrection of damnation." John v. 28,
29.   Should I hear a preacher, at the present day, use
such an expression as this, without any explanation, I
should naturally conclude that he believed, not only in
the future resurrection of the bodies of all the dead, but
of the subsequent happiness of the righteous, and misery
of the wicked.   This, I cannot doubt, is the conclusion
of ninety-nine in a hundred, the first time they hear the
expression.   It is truly astonishing then, that Christ, who
is supposed to have known that these doctrines are totally false, and extremely pernicious, should have used such
an expression.   Not one in fifty of those who now preach
universal salvation, would, it is presumed, have the imprudence to drop this expression, or any one similar to it,
without at the same time so explaining it, as to prepare
his audience to receive a meaning essentially different
from the most obvious sense of the words.

In his explanation of the parable of the tares and the
wheat, Christ says, "The field is the world; the good
seed are the children of the kingdom; but the tares are
the children of the wicked one; the enemy that sowed
them is the devil; the harvest is the end of the world;
and the reapers are the angels.   As therefore the tares
are gathered and burned in the fire; so shall it be at the
end of the world.   The Son of man shall send forth his
angels, and they shall gather out of his kingdom all things
that offend, and them which do iniquity.   And shall cast
them into a furnace of fire; there shall be wailing and
gnashing of teeth.   Then shall the righteous shine forth
as the sun in the kingdom of their Father." Matt. xxiii.

38—43. When I consider that this is an *explanation* of a parable which Christ had previously spoken; an attempt to make more *plain* to them what he had left in comparative obscurity, I have no words to express the astonishment which I feel at his language. Instead of finding the doctrine of universal salvation plainly and unequivocally taught, as we might expect, if Christ believed it himself, from such a parable as this, we find here a *distinction* made between the children of the kingdom and the children of the wicked one; an assertion that those who do iniquity shall be gathered out of the kingdom of God, and cast into a lake of fire; and an intimation that the *righteous* only shall shine forth in the kingdom of their Father. How much more like a Universalist would Christ have spoken, if he meant to intimate that all would be saved, how much more generally, as well as easily, would he have been understood, if he had been silent respecting a *distinction* between the children of the kingdom and the children of the wicked one, and called them all the children of God. And, instead of dooming a part to a lake of fire, as is frequently done in the pulpits of those now termed bigoted ecclesiastics, he had said, not that the *righteous* shall shine forth as the sun in the kingdom of their Father, but that *all the human race* " shall shine forth as the sun in the kingdom of their Father." Christ *was* honest and sincere, plain and faithful in his instructions. But *how* he could be so and use such language as is found in the explanation of this parable, if he believed that all would be saved, is certainly among the mysteries which are not yet understood.

" When the Son of man shall come in his glory, and all the holy angels with him, then shall he sit upon the throne of his glory; and before him shall be gathered all nations; and he shall separate them one from another, as a shepherd divideth his sheep from the goats; and he shall set the sheep on his right hand, and the goats on the left. Then shall the king say unto them on his right hand, Come, ye blessed of my Father, inherit the kingdom prepared for you from the foundation of the world. Then shall he say also unto them on the left hand, Depart, ye cursed, into everlasting fire, prepared for the devil and his angels. And these shall go away into everlasting pun-

nishment, but the righteous into life eternal." Matt. xxv.
31—34. 41. 46. Now if the opinion, that there is to be
a day of judgment at which all the human race will be
summoned before Christ, the righteous separated from the
wicked, the one received to endless happiness, and the
other consigned to ceaseless perdition, be groundless, it is
to me peculiarly *strange*, that Christ, who must have
known the falsehood of this doctrine, should so plainly
express it, as he does when he speaks of all nations being gathered before him, of his separating the righteous
from the wicked as a shepherd divideth the sheep from
the goats, of his inviting the one to the enjoyment of that
kingdom prepared for them by his Father, and of his bid-
ding the other depart accursed into everlasting fire, prepared for the devil and his angels. If he did not believe
this doctrine, it is certainly natural to suppose that he
would have been more cautious than to use language
which so unequivocally expresses it. That thousands of
honest inquirers after truth have understood him to assert
this doctrine, in the passage before us, is what few, if
any, will pretend to deny ; and that he knew they would
thus understand him is as generally acknowledged. It
appears to me *strange*, therefore, that he had not used expressions that would have clearly conveyed his meaning,
and prevented the numerous distressing fears, as well as
hurtful errors, which his language has occasioned. Let
my readers consider, that Christ *knew* the truth upon this
subject, that he was able to express it with the greatest
plainness, that he had no intention of frightening them by
false exaggerated representations, but that his real object
was to communicate the most important practical information ; and then let them tell me how he came to use
language which so much resembles that of those who
preach the gloomy doctrine of future and everlasting punishment.

The conduct of the apostles, upon this subject, appears
to me equally strange with that of Christ. If they were
Universalists, designing to teach that there will be no punishment after this life, I am wholly unable to reconcile
their expressions with truth and sincerity. Paul's language to the Corinthians, upon the future condition of
mankind, exactly resembles the language of those who

preach, in opposition to the Universalists, the doctrine of future punishment. "We must all appear before the judgment-seat of Christ; that every man may receive the things done in his body, according to that he hath done, whether it be good or bad." 2 Cor. v. 10. If Paul believed that there is no judgment after death, and no punishment but what is suffered in this life, it is very difficult, to say the least, to tell what he meant by our receiving, at the judgment, the things done in our *bodies*. Nor does there appear to be any propriety in his intimating, as he appears to do in the following passage, that mankind go to judgment *after* death. "It is appointed unto men once to die, and *after* this the judgment." Heb. ix. 27. A Universalist might, perhaps, in consequence of finding such expressions in the Scriptures, make use of them in his public discourses. But if he were a man of prudence, he would carefully guard the minds of his hearers against a misunderstanding of them, by his own explanations. When, therefore, I find Paul freely using such expressions, and accompanying them with no explanations that seem in the least to detract from their most obvious sense, I am compelled to conclude that he was a very imprudent preacher, or, that he was no Universalist.

I have often heard serious and worthy ministers of the Gospel, tinctured, however, with the belief of future and eternal punishment, censured for preaching too much terror. And there certainly has been, at times, some things in their awful denunciation against sinners, which were enough to make the stoutest heart tremble. But what has surprised me more than any thing else relative to this subject, is the fact, that Paul, and others of the apostles, use expressions upon this subject as strong, and as full of terror as any thing which ever dropped from their lips. I never heard the most offensive of these preachers say any thing which appeared to me more unequivocally to assert the doctrine of future and eternal punishment, more indicative of God's displeasure with the wicked, or more calculated to frighten them, than the following language of Paul: "The Lord Jesus shall be revealed from heaven, with his mighty angels, in flaming fire, taking vengeance on them that know not God, and that obey not the Gospel of our Lord Jesus Christ, who shall be punished with everlasting destruction from the presence of the Lord, and from the glory of his power." 2 Thess. i. 7—9. One thing must be obvious to all : should a Universalist preacher now make a free use of such expressions of the Apostles as that above quoted, without accompanying them with his own interpretations, his hearers would conclude that he had changed his sentiments.

These remarks may lead my readers to conclude, that Paul was more careless, or imprudent, in his language, than the rest of the Apostles. But I am far from thinking that this is a fact. Although I dislike to charge him or any of his brethren with imprudence or insincerity ; yet, upon the supposition that they believed in the salvation of all men, I say again, I cannot reconcile their language with their sentiments, or with any serious intention of communicating them. We will now suppose that John was a Universalist, and at the same time, consider, for a moment, the language which he uses in relating a vision which he had of future things. "I saw a great white throne, and him that sat on it, from whose face the earth and the heavens fled away. And I saw the dead, small and great, stand before God; and the books were opened ; and another book was opened which was the book of life; and the dead were judged out of those things which were written in the books, according to their works. And the sea gave up the dead which were in it, and death and hell delivered up the dead which were in them, and they were judged every man according to their works. And death and hell were cast into the lake of fire. This is the second death. And whosoever was not found written in the book of life was cast into the lake of fire." Rev. xx. 11—15. Here I cannot refrain from remarking that it is a *strange* thing, that John, who, as we have supposed, was perfectly free from any apprehension of a judgment after death, should have had just such a vision as this. And admitting, as we must, that he did have it, it is unaccountable that he should not have had the prudence to express himself a little differently, or to add some explanation to his words, which would have satisfied every honest reader, that he did not mean *all* which he seems to say. If he had told us, expressly, that he did not mean, by what he had said respecting the dead, small and great,

standing before God, to intimate that any of the human
race would ever be raised from the dead; that he did not
design, by the books being opened, and the dead being
judged out of the things written in the books, to be understood that any would hereafter be called to an account
for what they had done in this life; and that by his declaration, "Whosoever was not found written in the book
of life was cast into the lake of fire," he had not the most
distant thought of alarming any one with the fear of future punishment, although it would then have been impossible, upon any fair principles of interpretation, to ascertain what he did mean by his expressions, yet he might
have appeared honest, and sincere, and prudent. But to
leave his expressions in the unguarded form in which they
now stand, looks like a species of imprudence directly
calculated to lead honest, sincere, and even discerning
minds, into the gloomy belief of a day of judgment and
perdition of ungodly men : a species of imprudence which
we are sure would destroy the popularity, and essentially
injure the cause of any Universalist at the present day,
and of which none of this class, within my knowledge, is
ever guilty.

5. If there is no punishment after death, there appears
to me to be something *strange in God's treatment of his
creatures in this world.* Generally speaking, the righteous
and the wicked are here treated essentially alike. Although there are instances in which God does, by his
providence, inflict signal punishments upon the wicked,
and confer signal rewards upon the righteous in this life;
yet these instances, being comparatively rare, must be
considered among the *extraordinary* events of his providence. God's general rule of dealing with his creatures
in this life, a rule from which he never departs, except in
extraordinary cases and for special purposes, is expressed
in the following words : "He maketh his sun to rise on
the evil and on the good, and sendeth rain on the just
and on the unjust." Solomon seems to have been convinced that, as a general rule, God treats the righteous
and the wicked alike in this world. "All things," he says,
"come alike unto all; there is one event to the righteous,
and to the wicked." In another place, he says, "there
is a vanity done upon the earth; that there be just men,

unto whom it happeneth according to the work of the
wicked; again there be wicked men, to whom it happeneth according to the work of the righteous." Now if it
is a fact, as is unequivocally asserted in these words, that
rewards and punishments are not always distributed in this
life according to the deserts of men, it is *strange* to me
that there should not be a *future* retribution. To my mind,
there is no truth more indisputable than this: the goodness of God must lead him, sooner or later, to treat all his
creatures according to their characters.

Besides, upon the principle that all will be immediately happy after death, there is often something *strange*,
even in those instances in which God *makes* a distinction
between the righteous and the wicked in this world.
Whenever the judgments of God upon the wicked are such
as to carry them out of the world, they must, for aught I
can see, become blessings; as in such cases they are always instrumental of removing the subjects of them from
this world to heaven. Now the flood, which has uniformly been considered as a judgment upon those who
perished in its waters, must, upon the principle here assumed, be considered as a judgment upon Noah, and a
blessing to those who were destroyed! Reader, look at
this subject one moment. Those who perished, all went
immediately to heaven, where they were made perfectly
happy in the enjoyment of God; while Noah, after having
witnessed the agonies of a dying world, and enduring the
sorrows of this seemingly dreadful catastrophe for forty
days and forty nights, was left an afflicted, solitary individual, with no society but his own family, and no possessions but the ruins of his ark. To this solitary pilgrimage he was driven, for no other reason than for being
a good man; while the true cause of his companions all
being received so soon to heaven was, they had corrupted
their way before the Lord! A similar reason must be assigned why Lot, deprived of his wife, and dispossessed of
his inheritance, was obliged to linger out a pitiable existence in the little city Zoar, while the inhabitants of Sodom and Gomorrah, after one momentary pang from the devouring element in which they were enveloped, were all
received to the mansions of bliss; and why Moses was
required to endure the labours, and hardships, and self-

denial of a journey through the wilderness, and to hear, for the space of forty years, the murmurs and reproaches of a rebellious people ; while Pharaoh and his hosts, who maliciously pursued him, all safely entered the rest prepared for the people of God, the moment they were overwhelmed in the Red Sea.   This is the strange attitude in which the opinion under consideration presents all the judgments of God, which have ever swept the wicked from the earth.   So far from having been evils to them who suffered them, they appear to have been blessings !

On the whole, I cannot but think it *strange*, that a doctrine, attended with so many strange things, should be thought to be true.   There must be something strange in the structure of that mind, or in the feelings of which it is the subject, which can believe this doctrine, in the face of so much plain testimony, and in opposition to so many well known facts.   The mind which can believe this doctrine, in opposition to the scriptural facts and scriptural testimony which present themselves against it, cannot be prevented, by *Scripture*, from believing any thing which it wishes to be true.   Do you ask, Reader, what is the reason why so many readily receive the false and absurd doctrine which has now been considered.   In the following Scripture, you have an answer : " Having the understanding darkened ; being alienated from the life of God through the ignorance that is in them, because of the blindness of their heart."

No. 120.

HEAVEN LOST.

FROM BAXTER'S SAINTS' REST.

See page 15.

PUBLISHED BY THE

AMERICAN TRACT SOCIETY,

NO. 150 NASSAU-STREET, NEW-YORK.

D. Fanshaw, Printer.

HEAVEN LOST.

As " godliness hath a promise of the life that now is, and of that which is to come," and if we " seek first the kingdom of God and his righteousness," then all meaner things shall be added unto us, so also are the ungodly threatened with the loss both of spiritual and temporal blessings ; and because they sought not first God's kingdom and righteousness, therefore shall they lose both it and that which they did seek, and there shall be taken from them that little which they have. If they could but have kept their present enjoyments, they would not have much cared for the loss of heaven. If they had lost and forsaken all for Christ, they would have found all again in him; for he would have been all in all to them. But now they have forsaken Christ for other things, they shall lose Christ, and that also for which they forsook him ; even the enjoyments of time, besides suffering the torments of hell.

Among the enjoyments of time, they shall particularly lose their presumptuous belief of their interest in the favour of God and the merits of Christ; all their hopes ; all their false peace of conscience ; all their carnal mirth; and all their sensual delights.

They shall lose *their presumptuous belief of their interest in the favour of God and the merits of Christ.* This false belief now supports their spirits, and defends them from the terrors that would otherwise seize upon them. But what will ease their trouble, when they can believe no longer, nor rejoice any longer ? If a man be near to the greatest mischief, and yet strongly conceit that he is in safety, he may be as cheerful as if all were well. If there were no more to make a man happy, but to believe that he is so, or shall be so, happiness would be far more common than it is like to be. As true faith is the leading grace in the regenerate, so is false faith the leading vice in the unregenerate. Why do such multitudes sit still, when they might have pardon, but that they verily think they are pardoned already ? If you could ask thousands in hell, what madness brought them thither ; they would most of thém answer, " We made sure of being saved, till we found ourselves damned. We would have been more earnest seekers of regeneration, and the power of godliness, but we verily thought we were christians before.— We have flattered ourselves into these torments, and now there is no remedy." Reader, I must in faithfulness tell thee, that the confident belief of their good state, which the careless, unholy, unhumbled multitude so commonly boast of, will prove in the end but a soul damning delusion. There is none of this believing in hell. It was Satan's stratagem, that, being blindfolded, they might follow him the more boldly ; but then he will uncover their eyes, and they will see where they are.

They will lose also *their hopes.* In this life, though they were threatened with the wrath of God, yet their hope of escaping it bore up their hearts. We can now scarcely speak with the vilest drunkard, or swearer, or scoffer, but he hopes to be saved, for all this. O happy world, if salvation were as common as this hope! Nay, so strong are men's hopes, that they will dispute the cause with Christ himself at judgment, and plead their " having eaten and drunk in his presence, and prophesied in his name, and in his name cast out devils ;" they will deny that ever they neglected Christ in hunger, nakedness, or prison, till he confutes them with the sentence of their condemnation. O the sad state of these men, when they must bid farewell to all their hopes! " When a wicked man dieth, his expectation shall perish ; and the hope of unjust men perisheth." Prov. xi. 7. " The eyes of the wicked shall fail, and they shall not escape, and their hopes shall be as the giving up of the ghost." Job. xi. 20. The giving up the ghost is a fit, but terrible resemblance of a wicked man's giving up his hopes. As the soul departeth from the body not without the greatest pain ; so doth the hope of the wicked depart. The soul departs from the body suddenly, in a moment, which hath there delightfully continued so many years ; just so doth the hope of the wicked depart. The soul will never more return to live with the body in this world ; and the hope of the wicked takes an everlasting farewell of his soul. A miracle of resurrection shall again unite soul and body, but there shall be no such miraculous resurrection of the hope of the damned. Methinks, it is the most pitiable sight this world affords, to see such an ungodly person dying, and to think of his soul and his hopes departing together. With what a sad change he appears in another world! Then, if a man could but ask that hopeless soul, "Are you as confident of salvation as you were wont to be?" What a sad answer would be returned! O that careless sinners would be awakened to think of this in time! Reader, rest not till thou canst give a reason of all thy hopes, grounded upon Scripture promises: that they purify thy heart; that they quicken thy endeavours in godliness; that the more thou hopest, the less thou sinnest, and the more exact is thy obedience. If thy hopes be such as these, go on in the strength of the Lord, hold fast thy hope, and never shall it make thee ashamed. But if thou hast not one sound evidence of a work of grace on thy soul, cast away thy hopes. Despair of ever being saved, except thou be born again; or of seeing God, without holiness; or of having part in Christ, except thou love him above father, mother, or thy own life. This kind of despair is one of the first steps to heaven. If a man be quite out of his way, what must be the first means to bring him in again? He must despair of ever coming to his journey's end in the way that he is in. If his home be eastward, and he is going westward, as long as he hopes he is right, he will go on; and as long as he goes on hoping, he goes farther amiss. When he despairs of coming home except he turn back, then he will return, and then he may hope. Just so it is, sinner, with thy soul. Thou art born out of the way to heaven, and hast proceeded many a year; thou goest on and hopest to be saved, because thou art not so bad as many others. Except thou throw away these hopes, and see that thou hast all this while been quite out of the way to heaven, thou wilt never return and be saved. There is nothing in the world more likely to keep thy soul out of heaven, than thy false hopes of being saved, while thou art out of the way to salvation. See then how it will aggravate the misery of the damned, that, with the loss of heaven, they shall lose all that hope of it which now supports them.

They will lose *all that false peace of conscience* which makes their present life so easy. Who would think, that sees how quietly the multitude of the ungodly live, that

they must shortly lie down in everlasting flames? They
are as free from the fears of hell as an obedient believer;
and for the most part have less disquiet of mind than those
who shall be saved. Happy men, if this peace would prove
lasting! "When they shall say, Peace and safety; then
sudden destruction cometh upon them, as travail upon a
woman with child, and they shall not escape." 1 Thes.
v. 3. O cruel peace, which ends in such a war! The soul
of every man, by nature, is Satan's garrison; all is at peace
in such a man, till Christ comes and gives it terrible alarms
of judgment and hell, batters it with the ordnance of his
threats and terrors, forces it to yield to his mere mercy,
and take him for the Governor; then doth he cast out
Satan, "overcome him, take from him all his armour
wherein he trusted, and divideth his spoils;" (Luke, xi. 22.)
and then doth he establish a firm and lasting peace. If
therefore thou art yet in that first peace, never think it
will endure. Can thy soul have lasting peace, in enmity
with Christ? Can he have peace against whom God proclaims war? I wish thee no greater good, than that God
break in upon thy careless heart, and shake thee out of
thy false peace, and make thee lie down at the feet of
Christ, and say, "Lord, what wouldst thou have me to
do?" and so receive from him a better and surer peace,
which will never be quite broken; but be the beginning
of thy everlasting peace, and not perish in thy perishing,
as will the groundless peace of the world.

They shall lose *all their carnal mirth*. They will themselves say of their laughter, it is mad; and of their mirth,
what doeth it? Eccl. ii. 2. It was but "as the crackling
of thorns under a pot." Eccl. vii. 6. It made a blaze for
a while, but it was presently gone, and returned no more.
The talk of death and judgment was irksome to them, because it dampened their mirth. They could not endure
to think of their sin and danger, because these thoughts
sunk their spirits. They knew not what it was to weep
for sin, or to humble themselves under the mighty hand of
God. They could laugh away sorrow, and sing away cares,
and drive away those melancholy thoughts. To meditate,
and pray, they fancied would be enough to make them utterly miserable. Poor souls! what a misery will that life
be, where you shall have nothing but sorrow; intense,

heart piercing, multiplied sorrow; when you shall neither have the joys of saints nor your own former joys? Do you think there is one merry heart in hell; or one joyful countenance, or jesting tongue? You now cry, "A little mirth is worth a great deal of sorrow." But, surely, a little godly sorrow, which would have ended in eternal joy, had been worth much more than all your foolish mirth; for the end of such mirth is sorrow.

They shall also lose *all their sensual delights.* That which they esteemed their chief good, their heaven, their god, must they lose, as well as God himself. What a fall will the proud ambitious man have from the top of his honours? As his dust and bones will not be known from the dust and bones of the poorest beggar; so neither will his soul be honoured or favoured more than theirs. What a number of the great, noble, and learned, will be shut out of the presence of Christ? They shall not find their magnificent buildings, soft beds, and easy couches. They shall not view their curious gardens, their pleasant meadows, and plenteous harvests. Their tables will not be so furnished, nor attended. The " rich man " is there no more " clothed in purple and fine linen, nor faring sumptuously every day." There is no expecting the admiration of beholders. They shall spend their time in sadness, and not in sports and pastimes. What an alteration will they then find? They will have no more love of worldly pleasure. How will it even cut them to the heart to look each other in the face! What an interview will there then be, cursing the day that ever they saw one another? O that sinners would now remember, and say, " Will these delights accompany us into the other world? Will not the remembrance of them be then our torment? Shall we then take this partnership in vice for true friendship? Why should we sell such lasting, incomprehensible joys, for a taste of seeming pleasure? Come, as we have sinned together, let us pray together, that God would pardon us; and let us help one another towards heaven, instead of helping to deceive and destroy each other." O that men knew but what they desire, when they would have all things suited to the desires of the flesh! It is but to desire their temptations to be increased, and their snares strengthened.

As the loss of the Saint's rest will be aggravated by los-

ing the enjoyments of time, it will be much more so by
suffering the torments of hell.   The exceeding greatness
of such torments may appear by considering the principal
Author of them, who is God himself; the place or state
of torment; that these torments are the fruit of divine vengeance ; that Satan and sinners themselves shall be God's
executioners ; that these torments shall be universal, without mitigation, and without end.

The principal *Author* of hell-torments is God himself.
As it is no less than God whom sinners have offended, so
it is no less than God who will punish them for their offences. He hath prepared those torments for his enemies.
His continued anger will still be devouring them.   His
breath of indignation will kindle the flames.   His wrath
will be an intolerable burden to their souls. If it were but
a creature they had to do with, they might bear it ; but
wo to him that falls under the strokes of the Almighty !
" It is a fearful thing to fall into the hands of the living
God." Heb. x. 13.   It were nothing in comparison to this,
if the world were against them, or if the strength of all creatures were united in one to inflict their penalty.   They had
now rather venture to displease God, than displease a land-
-lord, a customer, a master, a friend, a neighbour, or their
own flesh ; but then they will wish a thousand times in
vain, that they had been hated of all the world, rather than
have lost the favour of God.   What a consuming fire is his
wrath ? If it be kindled here but a little, how do we with-
er like the grass ? How soon doth our strength decay, and
turn to weakness, and our beauty to deformity ? The flames
do not so easily run through the dry stubble, as the wrath
of God will consume these wretches.   They that could
not bear a prison, or gibbet, or fire, for Christ ; nor scarce
a few scoffs ; how will they now bear the devouring flames
of divine wrath ?

The *place*, or *state* of torment is purposely ordained to
glorify the justice of God.   When God would glorify his
power, he made the worlds.   The comely order of all his
creatures declareth his wisdom. His providence is shown,
in sustaining all things. When a spark of his wrath kindles
upon the earth, the whole world, except only eight persons, are drowned ; Sodom, Gomorrah, Admah, and Zebo-
im, are burnt with fire from heaven ; the sea shuts her

mouth upon some; the earth opens and swallows up others; the pestilence destroys by thousands. What a standing witness of the wrath of God, is the present deplorable state of the Jews? Yet the glorifying of the mercy and justice of God is intended most eminently for the life to come. As God will then glorify his mercy in a way that is now beyond the comprehension of the saints that must enjoy it; so also will he manifest his justice to be indeed the justice of God. The everlasting flames of hell will not be thought too hot for the rebellious; and when they have there burned through millions of ages, he will not repent him of the evil which is befallen them. Wo to the soul that must thus endure for ever the wrath of the Almighty, and burn in the flames of his jealousy, and never be consumed!

The torments of the damned must be extreme, because they are the effect of *divine vengeance*. When the great God shall say, " My rebellious creatures shall now pay for all the abuse of my patience. Remember how I waited your leisure in vain, how I stopped to persuade and entreat you. Did you think I would always be so slighted?" Then will he be revenged for every abused mercy, and for all their neglects of Christ and grace. O that men would foresee this, and please God better in preventing their wo! Wretched creatures! when "he that made them will not have mercy on them, and he that formed them will show them no favour." Isa. xxvii. 4. 11. " As the Lord rejoiced over them to do them good; so the Lord will rejoice over them to destroy them, and to bring them to nought." Deut. xxviii. 63. Wo to the souls whom God rejoiceth to punish! " He will laugh at their calamity, he will mock when their fear cometh ; when 'their fear cometh as desolation, and their destruction cometh as a whirlwind ; when distress and anguish cometh upon them." Prov. i. 26, 27. Terrible thing, when none in heaven or earth can help them but God, and he shall rejoice in their calamity! Though Scripture speaks of God's laughing and mocking, not literally, but after the manner of men ; yet it is such an act of God in tormenting the sinner, as cannot otherwise be more fitly expressed.

Consider, that *Satan and themselves* shall be God's executioners He that was here so successful in drawing them from Christ, will then be the instrument of their punishment, for yielding to his temptations. That is the reward he will give them for all their service; for their rejecting the commands of God, and forsaking Christ, and neglecting their souls, at his persuasion. If they had served Christ as faithfully as they did Satan, he would have given them a better reward. It is also most just, that they should be their own tormentors, that they may see that their whole destruction is of themselves; and then who can they complain of but themselves?

Consider also, that their torment will be *universal.* As all parts have joined in sin, so must they all partake in the torment. The soul, as it was the chief in sinning, shall be the chief in suffering; and as it is of a more excellent nature than the body, so will its torments far exceed bodily torments; and as its joys far surpass all sensual pleasures, so the pains of the soul exceed corporal pains. It is not only a soul, but a sinful soul, that must suffer. Fire will not burn, except the fuel be combustible; but if the wood be dry, how fiercely will it burn? The guilt of their sins will be to damned souls like tinder to gunpowder, to make the flames of hell take hold upon them with fury. The body must also bear its part. The body, which was so carefully looked to, so tenderly cherished, so curiously dressed; what must it now endure? How are its haughty looks now taken down? How little will those flames regard its comeliness and beauty? Those eyes which were wont to be delighted with curious sights, must then see nothing but what shall terrify them; an angry God above them, with those saints whom they scorned, enjoying the glory which they have lost; and about them will be only devils and damned souls. How will they look back, and say, " Are all our feasts, and games, and revels come to this?" Those ears which were accustomed to music and songs, shall hear the shrieks and cries of their damned companions; children crying out against their parents, that gave them encouragement and example in evil; husbands and wives, masters and servants, ministers and people, magistrates and subjects, charging their misery upon one another, for discouraging in duty, conniving at sin, and being silent, when they should have plainly foretold the danger. Thus will soul and body be companions in wo.

Far greater will these torments be because *without mitigation*. In this life, when told of hell, or conscience troubled their peace, they had comforters at hand; their carnal friends, their business, their company, their mirth. They could drink, play, or sleep away their sorrows. But now all these remedies are vanished. Their hard, presumptuous, unbelieving heart was as a wall to defend them against trouble of mind. Satan was himself their comforter, as he was to our first mother; "Hath God said, ye shall not eat? Ye shall not surely die." Doth God tell you that you shall lie in hell? It is no such matter. God is more merciful. Or if there be a hell, what need you fear it? Are not you Christians? Was not the blood of Christ shed for you?" Thus as the Spirit of Christ is the comforter of the saints, so Satan is the comforter of the wicked. Never was a thief more careful less he should awake the people, when he is robbing the house, than Satan is not to awaken a sinner. But when the sinner is dead, then Satan hath done flattering and comforting. Which way then will the forlorn sinner look for comfort? They that drew him into the snare, and promised him safety, now forsake him, and are forsaken themselves. His comforts are gone, and the righteous God, whose forewarnings he made light of, will now make good his word against him, to the least tittle.

But the greatest aggravation of these torments will be their *eternity*. When a thousand millions of ages are past, they are as fresh to begin, as on the first day. If there were any hope of an end, it would ease the damned to foresee it; but *for ever*, is an intolerable thought. They were never weary of sinning, nor will God be weary of punishing. They never heartily repented of sin, nor will God repent of their suffering. They broke the laws of the eternal God, and therefore shall suffer eternal punishment. They knew it was an everlasting kingdom which they refused, and what wonder if they are everlastingly shut out of it? Their immortal souls were guilty of the trespass, and therefore must immortally suffer the pains. What happy men would they think themselves, if they might have lain still in their graves, or might but there lie down again! How will they call and cry! "O death! whither art thou now gone? Now come and cut off this doleful life. O

that these pains would break my heart, and end my being!
O that I might once at last die! O that I had never had
a being!" These groans will the thoughts of eternity
wring from their hearts. They were wont to think sermons and prayers long; how long then will they think
these endless torments? What difference is there between
the length of their pleasures and their pains! The one
continued but a moment, the other endureth through all
eternity. Sinner, remember how time is almost gone.
Thou art standing at the door of eternity; and death is
waiting to open the door, and put thee in. Go, sleep out
a few more nights, and stir about a few more days on earth,
and then thy nights and days shall end; thy thoughts, and
cares, and pleasures, shall be devoured by eternity; thou
must enter upon the state which shall never be changed.
As the joys of heaven are beyond our conception, so are
the pains of hell. Everlasting torment is inconceivable
torment.

But methinks I see the obstinate sinner desperately resolving, "If I must be damned, there is no remedy; rather
than I will live as the Scriptures require, I will put it to
the venture; I shall escape as well as the rest of my
neighbours, and we will even bear it as well as we can."
Alas! poor creature, let me beg this of thee, before thou
dost so resolve, that thou wouldst lend me thy attention to
a few questions, and weigh them with the reason of a man.

Who art thou, that thou shouldst bear the wrath of God?
Art thou a God, or a man? What is thy strength? Is it
not the strength of wax or stubble to resist the fire; or
as chaff to the wind; or as dust before the fierce whirlwind? If thy strength were as iron, and thy bones as
brass; if thy foundation were as the earth, and thy power
as the heavens; yet shouldst thou perish at the breath of
his indignation! How much more, when thou art but a
piece of breathing clay, kept a few days from being eaten
with worms, by the mere support and favour of him whom
thou art thus resisting? Why dost thou tremble at the
signs of almighty power and wrath? At claps of thunder,
or flashes of lightning; or that unseen power which rends
in pieces the mighty oaks, and tears down the strongest
buildings; or at the plague, when it rages around thee?

If thou hadst seen the plagues of Egypt; or the earth
swallow up Dathan and Abiram; or Elijah bring fire from
heaven to destroy the captains and their companies, would
not any of these sights have daunted thy spirits? How
then canst thou bear the plagues of hell? Why art thou
dismayed with such small sufferings as befall thee here?
A tooth-ach; a fit of the gout, or stone; the loss of a
limb; or falling into beggary and disgrace? And yet all
these laid together, will be one day accounted a happy
state, in comparison of that which is suffered in hell.
Why does the approach of death so much affright thee?
O how cold it strikes to the heart! And would not the
grave be accounted a paradise, compared with that place
of torment which thou slightest? Is it an intolerable thing
to burn part of the body, by holding it in the fire? What
then will it be to suffer ten thousand times more for ever
in hell? Why does the thought or mention of hell occasion any disquiet in thy spirits? And canst thou endure
the torments themselves? Why doth the rich man complain to Abraham *of his torments in hell*? Or thy dying
companions lose their courage, and change their haughty
language? Didst thou never see or speak with a man
under despair? How uncomfortable was his talk? How
burthensome his life? Nothing he possessed did him
good; he had no sweetness in meat or drink; the sight
of friends troubled him; he was weary of life, and fearful
of death. If the misery of the damned can be endured,
why cannot a man more easily endure these foretastes of
hell? What if thou shouldst see the devil appear to thee
in some terrible shape? Would not thy heart fail thee,
and thy hair stand up? And how wilt thou endure to live
for ever, where thou shalt have no other company but devils and the damned, and shalt not only see them, but
be tormented with them and by them? Let me once more
ask, if the wrath of God be so light, why did the Son of
God himself make so great a matter of it? It made him
" sweat as it were great drops of blood falling down to the
ground." The Lord of Life cried, " My soul is exceeding
sorrowful, even unto death." And on the cross, " My God,
my God, why hast thou forsaken me?" Surely, if any one
could have borne these sufferings easily, it would have been
Jesus Christ. He had another measure of strength to bear

them than thou hast. Wo to thee, sinner, for thy mad security! Dost thou think to find that tolerable to thee, which was so heavy to Christ? Nay, the Son of God is cast into a bitter agony and bloody sweat, only under the *curse of the law;* and yet thou, a feeble worm, makest nothing to bear also the curse of the Gospel, which requires a "much sorer punishment." The good Lord bring thee to thy right mind by repentance, lest thou buy thy folly at too dear a rate!

And now, Reader, I demand thy resolution, what use wilt thou make of all this? Shall it all be lost to thee? or wilt thou consider it in good earnest? Thou hast cast away many a warning of God; wilt thou do so by this also? Take heed. God will not always stand warning and threatening. The hand of revenge is lifted up, the blow is coming, and wo to him on whom it lighteth! Dost thou throw away the book, and say, it speaks of nothing but hell and damnation? Thus thou usest also to complain of the preacher. But wouldst thou not have us tell thee of these things? Should we not be guilty of the blood of thy soul by keeping silent that which God hath charged us to make known? Wouldst thou perish in ease and silence, and have us to perish with thee, rather than displease thee, by speaking the truth? If thou wilt be guilty of such inhuman cruelty, God forbid we should be guilty of such folly. This kind of preaching or writing is the ready way to be hated; and the desire of applause is so natural, that few delight in such a displeasing way. But consider, are these things true, or are they not? If they were not true, I would heartily join with thee against any that fright people without a cause. But if these threatenings be the word of God, what a wretch art thou, that wilt not hear it and consider it? If thou art one of the people of God, this doctrine will be a comfort to thee, and not a terror. If thou art yet unregenerate, methinks thou shouldst be as fearful to hear of heaven, as of hell, except the bare name of heaven or salvation be sufficient. Preaching heaven and mercy to thee, is entreating thee to seek them, and not reject them; and preaching hell, is but to persuade thee to avoid it. If thou wert quite past hope of escaping it, then it were in vain to tell thee of hell; but as long as thou art alive, there is hope of thy recovery, and therefore all means must be used to awake thee from thy lethargy. Alas! what heart can now possibly conceive, or what tongue express, the pains of those souls that are under the wrath of God? Then, sinners, you will be crying to Jesus Christ, "O mercy! O pity, pity on a poor soul!" Why, I do now, in the name of the Lord Jesus, cry to thee, "O have mercy, have pity, man, upon thy own soul!" Shall God pity thee, who wilt not be entreated to pity thyself? If thy horse see but a pit before him, thou canst scarcely force him in; and wilt thou so obstinately cast thyself into hell, when the danger is foretold thee? "Who can stand before the indignation of the Lord? and who can abide the fierceness of his anger?" Nahum, i. 6. Methinks thou shouldst need no more words, but presently cast away thy soul-damning sins, and wholly deliver up thyself to Christ. Resolve on it immediately, and let it be done, that I may see thy face in rest among the saints. May the Lord persuade thy heart to strike this covenant without any longer delay! But if thou be hardened unto death, and there be no remedy, yet say not another day but that thou wast faithfully warned, and hadst a friend that would fain have prevented thy damnation.

And now, Reader, darest thou go on in thy common careless course, against the plain evidence of reason, and commands of God, and against the light of thy own conscience? Darest thou live as loosely, sin as boldly, and pray as seldom as before? Darest thou profane the Sabbath, slight the service of God, and think of thine everlasting state as carelessly as before? Or dost thou not rather resolve to "gird up the loins of thy mind," and set thyself wholly to the work of thy salvation, and break through the oppositions, and slight the scoffs and persecutions of the world, and "lay aside every weight, and the sin which doth so easily beset thee, and run with patience the race that is set before thee?" I hope these are thy full resolutions! Yet, because I know the obstinacy of the heart of man, and because I am solicitous thy soul might live, I once more entreat thy attention to the following questions; and I command thee from God, that thou stifle not thy conscience, nor resist conviction; but answer them faithfully, and obey accordingly:

If, by being diligent in godliness, you could grow rich, get honour or preferment in the world, be recovered from sickness, or live for ever in prosperity on earth; what a life would you lead, and what pains would you take in the service of God ? And is not the *Saint's rest* a more excellent happiness than all this ?—If it were felony to break the Sabbath, neglect secret or family worship, or be loose in your lives, what manner of persons would you then be ? And is not eternal death more terrible than temporal ? If God usually punished with some present judgment every act of sin, as he did the lie of Annanias and Sapphira, what kind of life would you lead ? And is not eternal wrath far more terrible ? If one of your acquaintance should come from the dead, and tell you that he suffered the torments of hell for those sins you are guilty of ; what manner of persons would you afterwards be ? How much more should the warnings of God affright you ? If you knew that this were the last day you had to live in the world, how would you spend it ? And you know not but it may be your last, and are sure your last is near. If you had seen the general dissolution of the world, and all the pomp and glory of it consumed to ashes, what would such a sight persuade thee to do ? Such a sight you shall certainly see. —If you had seen the judgment set, and the books opened, and the wicked stand trembling on the left hand of the Judge, and the godly rejoicing on the right hand, and their different sentence pronounced ; what persons would you have been after such a sight ? This sight you shall one day surely see.—If you had seen hell opened, and all the damned there in their endless torments ; also heaven opened, as Stephen did, and all the saints there triumphing in glory ; what a life would you lead after such sights ? These you will see before it be long.—If you had lain in hell but one year, or one day, or hour, and there felt the torments you now hear of ; how seriously would you then speak of hell, and pray against it ? And will you not take God's word for the truth of this, except you feel it ?—Or if you had possessed the glory of heaven but one year ; what pains would you take, rather than be deprived of such incomparable glory ? Thus I have said enough, if not to stir up the sinner to a serious working out his salvation, yet at least to silence him, and leave him inexcusable at the judgment of God. Only as we do by our friends when they are dead, and our words and actions can do them no good, yet to testify our affection for them we weep and mourn; so will I also do for these unhappy souls. It makes my heart tremble, to think how they will stand before the Lord confounded and speechless! When he shall say, "Was the world, or Satan, a better friend to you than I? Or had they done more for you than I had done? Try now whether they will save you, or recompense you for the loss of heaven, or be as good to you as I would have been." What will the wretched sinner answer to any of this? But, though man will not hear, we may hope in speaking to God. "O thou that didst weep and groan in spirit over a dead Lazarus, pity these dead and senseless souls, till they are able to weep and groan in pity to themselves! As thou hast bid thy servant speak, so speak now thyself; they will hear thy voice speaking to their hearts, who will not hear mine speaking to their ears. Lord, thou hast long knocked at these hearts in vain; now break the doors, and enter in."

ON THE

LORD'S PRAYER.

After this manner, therefore, pray ye: Our Father, which art in heaven; Hallowed be thy name. Thy kingdom come. Thy will be done, in earth, as it is in heaven. Give us this day our daily bread; and forgive us our debts, as we forgive our debtors. And lead us not into temptation; but deliver us from evil. For thine is the kingdom, and the power, and the glory, for ever. Amen.—MATTHEW, vi. 9—13.

PRAYER to God is the duty of all men. " In him we live, and move, and have our being." " Every good and perfect gift cometh down from the Father of lights." " Men ought therefore always to pray, and not to faint." We are so sinful, that we always need mercy. We are so weak, that we always need help. We are so empty, that we always need supplies. We are so exposed, that we always need protection. How reasonable then is it that we should continue in prayer!

But we greatly need direction in prayer. We know not how to pray, nor what to pray for, as we ought. Therefore Christ has been pleased to teach us in these words; which contain an excellent form and pattern of prayer. *After this manner* we are to pray. Now, as many persons constantly use this prayer, it may be very useful to explain it; because it may be feared that some repeat the words without knowing the meaning, which is formality at best; and some contradict every part of the prayer by their wicked lives, which is base hypocrisy. May we therefore be assisted by the good Spirit rightly to understand it, that so, whenever we use it hereafter, we may offer up a reasonable and spiritual sacrifice, acceptable to God, by Jesus Christ.

OUR FATHER, WHICH ART IN HEAVEN. We should always begin our prayers with proper thoughts of God. And what thoughts of him are so proper as those suggested by these words: namely, his *goodness* and his *greatness?* As a *Father*, he is good. As a *heavenly* Father, he is great. Thus we are taught to approach him both with confidence and with reverence.

As the Creator of all men, God may, in a general sense, be called the Father of all; but it is in a higher and more endearing sense that he is here called a Father: as being reconciled to believing sinners through the blood of Jesus Christ. God is angry with the wicked every day. He does not look down upon them with approbation, nor do they look up to him with confidence and love. Therefore this prayer is not fit for the use of a man who lives in sin; whose carnal mind is enmity against God. How dares the swearer, the liar, the drunkard, call God a Father? God will not own the relation. If such men pray, might they not rather cry, Our father, which art in *hell?* for Christ said to such persons, " Ye are of your father the devil, and the lusts of your father ye will do." John, viii. 44.

But when a person is convinced of his state as a sinner; when he is enlightened to know Christ as a Saviour; and when, by a lively faith, he comes to God through him; then God is reconciled to him; his anger is turned away, and he comforts him. Then he may look up to God, through Christ, as a merciful God, " forgiving iniquity, transgression, and sin ;" for, " to as many as receive him," and the atonement through him, " he giveth power to become the sons of God, even to them that believe in his name ;" and to such only is the " Spirit of adoption" given, whereby they cry, " Abba, Father." For it is one thing to use the word *Father*, and another to approach him, as an affectionate child comes to a tender parent, with a persuasion of his being able and willing to supply his wants. To such persons this name is full of comfort; for they are emboldened to believe, that if earthly parents, though evil, know how to give good gifts to their children, God, our heavenly Father, is much more disposed to do them good, and bless them with all spiritual blessings in Christ Jesus.

But this name teaches us also the *greatness* of God. Children ought to treat their earthly parents with great respect, but what reverence is due to the Father of spirits, whose throne is in the heavens! Not that God is confined to heaven; but he is said to dwell there, because there he displays the brightest beams of his glorious majesty, and there angels and saints bow low before his feet, crying, day and night, " Holy, holy, holy, is the Lord God Almighty!" Such thoughts as these should possess our minds, when we say, *Our Father, which art in heaven.*

HALLOWED BE THY NAME. This petition is placed first, to show us that our first and chief desire should be, *that God may be glorified.* The name of God signifies God himself, as he is pleased to make himself known to us by his titles, his words, and his works. In his Gospel, more especially, all his glorious perfections shine and unite. There he shows himself " a just God and a Saviour." Now, to *hallow* God's name is to *sanctify* it, to hold it sacred; for to sanctify any thing, is to set it apart from every profane and common use. In this petition, then, we pray that God would enable us to glorify him in all things whereby he makes himself known. We must glorify him in our *hearts*, by high, holy, reverent thoughts of him. We must glorify him in our *language*, by always speaking of him in the most solemn manner. We must glorify him in our *actions;* whether we eat or drink, all should be done with a view to the glory of God.

How far from this are many who say this prayer, and who no sooner rise from their knees than they profane this holy name. Think of this, you who curse and swear, or take the Lord's name in vain! When you say, in a thoughtless manner, God bless us! O God! O Christ! &c. is this to *hallow* the name of God? Leave off praying, or leave off swearing; for they cannot agree together.

But let every one that fears God remember, that the glory of God is the first and chief thing, that we are to ask for, and to desire, and to seek, even before our own good. That we and others may do this, we are taught, in the next place, to pray,

THY KINGDOM COME. This does not mean the kingdom of God's providence, which rules over all: this cannot be said to *come*, for it is come already, and will never cease: but it means that *spiritual* kingdom which Christ came to set up in the world; that kingdom of the Messiah, which the pious Jews had long expected, and which, when this prayer was given to the disciples, was said to be *at hand.* This kingdom of Christ did come soon after. It was set up when Christ ascended to heaven, and the Spirit descended from it. But still the prayer is as necessary as ever; for we pray that this kingdom may be established in our hearts, and extended to all the world.

The kingdom of Christ is erected on purpose to destroy the kingdom of Satan. The devil has usurped a dominion over all mankind; and though he does not now possess the bodies of men, as once he did, yet he "rules in the hearts of the children of disobedience," who are "led captive by him at his will;" and in some parts of the world he is actually worshipped. In order to destroy this infernal kingdom, Jesus Christ came into the world; he overcame him in all his attempts to seduce him; and on the cross he spoiled principalities and powers, and conquered when he fell: he deprived Satan of his power, and led captivity captive. Wherever he sends his Gospel, he proclaims liberty; and wherever he gives his grace to any person, there Satan is dethroned; and being made willing to submit to Christ, the believer is translated out of Satan's kingdom of sin and darkness into the holy and happy kingdom of God's dear Son.

When we say, *Thy kingdom come*, we pray that the light, power, liberty, and glory of Christ's spiritual kingdom, may be more fully experienced in our own hearts. For, as one observes, " In *worship* we pay our homage to God. In the *word*, we come to learn his laws. In the *Lord's Supper*, we renew our vows of allegiance. In *alms-giving*, we pay him tribute. In *prayer*, we ask him leave; and *praise* is our rent to the great Lord, from whom we hold our all." Thus also we express our soul's desire for our poor fellow-sinners. Deeply affected with the state of Heathens, Jews, Mahometans, and sinners of all descriptions, we pour forth our souls in holy longings for their conversion, earnestly desiring the joyful day when it shall be said, " The kingdoms of this world are become the kingdom of our Lord and of his Christ; and he shall reign for ever and ever."

THY WILL BE DONE, IN EARTH, AS IT IS IN HEAVEN. God, the glorious Maker of the world, has a right to govern it. His will is the proper rule of his creatures' actions; and it is obeyed by them all, except by men and devils. God has made known his will to us in his word. The law of the ten commandments shows what obedience he requires of us; but, as fallen creatures, we have broken it, and rendered ourselves incapable of obtaining life by it. God has graciously given us the law of faith, or the Gospel of salvation, by Jesus Christ; and " this is his commandment, that we should believe on the name of his Son Jesus Christ, and love one another." But the natural man refuses obedience to this also; he is either unconcerned about salvation, or dislikes the way of it; and while he remains in this state, he cannot do the will of God in any respect acceptably; for " without faith it is impossible to please him."

How necessary then is this petition, *Thy* will be done! It includes,

1. *A desire to know it;* as the Psalmist prays, " Teach me to do thy will, for thou art my God;" (cxliii. 10.) or, as converted Saul, " Lord, what wilt thou have me to do?"

2. *A heart to do it:* a heart on which God has written his laws. I remember a person who told me, when he was teaching his child to say this prayer, and came to this petition, " *Thy* will be done," the child refused to say it, and would have it, " *My will* be done." This poor simple child was far more honest than many of us, who say, " Thy will be done," and yet determine to follow our own will; but the real christian's desire is, " O that there were such a heart in me, to fear God, and to keep his commandments always!" Deut. v. 20. We pray also,

3. *For strength* to do the will of God; for *to will* may be present, and yet how to perform that which is good we may not find; but, knowing that the Lord worketh in his people both *to will* and *to do*, we hereby pray that he would " make us perfect in every good work, to do his will; working in us that which is well pleasing in his sight, through Jesus Christ." This petition also includes holy submission to the will of his providence, however afflictive; and that we may learn to bear it without murmuring.

We pray for grace to do all this, in imitation of the spirits of just men made perfect, and of the sinless angels in heaven. " God's will *is* done in *heaven.*"

GIVE US THIS DAY OUR DAILY BREAD. This petition implies our dependence on God for food and all the supports and comforts of life. Man, as a fallen creature, has forfeited the good things of this life, and deserves to be deprived of them all. The earth was cursed for man's sake, therefore in sorrow and labour he eats of it; but it is through the goodness of God that he has power to labour; that rain from heaven and fruitful seasons are granted. It is "he who gives us our corn, and wine, and oil;" and though the poor man works hard for his daily bread, it is no less the gift of God. To him also we owe the appetite that makes our food pleasant, and the power of digestion that makes it nourishing.

Moderation in our desires is here expressed. We are not taught to ask for riches and honours, which are often the destructive snares of those who possess them; but we may lawfully ask for food and raiment; "for our heavenly Father knoweth that we have need of these things," (Matt. vi. 32.) and having these, "we ought to be content."

We are not to ask for *weekly* bread, or *monthly* bread, or *yearly* bread; but for *daily* bread; for we must not boast of to-morrow, or depend on future years; but live in daily dependence on God, without anxious cares for a future time. "Sufficient to the day is the evil thereof;" and sufficient for the day is the good thereof; so that we are to exercise ourselves in daily prayer, and receive every meal and every morsel as the gift of a good God, which will make it sweet.

The christian will also ask for bread for his soul, as well as his body. Christ is to the believer's soul, what food is to the body. He is "the Bread of Life;" and if we are born of God, we shall daily desire to feed upon him in our hearts, by faith, with thanksgiving.

AND FORGIVE US OUR DEBTS, AS WE FORGIVE OUR DEBTORS. This petition is joined to the last by the word *and;* which may teach us, that without the forgiveness of sins, the comforts of this life can do no real good; "for what is a man profited, if he gain the whole world, and lose his own soul?" Every man is a sinner. There is not a creature, who wants daily bread, that does not also want daily pardon; and yet how few are sensible of it? Sin is here compared to a debt. There.is a debt of *duty* we owe to God; and in case of failure, we contract a new debt to the justice of God. The debts we owe to man expose us to misery here; but the debts we owe to God expose us to eternal misery. And be it remembered, we are not able to pay a single farthing of this debt. If ever we are delivered from going to the prison of hell, it must be by a free pardon; for so we here pray: " *Forgive us* our debts;" or, as it is elsewhere, " Forgive us our trespasses."

We can make no amends. It is not taking care not to contract a new debt, that will discharge an old one; this will not do with our neighbours, nor will it do with God. Free forgiveness alone will prevent our punishment. But, though a sinner is justified freely, it is only " through the redemption that is in Christ." With believing and penitent hearts we must go to God by Jesus Christ, and plead for his mercy for Christ's sake.

At the same time, we are here taught the necessity of a forgiving temper. " As we forgive our debtors," that is, as we forgive those who have injured us in our property, person, or name. Not that by our kindness to another we deserve forgiveness at the hand of God; but that, as we cannot expect pardon from God, while we refuse it to those who ask us for it, we may humbly hope, that, if we are enabled, by grace, to forgive others, God, whose thoughts and ways are infinitely above ours, will not reject our prayer for pardoning mercy through Jesus Christ.

AND LEAD US NOT INTO TEMPTATION, BUT DELIVER US FROM EVIL. Those whose sins are forgiven will be afraid of sinning again; and knowing the power of temptation, we pray to be kept from it. *Temptation* is any thing which makes *trial* of us, and proves what is in our hearts. Afflictions are God's trial of us, for our good; but all Satan's temptations are to lead us into evil. The person who uses this prayer aright is afraid of sin; and he offers up this petition to God, that he would keep him out of the way of such trials as would be too hard for him, or grant sufficient strength to resist and overcome the devil, *the evil one*, " who goeth about like a roaring lion, seeking whom he may devour." But this must be accompanied with *watching*, and avoiding all wilful occasion of sin, or else these words do but mock God.

The conclusion of the prayer is: FOR THINE IS THE KINGDOM, AND THE POWER, AND THE GLORY, FOR EVER. AMEN. This shows why we should pray to God, and why we may hope to be heard. The *kingdom* is his. God is king of all the world, and has a right to dispose of all things in it. The *power* is his, as

well as the authority. He therefore *can* answer our prayers;
and we hope he *will*. His then will be the *glory*. Whatever
God does is for his own glory; and if we are disposed to
give him all the glory of what he does for us, we may hope
that our petitions will be granted. This kingdom, this
power, this glory, are *for ever:* he will never want the
power to help; and if we are saved, we shall never cease
to give him praise.

The force of the prayer lies in the *first* and *last* words of
it—*Our Father*, and *Amen.* In the *first* we apply to God in
Christ, as reconciled to us; in the *last* we set our seal to
the whole, and say, *Amen; so let it be; so*, we humbly hope,
it shall be, for Christ's sake.

CONCLUSION.

How awfully is this prayer abused! Ignorant people
use it as a kind of charm; and think it enough to say the
words, without considering the meaning. O beware, as you
love your souls, of mocking God by thoughtless praying!
Can you call him a father, while you obey the devil? Will
you say, "Hallowed be thy name," and yet profane it
daily? What do you care for *his kingdom*, while you belong
to another? or talk of God's will, without wishing to do it?
Do you not forget him when you eat and drink?

Are you not careless about the forgiveness of your sins,
adding daily to the dreadful debt; and perhaps living in
malice and wrath? How can you pray that God will not
lead you into temptation, when you run wilfully into the
way of it; frequenting the ale-house, the play-house, and
the company of the lewd, the profane, and the drunken?
Dear fellow-creature, permit me to say, that thus contra-
dicting your prayers by your life, you cannot expect to be
heard; nay, God may justly say to you at last, "Out of
thine own mouth will I condemn thee, thou wicked servant." But God forbid! Think over this prayer before
you use it again: and beg of God to enable you to use it
with understanding and sincerity, that the rich blessings
asked for in it may be yours, and God be glorified in your
everlasting salvation.

PUBLISHED BY THE
AMERICAN TRACT SOCIETY.

THE

Criminal Court.

PUBLISHED BY THE

AMERICAN TRACT SOCIETY,

AND SOLD AT THEIR DEPOSITORY, NO. 150 NASSAU-STREET, NEAR
THE CITY-HALL, NEW-YORK; AND BY AGENTS OF THE
SOCIETY, ITS BRANCHES, AND AUXILIARIES, IN
THE PRINCIPAL CITIES AND TOWNS
IN THE UNITED STATES

THE

CRIMINAL COURT.

—◆◆◆—

ON my approach to the city of C——, I found the road
crowded with carriages, horsemen, and passengers on foot,
all pressing forward in the same direction. The Criminal
Court was to be held there on the morrow.

This awakened in my mind a train of serious reflections,
and I could not help presenting to my imagination the solemn scene which would most probably be displayed on this
occasion. By and by, the distant trumpets were heard, an-
nouncing the approach of the Judge. Again and again the
shrill sound pierced the air, as the procession moved along.
When they passed the jail, the trumpets penetrated the
darkest cell, and made the most hardened of the prisoners
to tremble. They had often pretended to try each other in
a mock court, and they had pronounced various sentences,
with the greatest levity, on those found guilty. Now, when
they were about to be put upon their trial before a real tribunal, which had power to condemn, and to execute its
sentence, their hearts began to fail. Conscience, an accus-
ing conscience, raised her voice ; and they could not help
foreboding the probable issue of their trial.

On the morrow, the Court was filled at an early hour.
The Judge entered, and taking his seat upon the bench,
opened his commission. The prisoners were arraigned,
and murder, robbery, and forgery, were among the black
offences which they were charged with having committed.
Around, and in the hall, were to be seen their relations
and friends, anxiously awaiting the verdicts of the jury.

In one place was a genteel and decent-looking young
woman, with an infant at her breast, and two little children by her side, who attracted particular notice. She had
married, contrary to her parents' advice, a young man,
who might have maintained her and his family comforta-

bly; but he was a man of expensive habits, and a lover of pleasure. These soon involved him in debt. He associated with gamblers and sharpers; and, after having himself practised the various arts of a swindler, he at length proceeded to forgery, for which crime he was about to take his trial.

In another part of the hall was an aged countryman, of respectable appearance, whose tears and dejected countenance bespoke his inward grief. The young man, his son, had been well brought up. His parents, who were sober and industrious, and who feared God, had set a good example before him. But in an evil hour he became acquainted with an artful female, who soon enticed him to break through the restraints of a good education. When in want of money to support her extravagance, he determined, at her instigation, to go on the highway, where he committed the robbery for which he stood indicted.

I observed another person, the very reverse of the old man already described; a father too, who manifested the most hardened indifference. He was one who disliked working, and preferred a boxing-match, or a horse-race, to the earnings of an honest subsistence for his family. To make up for the loss of time, he resorted to stealing poultry. He had, at an early age, taken his son (now in jail) with him on his nightly expeditions. The youth soon became expert in his low and mischievous employment; but trained up to habits of idleness and expense, he found it insufficient to support him. When unsuccessful in his pursuit of game, he proceeded to steal any thing which came in his way in his midnight rambles. But finding these all too little for his extravagance, he formed the dreadful resolution to rob and murder a rich old man, and his maid servant, who lived at a lone house a few miles distant. He committed the foul deed; and the better to cover his guilt, set fire to the house, thinking, by that expedient, to prevent all means of detection. But that God, whose eyes are as a flame of fire, and to whom the darkness and the light are both alike, by his Providence, soon led to a discovery of the dreadful deed.

These and similar crimes lead to punishment in the present life. They bring with them a train of wretchedness to the persons themselves, and their families and relations; for "the way of transgressors is hard;" and if there were no life beyond the present, honesty and industry would be the best policy.

To those readers (should there be any such) who are pursuing evil courses, on the presumption that they shall avoid detection, I would say, What will it profit you at the last, should you live all your days unsuspected; or though, shut up in prison, and arraigned at the bar, you should escape punishment, through a flaw in the indictment, an unwillingness to prosecute, or a deficiency in the evidence? There is a tribunal to which you are hastening, where no contrivance to evade the purposes of justice can for a moment avail.

Reader, have you been mercifully preserved from violating the laws of your country, and from gross outward sins? Bless God for it; but remember, you nevertheless stand condemned by his righteous and holy law. "There is none righteous, no, not one; for all have sinned and come short of the glory of God, that every mouth may be stopped, and all the world may become guilty before God." Rom. iii. 10. 19. 28. "The hour is coming, in the which all that are in the graves shall hear his voice, and shall come forth, they that have done good unto the resurrection of life, and they that have done evil unto the resurrection of damnation." John, v. 28, 29. "I saw a great white throne, and him that sat on it, from whose face the earth and the heaven fled away, and there was found no place for them. And I saw the dead, small and great, stand before God; and the books were opened, and another book was opened, which is the book of life; and the dead were judged out of those things which are written in the books, according to their works." Rev. xx. 11, 12.

Sinner, are you flattering yourself with a hope of escaping that day of trial? that but of the countless millions who shall appear, you may be able to avoid the eye of the Judge? Vain thought! His eye will be as fully upon you as if you were the only one to be tried. "Whither shall I go from thy Spirit, or whither shall I flee from thy presence? If I ascend up into heaven, thou art there; if I make my bed in hell, thou art there. If I take the wings of the morning, and dwell in the uttermost parts of the sea, even there shall thy hand lead me, and thy right hand shall hold me. If I say, Surely the darkness shall cover me, even the night shall be light about me. Yea, the darkness hideth not from thee, but the night shineth as the day : the darkness and the light are both alike to thee !" Psalm cxxxix. 7—12.

How altered the tone of the bold blasphemers and presumptuous sinners in that day! In this life they could laugh at every thing sacred; they could call on God to damn their souls, and sport with the Saviour's name, on the most trifling occasions. Hear them now " calling on the rocks and the mountains to fall on them, and hide them from the face of him that sitteth on the throne, and from the *wrath of the Lamb ;* for the great day of his wrath is come, and who shall be able to stand ?"

If you cannot escape the eye of the Judge, will you be able to justify yourself before him? Do you allege, that you do no harm, that you pay every one his own, that you have a good heart? Hear what the Judge says of your heart. " The heart is deceitful above all things, and desperately wicked : who can know it ?" Jer. xvii. 9. "For out of the heart proceed evil thoughts, murders, adulteries, fornications, thefts, false witness, blasphemies." Matt. xv. 19. The law by which you must be judged is so strict and holy, that the secret wish or look is a transgression. " Whosoever hateth his brother, is a murderer." 1 John, iii. 15. "Cursed is every one that continueth not in all things which are written in the book of the law to do them." Gal. iii. 10.

When the book shall be opened by the Judge, which contains a countless number of evil thoughts, spiteful words, and sinful actions, recorded against you, and conscience, awakened by ten thousand recollections, shall do her office, you will stand speechless and self-condemned.

If you can neither escape nor justify yourself, will you be able to contend with the Judge? Vain thought! " Can thy heart endure, or can thy hands be strong, in the day that I shall deal with thee ?" Ezek. xxii. 14. He who bore so long with your provocations, will then ascend the throne of judgment, to avenge the insulted Majesty of Heaven, and to vindicate his holy law.

Hear the blessed Judge addressing the sinner. " How

often would I have gathered you as a hen gathereth her
chickens under her wings, and ye would not.   How often
did I, as if in humble suit, knock at the door of your heart,
beseeching you to be reconciled; but ye refused. How
often when my hand has been lifted up to execute my
wrath upon you, did my patience and long-suffering prevail, and another trial was afforded you.   Yea, how often
did I follow you, saying, Turn ye, turn ye, why will ye die?
By my holy incarnation, my life of sorrows, my bloody
sweat, my pierced hands and feet, and wounded side, did
I plead with you; but all in vain.   Take now these mine
enemies, who would not that I should reign over them,
bind them hand and foot, and cast them into outer darkness, where there is wailing and gnashing of teeth."

And should you be neither able to escape nor justify your-
sel , nor contend successfully with the Judge, will you be
able to endure the dreadful sentence? Are you prepared
for an immortality of woe? It is a fearful thing to fall into
the hands of the living God. Who can conceive the full
meaning of these words, *The wrath of the Lamb*? Ye fallen spirits, thrones, and dominions, who kept not your first
estate, and who have been long confined in chains of
darkness, say what it is! Ye who have sunk deepest in
the fiery lake, tell us what *the wrath of the Lamb* is! And
ye sinners of mankind, condemned before the flood, declare if ye can, what is meant by quenchless fire and the
ever-gnawing worm.

Reader, listen not to those deceivers who would flatter
you into a belief, that after a season of punishment it will
be well. The irreversible sentence of the Judge is, "Depart from me, ye cursed, into *everlasting fire*, where the
worm dieth not, and the fire is not quenched."

Sinner, I have been endeavouring to set before you the
end of all your evil courses; for however different the
paths of transgressors are, (and the broad road has many
paths,) they all lead down to the chambers of death. Let
me affectionately entreat you to stop, before your feet
stumble on the dark mountains. Oh sinner, stop! Why in
such haste? Do not madly press forward in thy career of
sin. Say not, There is no hope. There *is* hope—hope for
the most abandoned sinner on the face of the earth. Hear
the heart-affecting address of that God, whose laws you

have broken, whose threatenings you have defied, whose
patience you have insulted, whose offers of mercy you
have rejected. Hear him addressing you as by name:
" As I live, saith the Lord God, I have no pleasure in the
death of the wicked; but that the wicked turn from his
way and live: turn ye, turn ye, from your evil ways; for
why will ye die ?" Ezek. xxxiii. 11. And lest you should
count your guilt too great to be pardoned, listen to the gracious invitation, " Come now, and let us reason together,
saith the Lord ; though your sins be as scarlet, they shall
be white as snow; though they be red like crimson, they
shall be as wool." Isa. i. 18. " For God so loved the world,
that he gave his only begotten Son, that whosoever believeth in him should not perish, but have everlasting life.
For God sent not his Son into the world to condemn the
world ; but that the world through him might be saved."
John, iii. 16, 17. " God was in Christ, reconciling the
world unto himself, not imputing their trespasses unto
them; and hath committed unto us the word of reconcilia-
tion. Now then we are ambassadors for Christ, as though
God did beseech you by us ; we pray you in Christ's stead,
be ye reconciled to God. For he hath made him to be sin
for us, who knew no sin; that we might be made the
righteousness of God in him." 2 Cor. v. 19, 20, 21.

How sweet is the voice of mercy to the miserable and
the guilty ! What a crowd of promises are pressing forward, as it were, to stop the sinner in his evil course !
Unfeeling indeed must be the heart which is unmoved,
on hearing such gracious tidings as these. " Behold the
Lamb of God, which taketh away the sin of the world !"
Hear him, with his dying breath, pleading for the pardon
of his murderers. See him with extended arms, ready to
receive you. Come, sinner, to the Gospel feast; come, for
all things are now ready. " Ho ! every one that thirsteth,
come ye to the waters, and he that hath no money, come,
buy wine and milk without money and without price."
Isa. iv. 1. Blessings of infinite value, which cost a sum so
great that an angel cannot estimate the value, are offered
to all who will receive them, without price. You are guilty : Jesus shed his blood as an atonement for sin. You are
unholy and polluted : there is a fountain opened for all un-
cleanness. Hear the gracious promise of the Holy Spirit :

" Then will I sprinkle clean water upon you, and ye shall be clean; from all your filthiness, and from all your idols will I cleanse you. A new heart also will I give you, and a new spirit will I put within you; and I will take away the stony heart out of your flesh, and I will give you a heart of flesh. And I will put my Spirit within you, and cause you to walk in my statutes, and ye shall keep my judgments and do them." Ezek. xxxvi. 25, 26, 27. " Ask, and it shall be given you; seek, and ye shall find; knock, and it shall be opened unto you. For every one that asketh, receiveth; and he that seeketh, findeth; and to him that knocketh it shall be opened. If ye, then, being evil, know how to give good gifts unto your children, how much more shall your Heavenly Father give the *Holy Spirit* to them that ask him!" Luke, xi. 9, 10. 13. Without delay hasten to the Saviour; the door of mercy is now open. " The Spirit and the Bride say, Come; and let him that heareth say, Come; and let him that is athirst come; and *whosoever will,* let him take of the water of *life* freely." Rev. xxii. 17.

The Last Judgment.

Think, O my soul, the dreadful day,
   When the incensed God
Shall rend the sky and burn the sea,
   And fling his wrath abroad!

What shall the wretch, the sinner do!
   He once defied the Lord!
But he shall dread the Thund'rer now,
   And sink beneath his word.

Tempests of angry fire shall roll,
   To blast the rebel worm;
And beat upon his naked soul,
   In one eternal storm.

END.

THE SUBSTANCE

OF

LESLIE'S METHOD

WITH

THE DEISTS;

AND

TRUTH OF CHRISTIANITY

DEMONSTRATED.

---•◉●◉•---

A SHORT AND EASY METHOD WITH THE DEISTS.

DEAR SIR—You are desirous, you inform me, to receive from me some one topic of reason, which shall demonstrate the truth of the Christian Religion, and at the same time distinguish it from the impostures of Mahomet, and the Heathen Deities : that our Deists may be brought to this test, and be obliged either to renounce their reason and the common reason of mankind, or to admit the clear proof, from reason, of the Revelation of Christ; which must be such a proof as no impostor can pretend to, otherwise it will not prove Christianity not to be an imposture. And you cannot but imagine, you add, that there must be such a proof, because every truth is in itself one : and therefore one reason for it, if it be a true reason, must be sufficient; and, if sufficient, better than many : because multiplicity creates confusion, especially in weak judgments.

Sir, you have imposed a hard task upon me : I wish I could perform it. For, though every truth be one, yet our sight is so feeble, that we cannot always come to it directly, but by many inferences and layings of things together. But, I think, that in the case before us, there is such a proof as you desire, and I will set it down as shortly and as plainly as I can.

I suppose, then, that the truth of the Christian Doctrines will be sufficiently evinced, if the matters of fact recorded of Christ in the Gospels are proved to be true; for his

P

miracles, if true, establish the truth of what he delivered. The same may be said, with regard to Moses. If he led the children of Israel through the Red Sea, and did such other wonderful things as are recorded of him in the book of Exodus, it must necessarily follow that he was sent by God : these being the strongest evidences we can require, and which every Deist will confess he would admit, if he himself had witnessed their performance. So that the stress of this cause will depend upon the proof of these matters of fact.

With a view, therefore, to this proof, I shall proceed,

I. To lay down such marks, as to the truth of matters of fact in general, that, where they all meet, such matters of fact cannot be false : and,

II. To show that they all do meet in the matters of fact of Moses and of Christ; and do not meet in those reported of Mahomet and of the Heathen Deities, nor can possibly meet in any imposture whatsoever :

I. The marks are these :

1. That the fact be such as men's *outward senses* can judge of;

2. That it be performed *publicly*, in the presence of witnesses;

3. That there be *public monuments and actions* kept up in memory of it; and,

4. That such monuments and actions shall be established, and commence, *at the time of the fact.*

The two first of these Marks make it impossible for any false fact to be imposed upon men at the time when it was said to be done, because every man's senses would contradict it. For example : Suppose I should pretend that, yesterday, I divided the Thames in the presence of all the people of London, and led the whole city over to Southwark on dry land, the waters standing like walls on each side :—it would be morally impossible for me to convince the people of London that this was true; when every man, woman, and child, could contradict me, and affirm that they had not seen the Thames so divided, nor been led over to Southwark on dry land. I take it then for granted, (and I apprehend with the allowance of all the Deists in the world,) that no such imposition could be put upon mankind at the time when such matter of fact was said to be done.

"But," it may be urged, "the fact might be invented, when the men of that generation in which it was said to be done were all past and gone; and the credulity of after-ages might be induced to believe that things had been performed in earlier times, which had not!"

From this the two latter Marks secure us, as much as the two first, in the former case. For whenever such a fact was invented, if it were stated that not only public monuments of it remained, but likewise that public actions or observances had been kept up in memory of it ever since, the deceit must be detected by no such monuments appearing, and by the experience of every man, woman, and child, who must know that no such actions or observances had ever taken place. For example: Suppose I should now fabricate a story of something done a thousand years ago, I might perhaps get a few persons to believe me; but if I were farther to add, that from that day to this, every man, at the age of twelve years, had a joint of his little finger cut off in memory of it, and that of course every man then living, actually wanted a joint of that finger, and vouched this institution in confirmation of its truth: it would be morally impossible for me to gain credit in such a case, because every man then living would contradict me, as to the circumstance of cutting off a joint of the finger; and that, being an essential part of my original matter of fact, must prove the whole to be false.

II. Let us now come to the second point, and show that all these Marks do meet in the matters of fact of Moses, and of Christ; and do not meet in those reported of Mahomet, and of the Heathen Deities, nor can possibly meet in any imposture whatsoever.

As to Moses, he, I take it for granted, could not have persuaded six hundred thousand men, that he had brought them out of Egypt by the Red Sea, fed them forty years with miraculous manna, &c. if it had not been true: because the senses of every man who was then alive would have contradicted him. So that here are the two first Marks.

For the same reason, it would have been equally impossible for him to have made them receive his Five Books as true, which related all these things as done before their eyes, if they had not been so done. Observe how positively he speaks to them. "And know you this day, for I

speak not with your children, which have not known, and
which have not seen the chastisement of the Lord your
God, his greatness, his mighty hand, and his stretched-out
arm, and his miracles;—but your eyes have seen all the
great acts of the Lord which he did." Deut. xi. 2—7.
Hence we must admit it to be impossible that these Books,
if written by Moses in support of an imposture, could have
been put upon the people who were alive at the time when
such things were said to be done.

"But they might have been written," it may be urged,
"in some age after Moses, and published as his!"

To this I reply, that, if it were so, it was impossible they
should have been received as such; because they speak of
themselves as delivered by Moses, and kept in the ark from
his time; (Deut. xxxi. 24—26.) and state that a copy of
them was likewise deposited in the hands of the king,
"that he might learn to fear the Lord his God, to keep all
the words of this law and these statutes, to do them."
Deut. xvii. 19. Here these Books expressly represent
themselves as being not only the civil history, but also the
established municipal law of the Jews, binding the king
as well as the people. In whatever age, therefore, after
Moses, they might have been forged, it was impossible
they should have gained any credit; because they could
not then have been found either in the ark, or with the
king, or anywhere else: and, when they were first published, every body must know that they had never heard
of them before.

And they could still less receive them as their book of
statutes, and the standing law of the land, by which they
had all along been governed. Could any man, at this day,
invent a set of Acts of Parliament for England, and make
it pass upon the nation as the only book of statutes which
they had ever known? As impossible was it for these
Books, if written in any age after Moses, to have been received for what they declare themselves to be, that is, the
municipal law of the *Jews;* and for any man to have persuaded that people that they had owned them as their
code of statutes from the time of Moses, that is, before
they had ever heard of them! Nay, more: they must
instantly have forgotten their former laws, if they could
receive these Books as such; and as such only could they

receive them, because such they vouched themselves to be. Let me ask the Deists but one short question : "Was a book of sham laws ever palmed upon any nation since the world began ?" If not, with what face can they say this of the law books of the *Jews* ? Why will they affirm that of them, which they admit never to have happened in any other instance ?

But they must be still more unreasonable. For the Books of Moses have an ampler demonstration of their truth than even other law books have ; as they not only contain the laws themselves, but give a historical account of their institution and regular fulfilment : of the Passover, for instance, in memory of their supernatural protection, upon the slaying of the first-born of Egypt; the dedication of the first-born of Israel, both of man and beast ; the preservation of Aaron's Rod which budded, of the pot of Manna, and of the Brazen Serpent, which remained till the days of Hezekiah. 2 Kings, xviii. 4, &c. And, besides these memorials of particular occurrences, there were other solemn observances, in general memory of their deliverance out of Egypt, &c. as their annual Expiations, their New Moons, their Sabbaths, and their ordinary Sacrifices : so that there were yearly, monthly, weekly, and daily recognitions of these things. The same books likewise farther inform us, that the tribe of Levi were appointed and consecrated by God as his ministers, by whom alone these institutions were to be celebrated; that it was death for any others to approach the altar; that their High-Priest wore a brilliant mitre and magnificent robes, with the miraculous Urim and Thummim in his breast-plate ; that at his word all the people were to go out, and to come in ; that these *Levites* were also their judges, even in all civil causes, &c.

Hence, too, therefore, in whatever age after Moses they might have been forged, it was impossible they should have gained any credit : unless indeed the fabricators could have made the whole nation believe, *in spite of their invariable experience to the contrary*, that they had received these Books long before, from their fathers; had been taught them when they were children, and had taught them to their own children ; that they had been circumcised themselves, had circumcised their families, and uniformly observed their whole minute detail of sacrifices and ceremonies; that they had never eaten any swine's flesh or other prohibited meats; that they had a splendid tabernacle, with a regular priesthood to administer in it, confined to one particular tribe, and a superintendant High-Priest, whose death alone could deliver those that had fled to the cities of refuge; that these priests were their ordinary judges, even in civil matters, &c. But this would surely have been impossible, if none of these things had been practised; and it would consequently have been impossible to circulate, as true, a set of books which affirmed that they had practised them, and upon that practice rested their own pretensions to acceptance. So that here are the two latter Marks.

"But," to advance to the utmost degree of supposition, it may be urged, "these things might have been practised prior to this alleged forgery; and those books only deceived the nation, by making them believe that they were practised in memory of such and such occurrences as were then invented!"

In this hypothesis, however groundless, the same impossibilities press upon our notice as before. For it implies that the Jews had previously kept these observances in memory of nothing, or without knowing why they kept them; whereas, in all their particulars, they strikingly express their original: as the Passover, instituted in memory of God's passing over the children of the Israelites, when he slew the first-born of Egypt, &c.

Let us admit, however contrary both to probability and to matter of fact, that they did not know why they kept these observances; yet, was it possible to persuade them that they were kept in memory of something which they had never heard of before? For example: Suppose I should now forge some romantic story of strange things done a long while ago; and, in confirmation of this, should endeavour to convince the Christian world that they had regularly, from that period to this, kept holy the first day of the week, in memory of such or such a man: a Cæsar, or a Mahomet: and had all been baptized in his name, and sworn by it upon the very book which I had then fabricated, and which of course they had never seen before in their public courts of judicature; that this book likewise contained their law, civil and ecclesiastical, which they had ever since his time acknowledged, and no other :—I ask any Deist, whether he thinks it possible that such a cheat could be received as the Gospel of Christians, or not? The same reason holds with regard to the books of Moses, and must hold with regard to every book which contains matters of fact accompanied by the abovementioned Four Marks. For these Marks, together, secure mankind from imposition, with regard to any false fact, as well in after ages, as at the time when it was said to be done.

Let me produce, as another and a familiar illustration, the *Stonehenge* of *Salisbury-plain*. Almost every body has seen, or heard of it ; and yet nobody knows by whom, or in memory of what, it was set up.

Now suppose I should write a book to-morrow, and state in it that these huge stones were erected by a Cæsar or a Mahomet, in memory of such and such of their actions ; and should farther add, that this book was written at the time when those actions were performed, and by the doers themselves, or by eye-witnesses ; and had been constantly received as true, and quoted by authors of the greatest credit in regular succession ever since ; that it was well known in England, and even enjoined by Act of Parliament to be taught our children, and that we accordingly did teach it our children, and had been taught it ourselves when we were children :—would this, I demand of any Deist, pass current in England? Or, rather, should not I, or any other person who might insist upon its reception, instead of being believed, be considered insane?

Let us compare, then, this rude structure with the Stonehenge, as I may call it, or "twelve stones" set up at *Gilgal*. Joshua, iv. 6. It is there said, that the reason why they were set up was, that when the children of the Jews, in after-ages, should ask their meaning, it should be told them. Ch. iv. 20—22. And the thing, in memory of which they were set up, the passage over Jordan, was such as could not possibly have been imposed upon that people at the time when it was said to be done : it was not less miraculous, and from the previous notice, preparations, and other striking circumstances of its performance, (iii.

5. 15.) still more unassailable by the petty cavils of infidel sophistry, than their passage through the Red Sea.

Now, to form our argument, let us suppose that there never was any such thing as that passage over Jordan; that these stones at Gilgal had been set up on some unknown occasion; and that some designing man, in an after-age, invented this book of Joshua, affirmed that it was written at the time of that imaginary event by Joshua himself, and adduced this pile of stones as a testimony of its truth:—would not every body say to him, "We know this pile very well, but we never before heard of this reason for it, nor of this book of Joshua. Where has it lain concealed all this while? And where and how came you, after so long a period, to find it? Besides, it informs us, that this passage over Jordan was solemnly directed to be taught our children, from age to age; and, to that end, that they were always to be instructed in the meaning of this particular monument: but we were never taught it ourselves, when we were children, nor did we ever teach it to our children. And it is in the highest degree improbable that such an emphatic ordinance should have been forgotten during the continuance of so remarkable a pile of stones, set up expressly for the purpose of preserving its remembrance."

If, then, for these reasons, no such fabrication could be put upon us, as to the stones in *Salisbury-plain;* how much less could it succeed, as to the stonage at *Gilgal?* If, where we are ignorant of the true origin of a mere naked monument, such a sham origin cannot be imposed, how much less practicable would it be to impose upon us in actions and observances, which we celebrate in memory of what we actually know; to make us forget what we have regularly commemorated; and to persuade us that we have constantly kept such and such institutions, with reference to something which we never heard of before! That is, that we knew something before we knew it! And, if we find it thus impossible to practise deceit, even in cases which have not the above Four Marks, how much more impossible must it be that any deceit should be practised in cases in which all these Four Marks meet.

In the matters of fact of Christ likewise, as well as in those of Moses, these Four Marks are to be found. The reasoning, indeed, which has been already advanced with respect to the Old Testament, is generally applicable to the New. The Miracles of Christ, like those of Moses, were such as men's *outward senses* could judge of; and were performed *publicly*, in the presence of those to whom the history of them, contained in the Gospel, was addressed. And it is related, that "about three thousand" at one time, (Acts, ii. 41.) and about "five thousand" at another, (iv. 4.) were converted in consequence of what they themselves saw and heard, in matters where it was impossible that they should have been deceived. Here, therefore, were the two first Marks.

And, with regard to the two latter, Baptism and the Lord's Supper were instituted as memorials of certain things, not in after-ages, but *at the time* when these things were said to be done; and have been strictly observed, *from that time to this*, without interruption. Christ himself also ordained Apostles, &c. to preach and administer his ordinances, and to govern his church "even unto the end of the world." Now the Christian ministry is as notorious a matter of fact among us as the setting apart of the tribe of Levi was among the Jews; and as the era and object of their appointment are part of the Gospel-narrative, if that narrative had been a fiction of some subsequent age, at the time of its fabrication no such order of men could have been found, which would have effectually given the lie to the whole story. And the truth of the matters of fact of Christ, being no otherwise asserted than as there were at the time (whenever the Deist will suppose the Gospel to have been fabricated) public ordinances, and a public Ministry of his institution to dispense them, and it being impossible, upon this hypothesis, that there could be any such things then in existence, we must admit it to be equally impossible that the forgery should have been successful. Hence, it was as impossible to deceive mankind, in respect to these matters of fact, by inventing them in after-ages, as at the time when they were said to be done.

The matters of fact, reported of Mahomet and of the Heathen Deities, do all want some of these Four Marks, by which the certainty of facts is established. Mahomet himself, as he tells us in his Koran, (vi. &c.) pretended to no miracles; and those which are commonly related of him pass, even among his followers, for ridiculous legends, and as such are rejected by their scholars and philosophers. They have not either of the two first Marks; for his converse with the moon, his night-journey from Mecca to Jerusalem, and thence to heaven, &c. were not performed before any witnesses, nor was the tour indeed of a nature to admit human attestation: and to the two latter they do not even affect to advance any claim.

The same may be affirmed, with little variation, of the stories of the Heathen Deities: of Mercury's stealing sheep, Jupiter's transforming himself into a bull, &c. besides the absurdity of such degrading and profligate adventures. And accordingly we find that the more enlightened Pagans themselves considered them as fables involving a mystical meaning, of which several of their writers have endeavoured to give us the explication. It is true, these gods had their priests, their feasts, their games, and other public ceremonies; but all these want the fourth Mark, of commencing *at the time* when the things which they commemorate were said to have been done. Hence they cannot secure mankind, in subsequent ages, from imposture, as they furnish no internal means of detection at the period of the forgery. The *Bacchanalia*, for example, and other heathen festivals, were established long after the events to which they refer; and the priests of Juno, Mars, &c. were not ordained by those imaginary Deities, but appointed by others in some after-age, and are therefore no evidence to the truth of their preternatural achievements.

To apply what has been said :

We may challenge all the Deists in the world to show any fabulous action accompanied by these Four Marks. The thing is impossible. The histories of the Old and New Testament never could have been received, if they had not been true; because the priesthoods of Levi and of Christ, the observance of the Sabbath, the Passover and Circumcision, and the ordinances of Baptism and the Lord's Supper, &c. are there represented as descending uninterruptedly from the times of their respective institution. And it would have been as impossible to persuade men in after-ages that they had been circumcised or baptized, and celebrated Passovers, Sabbaths, and other ordinances, under the ministration of a certain order of priests, if they had done none of those things, as to make them believe at the time, without any real foundation, that they had gone through seas on dry land, seen the dead raised, &c. But, without such a persuasion, it was impossible that either the Law or the Gospel could have been received. And the truth of the matters of fact of each being no otherwise asserted than as such public ceremonies had been previously practised, their certainty is established upon the FULL CONVICTION OF THE SENSES OF MANKIND.

I do not say that every thing which wants these Four Marks is false; but that every thing which has them all, must be true.

I can have no doubt that there was such a man as Julius Cæsar, that he conquered at Pharsalia, and was killed in the Senate-house, though neither his actions nor his assassination be commemorated by any public observances. But this shows that the matters of fact of Moses and of Christ have come down to us better certified than any other whatsoever. And yet our Deists, who would consider any one as hopelessly irrational, that should offer to deny the existence of Cæsar, value themselves as the only men of profound sense and judgment, for ridiculing the histories of Moses and of Christ, though guarded by infallible marks, which that of Cæsar wants.

Besides, the nature of the subject would of itself lead to a more minute examination of the one than of the other: for of what consequence is it to me, or to the world, whether there ever was such a man as Cæsar; whether he conquered at Pharsalia, and was killed in the Senate-house, or not? But our eternal welfare is concerned in the truth of what is recorded in the Scriptures; whence they would naturally be more narrowly scrutinized, when proposed for acceptance.

How unreasonable, then, is it to reject matters of fact so important, so sifted, and so attested; and yet to think it absurd, even to madness, to deny other matters of fact—which have not the thousandth part of their evidence—have had comparatively little investigation—and are of no consequence at all!

TRUTH OF CHRISTIANITY
DEMONSTRATED.

To the preceding Four Marks, which are common to the matters of fact of Moses and of Christ, I now proceed to subjoin Four additional Marks; the three last of which, no matter of fact, how true soever, either has had, or can have, except that of Christ.

This will obviously appear, if it be considered,

5. That the book, which relates the facts, *contains likewise the laws* of the people to whom it belongs;

6. That Christ was previously announced, for that very period, by a long train of *prophecies;* and,

7. Still more peculiarly prefigured by *types*, both of a circumstantial and personal nature, from the earliest ages; and,

8. That the facts of Christianity are such, as to make it impossible for either their relaters or hearers to believe them, if false, without supposing a *universal deception of the senses of mankind.*

The *fifth Mark*, which has been subordinately discussed in the former part of this Tract, in such a manner as to supersede the necessity of dwelling upon it in this, renders it impossible for any one to have imposed such a book upon any people. For example: Suppose I should forge a code of laws for Great Britain, and publish it next term; could I hope to persuade the judges, lawyers, and people, that this was their genuine statute-book, by which all their causes had been determined in the public courts for so many centuries past! Before they could be brought to this, they must totally forget their established laws, which they had so laboriously committed to memory, and so familiarly quoted in every day's practice, and believe that this new book, which they had never seen before, was that old book, which had been pleaded so long in Westminster-Hall, which has been so often printed, and of which the originals are now so carefully preserved in the Tower.

This applies strongly to the books of Moses, in which, not only the history of the *Jews*, but likewise their whole law, secular and ecclesiastical, was contained. And though, from the early extension and destined universality of the Christian system, it could not, without unnecessary confusion, furnish a uniform civil code to all its various followers

who were already under the government of laws in some
degree adapted to their respective climates and characters,
yet was it intended as the spiritual guide of the new
Church. And in this respect this Mark is still stronger
with regard to the Gospel, than even to the Books of
Moses; inasmuch as it is easier (however hard) to imagine
the substitution of an entire statute-book in one particular
nation, than that all the nations of *Christendom* should have
unanimously conspired in the forgery. But, without such
a conspiracy, such a forgery could never have succeeded,
as the Gospel universally formed a regular part of their
daily public offices.

But I hasten to the *sixth Mark*, namely, *Prophecy.*

The great fact of Christ's coming was previously announced to the *Jews*, in the Old Testament, " by all the
holy Prophets which have been since the world began."
Luke, i. 70.

The first promise upon the subject was made to Adam,
immediately after the fall. Gen. iii. 15. Compare Col. ii. 15.
and Heb. ii. 14.

He was again repeatedly promised to Abraham, (Gen.
xii. 3. xviii. 18. and xxii. 18. Gal. iii. 16.) to Isaac, (Gen.
xxvi. 4.) and to Jacob, Gen. xxviii. 14.

Jacob expressly prophesied of him, under the appellation
of " Shiloh," or *Him that was to be sent.* Gen. xlix. 10.
Balaam also, with the voice of inspiration, pronounced him
" the Star of Jacob, and the Sceptre of Israel." Numb.
xxiv. 17. Moses spake of him, as One " greater than
himself." Deut. xviii. 15, 18, 19. Acts, iii. 22. And Daniel hailed his arrival, under the name of " Messiah the
Prince." Chap. ix. 25.

It was foretold, that he should be born of a virgin, (Isa.
vii. 14.) in the city of *Bethlehem*, (Micah, v. 2.) of the
seed of Jesse; (Isa. xi. 1. 10.) that he should lead a life
of poverty and suffering, (Psalm xxii.) inflicted upon him,
" not for himself," (Dan. ix. 26.) but for the sins of others,
(Isa. liii.) and, after a short confinement in the grave,
should rise again; (Psalm xvi. 10. Acts, ii. 27, 31, and
xiii. 35—37.) that he " should sit upon the throne of
David for ever," and be called " the mighty God," (Isa.
ix. 6, 7.) " the Lord our Righteousness," (Jer. xxxiii. 16.)
" Immanuel, that is, God with us," (Isa. vii. 14. Matt.
i 23.) and by David himself, whose son he was accord-

ing to the flesh, " Lord." Psalm cx. 1. applied to Christ by nimself, Matt. xxii. 44, and by Peter, Acts, ii. 34.

The time of his incarnation was to be, before " the Sceptre should depart from *Judah*," (Gen. xlix. 10.) during the continuance of the second Temple, (Hag. ii. 7, 9.) and within seventy weeks, or 490 days, that is, according to the constant interpretation of prophecy, 490 years from its erection. Dan. ix. 24.

From these, and many other predictions, the coming of Christ was at all times the general expectation of the *Jews*; and fully matured at the time of his actual advent, as may be inferred from the number of false Messiahs who appeared about that period.

That he was likewise the expectation of the *Gentiles*, (in conformity to the prophecies of Gen. xlix. 10. and Hag. ii. 7. where the terms " People," and " Nations," denote the Heathen world,) is evinced by the coming of the wise men from the East, &c. a story which would of course have been contradicted by some of the individuals so disgracefully concerned in it, if the fact of their arrival, and the consequent massacre of the infants in and about Bethlehem, had not been fresh in every one's memory: by them, for instance, who afterward suborned false witnesses against Christ, and gave large money to the soldiers to conceal, if possible, the event of his resurrection; or them who, in still later days, every where zealously " spake against" the tenets and practices of his rising church.

All over the East, indeed, there was a general tradition, that *about that time a king of the* JEWS *would be born, who should govern the whole earth.* This prevailed so strongly at *Rome*, a few months before the birth of Augustus, that the Senate made a decree to expose all the children born that year; but the execution of it was eluded by a trick of some of the senators, who, from the pregnancy of their wives, were led to hope that they might be the fathers of the promised Prince. Its currency is also recorded with a remarkable identity of phrase by the pens of Suetonius and Tacitus. Now that in this there was no collusion between the *Chaldeans, Romans,* and *Jews,* is sufficiently proved by the desperate methods suggested, or carried into effect, for its discomfiture. Nor, in fact, is it practicable for whole nations of contemporary (and still less, if possible, for those of successive) generations, to concert a story perfectly harmonious in all its minute accompaniments of time, place, manner, and other circumstances.

In addition to the above general predictions of the coming, life, death, and resurrection of Christ, there are others which foretel still more strikingly several particular incidents of the Gospel narrative; instances unparalleled in the whole range of history, and which could have been foreseen by God alone. They were certainly not foreseen by the human agents concerned in their execution: or they would never have contributed to the fulfilment of prophecies referred even by themselves to the Messiah, and therefore verifying the divine mission of Him whom they crucified as an impostor.

Observe, then, how literally many of these predictions were fulfilled. For example: Read Psalm lxix. 21, "They gave me gall to eat, and vinegar to drink;" and compare Matt. xxvii. 34, "*They gave him vinegar to drink, mingled with gall.*" Again, it is said, Psalm xxii. 16—18, "They pierced my hands and my feet. They part my garments among them, and cast lots upon my vesture;"* as if it had been written *after* John, xix. 23, 24. It is predicted, likewise, Zech. xii. 10, "They shall look upon me whom they

---

* The soldiers did not tear his coat, because it was *without seam, woven from the top throughout;* and therefore they *cast lots for it.* But this was entirely accidental. With the passage in the Psalms, as *Romans,* they were not likely to be acquainted. The same remark applies to the next instance, from Zechariah.

And here it may be suggested, (in reply to those who insidiously magnify "the power of chance, the ingenuity of accommodation, and the industry of research," as chiefly supporting the credit of obscure prophecy,) that greater plainness would have enabled wicked men, as free agents, to prevent its accomplishment, when obviously directed against themselves. The *Jews,* not understanding what Christ meant by his "lifting up," (John, viii. 28. xii. 32, 33.) and not knowing that he had foretold his crucifixion to his apostles, (Matt. xx. 19.) instead of finally stoning him—the death appointed by their law (Levit. xxiv. 16.) for blasphemy, (Matt. xxvi. 65.) more than once menaced against the Saviour, (John, viii. 59. x. 33.) and actually inflicted upon Stephen (Acts, vii. 58.) for that offence—unconsciously delivered him to the predicted *Roman* cross. Again; the piercing of his side was no part of the Roman sentence, but merely to ascertain his being dead, previously to taking him down from the cross; "that the body might not remain there on the Sabbath-day," which commenced that evening, a few hours after the crucifixion. From his early *giving up the ghost,* however, it was not necessary that "a bone of him should be broken," (Exod. xii. 46. Numb. ix. 12. Psalm xxxiv. 20.) like those of the two thieves, his fellow-sufferers. John, xix. 32, 36.

have pierced;" and we are told, John, xix. 34, that " *one of the soldiers with a spear pierced his side.*"

Compare also Psalm xxii. 7, 8, " All they that see me laugh me to scorn : they shoot out their lips and shake their heads, saying, He trusted in God that he would deliver him; let him deliver him if he will have him," with Matt. xxvii. 39, 41, 43, " *And they that passed by reviled him, wagging their heads, and saying, Come down from the cross.   Likewise also the chief priests mocking him, with the scribes and elders said, He trusted in God: let him deliver him now, if he will have him ; for he said, I am the Son of God.*"   His very price, and the mode of laying out the money, previously specified, (Zech. xi. 13,) are historically stated by Matthew, in perfect correspondence with the prophet; chap. xxvii. 6, 7.   And his riding into Jerusalem upon an ass, predicted, Zech. ix. 9, (and referred by one of the most learned of the *Jewish* Rabbies to the Messiah,) is recorded by the same inspired historian, chap. xxi. 5. Lastly, it was foretold, that " he should make his grave with the wicked, and with the rich in his death;" (Isa. liii. 9.) or, as Dr. Lowth translates the passage, " his grave was appointed with the wicked, but with the rich man was his tomb;" which prediction was precisely verified by the very improbable incidents of his being crucified *between two thieves*, (Matt. xxvii. 38.) and afterwards *laid in the tomb of the rich man of* Arimathea. Ib. 57, 60.

Thus do the prophecies of the Old Testament, without variation or ambiguity, refer to the person and character of Christ.   His own predictions in the New, demand a few brief observations.

Those relating to the destruction of *Jerusalem,* which specified that it should be " laid even with the ground," and " not one stone be left upon another," (Luke, ix. 44.) " before that generation passed," (Matt. xxiv. 34.) were fulfilled in a most surprisingly literal manner, the very foundations of the temple being ploughed up by Turnus Rufus.   In another remarkable prophecy he announced the many false Messiahs that should come after him, and the ruin in which their followers should be involved. Matt. xxiv. 24, 26.   That great numbers actually assumed that holy character, before the final fall of the city, and led the people into the wilderness to their destruction, we learn from Josephus. Antiq. Jud. xviii. 12. xx. 6. and B. J. viii. 31.

Nay, such was their wretched infatuation, that under this delusion they rejected the offers of Titus, who courted them to peace. Id. B. J. vii. 12.

It will be sufficient barely to mention his foretelling the dispersion of that unhappy nation, and the triumph of his Gospel over *the gates of hell*, under every possible disadvantage—himself low and despised, his immediate associates only twelve, and those illiterate and unpolished, and his adversaries the allied powers, prejudices, habits, interests, and appetites of mankind.

But the *seventh Mark* is still more peculiar, if possible, to Christ, than even that of Prophecy. For whatever may be weakly pretended with regard to the oracular predictions of *Delphi* or *Dodona*, the Heathens never affected to prefigure any future event by *types*, or resemblances of the fact, consisting of analogies either in individuals, or in sensible institutions directed to be continued, till the antitype itself should make its appearance.

These types, in the instance of Christ. were of a twofold nature, *circumstantial*, and *personal*.

Of the *former* kind (not to notice the general rite of sacrifice) may be·produced, as examples : 1. *The Passover*, appointed in memory of that great night when the Destroying Angel, who slew all " the first-born of *Egypt*," passed over those houses upon whose door-posts the blood of the Paschal Lamb was sprinkled; and directed to be eaten with what the Apostle (1 Cor. v. 7, 8.) calls, " the unleavened bread of sincerity and truth." 2. *The annual expiation*, in two respects: first, as the High-Priest entered into the Holy of Holies (representing heaven, Exod. xxv. 40. Heb. ix. 24.) with the blood of the sacrifice, whose body was burnt without the camp, " wherefore Jesus also, that he might sanctify the people with his own blood, suffered without the gate;" (Heb. xiii. 12.) and " after he had offered one sacrifice for sin, for ever sat down at the right hand of God :" (x. 12.) and secondly, as " all the iniquity of the children of Israel was put upon the head" of the Scape Goat. Lev. xvi. 21. 3. *The brazen Serpent*, by looking up to which the people were cured of the stings of the fiery serpents; and whose " lifting up " was, by Christ himself, interpreted as emblematical of his being lifted up on the cross. John, iii. 14. 4. *The manna*, which repre-

sented " the bread of life, that came down from heaven."
John, vi. 31—35. 5. *The rock*, whence the waters flowed,
to supply drink in the wilderness; " and that rock was
Christ." 1 Cor. x. 4. 6. *The Sabbath*, " a shadow of
Christ;" (Col. ii. 16, 17.) and, as a figure of his eternal
rest, denominated " a sign of the perpetual covenant."
Exod. xxxi. 16, 17. Ezek. xx. 12, 20. And, lastly, to omit
others, *The temple*, where alone the shadowy sacrifices
were to be offered, because Christ, " the body," was to
be offered there himself.

Of *personal* types, likewise, I shall confine myself to such
as are so considered in the New Testament.

1. *Adam*, between whom and Christ a striking series of
relations is remarked. Rom. v. 12—21, and 1 Cor. xv. 45—
49. 2. *Noah*, who was " saved by water; the like figure
whereunto, even baptism, doth now save us, by the resurrection of Jesus Christ." 1 Peter. iii. 20, 21. 3. *Mel-
chisedec*, king of Salem, who was made " like unto the
Son of God, a priest continually." Heb. vii. 3. 4. *Abraham*,
" the heir of the world," (Rom. iv. 13.) " in whom all
the nations of the earth are blest." Gen. xviii. 18. 5. *Isaac*,
in his birth and intended sacrifice, whence also his father
received him in a figure, (Heb. xi. 19.) that is, of the resurrection of Christ. He too was the promised seed, (Gen.
xxi. 12. and Gal. iii. 16.) in whom all the nations of the
earth were to be blessed. Gen. xxii. 18. 6. *Jacob*, in
his vision of the ladder, (Gen. xxviii. 12. and John. i. 51.)
and his wrestling with the angel; whence he, and after
him the church, obtained the name of Israel. Gen. xxxii.
28. and Matt. xi. 21. The *Gentile* world also, like Jacob,
gained the blessing and heirship from their elder brethren
the Jews. 7. *Moses*, (Deut. xviii. 18. and John. i. 45.)
in redeeming the children of Israel out of Egypt. 8. *Joshua*, called also Jesus, (Heb. iv. 8.) in acquiring for them
the possession of the Holy Land, and as Lieutenant to the
" Captain of the host of the Lord." Josh. v. 14. 9. *David*,
(Psalm xvi. 10. and Acts. ii. 25—35.) upon whose throne
Christ is said to sit, (Isai. ix. 7.) and by whose name he is
frequently designated (Hos. iii. 5. &c.) in his pastoral, re-
gal, and prophetical capacity. 10. *Jonah*, in his dark imprisonment of three days, applied by Christ to himself.
Matt. xii 40.

The eighth *Mark* is, that the facts of Christianity are such as to make it impossible for either the relaters or the hearers to believe them, if false, without supposing a universal deception of the senses of mankind.

For they were related by the doers, or by eye-witnesses, to those who themselves likewise either were, or might have been present, and undoubtedly knew many that were present at their performance. To this circumstance, indeed, both Christ and his apostles often appeal. And they were of such a nature as wholly to exclude every chance of imposition. What juggler could have given sight to him "that was born blind;" have fed five thousand hungry guests with "five loaves and two fishes;" or have raised one, who had been "four days buried," from his grave?

When, then, we add to this, that none of the *Jewish* or *Roman* persecutors of Christianity, to whom its first teachers frequently referred as witnesses of those facts, ever ventured to deny them; that no apostate disciple, under the fear of punishment, or the hope of reward, not even the artful and accomplished Julian himself, ever pretended to detect them: that neither learning nor ingenuity, in the long lapse of so many years, has been able to show their falsehood: though, for the first three centuries after their promulgation, the civil government strongly stimulated hostile inquiry: and that their original relaters, after lives of unintermitted hardship, joyfully incurred death in defence of their truth—we cannot imagine the possibility of a more perfect or abundant demonstration.

It now rests with the Deists, if they would vindicate their claim to the self-bestowed title of "*men of reason*," to adduce some matters of fact of former ages, which they allow to be true, possessing evidence superior, or even similar, to those of Christ. This, however, it must at the same time be observed, would be far from proving the matters of fact respecting Christ to be false; but certainly without this, they cannot reasonably assert that their own facts alone, so much less powerfully attested, are true.

Let them produce their Cæsar, or Mahomet,

1. Performing a fact, of which men's *outward senses* can judge;

2. *Publickly*, in the presence of witnesses;

3. In memory of which *public monuments and actions* are kept up;

4. Instituted and commencing *at the time of the fact;*

5. Recorded likewise in a set of books, addressed to the identical people before whom it was performed, and containing their *whole code of civil and ecclesiastical laws;*

6. As the work of one previously announced for that very period by a long train of *prophecies;*

7. And still more peculiarly prefigured by *types,* both of a circumstantial and personal nature, from the earliest ages; and,

8. Of such a character as made it impossible for either the relaters or hearers to believe it, if false, without supposing a *universal deception of the senses of mankind.*

Farther; let them display, in its *professed eye-witnesses,* similar *proofs of veracity;* in some *doctrines* founded upon it, and *unaided by force or intrigue,* a like *triumph* over the *prejudices* and *passions* of mankind: among its *believers,* equal *skill* and equal *diligence* in *scrutinizing* its evidences, OR LET THEM SUBMIT TO THE IRRESISTIBLE CERTAINTY OF THE CHRISTIAN RELIGION.

And now, Reader, *solemnly consider* what that Religion *is,* the truth of which is proved by so many decisive marks. It is a declared Revelation from God; pronounces all men guilty in his sight; proclaims pardon, as his free gift through the meritorious righteousness, sacrifice, and intercession of his only Son, to all who trust alone in his mercy and grace, cordially repenting and forsaking their sins; requires fervent love, ardent zeal, and cordial submission toward himself, and the highest degree of personal purity and temperance, with rectitude and benevolence toward others; and offers the aid of the Holy Spirit for these purposes, to all who sincerely ask it. *Consider,* this Religion is the *only true* one, and this is *tremendously true;* while it promises peace on earth and eternal happiness to all who *do* receive and obey it, it denounces everlasting destruction against all who *do not.* It is in vain for you to admit its truth, unless you receive it as *your* confidence, and obey it as *your* rule. O study, O embrace it *for yourself:* and may the God of love and peace be with you. *Amen.*

A

TRAVELLER'S FAREWELL.

I SHALL SEE THY FACE NO MORE.

THERE is always something painful attending the separation of friends. When, for a length of time, we have enjoyed each other's company, and feel mutual respect and esteem, if we are compelled to part without the expectation of meeting again, we can scarcely bid the last farewell without regret. Thus, when the Apostle Paul bade farewell to the elders of the church at Ephesus, they sorrowed greatly; but " most of all for the words which he spake, that they should see his face no more." You and I have been fellow-travellers for a short time. We were strangers before, and must become strangers again. You must go your way, and I must go mine; and it is very probable *you will see my face again no more !*

Though our acquaintance has been so short as scarcely to be called an acquaintance, yet I cannot but feel, at the thought of parting, NEVER TO MEET AGAIN! We both belong to one great family, the family of man. We are both possessed of one great treasure, an immortal soul. We both are travelling toward one ultimate destination— an eternal world. Yes, my friend, for such I desire to consider you, I feel much at the thought of parting, never to meet again on earth. Give me leave, at least, cordially to bid you farewell.

And must we never see one another again ? Very likely not. Never, till our spirits have left their dying clay ! Never, till day and night have come to an end ! Never, till spring hath ceased to follow winter, and summer ceased to follow spring ! Never, till the sun hath ceased to shine, and the stars to twinkle ! Never, till months, and years, and ages, and time itself, are no more ! Never, till the voice of the archangel and the trump of God have summoned the dead to rise, and proclaimed the arrival of eternal judgment! And where shall our next place of meeting be:

SHALL WE MEET IN HELL?

Shall you and I lift up our eyes in torments, and find each other in that abode of misery, from which there is no deliverance? Oh! what a meeting will that be! What shocking salutations shall we utter! With what down-cast looks shall we gaze on each other, and wish that we had never met at all!

SHALL WE MEET IN HEAVEN?

Transporting thought, if so it may be. Your countenance will then shine like that of an angel, and so will mine. And the smile with which we shall welcome one another to that happy land, will be cheerful as the brightness of a clear morning. But are we prepared for heaven? Because none enter its holy gates but such as are "beforehand prepared unto glory." O my soul, art thou prepared? O my friend, are you? "Except a man be *born again*, he cannot see the kingdom of God." Are you born again? Except our sins are forgiven, we cannot see the face of God with joy. Are your sins forgiven? Without a wedding garment of perfect righteousness, we cannot sit down at the marriage supper of the Lamb. Are you sanctified and justified, in the name of the Lord Jesus and by the Spirit of the living God? Joyful anticipation! glorious prospect! If we are new creatures in Christ Jesus; if he is our hope; if we bear his image; we shall meet again—yes, we shall meet again—happy, triumphant, glorified! At all events

WE SHALL BOTH STAND BEFORE THE JUDGMENT SEAT OF CHRIST.

For we must all appear before the judgment seat of Christ, to give account of ourselves unto God, and receive for the things done in the body, according to that which we have done, whether it be good or bad. For God will bring every work into judgment, and every idle word, and every secret thing, whether it be good or evil. He shall sit on his "great white throne," with all the quick and the dead, small and great, before him. He shall divide the righteous from the wicked, as a shepherd divideth his sheep from the goats. He shall say to the righteous on his right hand: "Come, ye blessed of my Father, inherit the kingdom prepared for you from the foundation of the world."

He shall say to the wicked on the left hand: "Depart from me, ye cursed, into everlasting fire, prepared for the devil and his angels." Perhaps we may not see each other, but we shall both be there. Shall we both be on the right hand, or both on the left? Or shall we then stand in opposite divisions of the vast assembly? Shall the one be saved, the other lost? the one ascend to heaven, the other sink to hell? And shall we see each other's face no more, for ever, and ever, and ever?

Gladly, you answer, would you escape this; but then you know not the way. What was the reply of Jesus, when one of his apostles started a similar difficulty? "I am the way." "I am the way, the truth, and the life · no man cometh unto the Father, but by me." Would you know, then, how you are to be preserved from hell? Christ answers, "I am the way." Would you know how you may enter into heaven? He makes the same reply, "I am the way." I am the way by which you may depart from the shades of death. I am the way by which you may enter into life." "God so loved the world, that he gave his only begotten Son, that whosoever believeth in him should not perish, but have eternal life." "Should not perish." Here you have deliverance from perdition. —"But have eternal life." Here you have the offer of salvation. To this end Christ both died and rose again.

Consider what I say, and the Lord give you understanding in all things. Do not forget these admonitions. They are addressed to you by one who earnestly desires your eternal welfare. Most likely they are the last that you will receive from me. Regard them as the last words of a friend. If you have already attended to these things—if you enjoy a good hope through grace, consider if there is not some way in which you may promote, more extensively, the glory of God and the good of souls. Did you ever hear of one that, on a death bed, was sorry for having actively served the Lord? The more the light of eternity opens upon us, the more clearly we perceive the value of those opportunities of usefulness which are put into our hands. The nearer and nearer we approach the great tribunal, we hear more distinctly the words of that sentence: "Cast ye the unprofitable servant into outer darkness, there shall be weeping and gnashing of teeth." If, therefore, you are a lukewarm, inactive professor, mark well this curse, for it is yours : " Curse ye Meroz, said the angel of the Lord, curse ye bitterly the inhabitants thereof; because they came not to the help of the Lord, to the help of the Lord against the mighty." " When I die," said the zealous and indefatigable Grimshaw, " I shall have my greatest grief, and my greatest joy: my greatest grief, that I have done so little for Christ; my greatest joy, that Christ has done so much for me."

If you have hitherto lived unconcerned, oh ! reflect—the time is short—your days are fast spending and wasting. You are killing time. We expect a resurrection of dead bodies, but when will there be a resurrection of dead time ? Ah ! time slain in folly will revive no more ; except in its remembrance, as a swift witness against those who killed it ! You cannot call back an hour or a moment. The sun once stood still in Gibeon, but time did not stand still. The sun once returned ten degrees on the dial of Ahaz, but time proceeded on his journey with unremitted speed. Time is hasting onwards, and rapidly bearing you to the everlasting state. Your all, your eternal all, is at hazard. You can make one experiment, and if that fail, you are undone for ever ! Therefore, by the dread authority of the great God—by the terrors of death and the great rising day—by the joys of heaven and the torments of hell—by the value of your immortal soul, I entreat, I charge, I adjure you, to awake out of your security, and improve the gracious moments of life. This world is dying all around you. Can you rest easy in such a world, while unprepared for eternity ? Awake to righteousness, now, at the call of a friend ; before the last trumpet give you an alarm of another kind.

A mighty change awaits us, when the hour
Arrives, that lands us on th' eternal shore.
From glory then to glory we shall rise,
Or sink from deep to deeper miseries.
Ascend perfection's everlasting scale,
Or still descend from gulf to gulf in hell.

Now the God of hope fill you with all joy and peace in believing, that you may abound in hope, through the power of the Holy Ghost. FAREWELL.

PUBLISHED BY THE AMERICAN TRACT SOCIETY.

ON THE

TRAFFIC IN ARDENT SPIRIT.

ARDENT spirit is composed of alcohol and water, in nearly equal proportions. Alcohol is composed of hydrogen, carbon, and oxygen, in the proportion of about 14, 52, and 34 parts to the hundred. It is, in its nature, as manifested by its effects, a *poison*. When taken in any quantity it disturbs healthy action in the human system, and in large doses suddenly destroys life. It resembles opium in its nature, and arsenic in its effects. And though when mixed with water, as in ardent spirit, its evils are somewhat modified, they are by no means prevented. Ardent spirit is an enemy to the human constitution, and cannot be used as a drink without injury. Its ultimate tendency invariably is, to produce weakness, not strength; sickness, not health; death, not life.

Consequently, to use it is an immorality. It is a violation of the will of God, and a sin in magnitude equal to all the evils, temporal and eternal, which flow from it. Nor can the furnishing of ardent spirit for the use of others be accounted a less sin, inasmuch as this tends to produce evils greater than for an individual merely to drink it. And if a man knows, or has the opportunity of knowing, the nature and effects of the traffic in this article, and yet continues to be engaged in it, he may justly be regarded as an immoral man; and for the following reasons, viz.

Ardent spirit, as a drink, is *not needful*. All men lived without it, and all the business of the world was conducted without it, for thousands of years. It is not three hundred years since it began to be generally used as a drink in Great Britain, nor one hundred years since it became common in America. Of course it is not needful.

It is *not useful*. Those who do not use it are, other things being equal, in all respects better than those who do. Nor does the fact that persons have used it with more or less frequency, in a greater or smaller quantity, for a longer or shorter time, render it either needful, or useful, or harmless, or right for them to continue to use it. More than a million of persons in this country, and multitudes in other countries, who once did use it, and thought it needful, have, within five years, ceased to use it, and they have found that they are in all respects better without it. And this number is so great, of all ages, and conditions, and employments, as to render it certain, should the experiment be fairly made, that this would be the case with all. Of course, ardent spirit, as a drink, is not useful.

It is *hurtful*. Its whole influence is injurious to the body and the mind for this world and the world to come.

1. It forms an *unnecessary, artificial, and very dangerous appetite;* which, by gratification, like the desire for sinning, in the man who sins, tends continually to increase. No man can form this appetite without increasing his danger of dying a drunkard, and exerting an influence which tends to perpetuate drunkenness, and all its abominations, to the end of the world. Its very formation therefore is a violation of the will of God. It is, in its nature, an immorality, and springs from an inordinate desire of a kind or degree of bodily enjoyment—animal gratification, which God has shown to be inconsistent with his glory, and the highest good of man. It shows that the person who forms it is not satisfied with the proper gratification of those appetites and passions which God has given him, or with that kind and degree of bodily enjoyment which infinite wisdom and goodness have prescribed as the utmost that can be possessed consistently with a person's highest happiness and usefulness, the glory of his Maker, and the good of the universe. That person covets more animal enjoyment; to obtain it he forms a new appetite, and in doing this he rebels against God. That desire for increased animal enjoyment from which rebellion springs, is sin, and all the evils which follow in its train are only so many voices by which Jehovah declares " the way of transgressors

is hard. ' The person who has formed an appetite for ardent spirit, and feels uneasy if he does not gratify it, has violated the divine arrangement, disregarded the divine will, and if he understands the nature of what he has done, and approves of it, and continues in it, it will ruin him. He will show that there is one thing in which he will not have God to reign over him. And should he keep the whole law, and yet continue knowingly, habit- ually, wilfully, and perseveringly to offend in that one point, he will perish.   Then, and then only, according to the Bible, can any man be saved, when he has re- spect to all the known will of God, and is disposed to be governed by it. He must carry out into practice, with regard to the body and the soul, " not my will, but thine be done." His grand object must be to know the will of God, and when he knows it, to be governed by it, and with regard to all things. This, the man who is not con- tented with that portion of animal enjoyment which the proper gratification of the appetites and passions which God has given him will afford, but forms an appetite for ardent spirit, or continues to gratify it after it is formed, does not do. In this respect, if he understands the nature and effects of his actions, he prefers his own will to the known will of God, and is ripening to hear, from the lips of his Judge, " Those mine enemies, that would not that I should *reign* over them, bring them hither and slay them before me." And the men who traffic in this article, or furnish it as a drink for others, are tempting them to sin, and thus uniting their influence with that of the devil for ever to ruin them.   This is an aggravated immorality, and the men who continue to do it are im- moral men.

2. The use of ardent spirit, to which the traffic is ac- cessory, causes a great and wicked *waste of property.* All that the users pay for this article is to them lost, and worse than lost.   Should the whole which they use sink into the earth, or mingle with the ocean, it would be better for them, and better for the community, than for them to drink it.   All which it takes to support the pau- pers, and prosecute the crimes which ardent spirit occa- sions, is, to those who pay the money, utterly lost.   All the diminution of profitable labor which it occasions,

through improvidence, idleness, dissipation, intemperance, sickness, insanity, and premature deaths, is to the community so much utterly lost. And these items, as has often been shown, amount in the United States to more than $100,000,000 a year. To this enormous and wicked waste of property, those who traffic in the article are knowingly accessory.

A portion of what is thus lost by others, they obtain themselves; but without rendering to others any valuable equivalent. This renders their business palpably unjust; as really so as if they should obtain that money by gambling; and it is as really immoral. It is also unjust in another respect; it burdens the community with taxes both for the support of pauperism, and for the prosecution of crimes, and without rendering to that community any adequate compensation. These taxes, as shown by facts, are four times as great as they would be if there were no sellers of ardent spirit. All the profits, with the exception perhaps of a mere pittance which he pays for license, the seller puts into his own pocket, while the burthens are thrown upon the community. This is palpably unjust, and utterly immoral. Of 1969 paupers in different alms-houses in the United States, 1790, according to the testimony of the overseers of the poor, were made such by spiritous liquor. And of 1764 criminals in different prisons, more than 1300 were either intemperate men, or were under the power of intoxicating liquor when the crimes for which they were imprisoned were committed. And of 44 murders, according to the testimony of those who prosecuted or conducted the defence of the murderers, or witnessed their trials, 43 were committed by intemperate men, or upon intemperate men, or those who at the time of the murder were under the power of strong drink.

The Hon. Felix Grundy, United States senator from Tennessee, after thirty years extensive practice as a lawyer, gives it as his opinion that four-fifths of all the crimes committed in the United States can be traced to intemperance. A similar proportion is stated, from the highest authority, to result from the same cause in Great Britain. And when it is considered that more than 200 murders are committed, and more than 100,000 crimes

are prosecuted in the United States in a year, and that such
a vast proportion of them are occasioned by ardent spirit,
can a doubt remain on the mind of any sober man, that the
men who know these facts, and yet continue to traffic in
this article, are among the chief causes of crime, and ought
to be viewed and treated as immoral men? It is as really
immoral for a man, by doing wrong, to excite others to
commit crime, as to commit them himself; and as really
unjust wrongfully to take another's property with his
consent, as without it. And though it might not be desirable to have such a law, yet no law in the statute book
is more righteous than one which should require that
those who make paupers should support them, and those
who excite others to commit crimes, should pay the cost
of their prosecution, and should, with those who commit
them, bear all the evils. And so long as this is not the
case they will be guilty, according to the divine law, of
defrauding, as well as tempting and corrupting their fellow men. And though such crimes cannot be prosecuted, and justice be awarded in human courts, their
perpetrators will be held to answer, and will meet with
full and awful retribution at the divine tribunal. And
when judgment is laid to the line, and righteousness to
the plummet, they will appear as they really are, criminals, and will be viewed and treated as such for ever.

There is another view in which the traffic in ardent
spirit is manifestly highly immoral. It exposes the children of those who use it, in an eminent degree, to dissipation and crime. Of 690 children prosecuted and imprisoned for crimes, more than 400 were from intemperate families. Thus the venders of this liquor exert an
influence which tends strongly to ruin not only those
who use it, but their children; to render them more than
four times as liable to idleness, profligacy, and ruin, as
the children of those who do not use it; and through
them to extend these evils to others, and to perpetuate
them to future generations. This is a sin of which all
who traffic in ardent spirit are guilty. Often the deepest
pang which a dying parent feels for his children, is lest,
through the instrumentality of such men, they should be
ruined. And is it not horrible wickedness for them, by,

exposing for sale one of the chief causes of this ruin, to tempt them in the way to death. If he who takes money from others without an equivalent, or wickedly destroys property, is an immoral man, what is he who destroys character; who corrupts the children and youth, and exerts an influence to extend and perpetuate immorality and crime through future generations? This every vender of ardent spirit does, and if he continues in this business with a knowledge of the subject, it marks him as an habitual and persevering violater of the will of God.

3. Ardent spirit *impairs,* and often *destroys reason.* Of 781 maniacs in different insane hospitals, 392, according to the testimony of their own friends, were rendered maniacs by strong drink. And the physicians who had the care of them gave it as their opinion that this was the case with many of the others. Those who have had extensive experience, and the best opportunities for observation with regard to this malady, have stated, that probably from one half to three-fourths of the cases of insanity, in many places, are occasioned in the same way. Ardent spirit is a poison so diffusive and subtil that it is found by actual experiment to penetrate even the brain.

Dr. Kirk, of Scotland, dissected a man a few hours after death who died in a fit of intoxication: and from the lateral ventricles of the brain he took a fluid distinctly visible to the smell as whiskey; and when he applied a candle to it in a spoon it took fire and burnt blue; " the lambent blue flame," he says, " characteristic of the poison, playing on the surface of the spoon for some seconds."

It produces also in the children of those who use it freely, a predisposition to intemperance, insanity, and various diseases of both body and mind; which, if the cause is continued, becomes hereditary, and is transmitted from generation to generation; occasioning a diminution of size, strength, and energy; a feebleness of vision, a feebleness and imbecility of purpose, an obtuseness of intellect, a depravation of moral taste, a premature old age, and a general deterioration of the whole character. This is the case in every country, and in every age.

Instances are known where the first children of a
family who were born when their parents were temperate, have been healthy, intelligent, and active; while
the last children, who were born after the parents had
become intemperate, were dwarfish and idiotic. A medical gentleman writes, " I have no doubt that a disposition to nervous diseases of a peculiar character is transmitted by drunken parents." Another gentleman states,
that in two families within his knowledge, the different
stages of intemperance in the parents seemed to be
marked by a corresponding deterioration in the bodies
and minds of the children. In one case the eldest of
the family is respectable, industrious, and accumulates
property; the next is inferior, disposed to be industrious,
but spends all he can earn in strong drink. The third
is dwarfish in body and mind, and, to use his own language, " a poor miserable remnant of a man."

In another family of daughters, the first is a smart,
active girl, with an intelligent well-balanced mind; the
others are afflicted with different degrees of mental weakness and imbecility, and the youngest is an idiot. Another medical gentleman states, that the first child of a
family, who was born when the habits of the mother were
good, was healthy and promising; while the four last
children, who were born after the mother had become
addicted to the habit of using opium, appeared to be
stupid; and all, at about the same age, sickened and died
of a disease apparently occasioned by the habits of the
mother.

Another gentleman mentions a case more common,
and more appalling still. A respectable and influential
man early in life adopted the habit of using a little ardent
spirit daily, because, as he thought, it did him good. He
and his six children, three sons and three daughters, are
now in the drunkard's grave, and the only surviving
child is rapidly following after, in the same way, to the
same dismal end.

The best authorities attribute one half the madness,
three-fourths of the pauperism, and four-fifths of the
crimes and wretchedness in Great Britain to the use of
strong drink.

4. Ardent spirit increases the number, frequency, and

violence of *diseases*, and tends to bring those who use it
to a premature grave. In Portsmouth, New-Hampshire,
of about 7,500 people, twenty-one persons were killed
by it in a year. In Salem, Massachusetts, of 181 deaths,
twenty were occasioned in the same way. Of ninety-
one adults who died in New-Haven, Connecticut, in one
year, thirty-two, according to the testimony of the Medical Association, were occasioned, directly or indirectly,
by strong drink, and a similar proportion had been occasioned by it in previous years. In New-Brunswick,
New-Jersey, of sixty-seven adult deaths in one year,
more than one-third were caused by intoxicating liquor.
In Philadelphia, of 4,292 deaths, 700 were, in the opinion
of the College of Physicians and Surgeons, caused in
the same way. The physicians of Annapolis, Maryland,
state, that of thirty-two persons, male and female, who
died in 1828, above eighteen years of age, ten, or nearly
one third, died of diseases occasioned by intemperance;
that eighteen were males, and that of these, nine, or one
half, died of intemperance. They also say, " When we
recollect that even the temperate use, as it is called, of
ardent spirits, lays the foundation of a numerous train of
incurable maladies, we feel justified in expressing the
belief, that were the use of distilled liquors entirely discontinued, the number of deaths among the male adults
would be diminished at least one half."

Says an eminent physician, " Since our people generally have given up the use of spirit, they have not had
more than half as much sickness as they had before;
and I have no doubt, should all the people of the United
States cease to use it, that nearly half the sickness of the
country would cease." Says another, after forty years
extensive practice, " Half the men every year who die
of fevers might recover had they not been in the habit
of using ardent spirit. Many a man, down for weeks
with a fever, had he not used ardent spirit, would not
have been confined to his house a day. He might have
felt a slight headache, but a little fasting would have removed the difficulty, and the man been well. And many
a man who was never intoxicated, when visited with a
fever, might be raised up as well as not, were it not for
that state of the system which daily moderate drinking

occasions, who now, in spite of all that can be done, sinks down and dies."

Nor are we to admit for a moment the popular reasoning, as applicable here, " that the abuse of a thing is no argument against its use;" for, in the language of the late Secretary of the College of Physicians and Surgeons of Philadelphia, Samuel Emlen, M. D. " All use of ardent spirits (*i. e.* as a drink) is an abuse. They are mischievous under all circumstances." Their tendency, says Dr. Frank, when used even moderately, is to induce disease, premature old age, and death. And Dr. Trotter states, that no cause of disease has so wide a range, or so large a share, as the use of spiritous liquors.

Dr. Harris states, that the *moderate* use of spiritous liquors has destroyed many who were never drunk ; and Dr. Kirk gives it as his opinion, that men who were never considered intemperate, by daily drinking have often shortened life more than twenty years ; and that the respectable use of this poison kills more men than even drunkenness. Dr. Wilson gives it as his opinion, that the use of spirit in large cities causes more diseases than confined air, unwholesome exhalations, and the combined influence of all other evils.

Dr. Cheyne, of Dublin, Ireland, after thirty years practice and observation, gives it as his opinion, that should ten young men begin at twenty-one years of age to use but one glass of two ounces a day, and never increase the quantity, nine out of ten would shorten life more than ten years. But should moderate drinkers shorten life only five years, and drunkards only ten, and should there be but four moderate drinkers to one drunkard, it would in thirty years cut off in the United States 32,400,000 years of human life. An aged physician in Maryland states, that when the fever breaks out there, the men who do not use ardent spirit are not half as likely as other men to have it; and that if they do have it they are ten times as likely to recover. In the island of Key West, on the coast of Florida, after a great mortality, it was found that every person who had died was in the habit of using ardent spirit. The quantity used was afterward diminished more than nine tenths, and the inhabitants became remarkably healthy.

A gentleman of great respectability from the south, states, that those who fall victims to southern climes, are almost invariably addicted to the free use of ardent spirit. Dr. Mosely, after a long residence in the West Indies, declares, " that persons who drink nothing but cold water, or make it their principal drink, are but little affected by tropical climates; that they undergo the greatest fatigue without inconvenience, and are not so subject as others to dangerous diseases;" and Dr. Bell, " that rum, when used even moderately, always diminishes the strength, and renders men more susceptible of disease; and that we might as well throw oil into a house, the roof of which is on fire, in order to prevent the flames from extending to the inside, as to pour ardent spirits into the stomach to prevent the effect of a hot sun upon the skin."

Of seventy-seven persons found dead in different regions of country, sixty-seven, according to the coroner's inquests, were occasioned by strong drink. Nine-tenths of those who die suddenly after the drinking of cold water, have been habitually addicted to the free use of ardent spirit; and that draught of cold water, that effort, or fatigue, or exposure to the sun, or disease, which a man who uses no ardent spirit will bear without inconvenience or danger, will often kill those who use it. Their liability to sickness and to death is often increased ten fold. And to all these evils, those who continue to traffic in it, after all the light which God in his providence has thrown upon the subject, are knowingly accessory. Whether they deal in it by wholesale or retail, by the cargo or the glass, they are, in their influence, drunkard-makers. So are also those who furnish the materials; those who advertise the liquors, and thus promote their circulation; those who lease their tenements to be employed as dram-shops, or stores for the sale of ardent spirit; and those also who purchase their groceries of spirit dealers rather than of others, for the purpose of saving to the amount which the sale of ardent spirit enables such men, without loss, to undersell their neighbors. These are all accessory to the making of drunkards, and as such will be held to answer at the divine tribunal. So are those men who employ their shipping in transporting the liquors, or are in any way knowingly aiding and abetting in perpetuating their use as a drink in the community.

Four-fifths of those who are swept away by that direful malady the CHOLERA, are such as have been addicted to the use of intoxicating drink. Dr. Bronson, of Albany, who lately spent some time in Canada, and whose professional character and standing give great weight to his opinions, says, "Intemperance of any species, but particularly intemperance in the use of *distilled liquors*, has been a more productive cause of cholera than any other, and indeed than all others." And can men, for the sake of money, make it a business knowingly and perseveringly to furnish the most productive cause of cholera, and not be guilty of *blood?* not manifest a recklessness of character which will brand the mark of vice and infamy on their foreheads?" "Drunkards and tipplers," he adds, "have been searched out with such unerring certainty as to show that the arrows of death have not been dealt out with indiscrimination. An indescribable terror has spread through the ranks of this class of beings. They see the bolts of destruction aimed at their heads, and every one calls himself a victim. There seems to be a natural affinity between cholera and ardent spirit." What, then, in days of exposure to this malady, is so great a nuisance as the places which furnish this poison? Says Dr. Rhinelander, who, with Dr. De Kay, was deputed from New-York to visit Canada, "We may be asked who are the victims of this disease? I answer, the intemperate it invariably cuts off." In Montreal, after 1200 had been attacked, a Montreal paper states, that "not a drunkard who has been attacked has recovered of the disease, and almost all the victims have been at least *moderate* drinkers." In Paris, the 30,000 victims were, with few exceptions, those who freely used intoxicating liquors. Nine-tenths of those who died of the cholera in Poland were of the same class.

In Petersburg and Moscow, the average number of deaths in the bills of mortality, during the prevalence of the cholera, when the people ceased to drink brandy, was no greater than when they used it during the usual months of health—showing that brandy, and attendant dissipation, killed as many people in the same time as even the cholera itself, that pestilence which has spread sackcloth over the nations. And shall the men who know this, and yet continue to furnish it for all who can be induced to buy, escape the execration of being the destroyers of their race? Of more than 1000 deaths in Montreal, it is stated that only two were members of Temperance societies; and that as far as is known no members of Temperance societies in Ireland, Scotland, or England, have as yet fallen victims to that dreadful disease.

From Montreal, Dr. Bronson writes, " Cholera has stood up here, as it has done every where, the advocate of Temperance. It has pleaded most eloquently, and with tremendous effect. The disease has searched out the haunt of the drunkard, and has seldom left it without bearing away its victim. Even *moderate* drinkers have been but little better off. Ardent spirits, in any shape, and in all quantities, have been *highly* detrimental. Some temperate men resorted to them during the prevalence of the malady as a preventive, or to remove the feeling of uneasiness about the stomach, or for the purpose of drowning their apprehensions, but they did it at their peril."

Says the London Morning Herald, after stating that the cholera fastens its deadly grasp upon this class of men, " The same preference for the intemperate and uncleanly has characterized the cholera *every where*. Intemperance is a qualification which it never overlooks. Often has it passed harmless over a wide population of temperate country people, and poured down, as an over-flowing scourge, upon the drunkards of some distant town." Says another English publication, " All experience, both in Great Britain and elsewhere, has proved that those who have been addicted to drinking spiritous liquors, and indulging in irregular habits, have been the greatest sufferers from cholera. In some towns the drunkards are all dead. Rammohun Fingee, the famous Indian doctor, says, with regard to India, that people who do not take opium, or spirits, do not take this disorder even when they are with those who have it. Monsieur Huber, who saw 2,160 persons perish in twenty-

five days in one town in Russia, says, " It is a most remarkable circumstance, that persons given to drinking
have been swept away like flies. In Tiflis, containing
20,000 inhabitants, every drunkard has fallen—all are
dead, not one remains."

And Dr. Sewall, of Washington city, in a letter from
New-York, states, that of 204 cases of cholera in the
Park hospital, there were only six temperate persons,
and that those had recovered ; while 122 of the others,
when he wrote, had died, and that the facts were similar
in all the other hospitals.

In Albany, New-York, a careful examination was made
by respectable gentlemen into the cases of those who
died of the cholera in that city in 1832, over sixteen
years of age. The result was examined in detail by nine
physicians, members of the medical staff attached to the
Board of Health in that city—(all who belong to it, except two, who were at that time absent)—and published
at their request under the signature of the Chancellor of
the State, and the five distinguished gentlemen who com-
pose the Executive Committee of the New-York State
Temperance Society, and is as follows : Number of
deaths, 366 ; viz. intemperate, 140 ; free drinkers, 55 ;
moderate drinkers, mostly habitual, 131 ; strictly temperate, who drank no ardent spirit, 5 ; members of Tem
perance societies, 2 ; and when it is recollected that of
more than 5,000 members of Temperance societies in
the city of Albany, only 2, not one in 2,500, fell by this
disease, while it cut off more than one in 50 of the inhabitants of that city, we cannot but feel that men who
furnish ardent spirit as a drink for their fellow-men, are
manifestly inviting the ravages, and preparing the victims of this fatal malady, and of numerous other mortal
diseases ; and when inquisition is made for blood, and
the effects of their employment are examined for the
purpose of rendering to them according to their work,
they will be found, should they continue, to be guilty of
knowingly destroying their fellow-men.

What right have men, by selling ardent spirit, to increase the danger, extend the ravages, and augment and
perpetuate the malignancy of the cholera, and multiply
upon the community numerous other mortal diseases ?

Who cannot see that it is a foul, deep, and fatal injury inflicted on society? that it is in a high degree cruel and unjust? that it scatters the population of our cities, renders our business stagnant, and exposes our sons and our daughters to premature and sudden death? So manifestly is this the case, that the Board of Health of the city of Washington, on the approach of the cholera, declared the vending of ardent spirit, *in any quantity*, to be a *nuisance;* and as such ordered that it be discontinued for the space of ninety days. This was done in self-defence, to save the community from the sickness and death which the vending of spirit is adapted to occasion. Nor is this tendency to occasion disease and death confined to the time when the cholera is raging.

By the statement of the physicians in Annapolis, Maryland, it appears that the average number of deaths by intemperance for several years, has been one to every 329 inhabitants; which would make in the United States 40,000 in a year. And it is the opinion of physicians that as many more die of diseases which are induced, or aggravated, and rendered mortal by the use of ardent spirit. And to those results, all who make it, sell it, or use it, are accessory.

It is a principle in law, that the perpetrator of crime, and the accessory to it, are both guilty, and deserving of punishment. Men have been hanged for the violation of this principle. It applies to the law of God. And as the drunkard cannot go to heaven, can drunkard-makers? Are they not, when tried by the principles of the Bible, in view of the developments of Providence, manifestly immoral men? men who, for the sake of money, will knowingly be instrumental in corrupting the character, increasing the diseases, and destroying the lives of their fellow-men?

" But," says one, " I never sell to drunkards; I sell only to sober men." And is that any better? Is it a less evil to the community to make drunkards of sober men than it is to kill drunkards? Ask that widowed mother who did her the greatest evil? The man who only killed her drunken husband, or the man who made a drunkard of her only son? Ask those orphan children who did them the greatest injury? the man who made their once

sober, kind, and affectionate father a drunkard, and thus
blasted all their hopes, and turned their home, sweet
home, into the emblem of hell; or the man who, after
they had suffered for years the anguish, the indescribable
anguish of the drunkard's children, and seen their heart-
broken mother in danger of an untimely grave, only
killed their drunken father, and thus caused in their
habitation a great calm? Which of these two men brought
upon them the greatest evil? Can you doubt? You then
do nothing but make drunkards of sober men, or expose
them to become such. Suppose that all the evils which
you may be instrumental in bringing upon other children,
were to come upon your own, and that *you* were to bear
all the anguish which you may occasion; would you have
any doubt that the man who would knowingly continue
to be accessory to the bringing of these evils upon you,
must be a notoriously wicked man?

5. Ardent spirit destroys the *soul*.

Facts in great numbers are now before the public,
which show conclusively that the use of ardent spirit
tends strongly to hinder the moral and spiritual illumina-
tion and purification of men; and thus to prevent their
salvation, and bring upon them the horrors of the second
death.

A disease more dreadful than the cholera, or any other
that kills the body merely, is raging, and is universal,
threatening the endless death of the soul. A remedy is
provided all sufficient, and infinitely efficacious; but the
use of ardent spirit aggravates the disease, and with millions and millions prevents the application of the remedy
and its effect.

It appears from the Fifth Report of the American
Temperance Society, that more than four times as many,
in proportion to the number, over wide regions of country, during the preceding year, have apparently embraced
the Gospel, and experienced its saving power, from among
those who had renounced the use of ardent spirit, as from
those who continued to use it.

The Committee of the New-York State Temperance
Society, in view of the peculiar and unprecedented attention to religion which followed the adoption of the plan
of abstinence from the use of strong drink, remark, that

when this course is taken, the greatest enemy to the work of the Holy Spirit on the minds and hearts of men, appears to be more than half conquered.

In three hundred towns, six tenths of those who two years ago belonged to Temperance societies, but were not hopefully pious, have since become so; and eight tenths of those who have within that time become hopefully pious, who did not belong to Temperance societies, have since joined them. In numerous places, where only a minority of the people abstained from the use of ardent spirit, nine-tenths of those, who have of late professed the religion of Christ, have been from that minority. This is occasioned in various ways. The use of ardent spirit keeps many away from the house of God, and thus prevents them from coming under the sound of the Gospel. And many who do come it causes to continue stupid, worldly minded, and unholy. A single glass a day is enough to keep multitudes of men, under the full blaze of the Gospel, from ever experiencing its illuminating and purifying power. Even if they come to the light, and it shines upon them, it shines upon darkness, and the darkness does not comprehend it. While multitudes who thus do evil will not come to the light lest their deeds should be reproved. There is a total contrariety between the effect produced by the Holy Spirit, and the effect of spiritous liquor upon the minds and hearts of men. The latter tends directly and powerfully to counteract the former. It tends to make men feel in a manner which Jesus Christ hates, rich spiritually, increased in goods, and in need of nothing; while it tends for ever to prevent them from feeling, as sinners must feel, to buy of him gold tried in the fire, that they may be rich. Those who use it, therefore, are taking the direct course to destroy their own souls; and those who furnish it are taking the course to destroy the souls of their fellow-men.

In one town, more than twenty times as many, in proportion to the number, professed the religion of Christ during the past year; and in another town more than thirty times as many of those who did not use ardent spirit, as of those who did. In other towns, in which from one-third to two-thirds of the people did not use it, and from twenty to forty made a profession of religion, they were all from the same class. What then are those men doing who furnish it, but taking the course which is adapted to keep men stupid in sin till they sink into the agonies of the second death? And is not this an immorality of a high and aggravated description? and one which ought to mark every man who understands its nature and effects, and yet continues to live in it, as a notoriously immoral man? What though he does not live in other immoralities—is not this enough? Suppose he should manufacture poisonous miasma, and cause the cholera in our dwellings; sell, knowingly, the cause of disease, and increase more than one-fifth over wide regions of country the number of adult deaths, would he not be a murderer? " I know," says the learned Judge Cranch, " that the cup (which contains ardent spirit) is poisoned; I know that it may cause death, that it may cause more than death, that it may lead to crime, to sin, to the tortures of everlasting remorse. Am I not then a murderer? worse than a murderer? as much worse as the soul is better than the body? If ardent spirits were nothing worse than a deadly poison—if they did not excite and inflame all the evil passions—if they did not dim that heavenly light which the Almighty has implanted in our bosoms to guide us through the obscure passages of our pilgrimage—if they did not quench the Holy Spirit in our hearts, they would be comparatively harmless. It is their moral effect—it is the ruin of the *soul* which they produce, that renders them so dreadful. The difference between death by simple poison, and death by habitual intoxication, may extend to the whole difference between everlasting happiness and eternal death."

And, say the New-York State Society, at the head of which is the Chancellor of the State, " Disguise that business as they will, it is still, in its true character, the business of destroying the bodies and souls of men. The vender and the maker of spirits, in the whole range of them, from the pettiest grocer to the most extensive distiller, are fairly chargeable, not only with *supplying* the appetite for spirits, but with *creating* that unnatural appetite; not only with supplying the drunkard with the fuel of his vices, but with *making* the drunkard.

" In reference to the taxes with which the making and

vending of spirits loads the community, how unfair toward others is the occupation of the maker and vender of them! A town, for instance, contains one hundred drunkards. The profit of making these drunkards is enjoyed by some half a dozen persons; but the burden of these drunkards rests upon the whole town. We do not suggest that there should be such a law; but we ask whether there would be one law in the whole statute book more *righteous* than that which should require those who have the profit of making our drunkards to be burdened with the support of them.''

Multitudes who once cherished the fond anticipation of happiness in this life, and that to come, there is reason to believe are now wailing beyond the reach of hope, through the influence of ardent spirit; and multitudes more, if men continue to furnish it as a drink, especially sober men, will go down to weep and wail with them to endless ages.

" But," says one, " the traffic in ardent spirit is a lawful business; it is approbated by law, and is therefore right." But the keeping of gambling houses is, in some cases, approbated by human law. Is that therefore right? The keeping of brothels is, in some cases, approbated by law. Is that therefore right? Is it human law that is the standard of morality and religion? May not a man be a notoriously wicked man, and yet not violate human law? The question is, is it right? Does it accord with the divine law? Does it tend in its effects to bring glory to God in the highest, and to promote the best good of mankind? If not, the word of God forbids it; and if a man who has the means of understanding its nature and effects continues to follow it, he does it at the peril of his soul.

" But," says another, " if I should not sell it I could not sell so many other things." If you could not, then you are forbidden by the word of God to sell so many other things. And if you continue to make money by that which tends to destroy your fellow-men, you incur the displeasure of Jehovah. " But if I should not sell it I must change my business." Then you are required by the Lord to change your business. A voice from the

throne of his excellent glory cries, "Turn ye, turn ye
from this evil way; for why will ye die?"

"If I should turn from it I could not support my
family." This is not true; at least no one has a right to
say that it is true, till he has tried it and done his whole
duty, by ceasing to do evil and learning to do well, trusting in God, and has found that his family is not supported.
Jehovah declares, that such as seek the Lord, and are
governed by his will, shall not want any good thing.
And till men have made the experiment of obeying him
in all things, and found that they cannot support their
families, they have no right to say that it is necessary
for them to sell ardent spirit. And if they do say this,
it is a libel on the divine character and government.
There is no truth in it. He who feeds the sparrow and
clothes the lilly, will, if they do right, provide for them
and their families; and there is no shadow of necessity,
in order to obtain support, for them to carry on a business which destroys their fellow-men.

"But others will do it, if I do not." Others will send
out their vessels, steal the black man, and sell him and
his children into perpetual bondage, if you do not. Others
will steal, rob, and commit murder, if you do not; and
why may not you do it, and have a portion of the profit,
as well as they? Because, if you do you will be a thief,
a robber, and a murderer, like them. You will here be
partaker of their guilt, and hereafter of their plagues.
Every friend therefore to you, to your Maker, or the
eternal interests of men, will, if acquainted with this
subject, say to you, As you value the favor of God, and
would escape his righteous and eternal indignation, renounce this work of death; for he that soweth death,
shall also reap death.

"But our fathers imported, manufactured, and sold
ardent spirit, and were they not good men? Have not
they gone to heaven?" Men who professed to be good
once had a multiplicity of wives, and have not some of
them too gone to heaven? Men who professed to be good
once were engaged in the slave trade, and have not some
of them gone to heaven? But can men who understand
the will of God with regard to these subjects, continue
to do such things now, and yet go to heaven? The prin-

ciple which applies in this case, and which makes the difference between those who did such things once, and those who continue to do them now, is that to which Jesus Christ referred when he said, If I had not come and spoken to them, they had not had sin; but now they have no cloak for their sin. The days of that darkness and ignorance which God may have winked at have gone by, and he now commandeth all men to whom his will is made known to repent. Your fathers, when they were engaged in selling ardent spirit, did not know that all men, under all circumstances, would be better without it. They did not know that it caused three-quarters of the pauperism and crime in the land—that it deprived many of reason—greatly increased the number and severity of diseases, and brought down such multitudes to an untimely grave. The facts had not then been collected and published. They did not know that it tended so fatally to obstruct the progress of the Gospel, and ruin, for eternity, the souls of men. You do know it, or have the means of knowing it. You cannot sin with as little guilt as did your fathers. The facts, which are the voice of God in his providence, and manifest his will, are now before the world. By them he has come and spoken to you. And if you continue, under these circumstances, to violate his will, you will have no cloak, no covering, no excuse for your sin. And though sentence against this evil work is not executed at once, judgment, if you continue, will not linger, nor will damnation slumber.

The accessory and the principal, in the commission of crime, are both guilty. Both by human laws are condemned. The principle applies to the law of God; and not only drunkards, but drunkard-makers—not only murderers, but those who excite others to commit murder, and furnish them with the known cause of their evil deeds, will, if they understand what they do, and continue thus to rebel against God, be shut out of heaven.

Among the Jews, if a man had a beast that went out and killed a man, the beast, said Jehovah, shall be slain, and his flesh shall not be eaten. The owner must lose the whole of him as a testimony to the sacredness of human life, and a warning to all not to do any thing, or

connive at any thing that tended to destroy it. But the
owner, if he did not know that the beast was dangerous,
and liable to kill, was not otherwise to be punished.
But if he did know, if it had been testified to the owner
that the beast was dangerous, and liable to kill, and he
did not keep him in, but let him go out, and he killed a
man, then, by the direction of Jehovah, the beast and
the owner were both to be put to death. The owner,
under these circumstances, was held responsible, and
justly too, for the injury which his beast might do.
Though men are not required or permitted now to execute this law, as they were when God was the Magis-
trate, yet the reason of the law remains. It is founded
in justice, and is eternal. To the pauperism, crime, sickness, insanity, and death, temporal and eternal, which
ardent spirit occasions, those who knowingly furnish the
materials, those who manufacture, and those who sell it,
are all accessory, and as such will be held responsible at
the divine tribunal. There was a time when the owners
did not know the dangerous and destructive qualities of
this article—when the facts had not been developed and
published, nor the minds of men turned to the subject;
when they did not know that it caused such a vast portion of the vice and wretchedness of the community,
and such wide-spreading desolation to the temporal and
eternal interests of men; and although it then destroyed
thousands, for both worlds, the guilt of the men who
sold it was comparatively small. But now they sin
against light, pouring down upon them with unutterable
brightness; and if they know what they do, and in full
view of its consequences continue that work of death—
not only let the poison go out, but furnish it, and send
it out to all who are disposed to purchase—it had been
better for them, and better for many others, if they had
never been born. For,

1. It is the selling of that, without the use of which
nearly all the business of this world was conducted, till
within less than three hundred years, and which of course
is not *needful*.

2. It is the selling of that which was not generally
used by the people of this country for more than a hundred years after the country was settled, and which by

hundreds of thousands, and some in all kinds of lawful business, is not used now. Once they did use it, and thought it needful or useful. But by experiment, the best evidence in the world, they have found that they were mistaken, and that they are in all respects better without it. And the cases are so numerous as to make it *certain*, that should the experiment be fairly made, this would be the case with all. Of course it is not *useful*.

3. It is the selling of that which is a real, a subtil and very destructive *poison;* a poison which by men in health cannot be taken without deranging healthy action, and inducing more or less disease, both of body and mind; which is, when taken in any quantity, positively *hurtful;* and which is of course forbidden by the word of God.

4. It is the selling of that which tends to form an unnatural, and a very dangerous and destructive appetite; which, by gratification, like the desire of sinning in the man who sins, tends continually to increase, and which thus exposes all who form it to come to a *premature grave.*

5. It is the selling of that which causes a great portion of all the pauperism in our land; and thus for the benefit of a few (those who sell) brings an enormous tax on the whole community. Is this fair? Is it just? Is it not exposing our children and youth to become drunkards? And is it not inflicting great evils on society?

6. It is the selling of that which excites to a great portion of all the crimes that are committed, and which is thus shown to be in its effects hostile to the moral government of God, and to the social, civil, and religious interests of men; at war with their highest good, both for this life and the life to come.

7. It is the selling of that, the sale and use of which, if continued, will form intemperate appetites, which, if formed, will be gratified, and thus will perpetuate intemperance, and all its abominations, to the end of the world.

8. It is the selling of that which makes wives widows, and children orphans; which leads husbands often to murder their wives, and wives to murder their husbands; parents to murder their children, and children to murder their parents; and which prepares multitudes for the prison, for the gallows, and for hell.

9. It is the selling of that which greatly increases the amount and severity of sickness; which in many cases destroys reason; which causes a great portion of all the sudden deaths, and brings down multitudes who were never intoxicated, and never condemned to suffer the penalty of the civil law, to an untimely grave.

10. It is the selling of that which tends to lessen the health, the reason, and the usefulness, to diminish the comfort, and shorten the lives of all who habitually use it.

11. It is the selling of that which darkens the under·standing, sears the conscience, pollutes the affections, and debases all the powers of man.

12. It is the selling of that which weakens the power of motives to do right, and increases the power of motives to do wrong, and is thus shown to be in its effects hostile to the moral government of God, as well as to the temporal and eternal interests of men; which excites men to rebel against him, and to injure and destroy one another.　And as no man can sell it without exerting an influence which tends to hinder the reign of the Lord Jesus Christ over the minds and hearts of men, and to lead them to persevere in iniquity, till, notwithstanding all the kindness of Jehovah, their case shall become hopeless.

Suppose a man, when about to commence the traffic in ardent spirit, should write in great capitals on his signboard, to be seen and read of all men, what he will do, viz. that so many of the inhabitants of this town or city, he will, for the sake of getting their money, make paupers, and send them to the alms-house, and thus oblige the whole community to support them and their families; that so many others he will excite to the commission of crimes, and thus increase the expenses, and endanger the peace and welfare of the community; that so many he will send to the jail, and so many more to the state prison, and so many to the gallows; that so many he will visit with sore and distressing diseases; and in so many cases diseases which would have been comparatively harmless, he will by his poison render fatal; that in so many cases he will deprive persons of reason, and in so many cases will cause sudden death; that so many wives he will make widows, and so many children he will make orphans, and that in so many cases he will cause the children to grow up in ignorance, vice, and crime, and after being nuisances on earth, will bring them to a premature grave; that in so many cases he will prevent the efficacy of the Gospel, grieve away the Holy Ghost, and ruin for eternity the souls of men. And suppose he could, and should give some faint conception of what it is to lose the soul, and of the overwhelming guilt and coming wretchedness of him who is knowingly instrumental in producing this ruin; and suppose he should put at the bottom of the sign this question, viz. What, you may ask, can be my object in acting so much like a devil incarnate, and bringing such accumulated wretchedness upon a comparatively happy people? and under it should put the true answer, MONEY; and go on to say, I have a family to support; I want money, and must have it; this is my business, I was brought up to it. And if I should not follow it I must change my business, or I could not support my family. And as all faces begin to gather blackness at the approaching ruin, and all hearts to boil with indignation at its author, suppose he should add for their consolation, " If I do not bring this destruction upon you somebody else will." What would they think of him? what would all the world think of him? what *ought* they to think of him? And is it any worse for a man to tell the people beforehand honestly what he will do, if they buy and use his poison, than it is to go on and do it? And what if they are not aware of the mischief which he is doing them, and he can accomplish it through their own perverted and voluntary agency? Is it not equally abominable, if *he knows* it, and does not cease from producing it?

And if there are churches whose members are doing such things, and those churches are not blessed with the presence and favor of the Holy Ghost, they need not be at any loss for the reason. And if they should *never* again, while they continue in this state, be blessed with the reviving influence of God's Spirit, they need not be at any loss for the reason. Their own members are exerting a strong and fatal influence against it; and that

too after Divine Providence has shown them what they
are doing. And in many such cases there is awful guilt
with regard to this thing resting upon the whole church.
Though they have known for years what these men were
doing ; have seen the misery, heard the oaths, witnessed
the crimes, and known the wretchedness and deaths which
they have occasioned, and perhaps have spoken of it, and
deplored it among one another ; many of them have never
spoken on this subject to the persons themselves. They
have seen them scattering firebrands, arrows, and death,
temporal and eternal, and yet have never so much as
warned them on the subject, and never besought them to
give up their work of death. An individual lately conversed with one of his professed Christian brethren who
was engaged in this traffic, and told him not only that he
was ruining for both worlds many of his fellow-men,
but that his Christian brethren viewed his business as
inconsistent with his profession, and tending to counteract all efforts for the salvation of men; and the man,
after frankly acknowledging that it was wrong, said that
this was the first time that any of them had conversed
with him on the subject. This may be the case with
other churches; and while it is, the whole church is conniving at the evil, and the whole church is guilty. Every
brother, in such a case, is bound, on his own account, to
converse with him who is thus aiding the powers of
darkness, and opposing the kingdom of Jesus Christ,
and try to persuade him to cease from this destructive
business. And the whole church is bound to make efforts,
and use all proper means to accomplish this result. And
before half the individual members have done their duty
on this subject, they may expect, if the offending brother
has, and manifests the spirit of Christ, that he will cease
to be an offence to his brethren, and a stumbling block
to the world, over which such multitudes fall to the pit
of wo. And till the church, the whole church, do their
duty on this subject, they cannot be freed from the guilt
of conniving at the evil. And no wonder if the Lord
leaves them to be as the mountains of Gilboa, on which
there was neither rain or dew. And should the church
receive from the world those who make it a business to
carry on this notoriously immoral traffic, they will greatly

increase their guilt, and ripen for the awful displeasure of their God. And unless members of the church shall cease to teach, by their business, that fatal error that it is right for men to buy and use ardent spirit as a drink, the evil will never be eradicated, intemperance will never cease, and the day of millennial glory never come. And each individual who names the name of Christ, is called upon, by the providence of God, to act on this subject openly and decidedly for him, and in such a manner as is adapted to banish intemperance, and all its abominations from the earth, and to cause temperance, and all its attendant benefits, universally to prevail. And if ministers of the Gospel, and members of Christian churches, do not connive at the sin of furnishing this poison as a drink for their fellow-men; and men who, in opposition to truth and duty, continue to be engaged in this destructive employment, are viewed and treated as wicked men; the work which the Lord hath commenced and carried forward with a rapidity, and to an extent hitherto unexampled in the history of the world, will continue to move onward till not a name, nor a trace, nor a shadow of a drunkard or a drunkard-maker shall be found on the globe.

PROFESSED CHRISTIAN,—In the manufacture or sale of ardent spirit as a drink, you do not, and you cannot honor God; but you do, and so long as you continue it you will, greatly dishonor Him. You exert an influence which tends directly and strongly to ruin, for both worlds, your fellow-men. Should you take a quantity of that poisonous liquid into your closet, present it before the Lord; confess to him its nature and effects, spread out before him what it has done and what it will do, and attempt to ask him to bless you in extending its influence; it would, unless your conscience is already seared as with a hot iron, appear to you like blasphemy. You could no more do it than you could take the instruments of gambling and attempt to ask God to bless you in extending them through the community. And why not, if it is a lawful business? Why not ask God to increase it, and make you an instrument in extending it over the country, and perpetuating it to all future generations. Even the worldly and profane man, when he hears about professing Christians offering prayer to God that he

would bless them in the manufacture or sale of ardent
spirit, involuntarily shrinks back and says, "That is too
bad." He can see that it is an abomination. And if it is
too bad for a professed Christian to pray about it, is it
not too bad for him to practise it? If you continue, under
all the light which God in his providence has furnished
with regard to its hurtful nature and destructive effects,
to furnish ardent spirit as a drink for your fellow-men,
you will run the fearful hazard of losing your soul, and
you will exert an influence which powerfully tends to
destroy the souls of your fellow-men. Every time you
furnish it you are rendering it less likely that they will
be illuminated, sanctified, and saved, and more likely
that they will continue in sin and go down to the chambers of death.   .

, It is always worse for a church member to do an immoral act, and teach an immoral sentiment, than for an
immoral man, because it does greater mischief. And this
is understood, and often adverted to by the immoral
themselves. Even drunkards are now stating it to their
fellow drunkards, that church members are not better
than they. And to prove it, are quoting the fact, that
although they are not drunkards, and perhaps do not
get drunk, they, for the sake of money, carry on the
business of making drunkards. And are not the men
and their business of the same character? "The deacon," says a drunkard, "will not use ardent spirit himself: he says 'It is poison!' But for six cents he will
sell it to me. And though he will not furnish it to his
own children, for he says, 'It will ruin them,' yet he
will furnish it to mine. And there is my neighbor, who
was once as sober as the deacon himself, but he had a
pretty farm, which the deacon wanted, and for the sake
of getting it he has made him a drunkard. And his
wife, as good a woman as ever lived, has died of a broken
heart, because her children would follow their father."
No, you cannot convince even a drunkard, that the man
who is selling him that which he knows is killing him,
is any better than the drunkard himself. Nor can you
convince a sober man, that he who for the sake of money
will, with his eyes open, make drunkards of sober men,
is any less guilty than the drunkards he makes.

Is this writing upon their employment " Holiness unto the Lord," without which no one, from the Bible, can expect to be prepared for the holy joys of heaven? As ardent spirit is a poison which, when used even moderately, tends to harden the heart, to sear the conscience, to blind the understanding, to pollute the affections, to weaken, and derange, and debase the whole man, and to lessen the prospect of his eternal life, it is the indispensible duty of each person to renounce it. And he cannot refuse to do this without becoming, if acquainted with this subject, knowingly accessory to the temporal and eternal ruin of his fellow-men. And what will it profit him to gain even the whole world by that which ruins the soul? My friend, you are soon to die, and in eternity to witness the influence, the whole influence which you exert while on earth, and you are to witness its consequence in joy or sorrow to endless being. Imagine yourself now, where you soon will be, *on your death-bed.* And imagine that you have a full view of the property which you have caused to be wasted, or which you have gained without furnishing any valuable equivalent; of the health which you have destroyed, and the characters which you have demoralized; of the wives that you have made widows, and the children that you have made orphans; of all the lives that you have shortened, and all the souls that you have destroyed. O! imagine that these are the only " rod and staff" which you have to comfort you as you go down the valley of the shadow of death, and that they will all meet you in full array at the judgment and testify against you. What will it profit you though you have gained more money than you otherwise would; when you have left it all far behind in that world which is destined to fire, and the day of perdition of ungodly men? What will it profit when you are enveloped in the influence which you have exerted, and are experiencing its consequences to endless ages; finding for ever that as a man soweth so must he reap, and that if he has sowed death he must reap *death?* Do not any longer assist in destroying men, nor expose yourself and your children to be destroyed. Do good, and good only, to all as you have opportunity, and good shall come unto you.

RELIGION WITHOUT LEARNING,

OR

THE HISTORY

OF

SUSAN WARD

"The rich and the poor meet together: the Lord is the Maker of them all."—*Prov.* 22 : 2.

PUBLISHED BY THE

AMERICAN TRACT SOCIETY,

NO. 150 NASSAU-STREET, NEW-YORK.

D. Fanshaw, Printer.

THE HISTORY

OF

SUSAN WARD.

WHEN the important truths of religion are urged, there are those who are ready to reply : " *We are no scholars,*" and who seem to consider their ignorance an excuse for their not being true christians. Most certainly, they who enjoy the advantages of education, particularly if their minds are naturally strong, have an important talent committed to them; and for the use they make of it, they must give a solemn account at the day of judgment. But the truths necessary to be known, in order that the soul may be saved, are so few; and the way of obtaining a knowledge of them is so clearly revealed in the Bible, that the " wayfaring man, though a fool, shall not err therein." The reason why so much ignorance prevails among a large class of the community, is *this:* they are indifferent about their immortal souls; their bodies have wants, and they perhaps work hard to supply those wants; but they neglect the wants of the soul. No care is taken of that which must live *for ever;* while that which may any day, or hour, or moment, become a breathless corpse, is laboured for with unceasing care. Let me ask you, who are reading this Tract, Is this the case with you? Do you labour with more diligence, and with more earnestness, " for the meat that perisheth," than you do " for that which endureth unto everlasting life?" Do you bestow more anxious thoughts about earning a maintenance for yourself, or your family, than you do for the pardon of your sins and the salvation of your soul? You have taken great pains perhaps to acquire the means of subsistence for yourself and your family; but have you taken pains to learn the way of salvation? If not, can you wonder that you should be ignorant of it? And can you suppose that wilful ignorance, in such an all-important concern, will be allowed as an excuse by an all-wise God? Allow me to point out those truths, which *all* must learn before they are made "wise unto salvation."

The first thing which I am anxious that you should deeply feel is, *that you are a sinner:* a transgressor of God's holy law, without any worthiness in yourself, and altogether lost. I would then, with unspeakable joy, inform you, that *Jesus Christ is appointed to save you* from that ruin to which your sins have made you liable. Dependance on Him, without vainly trusting to any thing which you do, is necessary, whether you consider the pardon of your sins, the change of your heart, or the eternal enjoyment of God in heaven. Again, I would direct you to the great duty of *prayer.* God has graciously promised to instruct those who, in sincerity, ask him for wisdom; but if we are too proud or too slothful to ask, it is a just punishment that we should continue in ignorance.

Permit me now to inquire, as a friend to your immortal soul, Do you rightly apprehend what you have just read? Do you acknowledge that you are a sinner, deserving of eternal misery, and exposed to it; that you may escape by applying heartily to Jesus Christ for salvation; and that this sense of your need of mercy and faith in Christ can be obtained only by the assistance of the Holy Spirit? If you have properly learned these three important things, you have knowledge sufficient to guide you into the paths of peace, and the fulness of joy. This you will the more clearly perceive, when you have read the following narrative.

In the parish of L———n, in Leicestershire, there lived a very poor woman, named SUSAN WARD. She had been neglected by her parents in her youth, as, alas! many are; so that she was not taught even to read. Where there was *this* neglect, it is easy to suppose that she had never had any religious instruction given her. Though she possessed an immortal soul, she had never been told it; and she knew not that there was either a heaven or a hell: she had neither been exhorted to seek the one, nor warned to escape the other. In this sad state of ignorance she lived, and was married to one with but little more understanding of spiritual things than herself. Some time after, her health declined, and a consumption threatened speedily to convey her from time into eternity. How melancholy was her prospect! She was a *sinner*, and God has said, " The soul that sinneth, it shall die." The Bible no where tells us that people who are ignorant, when they might have known better, will, by pleading this ignorance, be saved from everlasting punishment. Happily for Susan, though she had lived, she did not die in ignorance. A Clergyman taking a morning walk, saw this poor woman sitting under a hedge, near to a sheep-fold; for she had been told that the breath of sheep was good for her complaint. Little did she think, when she sat down there, that she was about to be numbered with the "little flock" of Christ; to be gathered unto that happy fold, which is constantly watched and defended by the gracious Shepherd of Israel; that his rod and his staff would be her defence and support when passing through the valley of the shadow of death, upon which she was soon to enter. The Clergyman feeling for a fellow-creature bowed down by disease, and concluding, from her sickly appearance, that " her spirit " would shortly " return to God who gave it," began to talk to her respecting her soul; but she was so very ignorant, that she did not know that she *had* a soul; and therefore could know nothing of its dangerous state, or of the way of salvation. What a wretched case did this appear! She suffered so much from disease, that it was difficult for her to bear a part in conversation; and the hope therefore of doing her any good was very small. " But with God all things are possible." Under this conviction, the Minister directed her to the Lord Jesus Christ, as crucified for our sins, and explained to her the way of salvation through him. He entreated her to pray that God would teach her, and pointed out to her that very encouraging promise in the first chapter of St. James, and the fifth verse, " If any of you lack wisdom, let him ask of God, that giveth to all men liberally, and upbraideth not." He also told her not to be discouraged at finding herself so ignorant; for that no one could be made truly wise but by Divine teaching, and that God could as easily teach *her*, as he could the wisest man in the world. Poor Susan listened with great attention to all that she heard, and was enabled to pray for the aid of that Teacher to whom the Clergyman directed her. Her petitions were answered. She discovered all she wanted. The

Lord appears to have enlightened her mind in an unusual degree : compassionating her as she lay on the bor
ders of the world to come.

It should be recollected, for the encouragement of all who
plead before the throne of grace, that God has promised
to give the Holy Spirit to them that ask him. The Clergyman, having learned from her where she lived, took an
early opportunity of going to see her ; when he was much
surprised to find the state of her mind totally changed from
what it was when he first saw her. The stupidity which
she had before manifested, was now entirely removed ;
and she was all anxiety to know something more from his
lips, respecting her immortal soul, and the means of saving it from ruin. O how pleasant now was this work, to
point her to the Saviour, and say, " Behold the Lamb of
God, which taketh away the sins of the world !" God
was pleased to give her an understanding heart, so that,
in a very short time, she knew the things which belonged
to her peace. In about six weeks after she first began to
pray, her complaint so much increased, that she was confined to her bed, *that* bed from which she was never more
to rise. But how shall I describe her happiness ! She
spoke on religious subjects like one that had been acquainted with them for years ; and I have often heard the Clergyman say, that he was glad, at the last, to visit her, for
the sake of the instruction he received from her faultering
tongue. She had such bright prospects before her, in consequence of putting all her trust in the Saviour, that her
joy astonished every beholder. The evening before her
departure, she said to one standing by her bed-side, " Give
my love to Mr. ————," (the Clergyman who had been the
happy means of directing her thoughts to God,) " and tell
him, I shall meet him in heaven—O thank him for what
he has done for me." Shortly after, she seemed to have
breathed her last ; but, having lain to all appearance dead
for a considerable time, she revived, and begged the neighbours, who were sitting by her, not to be alarmed, at the
same time desiring that her husband might be called, and
her little child brought to her. When they were come,
she thus addressed the former : " Husband, I hope you
will attend to the words of a dying wife : in a very short
time I shall be with my Saviour, but you will be left in

a wicked world. O give your heart to God. Pray to him to teach you your undone state without a Saviour; pray that you may have an interest in the salvation of Christ. *You* can read a little; O be diligent in reading your Bible, and go to hear the Gospel preached; it has made me happy in death, and it can make you happy both in life and death. Attend to these things, and the Lord will bless you, and we shall meet in heaven. Bring my dear child up in the fear of God; let her go to school both on the week-days and on the Sabbath. O set her a good example in all things; and then, I trust, I shall meet my child with you in glory." She then blessed them both in a most solemn manner, and resigned them to the Lord. After she had done speaking she desired them to go to bed. But her tender concern for immortal souls was not confined to those who were dear to her by nature; she wished to benefit her neighbours also. As soon, therefore, as she was a little recovered from the fatigue and pain of parting from her husband and child, she earnestly exhorted those that were sitting up with her, to seek the Lord while they were in health, by giving him their hearts; by praying to him for his teaching, by reading their Bibles, and by hearing the Word where it was preached with faithfulness; and assured them, that by so doing, in humble reliance on divine aid, they would obtain a blessing from the Lord. Her strength at length became exhausted, never more to be renewed; her lips were sealed in silence for nearly an hour; but her enlivened countenance continued to express the triumph of her mind, till her work was done on earth, and she entered on her glorious employment of praising her God and Saviour through a countless eternity.

This short account of poor Susan would give rise to many remarks. I shall confine myself to the following:

1. However ignorant any readers of this narrative may be, they cannot be more so than Susan was; and therefore they need not despair of becoming wise in the things of God, if they, like her, *pray from the heart, for Divine teaching.* None that can read this account of her, are so ignorant as she was; for she did not know a single letter. But though you may not be so ignorant, you are certainly no less sinful. Were I to ask you, as the clergyman did her. "What is the state of our soul?" would you be able to an-

swer better than she did? That you have a soul you may
believe; but of its fallen state, of the danger of its being for
ever lost, or how it is to be saved from endless ruin, you perhaps could tell me but little. If you do not know the way
of salvation, nothing can be clearer than this, that you are
not *in* it; and if you die without knowing it, favoured as
you are with the means of grace, your soul *must* be ruined; for it is written in the Bible, " The wicked shall be
turned into hell, and all the people that *forget God.*" O
let me now persuade you to " seek the Lord while he
may be found," and to call upon him while he is near.
Pray to him to show you your real character; for indeed
unless he gives you a new heart, if you die, you will be
wholly unfit for heaven. Perhaps you may never have prayed to God in your life: neither had poor Susan; for she
knew nothing of that good and great Being; yet in the use
of the means recommended, she " fled for refuge to lay
hold on the hope set before her," and found mercy and
grace suited to her case, and so may you : God is as willing to bless *you*, as he was *her.* Though to this hour you
may have lived in perfect ignorance, and without any
real prayer to God, yet think of poor Susan: she lacked
wisdom as much as you do; the pious Clergyman met her,
and directed her to seek to God for mercy : this little book
may meet you likewise in an unexpected way, and it urges
you to the same duty. Do not turn a deaf ear to what it has
said to you; nor say that you will attend to the concerns
of your soul when, like Susan, you are brought near to
the grave. This delay might prove fatal to you, for you
have no assurance that *you* shall die of a lingering consumption. You may die by some sudden stroke; or you
may be seized with a fever, and your senses may fail in a
moment. You may have often seen people, when lying
on a sick-bed, bewildered in their thoughts; so that when
christian friends have talked to them about prayer, or heaven, or hell, they have plainly shown, either by their
words or their looks, that the subject was all new to them.
And will *you* also leave what is of so much consequence,
to such a dreadful hazard? What though you should have
your senses to the last; if you neglect *this* warning, your
heart may be hardened, and you may not again have the
wish excited to partake of God's salvation. That you

may not defer to a future time, what you should instantly attend to, I will tell you what the Lord your God says
in the first chapter of Proverbs, beginning at the 24th
verse. "Because I have called, and ye refused, I have
stretched out my hand, and no man regarded; but ye have
set at nought all my counsel, and would none of my reproof: I also will laugh at your calamity, I will mock
when your fear cometh : when your fear cometh as desolation, and your destruction cometh as a whirlwind; when
distress and anguish come upon you. Then shall they
call upon me, but I will not answer; they shall seek me
early, but they shall not find me." After having read this
very awful passage, dare you *now* venture to say, "I will
seek God at some future season." If you should, your case
and poor Susan's would materially differ; and therefore
I should cease to urge her example as an encouragement
to *you*. *She* went immediately to Christ, and besought him
to have mercy upon her soul; and you have been told the
happy consequences. But if you put off the advice this
little book gives you, and make yourself easy by resolving,
that at some more convenient season you will attend to it,
I cannot entertain a hope that you will ever be benefited
by what has been said to you. Susan, in her health, never
had the warning and the exhortations you have now had
given *you*. She therefore never hardened her heart against
the same calls. When she was invited to return to the
God whom she had offended, she did not refuse. *The very
day* in which she was told of her danger, she sought for
a remedy; the very day on which she learned that she had
an immortal soul, she sought its salvation; the very day
on which she heard there was a Divine Teacher, she
bowed her knees and entreated that he would teach *her*.
But if you refuse to hear, now that God calls you; if
you set at nought his counsel, and turn a deaf ear to its
kindest invitations—when your calamity and your fear
come, he may awfully fulfil the threatening you have
just read. O! think of the shortness of life at the long-
est; the uncertainty of it, even under the most promising appearances for its continuance; and the variety
of circumstances that may render a death-bed repentance impossible. Think likewise of the vast difference
there will be between having a station, in the last day, on

the *right hand* of your Judge, and being driven to the *left:* and *then* determine whether you will, like poor Susan, begin *to-day* to implore Divine teaching, or whether you will put to hazard your everlasting welfare.

2. The next remark suggested by the account of Susan Ward is this: Divine teaching is *necessary* and *efficacious.* It is *necessary*, because none can be made "wise unto salvation" without it. The learned and the ignorant are upon a level here. It is only the *Spirit of God* that can discover to us our condition as sinners, or the grand mystery of our redemption by Jesus Christ. How clearly is this stated in the second chapter of the first of Corinthians, and the 14th verse: "The natural man receiveth not the things of the Spirit of God; for they are foolishness unto him; neither *can* he know them, *because* they are *spiritually discerned.*" Divine teaching is likewise *efficacious:* because no case can occur, in which this Teacher cannot remove all the darkness of the soul. How very different, both in *kind* and degree, was poor Susan's knowledge from that which is acquired merely by studying and reasoning. God, in this instance, as in many others, chose the "foolish things of this world to confound the wise." "Man by wisdom knows not God." There are many learned men who do not believe this; but they will one day wish that they, like poor Susan, had been without human learning, rather than that it should have proved a hinderance to their seeking for that wisdom which cometh from God.

3. The third remark which I make, is this: Where there is a change of heart wrought by the Spirit of God, there will be an earnest desire excited, *that others may be partakers of the same grace.* When Susan had learned the worth of her *own soul*, she felt for her husband's and her child's, and then for her friends' and her neighbours'. Nor did she satisfy herself with *wishing* them well: she exhorted, she warned, she prayed; and what she had found so efficacious in her own case, she earnestly recommended to others. It may with truth be affirmed, that where the worth of the soul is truly felt, there will be active endeavours to make others sensible of its value also. Those parents who neglect the religious instruction of their children, know nothing of that renewed state which leads to these active endeavours. This those of you who are pa-

rents may know, by the answers which you can give to the following inquiries : Do you exercise your authority, and restrain your children from breaking the Sabbath? Where were they on the last Sabbath? Were they permitted to play in the streets or fields, or did you conduct them to God's house? Did you endeavour to instruct them at home; or, if you found yourself incapable of doing this, did you send them where they might obtain such instruction? Did you *read* to them in the evening out of God's Word, or did you endeavour to impress their minds with serious conversation? Did you examine them in what they had heard at church, or tell them that they had immortal souls that must be happy or miserable for ever? Now if you answer to these inquiries, that *nothing* of this care was manifested by you, surely you know nothing of the worth either of *their* souls or your *own*. If you thought of *theirs*, you would warn them to "flee from the wrath to come." When you thought of *your own*, you would look forward to that solemn day of account, when parents and children must stand at the tribunal of God. When children perish through the neglect of parents, how awful the doom of those parents will be, no tongue can tell! O parents, if you would be spared the unutterable anguish of finding yourselves contributers to the eternal misery of your dear children, endeavour to turn them from the broad path in which so many are going to destruction, and try to allure them, *especially by your example*, into the narrow one, which leadeth unto eternal life.

There is another deceit which many poor people practise upon themselves, which, though not suggested by the subject immediately before us, I take the present opportunity of exposing. How have I been grieved to hear a poor afflicted man or woman say, "Well, I shall have all my sufferings in *this* life; my troubles *here* will prevent my suffering hereafter." If this delusion should have fastened on *your* mind, what can I say to convince you how false your conclusions are? There is not one passage in your Bible, that, even in the most distant way, speaks a language like this. If an *eternity* of misery is threatened to *every* transgressor, who does not repent and believe in Christ for salvation, how can it be imagined that even the most severe sufferings, for the short time of three-score

years and ten, can atone for your numberless transgressions of the Divine Law? Your Bible says, "The wicked" (whether rich or poor) "shall go away into *everlasting* punishment," and "the righteous" (and the righteous
only) "into life eternal." None but holy beings can be
admitted into heaven; therefore, whoever dies *unholy* must
rise at the last unholy; must have his portion with unholy
spirits, and remain unholy *for ever and ever.*

4. The last remark which I shall make is this: Those
who know the way to heaven, seize every opportunity to
direct others thither, even when there is but the shadow
of a probability that the attempt will be successful. If the
Clergyman had said within himself, "This woman is so
ignorant, and at the same time so near her end, that to try
to instruct *her* would be a useless effort," he would not
now have had occasion to bless God for being made the
happy means of turning a fellow-sinner "from the error
of her ways;" and she might have sunk into the grave under her dark cloud of ignorance, and have risen at the
last to shame and everlasting contempt. What a very important event took place from what appeared a trivial circumstance, that of meeting with a poor diseased woman,
sitting by a sheep-fold. Here an opportunity presented
itself of doing good; it was seized; God gave *his* blessing
to what was said; and now, instead of howling for anguish
of spirit, an immortal being, we have reason to hope, is
admitted into that blessed state where there is no more
pain, nor sickness, nor death; and the praises of her Redeemer are her blissful employment day and night. Though
when on earth she was poor and ignorant, yet, being enriched with the righteousness of her Saviour, and taught
by the Spirit of God the way of salvation, she is now one
in that vast assembly which no man can number, who
cast their crowns at the foot of the Lamb, saying: "Thou
art worthy to receive all honour, and glory, and power;
for thou hast redeemed us to thyself by thy blood!"

Before I finish this little book, let me inquire, What
impression has been made on your mind while reading it?
Are you convinced, that though you are ignorant, your ignorance will be no hinderance to your becoming a true
christian, provided you pray, from the heart, for Divine
teaching? Do you believe the things that have been told

you? If you do, surely some effects will follow. Like poor Susan, you will begin *to-day* to attend to what has been said to you. But if you lay the book, and all concern about its contents aside together, you have read to no purpose, but to increase your future condemnation. If you have derived any benefit from reading it, you will make application, before you sleep this night, to that Divine Teacher who has promised to enlighten your mind, and has graciously offered to bestow wisdom on all who will ask him for it. Now do you feel thankful for being told this? If not, I think that you must be convinced that you are more alive to the concerns of your body than to those of your soul? you are more anxious to attain "the meat that perisheth, than that which endureth unto everlasting life." Let me entreat you to think seriously what is the meaning of such passages in your Bible as the following: "Give *diligence* to make your calling and election sure." "*Strive* to enter in at the strait gate." "Pray *without ceasing.*" "So *run*, that ye may obtain." "The kingdom of heaven suffereth *violence*, and the violent take it by force." Are you cold and careless? How then can you claim the character of a christian? And what then can be more plain than this, that you remain, to the present moment, without that change of heart which your Saviour, with a *verily, verily*, has told you *must* take place before you can be admitted into the kingdom of heaven? Read, with serious attention, the third chapter of St. John, and the third verse: He there says, *Ye must be born again.* Whoever, therefore, reads this little book, if he knows of no change of heart, if he finds that he does not strive to love and serve God *more* than he once did: if he does not feel that he hates and avoids sin more than he once did; if he does not love real christians more than he once did; if he does not try to benefit his fellow-creatures, and endeavour to promote the glory of God more than he once did: whether the reader be rich or poor, he is to this moment in his sins; old things are not passed away, all things are not become new. Nothing, therefore, can be more certain, than that if death should find him in this unrenewed state, his portion could not be with holy beings; his everlasting abode must be in that hell, into which not only all the wicked are turned, but likewise all the people that *forget God.*

END.

OBLIGATIONS

OF A GUARDIAN.

By an eminent Counsellor at Law.

THE trust of Guardian to the fatherless, which you have taken upon yourself, is one of the most momentous of all responsibilities. The relation of a parent is deeply interesting; for the principles he may instil into the mind of his child, may be the means of scattering blessings upon thousands, or of entailing on them unnumbered miseries. And a guardian stands in the place of a parent. If the law of the land invests him, as it certainly does, with a parent's powers, he cannot but be bound by a parent's obligations. The property, the health, the habits, the morals, the religious principles, and consequently the happiness of your ward, both in this life and in the world to come, all depend on your faithfulness. And you are especially accountable to that God, who has declared the widow and the fatherless to be the objects of his peculiar care. He is "the helper of the fatherless." Psalm x. 14. In Him "the fatherless findeth mercy." Hosea, xiv. 3. "He executeth the judgment of the fatherless and widow." Deut. x. 18. Psalm x. 18. "A father of the fatherless, and a judge of the widows, is God in his holy habitation." Psalm lxviii. 5. "He will be a swift witness against those that oppress the hireling in his wages, the widow and the fatherless." Mal. iii. 5. And he has thus distinctly denounced his vengeance against those who do them wrong: "Ye shall not afflict any widow or fatherless child. If thou afflict them in any wise, and they cry at all unto me, I will surely hear their cry. And my wrath shall wax hot, and I will kill you with the sword; and your wives shall be widows, and your children fatherless." Exod. xxii. 22—24.

Secured as the performance of your duty thus is, by the most solemn sanctions; while you are impelled, by every sacred principle, to its faithful discharge, you will find such a performance of it proportionably delightful. And happy, thrice happy may you finally be, in meeting both the grateful child and its departed parent, in the presence of an omniscient and approving Judge!

It is not enough to suppose, that, while you do not literally oppress, or defraud, or afflict the orphan, no part of your duty is neglected. They are entitled to your guardian care, to your kindness and sympathy, and to your vigilance over their persons, their minds, and their estates.

Of the management of their estates it is not my present purpose to speak. This may be the most laborious of your duties, but at the same time the least perplexing. Common vigilance and prudence will guide you through this department with safety, and insure a favorable event in the settlement of your accounts. But even here it is to be remembered, that the orphan's estate is entitled to the same care with your own. Nay, to more, if you are in the habit of neglecting your own; for his is not to be neglected. It must be kept in repair; be protected from injury and waste; be preserved from embarrassment; be managed with the least possible cost and expense; the debts due to your ward must be carefully and prudently collected; if his property is decreed to be sold, it must be done openly, with the diligent use of all lawful means to bring it to its fair value, and without collusion. The law, in its solicitude to preserve your integrity, will not suffer you to become the purchaser of your ward's estate.. It requires you to keep an exact account of every sum of money you receive and expend, and to be always prepared to exhibit a particular statement of all your proceedings; and it allows you, at the close, a just reward. All this, common talents and common honesty may accomplish; and advice on these subjects can always be obtained, whenever occasion may require. My object is rather to animate and encourage you to a faithful and punctual discharge of that portion of a guardian's duty, for the neglect of which he is not so strictly amenable to human tribunals.

In the *education* of your ward, he is to receive from you the impulses of his future life; and before he is able to regulate his own conduct, if you have awakened his affections, or gained his confidence, he will implicitly follow your footsteps, adopt your habits and principles, and be governed by the like motives with your own. How important, then, that the *examples* you hold out to him should be correct; that the whole course of your life should be such as he may safely follow! Here commences the duty you owe to him. How can you successfully impress him with the fear of God, unless it is apparent that his fear is ever present with you? Will he reverence the Being whose name he hears his guardian profane? Or will he respect those laws which he perceives you dispense with at pleasure? Of what value will he esteem truth and sincerity, while these are habitually disregarded by his instructer and guide? Would you train him to industry, and sobriety, and temperance? Let him see that your own conduct is steadily regulated by these virtues. If your precepts and your practice are at variance, he will surely copy the latter: esteeming it, as all men do, the living and practical exposition of your real faith. Your life will act upon his life. His heart will catch the spirit and the passions of yours. It is therefore among the first of duties, that you should give him the benefit of a good example. Without this, all attempts to train him to a life of virtue and religion will be vain.

Whether your ward is confided to your care at an early or at a more advanced age, it is necessary that he be furnished with constant *employment*. It is proverbially true, that idleness is the bane of virtue, and the fruitful parent of all vice. It both enervates the body and paralyzes the energies of the mind. Children and youth are naturally busy; they delight in motion; and are most happy when in the active pursuit of some object. This law of their very being and constitution must be made subservient to their happiness, or it will work to their ruin. Give them, therefore, useful and virtuous employment. No matter whether they are rich or poor. If the former, do not suppose, that, because their wealth in your hands is adequate to their support, it is therefore your duty to suffer them to live idly, and of course unprofitably to the community, and miserably to themselves. Such mistaken views of their duty in some guardians, have, doubtless, deprived society of those who might have been numbered among its brightest ornaments. Propose to your ward an object worthy of his character. In his early life teach him to labor and to think. Let his mind and his body be kept in activity, by proper alternations of instruction, of amusement, and of toil. Let him feel that he is born to be useful; that every grade in society is within his power to attain; and that for the right use of his talents and means he is deeply responsible to God.

Teach him *punctuality* in the fulfilment of all his engage-ments, and a *scrupulous and sacred regard to truth.* Let him know that every assertion which is not true, is false ; and that all falsehood is hateful in the sight of Him, who is " not man, that he should lie." There is no deception in heaven. " Whatsoever loveth or maketh a lie," cannot enter there. One of the distinguishing traits in the cha-racter of Christ, our great exemplar, was his sincerity. " If it were not so," said he, " I would have told you." He would not give countenance, by his silence, even to an error. If, as we are constantly taught, our characters for eternity are formed on earth, let children be early divested of all duplicity and falsehood, and be trained to an ardent love and the steady practice of truth, even in their most sportive moments. If you admit any deviations from truth, even of the most venial character, by what rule will you fix the limit at which falsehood becomes a crime ? Perhaps by indifference to this subject in early life, the foundation has been laid for perpetual unhappiness, from the invete-rate habit of speaking whatever, at the moment, appeared most convenient, without regard to its consistency with truth. And from the neglect to preserve and cultivate a conscientious and habitual reverence for strict veracity in all our conversation, the mind, after a lapse of time, loses its accurate perception of truth, and wanders disgracefully into the regions of falsehood ; the miserable victim being alike unable to fix his faith and to regulate his conduct.

Observe his *master-passion,* and begin early in the work of rendering it subservient to the great design of his ex-istence. If his mind is active, and vigorous, and grasping ; if his thirst for knowledge is strong ; excite in him also the desire to impart knowledge to others, and to advance es-pecially that which is most useful to the mass of mankind. If he is ambitious of fame and distinction, direct him to aspire after that honor which cometh from God alone ; and let him seek it in advancing the real happiness of his fel-low-men.

Direct him wisely and carefully in *his choice of books and company.* It is the happiness of our country, that the means of instruction are within the reach of all. Schools and books are multiplied without limit ; and the facility with which subsistence is required, affords opportunity for improvement to all classes and all ages. The sale of books too, of some kind or other, is become part of the employment of very many shopkeepers and dealers, as well as of itinerant traders. So that the young will furnish themselves with books; and an influence, often before parents are aware of it, will be thus exerted over their minds, and a direction given to their future lives. Your ward will choose his own books, unless you select them for him; or rather, he will read such as most delight his fancy, and awaken his imagination and his passions, without considering whether their tendency is evil or good. O what a weight of responsibility rests on parents and guardians, respecting the principles they suffer to be instilled, through this channel, into the minds of the young! And how many are the mischiefs which enter through this polluted avenue! It is thus that the poison of atheism is infused, and the hopes of religion blighted for ever. It is thus that the first germ of manhood is melted away in the lap of debauchery and libidinous appetite. Let their books, therefore, and their companions, be selected with equal care; and let both be such as have a tendency to promote their present advantage and their future well-being. Lead your ward into the path of virtuous emulation. Teach him that there is nothing beneath the desire of a wise man to know, if it can possibly render him more useful to his fellow-men. Let him be ambitious of filling a wide circle of activity and beneficence; and accustom him early to make even his pleasures and recreations conducive to the great object he proposes to accomplish by his life.

And this leads me to suggest the importance of calling strongly to the mind of every youth, the advantage of *commencing life with some settled plan of usefulness*, to be accomplished by the means which Providence may have placed within his reach. If he is rich, he must be taught that his wealth is to be employed. It is a sacred deposit in his hands from God. If he is poor, still he owes to God the full and unwearied application of all his energies to the service of his fellow-men. In what manner this wealth and these energies can be best applied, must depend on the particular circumstances of each case. But if a plan is once formed, and the mind of a youth is properly excited and interested in its accomplishment, this object becomes the pole-star of his life, and gives regularity and consistency to his conduct. To every solicitation of vice, or of idle company, or of his own strong passions, he will be ready to reply: " I am doing a great work, and I cannot come down." So every day will be allotted a time for the performance of its appropriate duties, from which pleasure will no longer have the power to allure him. Thus his bark will be poised and ballasted for the voyage of life, and every sail be spread to every breeze which can aid in wafting him to the haven where he would be.

Above all, seek his *eternal happiness in the conversion of his soul.* Its redemption is precious. Man is an immortal being. He only puts off the earthly house of this tabernacle, to be clothed with immortality. But short and fleeting as this life is, it is long enough to form the character for eternity. It is our warfare, which must be accomplished; and if we steadily contend under the banners of the great Captain of our salvation, he will make us more than conquerors. It is the laboratory, in which the man of the other world is formed; the mould, in which his destiny is cast for the life to come. He is daily painting his future likeness, heightening the touches of its brightness and glory, or deepening its shades of deformity and darkness. At death, how sudden soever the messenger may arrest his hand, this character is fixed. The blood of Jesus, which cleanseth from all sin, is no longer applied to wash away the stains of his guilt. He that is unholy at that moment, remains unholy for ever. The soul, disembodied, goes to its own place. It seeks its kindred. If Christ be formed within it the hope of glory, it ascends to his presence, to dwell with the spirits of the just made perfect for ever. But if the great business of preparation for eternity has been neglected, and the numerous sins of this life be unforgiven, because unrepented of—if the enmity that is in it have not been slain—it still seeks the company of its fellows; and finds its home among those, who, as they lived without God in this world, are doomed to pass a dreary eternity, without the light of his presence in the world to come. If, with all the intelligence and light which pervade our country at the present day, all the restraints of law, and religion, and public opinion, and the fear of punishment, were at once removed; who could dwell amid the robberies, and murders, and violence, and debaucheries, and blasphemies which would ensue? And who then can look, unappalled, upon the future condition of those, who, not having been willing to enroll themselves under Christ's banner here, will be compelled to associate with his enemies for ever? If men will live without God, let them remember that he can be happy without them.

And can *motives* be wanting to the performance of these duties? Your country demands it of your patriotism; for she looks with solicitude to the rising generation, as her future hope and protection. To them are to be confided her reputation, her virtue, her institutions, her liberties, and consequently her safety. Upon these, the youth entrusted to your care is hereafter to exert an influence, either to build up and preserve, or to undermine and destroy. Nay, more, the God of the fatherless himself requires you to *bring up this child for him*: on the one hand, denouncing his malediction against those who defraud or wrong the orphan; and, on the other, assuring to every faithful guardian a glorious reward in the retributions of eternity.

TO THE

RELATIVES AND FRIENDS OF THE WARD.

You are, in a moral sense, the guardians of the ward, till a special guardian is appointed. It is not to be supposed that the proper tribunal, by which such guardian is to be appointed, can, in many cases, have personal knowledge of the one proper to be appointed to such trust. Much will depend upon your judgment and information. Nor can you be indifferent to the momentous subject, without guilt. It is your duty to consider and recommend the person who, in your deliberate opinion, is best qualified to act as guardian. You are bound to do all in your power to prevent the appointment of an unsuitable person. Should you neglect the duty that naturally devolves upon you toward the ward, you may be indirectly the means of his temporal and eternal ruin. From a due regard to his best interests, therefore, and to your accountability to God, be faithful in selecting and recommending to the proper tribunal, the most suitable person to be appointed as guardian.

TO THE WARD.

Your guardian, in point of duty, stands in the place of a parent. His station, therefore, is one of most solemn responsibility. His counsel and authority you are bound to regard as those of a parent. They bear a divine sanction. Him you are bound to love and reverence, and you must manifest your love and reverence for him in all your words and actions. Remember that his counsels and instructions are the result of observation and experience. Submit to them in the fear of God. Be not impatient of wholesome restraint. Avoid all recreations and amusements, upon which you cannot conscientiously ask the blessing of God. Choose for associates those who are possessed of a correct taste, and who appear to derive satisfaction from those pursuits that virtuous minds alone can relish. A man is known by the company he keeps. Acquire a habit of cleanliness as to your person, and correctness as to your deportment. Treat all persons, at all times, with civility and respect. Avoid all appearance of profaneness. Never be guilty of deception or falsehood. Remember the Sabbath-day to keep it holy. Read your Bible daily. Read it prayerfully. Search it as for hid treasure, and with a desire to know its sacred truths. Make it the man of your counsel in all the duties you owe to God, your fellow-men, and yourself. Above all, give your heart to Christ, the great Redeemer, who died that sinners might be pardoned and justified through his blood. On this depends your happiness in life, in death, and in eternity. Think much, therefore, on these things.

Note.—This Tract, which was written by an eminent Counsellor at Law, is perpetuated, through the liberality of "An old Judge of Probate."

Other Solid Ground Titles

In addition to the volume which you hold in your hand, Solid Ground is honored to offer many other uncovered treasure, many for the first time in more than a century:

THE CHILD AT HOME by John S.C. Abbott
THE KING'S HIGHWAY: *10 Commandments for the Young* by Richard Newton
HEROES OF THE REFORMATION by Richard Newton
FEED MY LAMBS: *Lectures to Children on Vital Subjects* by John Todd
LET THE CANNON BLAZE AWAY by Joseph P. Thompson
THE STILL HOUR: *Communion with God in Prayer* by Austin Phelps
COLLECTED WORKS of James Henley Thornwell (4 vols.)
CALVINISM IN HISTORY *by Nathaniel S. McFetridge*
OPENING SCRIPTURE: *Hermeneutical Manual by Patrick Fairbairn*
THE ASSURANCE OF FAITH *by Louis Berkhof*
THE PASTOR IN THE SICK ROOM *by John D. Wells*
THE BUNYAN OF BROOKLYN: *Life & Sermons of I.S. Spencer*
THE NATIONAL PREACHER: *Sermons from 2nd Great Awakening*
FIRST THINGS: *First Lessons God Taught Mankind Gardiner Spring*
BIBLICAL & THEOLOGICAL STUDIES *by 1912 Faculty of Princeton*
THE POWER OF GOD UNTO SALVATION *by B.B. Warfield*
THE LORD OF GLORY *by B.B. Warfield*
A GENTLEMAN & A SCHOLAR: *Memoir of J.P. Boyce by J. Broadus*
SERMONS TO THE NATURAL MAN *by W.G.T. Shedd*
SERMONS TO THE SPIRITUAL MAN *by W.G.T. Shedd*
HOMILETICS AND PASTORAL THEOLOGY *by W.G.T. Shedd*
A PASTOR'S SKETCHES 1 & 2 *by Ichabod S. Spencer*
THE PREACHER AND HIS MODELS *by James Stalker*
IMAGO CHRISTI: *The Example of Jesus Christ by James Stalker*
A HISTORY OF PREACHING *by Edwin C. Dargan*
LECTURES ON THE HISTORY OF PREACHING *by J. A. Broadus*
THE SCOTTISH PULPIT *by William Taylor*
THE SHORTER CATECHISM ILLUSTRATED *by John Whitecross*
THE CHURCH MEMBER'S GUIDE *by John Angell James*
THE SUNDAY SCHOOL TEACHER'S GUIDE *by John A. James*
CHRIST IN SONG: *Hymns of Immanuel from All Ages by Philip Schaff*
COME YE APART: *Daily Words from the Four Gospels by J.R. Miller*
DEVOTIONAL LIFE OF THE S.S. TEACHER *by J.R. Miller*

Call us Toll Free at 1-866-789-7423
Send us an e-mail at sgcb@charter.net
Visit us on line at solid-ground-books.com
Uncovering Buried Treasure to the Glory of God

LaVergne, TN USA
04 December 2010
207252LV00006B/4/A